PG 2026 .A76 N48 1987

New studies in Russian language and
literature

NEW STUDIES IN
RUSSIAN LANGUAGE AND LITERATURE

NEW STUDIES IN RUSSIAN LANGUAGE AND LITERATURE

edited by

Anna Lisa Crone
University of Chicago

Catherine V. Chvany
MIT

Slavica Publishers, Inc.
Columbus, Ohio

Slavica publishes a wide variety of books and journals dealing with the peoples, languages, literatures, history, folklore, and culture of the peoples of Eastern Europe and the USSR. For a complete catalog with prices and ordering information, please write to:

Slavica Publishers, Inc.
P.O. Box 14388
Columbus, Ohio 43214
USA

ISBN: 0-89357-168-7.

Copyright © 1986 by the authors. All rights reserved.
This book was published in 1987.

Text set by Randy Bowlus at the East European Composition Center, supported by the Department of Slavic Languages and Literatures and the Center for Russian and East European Studies at UCLA.

Printed in the United States of America.

CONTENTS

BAYARA AROUTUNOVA, AN APPRECIATION

Dr. Bayara A. Aroutunova received her Ph.D. in Slavic Languages and Literatures from Harvard University in 1958. She joined the full-time teaching staff of the Harvard Department of Slavic Languages and Literatures as a Lecturer in the same year, becoming a Senior Lecturer in 1963. For 28 years she has taught courses, conducted entirely in Russian, in advanced Russian language and in the analysis of difficult literary texts. Throughout this time her teaching has been informed by scholarly interests spanning areas of Russian literature, poetics and literary theory, Slavic linguistics and language pedagogy. Her publications include a study of the semiotics of gesture in Russian idioms and proverbs, and articles on Vladimir Maya-kovsky and Boris Pasternak. Most recently, she has participated in two international symposia devoted to Pasternak's poetry. A long-term project on the archive of Zinaida Volkonskaja is nearing completion, with the first of two volumes now being readied for publication by Slavica Publishers, Inc.

In her courses, Dr. Aroutunova endeavored to instill in her students a sense of the importance to their chosen specialty of a command of both spoken and written Russian, thus motivating them to improve their Russian throughout their professional lives. Dr. Aroutunova possessed a knowledge of linguistics, poetics and literary texts exceptional among teachers of language, and this enabled her to relate advanced language study to these disciplines in a way that helped students integrate Russian language into their overall Slavic program.

New Studies in Russian Language and Literature is offered to Bayara Artemevna Aroutunova as a token of appreciation and esteem to a talented and dedicated teacher who has probably trained more active Slavic scholars-teachers than anyone else in the United States. Many of the contributors expressed their gratitude for Dr. Aroutunova's continued interest in their careers and scholarly progress, as well as for the extra time she devoted to perfecting their Russian during their student days—well beyond what could have been reasonably expected. The volume contains refereed scholarly articles, mostly by her former students, in the fields of Russian language, linguistics, translation, literature and folklore. Because of the wide range of fields, we did not aim for across-the-board uniformity of style or even transliteration, leaving the authors free to follow the conventions they prefer. The idea of a volume dedicated to Bayara Artemevna is not a new one. Former students of several generations had suggested the idea repeatedly over the years. This volume could easily have been much bigger, but practical constraints forced us to limit it to its present size. Our aim was to be representative rather than exhaustive. Some whose current work was already committed, or whom our informal call for papers did not reach in time, will be publishing articles dedicated to Bayara Artemevna elsewhere. Others provided editorial and clerical assistance. Typesetting costs were defrayed in large part by the contributors' institutions and the contributors themselves. We wish to thank all who provided support for the venture and, in particular, Charles E. Gribble of Slavica Publishers for his enthusiastic encouragement at every stage of the volume's preparation.

The editors also extend warm thanks to Mark Elson, Charles Isenberg, Paul Friedrich, Horace Lunt, Diana Burgin, Sam Driver, Emily Klenin, Ernest Scatton, David Sloane, and especially Stanley Rabinowitz, for editorial help with one or more papers; to David J. Birnbaum and Betty Y. Forman who helped with proofreading; to Vladimir Donchik who designed and executed the cover; to Dean S. Worth, Director of the UCLA East European Composition Center, and to Randy Bowlus of the Center for the excellent job he did in typesetting varied and often difficult texts.

Anna Lisa Crone
Catherine V. Chvany
May 26, 1986

JOINING THE AUTHORS AND EDITORS IN BEST WISHES FOR BAYARA AROUTUNOVA ARE:

Vladimir and Sybil Alexandrov
Anna Bobrov
Louise and Loring Conant, Jr.
Donald and Margot Fanger
George and Oksana Grabowicz
Charles E. Gribble
Morris Halle
Janet Marin King
Lena Lencek
Madeline G. Levine

Horace G. Lunt
John E. Malmstad
Ann Weiler Perkins
Robert A. Rothstein
Elena Semeka-Pankratov
M. and V. Setchkarev
Edward and Florence Stankiewicz
Vera and Kiril Taranovsky
Maria E. and Wiktor Weintraub
Irene and Thomas Winner

And many others, to be announced during the festivities surrounding Dr. Aroutunova's retirement from Harvard University in June 1987.

DEPARTICIPIAL ADVERBS IN RUSSIAN

Leonard H. Babby

1.0 Introduction. This paper will deal with the morphosyntactic properties of a relatively new verbal category in Russian, namely, departicipial manner adverbs formed with the suffix -*šče* (/ʃ,o/), e.g., *udručajušče* 'depressingly', *obeščajušče* 'promisingly', *ugrožajušče* 'threateningly', *draznjašče* 'teasingly', etc. Its main purpose is to shed some new light on the classic problems of "hybrid" verbal categories, i.e., categories that combine the properties of verbs and non-verbal categories like noun, adjective, or adverb.

In the first part of the paper I will describe the relations between these *šče*-adverbs and both the corresponding active participle in -*ščij* (*udručajuščij* 'depressing', *obeščajuščij* 'promising') and the corresponding gerund in -*a* (*udručaja* 'depressing', *obeščaja* 'promising'), since the former bears an obvious **formal** relation to *šče*-adverbs, while the latter bears a **functional** relation (they are sometimes referred to as verbal adverbs). In the second part I will propose an explicit account of the relations between these three verbal categories in terms of recent morphological theory, and will argue that they make a unique contribution to our understanding of the relation between **word structure** (the internal organization of morphologically complex words) and **phrase structure** (the internal organization of the phrases that these words head). But first a few preliminary remarks are necessary.

1.1 Active participles (verbal adjectives) in modern Russian have an exclusively attributive function which is close to that of relative clauses; their endings are the same as primary adjectives in the **long form**, i.e,. they are inflected for gender, number, and case.[1] Gerunds (verbal adverbs) have a function close to that of adverbial clauses, and, like all adverbs in Russian (including *šče*-adverbs), they are uninflected. One of our goals will be to characterize the differences between gerunds and *šče*-adverbs, which appear at first glance to have the same (adverbial) function; e.g., see the discussion of sentences like the following in Gvozdev (1955:256).

(1) Rebenok govoril, *umoljaja*   pustiť   ego   na   spektakľ.
     child   spoke   imploring   to-admit him   to   show

(2) Rebenok smotrel *umoljajušče*   na   mať.
     child   looked imploringly   at   (his) mother

2.0 *šče*-Adverbs and Deadjectival Adverbs.

The following sets of examples demonstrate that *šče*-adverbs have the same function and syntactic distribution as manner adverbs formed from primary adjectives.[2]

(3) a. Daže kogda ona ulybalas', oni (=glaza) smotreli *voprošajušče.*
        'Even when she smiled, they (=her eyes) looked inquiringly.
     b. Kolesa postukivali *usypljajušče.*
     c. On *ponimajušče* kivnul.
     d. Ona ulylabalas' *znajušče/manjašče/zaiskivajušče.*
     e. On *protestujušče* zadvigal brovjami.
     f. Èto legkaja smerť, — *utešajušče/uspokaivajušče* skazal vrač.
     g. Ona *vyžidajušče/izučajušče/ožidajušče* smotrela na menja.
     h. Ivan *plačušče* zaoral na ves' gorod.
     i. Stoľ naprjažennyj trud dolžen *sootvetstvujušče* oplačivaťsja. (*Izvestija*, 1979)
     j. On *osuždajušče* pokačal golovoj.
     k. Glaza Ivana skoľznuli *ocenivajušče* po èlegantnomu kostjumu Viktora.

Like manner adverbs formed from primary adjectives, *šče*-adverbs also modify adjectives and participles, e.g.:

(4) a. *slepjašče* belyj 'blindingly white'
     b. On xodit v *užasajušče* rvanyx bašmakax.
     c. Počemu on govorit s nami takim *issušajušče* naučnym jazykom?
     d. *podkupajušče* širokaja ulybka.
     e. Samye neznačiteľnye političeskie sluxi kazalis' *zaxvatyvajušče* interesnymi.

šče-adverbs freely conjoin with deadjectival manner adverbs in *-o*, as in (5), or can be used in parallel constructions with them, as in (6).

(5) a. Pljasali dve obnažennye ženščiny, ulybalis' *zazyvno i obeščajušče.*
     b. Fedor *nasmešlivo i sožalejušče* posmotrel na devušku.
     c. Tanja sprašivala *trebovateľno i moljašče.*
     d. Golos ego zvučal *tverdo i obodrjajušče.*
     e. Oni vygljadeli *i vyzyvajušče i trogateľno.*

(6) a. Ona *vnimateľno, izučajušče* posmotrela na muža.
     b. Glaza smotreli *pristaľno, ispytujušče.*
     c. Na kuxne dolžno xorošo paxnuť. *Vkusno. Vozbuždajušče.*
     d. Zdes' razgovarivali po-osobennomu — *korotko, predosteregajušče.*

Finally, like true manner adverbs, *šče*-adverbs can both modify and be modified by other manner adverbs, e.g.:

(7) a. Pticy teper' peli *pugajušče gromko.*
     b. Oni pisali *poraziteľno udručajušče.*
     c. Pridonnaja voda *ostužajušče-sladostno* zaskoľzila vokrug ee tela.

3.0 The Morphosyntactic Properites of *šče*-adverbs and *ščij*-participles.

The examples in (3)–(7) suggest that the relation between *ščij*-participles and the corresponding adverb in -*šče* is entirely parallel to the relation between primary adjectives and their corresponding manner adverb in -*o* (i.e., *gromkij* : *gromko* :: *umoljajuščij* : *umoljajušče*, etc.). But it turns out on closer inspection that this parallelism is not complete: while primary adjectives that have corresponding manner adverbs in -*o* normally have predicate short forms as well as attributive long forms, *ščij*-participles in Modern Russian do not have short forms and are not used in the predicate (e.g., **Ona byla sidjašča za stolom* 'She was sitting at the table'). Since it is normally assumed that primary manner adverbs in -*o* (*gromk-o* 'loudly') are related to neuter singular short forms of the same adjective (*gromk-o* 'loud'), we cannot therefore simply claim that the relation between *ščij*-participles, which have long forms only, and *šče*-adverbs is identical to the relation between primary adjectives and the corresponding manner adverb, and leave the matter at that; *ščij*-participles and their relation to *šče*-adverbs must be considered separately.

3.1 Primary Adjectives in -*ščij*. The analysis of the relation between *ščij*-participles and *šče*-adverbs is complicated by the existence of what appear to be predicate short forms of *ščij*-participles, e.g.:

(8) a. Spiski nepravil'nyx form *isčerpyvajušči*.
      'The lists of irregular forms are *exhaustive*'
  b. On byl privlekatelen i *ottalkivajušč* odnovremenno. (Tokareva)
      'He was attractive and *repulsive* at the same time'
  c. Ljubaja dejatel'nost', kotoroj zanimajutsja deti pod rukovodstvom nasto-
      jaščego pedagoga, vsegda *vospityvajušča*. (*Izvestija*, 1979)
      'Any activity in which children participate under the direction of a real
      pedagogue is always *educational*'

It turns out on closer inspection, however, that the predicate short forms in (8) are synchronically **primary adjectives**, not participles. What happened historically is this: Short forms like the ones in (8) were *ščij*-participles that underwent a diachronic process which reanalyzed them as primary adjectives, and these adjectives are listed in the lexicon of Modern Russian along with all the other primary adjectives. The most convincing evidence for this reanalysis (Selkirk 1982:104 suggests the term "recategorization") comes from the meaning of these forms. Participles always have the same meaning as the corresponding verb stem, but, as the English glosses demonstrate, the meaning of the predicate forms in (8) differ from that of the corresponding verb (and participle). For example, the verb *isčerpyvat'* means 'to exhaust, use up', and the *ščij*-participles formed from it has the same lexical meaning. But the "departicipial" adjective *isčerpyvajušč(-ij)* in (8a) means 'complete, exhaustive' (not 'exhausting'), and, since it is synchronically a primary adjective, it can have predicate short forms as well as attributive long ones. This difference in meaning between *ščij*-participles and the corresponding *ščij*-primary adjectives is particularly clear in the case of (8c). Thus Modern Russian has a large number of homophonous pairs in -*ščij*, one a primary adjective listed in the lexicon, the other a participle, which is part of the corresponding verb's paradigm and, since its form and meaning are entirely predictable, is not entered in the lexicon (see Halle 1973 for a different viewpoint). Given this analysis of the predicate short forms in (8), we are indeed justified in asserting that *ščij*-participles do not have short forms in Modern Russian.

It should also be noted here that while some *šče*-adverbs correspond to *ščij*-participles that have been recategorized as adjectives, most *šče*-adverbs do not (e.g., there is no *ščij*-adjective corresponding to the adverb *protestujušče* 'protestingly'). We cannot therefore claim that the *šče*-adverb is nothing more than a manner adverb in -/o/ that is formed from a primary adjective whose stem happens to end in -*šč*-.[3]

4.0 Gerunds and *šče*-Adverbs.

The preceding section was devoted to an informal discussion of participles (*umoljajuščij*) and the *šče*-adverbs associated with them. Now we will consider the relationship between *šče*-adverbs (*umoljajušče*) and gerunds (*umoljaja*).

It is a relatively easy matter to characterize the functional similarity of gerunds and *šče*-adverbs: both are adverbial forms of the verb. The crucial difference between them is this: *šče*-adverbs function exclusively as **manner** adverbs, while gerunds in Russia have a wide range of adverbial and quasi-adverbial functions, including that of manner adverbs. Speaking in the broadest possible terms, gerunds in Russian denote actions that are both related and subordinate to the action denoted by the main verb of the clause in which they are contained. The precise semantic interpretation of the gerund depends on a number of parameters (e.g., overall context, aspect, word order, lexical meaning). Thus *šče*-adverbs are manner adverbs whereas gerunds may function as manner adverbs (especially when they have no complements).

The use of gerunds as manner adverbs is illustrated in the following examples. In (9) gerunds are conjoined with manner adverbs formed from primary adjectives; in (10) they are conjoined with *šče*-adverbs.

(9) a. On govoril *bystro* i *ne umolkaja.*
'He spoke *quickly* and *without stopping*'
b. On šagal po ulice *bodro* i *ne ustupaja dorogu.*
'He walked down the street *boldly* and *not getting out of anyone's way*'
c. *Spokojno* i *ne toropjas'*, on prileg.
'He lay down *calmly* and *without rushing*'

(10) Ona *neponimajušče* i *vse ešče vsxlipyvaja* podnjala na nego lico (Rasputin)
'She lifted her faced to him *uncomprehendingly* and *still sobbing*'

4.1 Syntactic Differences.

Despite the fact that gerunds and *šče*-adverbs belong to the same category and have similar functions, there is a crucial syntactic difference between them. Gerunds have the same objects, modifiers, and complements that the corresponding finite verb does, whereas *šče*-adverbs do not. For example, a gerund formed from a transitive verb takes a direct object noun phrase in the accusative case, and, like the finite verb, its direct object is marked genitive rather than accusative if it is in the scope of sentence negation. But *šče*-adverbs formed from the same transitive verb cannot take an object noun phrase in any case. In the following examples, *uspokaivaja* is the gerund and *uspokaivajušče* is the *šče*-adverb formed from the transitive verb *uspokaivat'* 'to calm, soothe'; *nas* 'us' is the direct object.

(11) a. On govoril medlenno, tixo, *uspokaivaja nas* (svoim nizkim golosom).
'He spoke slowly, quietly, *soothing us* (with his low voice).
b.*On govoril medlenno, tixo, *uspokaivajušče nas* (svoim nizkim golosom).
c. On govril medlenno, tixo, *uspokaivajušče.*
'He spoke slowly, quietly, soothingly'

(12) a. On kivnul, *obodrjaja nas prodolžat'.*
'He nodded, encouraging us to continue'
b.*On kivnul, *obodrjajušče nas prodolžat'.*
c. On kivnul *obodrjajušče.*
'He nodded encouragingly'

Note also that gerunds, like finite verbs, can occur with the voice morpheme -*sja*, and can be used in either aspect; *šče*-adverbs cannot be inflected for voice and are formed from imperfective verbs only. On the other hand, *šče*-adverbs, like manner adverbs formed from primary adjectives, can be used to modify adjectives and adverbs (see (7)); gerunds cannot.

We can conclude on the basis of these syntactic properties that gerunds are heads of complete verb phrases, while *šče*-adverbs are not; they behave syntactically like simple adverbs.

ščij-participles also have the same objects, modifiers, complements, voice morphology, etc., as the corresponding gerund and finite verb. We can therefore conclude that gerunds head phrases that have the "internal" structure of verb phrases, but are "externally" adverb phrases, and that *ščij*-participles head phrases that are internally verb phrases and externally adjective phrases. In contrast, *šče*-adverbs head phrases that are both internally and externally adverb phrases. These structures can be schematically represented as follows (V– stands for a verb stem and AP for 'adjective phrase').

(13)

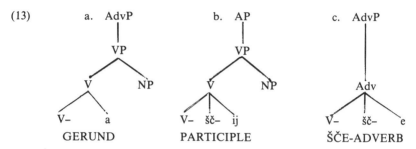

Given the structure in (13c), *šče*-adverbs associated with transitive verb stems do not have direct objects because they do not have the internal structure of a verb phrase.

The schematic representations in (13) are intended to capture the fact that *ščij*-participle phrases and gerund phrases are full verb phrases whose heads are verb stems to which have been affixed nonfinite suffixes that determine the phrase's overall adjectival or adverbial function in the sentence. But *šče*-adverbs are verb stems which are made adverbs when the suffix -*šč-e* is affixed to them; they cannot therefore have any of the properties of verb phrases (object noun phrases, complements, voice, etc.).

Note finally that while *ščij*-participles and gerunds can be formed from all regular verb stems, this is not the case with *šče*-adverbs, which appear to have various kinds of restrictions on their formation (e.g. not all verbs denote actions that can be used as adverbial modifiers, cf. **čitajušče* 'readingly', **sidjašče* 'sittingly', etc.). Thus the formation of *ščij*-participle phrases and gerund phrases appears to be a productive morphosyntactic process, while the formation of *šče*-adverbs appears to be a restricted lexical process, i.e., appears to be a product of **word formation** rather than **phrase formation** (this distinction is reminiscent of the distinction between gerundive and derived nominals made in Chomsky, 1970; cf. also Chvany 1977).

The King's Library

5.0 Formal Representation.

The first part of this paper (sections 1–4) contains an informal discussion of *šče*-adverbs and their relation to gerunds and participles. In this section we shall explore the theoretical implications of the relations between these verbal categories.

5.1 The most straightforward approach to the relation between *šče*-adverbs and *ščij*-participles is this: A rule combines an imperfective verb stem V– with the (derivational) suffix -*šč*- to form a derived adjectival stem (*umoljajušč-*, *utešajušč-*, *protestujušč-*, etc.), i.e.:

(14)   A   or   [V – šč –]$_A$

These deverbal adjectives then behave like primary adjectives with respect to their inflectional endings: the suffix /o/ is added to form manner adverbs, and the long form ending -*ij* (masc. sg. nom.), -*emu* (masc. sg. dat.), etc., are added to produce attributive forms, i.e., participles. Under this hypothesis, -*šč*- in participles and -*šč*- in *šče*-adverbs are the same suffix.

5.2 This approach works perfectly well for *šče*-adverbs. If we assume that Russian manner adverbs in -/o/ are adjectives that are used in the verb phrase to modify verbs, then -/o/ (realized as *e* after *šč*) is the neuter singular short form **inflectional** suffix that is normally used in Russian to mark the absence of agreement (see (15a)). If, on the other hand, we assume that manner adverbs are deadjectival adverbs, then -/o/ must be a **derivational** suffix (homophonous with the neuter singular short form ending) that marks the derivation of an adverb from an adjective (see (15b)). It is assumed in (15) that inflectional suffixes do not affect the stem's category.

(15)   a.   A   b.   Adv

There is considerable evidence from Russian and other languages (esp. Polish) that manner adverbs are not merely adjectives used as a verbal modifier, but are a separate category (see (15b)); but space does not allow for further discussion of this point.

5.3 But the hypothesis outlined above in section 5.1 is patently incorrect when applied to *ščij*-participles. If we start out with a derived structure like (14), then *ščij*-participle phrases would have to have the internal structure of an adjective phrase (see (16)) since, according to X-bar theory (Jackendoff, 1977), the phrasal category that dominates all the phrase's constituents must be a projection of the head.

(16)

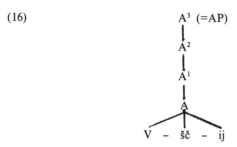

But, as we saw above in section 4.1, *ščij*-participle phrases have the internal organization of verb phrases, not adjective phrases. We must therefore abandon the hypothesis that *šče*-adverbs and *ščij*-participles share a commonly derived stem (see (14)) and consider an alternative hypothesis according to which the -*šč*- in *šče*-adverbs and *ščij*-participles are different suffixes in Modern Russian. This hypothesis must somehow capture the fact that the -*šč*- suffix in participles and the -*a* suffix in gerunds (and the -*ti* suffix on infinitives for that matter) are suffixes that are associated with entire verb phrases (i.e., affixed only to verbs that head verb phrases), while the -*šč*- suffix in *šče*-adverbs is associated with the verb stem only, not with verb phrases (i.e., it cannot be affixed to a verb that heads a verb phrase). This alternative hypothesis should also ideally explain the obvious diachronic relation between -*šč*- in *šče*-adverbs and -*šč*- in participles.

5.4   The same kinds of problems that we have been considering above arise in the analysis of gerundive nominals in English. While they have the internal organization of a verb phrase, they have the "external" distribution of a noun phrase (e.g., *We were all against John's buying a new house*). Although the suffix -*ing* is affixed to the verb, its function is to convert a verb phrase into a superficial noun phrase; the same is true of the suffix -*DIK*- in Turkish. The solution to the problem of nonfinite verbal categories in Russian therefore has significance beyond the boundaries of Russian grammar; it can contribute to the characterization of "hybrid" category in universal grammar. In the next section we will look briefly at R. Jackendoff's treatment of English gerundive nominals within the X-bar framework. I will argue that the **deverbalization** rules he proposes account remarkably well for Russian data presented in this paper.[4]

6.0   Deverbalizing Rules and X-bar Theory.

In his 1977 book on phrase structure (X-bar theory), R. Jackendoff proposed the Uniform Three-Level Hypothesis, which is a universal constraint on the form of phrase structure. According to this hypothesis, a phrase headed by the lexical category X will have the following skeletal structure (determiners, complements, and quantifiers are ignored).

(17)

$$
\begin{array}{c}
X^3 \\
| \\
X^2 \\
| \\
X^1 \\
| \\
X
\end{array}
$$

In other words, (17) claims that between the lexical category X and its maximal projection X^3 there are two intermediate categories (levels), each with its own determiners, complements, etc.[5]

In Chapter Nine Jackendoff introduces **deverbalizing rules**, which, he notes, constitute a principled class of exceptions to (17) since they generate structures in which the prhase's head (V) and "maximal projection" belong to different categories. These rules are also appropriately referred to as category changing rules, and they can be schematically represented as follows.

(18) $X^i \rightarrow af\ V^i$

Jackendoff notes (p. 221) that the rule in (18) "expands a supercategory of the lexical category X as a supercategory of the verb of the same level, plus a grammatical formant or affix" (*af* in (18) stands for affix). An X^3 involving a deverbalizing rule will display some properties of X^3 and some properties of verb phrases. The possible skeletal structures of phrases involving category switching rules in a theory in which the maximal projection of a phrase is X^3 are (see p. 221):

(19)   a.   b.   c.

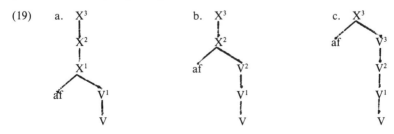

The structures grow less X-like and more verb-like as i in (18) goes from 1 to 3, i.e., the higher the level at which the category switching rule operates, the more verb phrase-like and the less X-like the phrase will become. At the level where a category is switched by a deverbalizing rule, there are no complements or determiners. This means, for example, that a phrase with the structure represented in (19c) will have the "internal organization" of a V^3, but will have the syntactic distribution ("external structure") of an X; it will have no X-type determiners or complements since the category switch takes place at X^3. In (19a) and (19b), however, there will be determiners and complements associated with both X-phrases and verb phrases.

6.1   Gerundive Nominals in English.

Gerundive nominals in English can serve as a concrete example of a category switching rule. They have the structure of a **verb phrase** up to the V^2 level and that of a **noun phrase** above, i.e., X^3 = NP (Jackendoff, p. 223). The phrase structure rule generating such a structure can be represented as follows: $N^2 \rightarrow ing\ V^2$; the structure of the gerundive nominal in (20a) can accordingly be represented by (20b).

(20)   a. Noam's inventing a new theory.

      b.

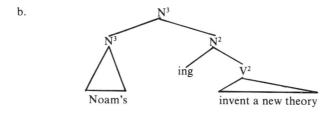

The deverbalizing suffix (or, from another perspective, the **nominalizing** suffix) *-ing* is positioned after the verb *invent* by a transformational rule.

This analysis is appealing because it provides a relatively straightforward way of capturing the fact that gerundive nominals are "hybrid" categories, i.e., that they are "internally" verb phrases and "externally" noun phrases; it also succeeds in representing the deverbalizing suffix *-ing* as associated with the entire V^2 rather than just the lexical head of V^2, to which it is eventually affixed.

6.2   Word Formation and Phrase Formation.

Jackendoff also notes that i in (18) can be zero, i.e.:

(21) $X \rightarrow af\ V$

Category switching rules like (21) are "congruent with a subset of the word formation rules in the lexicon, for example, those relating derived nominals to verbs" (see p. 235). Consider, for example, the word *building*, which is either a noun (derived nominal), as in (22a), or a gerundive nominal, as in (22b).

(22) a. This building is very old.
      b. John's building a new house is news to me.

The skeletal structure of (22a) and (22b) can be represented by (23a) and (23b).

(23)   DERIVED NOMINAL   GERUNDIVE NOMINAL

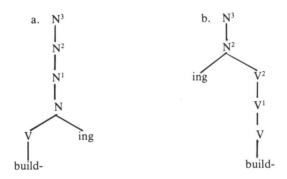

Jackendoff considers (23b) to be the result of a diachronic process, i.e., a word formation rule (see (23a)) develops into a phrase structure rule (see (23b)) (see p. 235).

7.0 Deverbalizing Rules in Russian.

The English deverbalizing rules presented above are able to represent precisely the relations we have observed in Russian between *ščij*-participles and *šče*-adverbs. *ščij*-participles, like all true participles, have the internal structure of a verb phrase and the external structure of an adjective phrase. This fact can be expressed in Jackendoff's framework by means of the following deverbalizing rule (assuming that the maximal projection of both adjective phrases and verb phrases to be A^3 and V^3 respectively).

(24) $A^3 \rightarrow af\ V^3$ (or $A^3 \rightarrow$ -šč- V^3)

The endings *-ij* (m. sg. nom.), *-aja* (f. sg. nom.), *-uju* (f. sg. acc.), etc., are inflectional; they are identical to the endings of primary attributive adjectives (i.e., long forms), and their values are determined by the same principles of noun phrase-internal agreement. Further details in Babby 1985.

The skeletal structure of a *ščij*-participle is given in (25a) and a concrete example in (25b); since the category switch takes place at the A³ level, *ščij*-participle phrases do not have any of the determiners or complements associated with adjective phrases.

(25a)

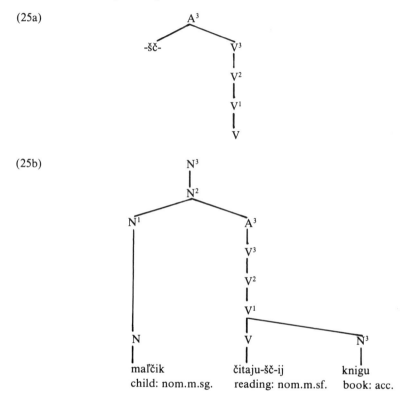

(25b)

```
malčik              čitaju-šč-ij           knigu
child: nom.m.sg.    reading: nom.m.sf.     book: acc.
```

Despite the fact that *ščij*-participles have adjectival inflectional morphology (i.e., *-ij, -aja,* etc.), they "govern" the accusative case on their direct objects, just as finite forms, gerunds, and infinitives do (primary adjectives do not have accusative complements). This is because, according to (25), the *ščij*-participle is a V that heads a V³, which contains the syntactic configuration that determines accusative marking on the objects of transitive verbs (see Babby 1980). In other words, the case marking on A³ (nominative in (25b)) percolates to the participial head (*čitajuščij* (nom. sg. m.)), but not to its direct object (*knigu* (acc.)) (cf. *mal'čiku* (dat.), *čitajuščemu* (dat.) *knigu* (acc.)/ **knige* (dat.)).

(24) and (25) capture precisely what we set out to capture at the beginning of this article, namely, that the participle suffix *-šč-* is associated with

the entire verb phrase, not just the verb, and that *ščij*-participle phrases have the internal structure of a verb phrase, but the syntactic distribution and morphology of an adjective phrase.

7.1 *šče*-adverbs and Deverbalizing Rules.

We established above in section 4.1 that the manner adverb suffix -*šče* is associated with verbs, not verb phrases (recall that they do not have any of the determiners or complements found in verb phrases (cf. (11) and (12)). This can be represented by the following deverbalizing rule (cf. section 6.2):

(26)   A → af V   (or A → -šč- V)

The skeletal structure of a Russian *šče*-manner adverb is given in (27a) and a concrete example in (27b).

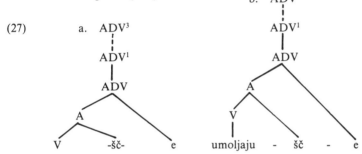

(26) and (27) capture the crucial fact that the *šče*-adverb suffix is associated with the verb, not the verb phrase (cf. (25a)), and that *šče*-adverbs have the distribution, function, and morphology of manner adverbs. See section 5.2.

7.2   According to the analysis presented above, the suffix -šč- is introduced by two different rules at two different bar-levels, at the word level (lexical V level) in the case of *šče*-adverbs, and at the phrase level (V³ level) in the case of participles. Thus the deverbalizing suffix -šč- in Russian is similar to the suffix -*ing* in English, which combines with verb stems at the word level (to form nouns) and combines with phrasal categories (to form gerundive nominals) (see the discussion of the word *building* above in section 6.2).

But there does appear to be one significant historical difference between -*ing* in English and -šč- in Russian. According to Jackendoff, gerundive nominals resulted from a diachronic process whereby a word formation rule developed into a phrase structure rule (see 6.2). The opposite appears to have taken place in Russian: a phrase structure rule (A³ → V³ -šč-) developed into a word formation rule (A → V -šč-); Jackendoff explicitly mentions this possibility on page 237.

7.3   Gerunds and Deverbalizing Rules.

It is now a relatively simple matter to account for the structure of gerunds (*umoljaja*) and their relation to both participles (*umoljajuščij*) and *šče*-adverbs (*umoljajušče*). Like *ščij*-participles, gerunds have the internal structure of a verb phrase, and, like *šče*-adverbs, they have the function and distribution of an adverb (adverbial clause). These properties can be captured by the deverbalizing rule in (28); the skeletal structure of a gerund phrase is given in (29).

(28) $ADV^3 \rightarrow af\ V^3$ (or $ADV^3 \rightarrow$ -a V^3)

(29)

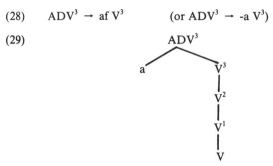

Since *ščij*-participle phrases are externally adjective phrases (see (25a)), they have the same inflectional morphology as primary adjectives, i.e., they are inflected for gender, number, and case; both *šče*-adverbs and gerunds are externally adverbs (see (27) and (29)) and, accordingly, both are uninflected (primary adverbs in Russian are all uninflected). Note finally that participles and gerunds (and infinitives) are formed by phrase structure rules and, therefore, they are completely productive, as we would expect them to be. But *šče*-adverbs are generated by a word structure rule which combines -*šč*- with a specific lexical item and semantic constraints naturally come into play; *šče*-adverbs are therefore only semiproductive (cf. derived nominals in English).

7.4   Summary.

The derivational suffix -*šč*-, like -*ing* in English (see (23)), is introduced by two different deverbalizing rules, one a phrase structure rule (which combines -*šč*- with V^3), the other a word structure (word formation) rule (which combines -*šč*- with a verb stem, forming a morphologically complex *word*).

8.0   Conclusions.

I have argued in this paper that the theory of deverbalizing rules proposed in Jackendoff 1977 is an important contribution to the characterization of hybrid categories in universal grammar. This is primarily because it

enables us to explicitly represent the fact that verbal suffixes can be associated either with verb phrases (i.e., with verbs that head verb phrases) or
with simple verb stems (i.e., with verbs that do not head verb phrases). The
former can be exemplified by *ščij*-participles, gerunds, and infinitives in
Russian, participles and gerundive nominals in Turkish, and gerundive
nominals in English; the latter can be exemplified by *šče*-adverbs in Russian. But there are a number of problems with Jackendoff's approach to
hybrid categories, some of them rather obvious, and it will therefore either
have to be radically revised, or his insights will have to be incorporated
into another theory. Since space does not allow for adequate discussion, I
will limit myself to a few general observations.

8.1 The most obvious problem with deverbalizing rules is that, as
Jackendoff himself points out, they violate a basic principle of X-bar theory, namely, in structures like those in (19), (25a), (27), and (29), V, the
head of the hybrid phrase (i.e., the phrase containing a category switching
rule), and the phrase's highest node belong to different categories (cf. the
Uniform Three-Level Hypothesis in (17)). For example, English gerundive
nominal phrases are headed by a V, but the phrase's highest node is N^3
(=NP).

According to the deverbalizing rules proposed in Jackendoff, 1977,
derivational suffixes are introduced by phrase structure rules at various
bar-levels (cf. (18)) and subsequently affixed to the lexical verb stems heading these phrases by means of specialized syntactic rules. Since it stands to
reason that not all derivational suffixes are to be introduced by phrase
structure rules and positioned by transformations (see Selkirk 1982), Jackendoff's theory entails a rather heterogeneous, unintuitive model of derivational morphology. Bowers 1984 makes the same point about the treatment
of inflectional morphology in recent theories of syntax (note that deverbalizing rules say nothing about inflectional morphology, but it can nevertheless serve as a valid criticism of the treatment of derivational morphology
in Jackendoff's theory).

> . . . such approaches are quite unconstrained, since inflectional features can
> be generated in a variety of different places in syntactic representations of the
> categorial component and may be related to actual morphological forms in
> ways that are quite indirect. Analyses such as those mentioned above, permit,
> in effect, no principled distinction at all to be made between syntax and mor-
> phology (Bowers 1984:24)

Note finally that since both primary adjective phrases and participle
phrases have the same "maximal projections" (A^3), it follows from Jackendoff's theory that both should have the same syntactic distribution. But, as

was noted in sections 3.0 and 3.1, they do not: participle phrases have only
an attributive function (and therefore have only long form endings), while
primary adjectives have both an attributive and predicate function (and
therefore have short form as well as long form endings).

8.2 Autonomous Morphology.

Bowers argues that morphology is autonomous, i..e, it constitutes "an
independent module whose basic units and principles of organization are
distinct from those of any other component of the grammar" (Bowers
1984:24). Morphologically complex words, i.e., words consisting of a stem
+ derivational suffix + inflectional suffix, are accordingly formed in an
autonomous morphological component and only then are inserted into the
syntactic representation of phrases and sentences. The acid test of the theory of autonomous morphology is whether or not it can account for the
properties of hybrid vebal categories discussed above in a natural, insight-
ful way.

If we assume that lexical categories (V, A, N, etc.) are composed of category features (see Chomsky 1970, Jackendoff 1977), and, furthermore, if
we assume that derivational as well as inflectional suffixes have features
associated with them, and that these features percolate (or "project") up to
the phrase's maximal projection along with the head's features, then it
seems, at least in principle, that such a theory is capable of capturing the
same insights as Jackendoff's, but without the defects mentioned above in
section 8.1.

ščij-participles would be formed by combining a verb stem, the derivational suffix -*šč*-, which contributes an adjectival feature, and an inflectional ending, which contributes the features of gender, number, and case.
The resulting word (formed entirely in the morphological component) will
head a phrase whose maximal projection is composed of an adjectival as
well as a verbal feature (whence its "hybrid" nature), in addition to inflectional features of gender, number, and case.[6] This phrase does not violate
the Uniform Three-Level Hypothesis since the feature complexes of the
head and maximal projection are identical. Note too that according to this
theory, the maximal projections of participle phrases and adjective phrases
are similar, but are not identical; we would therefore not expect their distribution in the sentence to be identical.

šče-adverbs would be formed as follows: the verb stem would combine
with the derivational suffix -*šč*- to form a deverbal adjective (cf. *ščij*-
participles), and this structure would in turn combine with the derivational
suffix -*o* to form an adverb, i.e., $[[\text{ V} + \text{šč}]_A + \text{o}]_{\text{ADV}}$, which then serves

as the head of an adverb phrase, just as primary adverbs do.

According to this "autonomous" analysis, -šč- is the "same" derivational suffix in šče-adverbs and ščij-participles, i.e., in both cases it combines with a verb stem, contributing an adjectival feature to the resulting derived lexical category. The major difference between šče-adverbs and ščij-participles is this: the former is less verb-like because two derivational (deverbalizing) suffixes have been combined with a verb stem in the morphological component; the latter is more verb-like (and has the same determiners and complements as a finite verb phrase) because its formation involves only one derivational (deverbalizing) suffix. Thus šče-adverbs have been completely deverbalized, while ščij-participles have been only partially deverbalized in the morphological component.

This analysis of deverbal participles and adverbs in the framework of Bowers' theory of autonomous morphology is intentionally sketchy—it is meant only to serve as the basis for future discussion of hybrid categories and their contribution to our understanding of the proper relation between morphology (word structure) and syntax (phrase structure). See Babby, forthcoming.

Cornell University

NOTES

[1]In Babby 1978 I argue that "active" participles in Russian are not always in the active voice, and "passive" participles are not inherently passive.

The short forms of primary adjectives and "passive" participles have an exclusively predicate function, i.e., they cannot be NP constitutents; they are therefore inflected for number and gender only, not case. Long forms of primary adjectives and participles are NP constituents and accordingly are marked for case (see Babby 1973, 1974, 1975, 1976).

[2]The term "primary adjective" is used to designate adjectives listed in the lexicon. It contrasts with "derived adjective" or "deverbal adjective," which is derived from the corresponding verb stem by means of a productive morphological or syntactic process. Since deverbal adjectives are part of the verb's paradigm, their form and meaning are entirely predictable, and there is no need to list them in the lexicon.

[3]It appears to be a universal for productively derived, paradigmatic verbal forms to acquire specialized lexical meanings and be reanalyzed as independent words with their own lexical entries. Turkish causatives are a particularly good example of this diachronic process. For example, *art-tir-mak*, the causative of *art-mak* 'to increase (intransitive)', must have its own lexical entry since, in addition to its predictable, causative meaning (make/let increase), it has acquired the meaning 'to save, economize' (See Türkçe-Ingilizce Büyük Lûgat, Ankara, 1959).

[4]I learned after writing the first draft of this paper that a similar proposal has been made for Latin participles (see J. Jensen 1981).

[5]I have argued elsewhere that the maximal projection of N in Russian is N^5, not N^3 (see Babby 1985), but, since nothing hinges on this in the following discussion, I will adopt Jackendoff's more familiar hypothesis.

[6]There must of course be some way to indicate that the phrase is predominantly verbal (not adjectival), and, therefore, has the determiners and complements associated with finite verb phrases (e.g., accusative direct objects). An adequate discussion of this formalism would have to include the notion "head of the word" and is therefore beyond the scope of this paper (see Selkirk 1982).

REFERENCES

Babby, L., "The deep structure of adjectives and participles in Russian." *Language* 49, 1973, 349-360.

Babby, L., "Towards a formal theory of 'part of speech.'" In R. Brecht and C. Chvany (eds.), *Slavic transformational syntax* (= Michigan Slavic materials 10). Ann Arbor: Department of Slavic languages and literatures, The University of Michigan, 1974, 151-181.

Babby, L., *A Transformational Grammar of Russian Adjectives* (= Janua Linguarum, Series Practica, 234). The Hague: Mouton, 1975.

Babby, L., "Morphology in a transformational grammar of Russian: inflectional categories." *International Review of Slavic Linguistics*, 1, No. 2/3, 1976, 241-272.

Babby, L., "Participles in Russian: attribution, predication, and voice." *International Review of Slavic Linguistics*, 3, No. 1/2, 1978, 5-25.

Babby, L., "The syntax of surface case marking." In W. Harbert and J. Herschensohn (eds.), *Cornell Working Papers in Linguistics*, No. 1, Spring 1980.

Babby, L., "Case, prequantifiers, and discontinuous agreement in Russian." Cornell manuscript (submitted for publication), 1985.

Babby, L., forthcoming. *The syntax of case and quantifiers in Russian.*

Bowers, J., "On the autonomy of inflectional morphology." In W. Harbert (ed.), *Cornell Working Papers in Linguistics* (Papers from the Second Cornell Conference on Government and Binding Theory). Spring 1984.

Chomsky, N., "Remarks on nominalization." In R. Jacobs and P. Rosenbaum (eds.), *Readings in English transformational grammar.* Waltham, Mass.: Ginn and Co., 1970.

Chvany, C. V. "Syntactically Derived Words in a Lexicalist Theory (Toward a Restudy of Russian Morphology)," *Folia Slavica* 1, 1977, 43-58.

Gvozdev, A.N., *Očerki stilistiki russkogo jazyka.* Moskva, 1955.

Halle, M., "Prolegomena to a theory of word formation." *Linguistic Inquiry* 4, 1973, 3-16.

Jackendoff, R., $\bar{X}$ *Syntax: A study of phrase structure.* Cambridge, Mass: MIT Press, 1977.

Jensen, J., "$\bar{X}$ Morphology." In V. Burke and J. Pustejovsky (eds.), *Proceedings of the Eleventh Annual Meeting North Eastern Linguistics Society.* University of Mass., Amherst, Mass., 1981.

Kibrik. A. E. and T. V. Bulygina, eds. *Novoe v zarubežnoj lingvistike*, XV. *Sovremennaja zarubežnaja rusistika.* Moscow: Progress, 1985. Contains Russian translations of Babby 1973, 1974, and Chvany 1977.

Selkirk, E, *The syntax of words.* Cambridge, Mass.: MIT Press, 1982.

JUNGIAN DACTYLS ON DEATH AND TOLSTOY[1]
(Verses Burlesque with Notations in Earnest)

Diana Lewis Burgin

> "When I've already one foot in the coffin,
> I shall the truth about women avow,
> tell it, jump in, close the lid, and [sign óff in]
> say[ing to *her*], — Go ahead! Take me now!"
> — L.N. Tolstoy[2]

Gorky has noted Tolstoy's deep hostility
towards all the women he wrote of and knew,
and to a reader with Jung's sensibility
what Gorky said in this instance rings true.[3]

First, there's Andrey, so in love with Natasha!
Yet, their first kiss leaves him fearing its thrill.[4]
Last, recall Pozdnyshev: he knew that passion
gave love the lie with its license to kill.[5]

Midways, Bezukhov, that lovable tippler,
married Hélène with her bosom so bare.
All he could think of was when he could stríp 'er—
Heavens! belle Helen was Hell an' unfair.[6]

Then, we have Anna, who, falling for Vrónsky,
murdered the corpse of their love with her sin.
Horrible guilt put her so in the wróng, she
animus-istic'lly did herself in.[7]

Levin explains, fills in Lev's views on women—
only two kinds—either mothers or whores.[8]
Treach'rous the latter who charm, tease, and woó men,
make them all . . . fear death will stalk through the doors.[9]

Why? (you might ask). But the answer is easy.
Arch-typal images make it quite clear—
"swallowing nothingness" gives man a queasy
fear for the loss of some thing he holds dear.[10]

'Even a lover of praiseworthy stamina
will,' warns Tolstoy, 'surely run out of breath
when he encounters the Arzamas anima,
noiselessly saying, "I'm here. I am Death." '[11]

'Death!' gulps our hero, by reason forsaken,
'How has she come to be anguishing me?
She was my mother, I can't be mis/taken!
Yet, "she will come, she, but she should not be." '

She soon became for Tolstoy an obsession,
led him to stasis, hysteria, one helluva
crisis. Paralysis penned his *Confession*
where we find images, fables, that téll-of-a

dragon of death.[12] That's a symbol, notes Cárl-Gustav
Jung of the negative anima. She
gapes in a waterless well, and her márl-must-'ave
Lev, who thinks [k]nots and naught else but to flee.

Fleeing, however, is one of the shán'ts-of-Him,
"Someone" who calls man to union with God.[13]
Thus, Lev must struggle with what-scares-the-pánts-off-him,
meaning, not Mother, but Other, the bawd.

Other/wise death, black sensation of sinning,
outmeasures pleasure to prove life's true worth.
Anima-ending-maternal-beginning
death fear remembers the trauma of birth.[14]

When, in "On Life," Lev discusses mortality,
he is enlightened by Reason above:
death (like bad women) exists in carnality;
life, (like good mothers) 's incarnate in Love.

Death, Tolstoy senses, means knowing your mother;
fear, he implies, is the incest taboo,
w[h]i[t]ch was what made you chase after the Other
Woman, who lied in submitting to you.

Snake! She recoiled from all of your offerings!
But, quake no more! You shall rise in a thrice.
Even Ivan could find God for his sufferings—
dying, he went through the Good Mother twice.[15]

Jung would say, Ívan's black sack is the wómb-of-his
spirit which stubbornly struggles in pain.
Knowing his self finally ruptures the tómb-of-his
body, so Ívan is born once again.[16]

'Death ends in birth,' Tolstoy preached, fulmináting,
'Man comes to life through that swallowing [w]hole
if, in great labor, his ma[w] emulating,
finally he finishes, birthing his soul.'

This is the truth shown by Master, Andréyevich.[17]
Lying, UNABLE, atop his man/wife,
he, still, can see, hear, move faster, and sáy, 'Ey, it's
over. I KNOW now, "I'm coming" to life!'

Everyman's spiritual parthenogeneses
realize his birthright—perfection of self,
rival and conquer his animae-nemeses:
IUD's*, doctors, bad women, and wealth.

Thus, in conclusion, it isn't surprising,
what Lev Tolstoy wished to get off his chest
spews forth that Truth which Carl Jung was surmising,
namely, rebirth is an arch-typal quest.

*Iniquitous Ultimate Dichotomy. See note 7 [D.L.B.]

NOTATIONS

[1]Working through the [Good] Title backwards we describe the long travail of this piece to see the light and its various rebirths, from my interest in Tolstoy's depiction of women and death (delivered but unpublished papers of 1978/1979: "Tolstoy's Pronominal Dance with Death," "The Anima of Death and Man's Struggle For Transcendence In Tolstoy," and "Tolstoy and Death, Or The Truth About Women"—is "the thought articulated a lie?"). This lengthy expect/oration on death in the archetypal family and its possible creative implications culminated in June, 1979 when I delivered "The Anima of Death and the Creative Impulse in Tolstoy's Art" at perhaps an unlikely conference for a Slavist, Jungian Perspectives on Creativity and the Unconscious (Miami University). During my subsequent struggle for transcendence (Other/Wise known as my fight for tenure—how the archetypes have fallen), which began in July of 1979, the presence of my real-life anima killed any desire for further exploration of Tolstoy's fictional one. In April, 1981, however, my father died. This horrifying event, which I really had feared all my life, brought me back to Tolstoy and appears, again archetypically, in the light of its issue, a *Life*, to have led to the partial realization of my animus through Pushkin, "the father of Russian literature," but with not a little push from Tolstoy. *Richard Burgin, A Life in Verse*, RB ALIV, [E]ntered the world of my written, but unpublished opus in June, 1983. Its gestation had endured a crisis in mid-life (at the beginning of Chapter Four):

> "We'll stop this futile versifying,
> my darling Muse, and work instead
> on something far more gratifying
> to you, who have been born and bred
> on modes and musings academic."
> "Your flattery is stratagemic,"
> she said, "but since I caused this breach,
> I owe you. Where's your Tolstoy speech?"
> Thus *Richard Burgin* was forgotten
> for "Death and Women in Tolstoy:
> A Jungian View." My Slavist's ploy
> was happily not misbegotten.
> Tolstoy revived her Muse's breath
> and thus has saved my *Life* from death (RBALIV, IV:7)

The title referred to was delivered at the Russian Research Center (Harvard University) in February, 1983 to a receptive audience made up almost w/holly of women (but I shan't bore you with an expatiation on my "little notions" concerning Harvard bore/ocracy (see Mary Daly, *Pure Lust*, Beacon Press, 1983)). Suffice to say, many who attended the delivery encouraged me to bring the work up to publication. Having thus explained the content and history of the present work, I should perhaps comment on the form, i.e., whence the dactyls? How did the three joints—Tolstoy/Death/Jung—of my callused writing finger become meterized? It happened in the spring of 1982, one year after the Death and one year before the Birth: "In those days, doing preparations/for classes—versified translations/of lyric Russian poetry—/I felt my Muse first come to me./ My dark apartment (not idyllic!)/was lightened by her bubbly wit./At first she parodied a bit,/burlesqued Tolstoy in rhymes dactylic,/then into verse perversely chose/to put my academic prose./" (RBALIV, VIII:1) The versified translations included one of *"Edu li noč'ju po ulice temnoj . . ."* The first version of "Jungian Dactyls (. . .)" emerged from Nekrasov, that is, from the "woman question." But now we are back to Tolstoy, have gone through the Title and reached the Epigraph.

[2]In spite of Tolstoy's acknowledgement in "On Life" that "man cannot know his own death and will never be able to know her" (*O žizni*, N.Y., Russian Library Press, 127, trs. mine—D.L.B.) he apparently never ceased trying. The works on death he left behind provide symbolic clues to the knowledge he desired and testify to the immortality of his "special attitude" to life. For the rest, we have only our imaginations and the beguiling words that the old man was reported by Gorky to have uttered to a group of writers during a conversation about women (English translation by Koteliansky & Woolf in Gorky, *Reminiscences of Tolstoy, Chekhov, and Andreev*, N.Y., Viking Press, 1959, 44). Tolstoy's triangular focus on Truth(telling)—Women—Death points us to the archetypal symbolic matrix of his creative works, "a considerable portion" of which, as Lavrin has remarked, "can be defined as a duel with death." (*Tolstoy—An Approach*, 1946, 86). The combatants in the duel are typically a hero who is consumed by a desire to know death, yet resists, out of fear, the knowledge he seeks; and a fearsome, provocative, rapacious, horrifyingly attractive, female presence, SHE/*ONA*. The combatants' struggle for dominance is very similar to the "battle of the sexes" as Tolstoy portrays it, particularly in relationships born of lust. Negative projections such as those we see in Tolstoyan male/female relationships indicate the presence of the anima.

[3]Certainly the testimony of Tolstoy's works, if not the projections that seem to have overshadowed his own marriage and family happiness bear out Gorky's opinion that Tolstoy regarded women with "implacable hostility, . . . the hostility of the male who has not succeeded in getting all the pleasure he could, or . . . the hostility of spirit against 'the degrading impulses of the flesh.'" (Gorky, 14) And death is nothing in Tolstoy if it is not "fleshly" (*plotskaja*). In "On Life" he reaches the conclusion that the only death is "fleshly death," which, like "fleshly [carnal] life" is false. Tolstoy's works reveal the writer's increasingly obvious effort to establish a definitive connection between sexual desire and killing on one hand, and the sexual woman (not the real woman, who is Mother) and death on the other. Tolstoy's obsession with these and other binary oppositions make his writing and thinking congenial to Jungian analysis.

[4]Prince Andrei is caught in a typically Tolstoyan dualism in his love for Natasha. His poetic love for her (similar to youthful Nikolai's love, in *Youth*, for his fantasy beloved, *she*, an eroticized, incestuous mother-imago) disappears in the physical reality of their first kiss, after which he "could find in his heart not a trace of his former love for her." In place of "the former poetic and mysterious charm of desire . . . was a feeling of pity . . . [and] a heavy and at

the same time joyful recognition of the obligation that bound him to her forever." (Tolstoy, *Polnoe sobranie sočinenii v 90 tomax*, Moscow, 1935, X, 225, translation mine—D.L.B. Henceforth this edition will be referred to as PSS.) Andrei's experience illustrates Jung's comment in "The Dual Mother" (henceforth DM) that "human love presents such a thorny problem to man that he would rather creep into the remotest corner than touch it with his little finger." (Jung, *Symbols of Transformation*, transl. R.F.C. Hull, Princeton, 1976, 308). Natasha later fulfills the role of negative anima for Andrei. In proposing to her he unconsciously senses that his human love cannot satisfy his striving for "the highest beauty and bliss," i.e. God, divine love. Like Nikolai in *Youth* (PSS: II/179) Andrei ultimately, in fact before his death, transfers his desire for union with real beauty and bliss away from "her" (the incestual mother imago) to "him" (God), or the self that yearns to become one with God. This suggests that Andrei is the kind of hero, who, "even more than the rest of mankind, finds his mother in the woman he loves, so that he can become a child again and win to immorality" (DM:332). His fears about Natasha are confirmed by his readiness to postpone his marriage in deference to his father's will, and his father seems to acquire archetypal significance as "the representative of the spirit whose function is to oppose pure instinctuality" (Jung, "Symbols of the Mother and Rebirth" [henceforth SMR], in *Symbols of Transformation*, 261). Andrei's repression of his desire for Natasha illustrates the quandary of the hero who desires both God and Wisdom (the Mother). Natasha's "fall," the fulfillment of the Old Prince's negative prophecy, and for Andrei, surely, a reaffirmation of his father's omnisicence, destroys Andrei's desire for her, but also his chances for (earthly) happiness. When seriously wounded he meets Natasha again and forgives her, but he is already caught up in a new striving for perfect Love in union with God. The only way to this union is through death, and thus death, however feared, becomes Prince Andrei's object of desire. Interestingly, in Andrei's dream of death, he perceives death (*smert'*, feminine) as awakening (*probuždenie*, neuter). The strength of his desire for the latter neuterizes/neutralizes the unacceptable (fleshly) reality (gender identity) of death.

[5]No such replacement is possible for Pozdnyshev who asserts implicitly that in sleeping with their wives men are, in fact, "killing" (*ubivajut*) them, and being killed—spiritually. His description of the actual murder of his wife has strong, sexual overtones. He remembers "the momentary resistance of her corset and of something else, and then the plunging of the dagger into something soft." The knifing bears a striking resemblance to *coitus interruptus*: "Having plunged the dagger in I pulled it out immediately, trying to remedy what had been done and to stop it." (*Great Short Works of Leo Tolstoy*, Perennial Classics, 1964, 424). *Coitus interruptus*, of course, as birth control, realizes the metaphor (or, climaxes it falsely) of the lie that Pozdnyshev asserts marriage "in his set" to be, marriage controlled by (bad) mothers, uninformed daughters, doctors, and birth control that necessarily ends in the death of real women (good, nurturing mothers) and self-realized men.

[6]The first such marriage-license to kill is issued, without issue, to Pierre Bezukhov in *War and Peace*. The parallels between Pierre's behavior at his father's death-bed and his ensuing courtship of his "false father" Prince Vasilii's daughter, the *femme fatale*, Hélène, reveal the negative anima in operation. Both experiences are set against the backdrop of high society's false values. Fear and incomprehension render Pierre helpless in going through both funereal and courtship rituals. He feels there is something horrifying about his father's last moments and something "bad" and "shameful" about the feelings Hélène's "bare bosom and naked shoulders" evoke in him. Throughout his disastrous marriage Pierre projects his guilt onto his wife and comes to view her as the source of his own evil spirit of negation, the major obstacle to his discovery of life's meaning. No wonder that in Pierre's worst moment of existential despair he visualizes an encounter with a "*she*" (*ona*), personified "lie" (*lož'*) and metaphor of death, which, like his desire for Hélène, expresses the paradoxical nature of his anima: she is and she is lie, exists while denying existence. Resistance to his fear at first compels Pierre to run from "her": "There's nothing worthwhile, nothing important, it's all the same: all one can do is to try as hard as one can to save oneself from her, thought Pierre. If only not to see *her* [*ee*], that terrible *her*." (PSS: X/297)

[7]The "she" that pursues Pierre (and with which he comes to terms by ultimately accepting in "her" place, as the pronoun of the "force that governs all," a neuter "it" (*ono*)) takes on fictional flesh in that side of Anna Karenina (she being the ultimate Tolstoyan dualism, she being Woman) which lusts for Vronsky, and counters her real feminine (maternal) nature. If we were to extend the already extended metaphor of Anna and Vronsky's relationship as co-criminals in the grisly murder of their "love," then their marriage constitutes the seemingly endless cutting up of its flesh until she (Anna) destroys herself in the grip of her own animistic spirit of negation. Anna's animus—Tolstoy—is implied by the vengeful God of the epigraph and is personified in the patriarchal figure (stooping peasant) in her dream, which she interprets as a pre-/admonition of death. Anna's negative animus beats in upon her battered self just as the bearded peasant, muttering foreign words, symbolic of a culture alien to her real "maternal" self (oh, those French!), beats upon the iron. Since Anna views death as self-obliteration, a gesture of revenge against moral author(ity), when she dies, cut in two by a train, she is symbolically emasculated, sees no light—the light in her eyes (psychic force or libido) goes out forever. Thus does Anna's anima (anna/ma?)-wracked author/God attempt to solve the Iniquitous Ultimate Dichotomy (IUD) by cleaving the iniquitous side of his hero/ine (her body) from her ultimate side (her reason). "Love" after all is "the most rational activity of mankind" ("On Life"), and "reason puts man on the only life path which, like a conically-shaped, everwidening tunnel in the middle of walls on all sides that close him in opens to him in the distance the indubitable non-endingness of life and his bliss." (164)

[8]While Lev-author cleaves the IUD in two, Levin-hero escapes from fear of "fallen creatures" (whom he refuses to call "women" but identifies as "painted Frenchwomen" and "scum" (PSS:XVIII/45)), as well as from his fear of death,

through rational acceptance of "the other great enigma," birth, that is, the maternal realization of the procreative spirit (God). "Hardly had he witnessed with his own eyes the one unresolved enigma and mystery of death [his brother's] than another confronted him, just as unresolved [Kitty's approaching maternity], and calling him to love and life." (PSS:XIX/75) The mystery of the IUD (more frequently known as the Madonna-Whore dichotomy), the enigmas of death and birth, of Woman, the "leaky vessel" of both, challenge Levin (and Lev) with an ultimatum to know the meaning of life and come back to God.

⁹But in order to come back to God man has to confront death, that is, pass out through the "exit doors." In Prince Andrei's dream, death enters the sickman's room (his self) through opening and closing double doors. In "On Life" Tolstoy opines that the "exit doors" of death are the same as the "entrance doors" we passed through at birth (157). These images are maternal symbols, and Tolstoy's ultimate rationalization of death as re/birth appears rooted in the "primitive idea of reproducing oneself by entering into the mother's body" (SMR:262). The trick is, of course, to accomplish this without despoiling her. For Tolstoy, Love Without Fear is Birth Without Sex.

¹⁰The incest taboo that underlies the Tolstoyan hero's fear of death surfaces in archetypal images of the Terrible, or Devouring Mother, i.e. the paradoxical essence conveyed by the idea of the Dual Mother, the mother of life and death. Tolstoy himself seems to have confronted this idea in witnessing his brother's death, about which he wrote to Fet in a letter of October, 1860: "A few minutes before he died he dozed off, then suddenly came to and whispered in horror, 'And what is this?' That was when he caught sight of her/it [ee]—that swallowing of oneself into nothing." (PSS:LX/357) Tolstoy's frequent personification of death as a rapacious "she" (ona) as well as his use of the same, italicized pronoun to designate the child's eternal image of his mother (see Childhood, PSS:I/85, "I forgot that the dead body which lay before me [Nikolka's mother's corpse] . . . was she."), and the adolescent's ideal beloved (in Youth), lead the reader to the same archetype of the feminine, the anima. In "The Dual Mother" Jung shows how the anima archetype underlies man's psychic struggle with the unconscious for self-realization and informs the symbolic meaning of the typical battle of the hero for rebirth (330-31). Tolstoy's personal struggle with death-fear appears, in the light of Jungian analysis, to have similarly archetypal significance.

¹¹Shortly after completing War and Peace Tolstoy endured his worst attack of existential panic/horror in the town of Arzamas where he had stopped for the night while travelling on business. As described by his autobiographical hero, the madman, in the unfinished 1883 story, "Notes Of A Madman," Tolstoy's "Arzamas Horror" appears to be what Jung has called the "rare and shattering experience [of] . . . gaz[ing] into the face of absolute evil," i.e. of realizing the anima ("Phenomenology of the Self," The Portable Jung, N.Y., Viking, 1971, 148). Unable to sleep because of tormenting thoughts, the madman walks into the corridor outside his hotel room. "But it followed me out and cast a pall over everything. . . . 'What causes me anguish, what do I fear?' "Me," the voice of

death replied noiselessly. "I am here." Yes, death. She will come, she, here she is, but she shouldn't be." (PSS:XXVI/469) About a decade after Arzamas, Tolstoy's anima (not to mention his guilt over killing his beloved heroine, Anna) surfaced again and plunged him into an existential crisis so profound that he too contemplated suicide. Ultimately, rather than iniquitously, he chose not the naught of the knot to re/lease his pent-up [w]horror, but the repentance of the pen. Like every true realization of the anima Tolstoy's was productive of faith, as seen in his spiritual autobiography, the *Confession.*

[12]"I see one thing only—the inescapable dragon, and I can't tear my eyes away." (PSS:XXIII/) The dragon of death, archetypal symbol of the Terrible Mother, yawns at the center of Tolstoy's *Cofession*, his creative opus, his life, and my "Jungian Dactyls (. . .)," challenging the artist and the [wo]man to an heroic quest: the discovery and revelation of the "indisputable truth that every man understands." The revelation of the truth about "her" constitutes the symbolic plot of the narrative, a plot that concerns rebirth and begins where all mythic quests for rebirth do, with the Mother, and the loss of "her." "Where is she, [my] mother? If I've been thrown out, then who threw me out? I can't hide from myself the fact that in loving, someone engendered me. Who is that someone? Again, God. . . . God is life." (PSS:XXIII/44) If the Mother (who bore life) and God (who is life) are one, then, the orphaned "I" is the hero-son who must attain to God through the Mother. God has incarnated Himself in the son while at the same time resisting incarnation ("throwing him out of the nest"). The Tolstoyan struggle for self-regeneration begins in this resistance which forces the son to search for himself and a way back to God and Mother (DM:331). The way back to God (self-realization—though a daughter, I have taken Tolstoy's trip) is blocked by fear, the unconscious, the incest taboo (forbidden fragrance), which threatens to swallow man into nothingness (produces asthma in women)—i.e., death. Besides the dragon and its lair, a waterless well (leaked out vessel), death/the anima/ Terrible Mother is present symbolically in the images of the rapids/crashing rocks (which threaten to destroy the "I's" boat as it rushes downstream), and "the infinity below" (see SMR:213,245,251 and DM:355-56).

[13]These images are developed into three metaphoric "fantasies" that analogize progressive stages in the hero-son's quest to conquer the Terrible Mother and attain to immortality, i.e. union with God, metaphorized as the "other shore" and, in the dream which concludes and summarizes the *Confession*, the "infinity above." (XXIII/58). The dreamer learns that by training his gaze on the "infinity above," aided by a disembodied voice from up there that tells him to 'Take note of "it"' [*ono*], and by giving up his futile (regressive and phallic) kicking motions (signifying re-entry into the womb, DM:315), he successfully dispels/ neuterizes the paralyzing fear that came over him from staring at the abyss down there, the "infinity below." The dreamer also sees and accepts that the ladder he is lying on from the waist up, that his mortal, but not carnal, existence, is securely fastened to a column (tree of life, symbol of the Good Mother, SMR:233). He rests comfortably on a circular loop (noose, the naught(y) knot) that extends from the column. A paradox resolves the paradox of "her" (she is,

but she shouldn't be): the noose that could have destroyed him turns out in reality to be his support: "All this was clear to me and I was happy and calm."

[14]The salutary outcome of Tolstoy's crisis is expressed in the didactic message of his late works on sex and death: "Do not think carnally, or you will be flesh, but think symbolically, and then you will be spirit" (SMR:226). To use Tolstoy's maternal imagery from "On Life," the key to immortality is in understanding one's self not as a separate wave, but part of the whole, eternal sea (i.e., the Mother). Knowledge of the true self constitutes reunion with the Mother, and death is the conduit to that eternity. "Every experience," comments Jung, "entails a change and a guarantee of life's unity." (DM:325) In "On Life" Tolstoy finds that guarantee in the conviction/hope that the change which will come about at death will reenact the change that happened at birth. The post-crisis heroes, the madman, Ivan Ilich, and Vasily Andreyich effect this change/consummation by acts of spiritual parthenogenesis, reproducing their selves by entering/emulating their mothers.

[15]As Helen Dinar points out in *Mothers and Amazons* (N.Y., Julian Press, 1965, 21), at the heart of the idea of 'going through the mother twice' is the perception of the Great Mother goddesses as intensely ambivalent figures, the mothers of life and death: "The problem of immortality for the son consists in being born through the body of the black as he was through the body of the white Great Mother. Once his problem has been solved, she is no more to him than a dark soft portal of eternal resurrection."

[16]In dying, Ivan Ilyich is forced to come to terms with the 'motherlessness' and spiritual bankruptcy of his so-called life. The unconscious self Ivan has avoided pursues him with a vengeance, compelling him finally to lie with her, to look her in the face, to know her: "Is it possible only *she* is true? . . . He could not escape *her*. . . . *She* penetrated through everything. . . . He would go to his study, lie down, and again remain alone with *her*. Eyeball to eyeball with *her*, and there was nothing to be done with *her* except to look at *her* and grow cold." (PSS:XXVI/95) The personified feminine pronoun *ona* ("she"), quite divorced from its noun referent, *bol'* (pain, metonym of death), runs amok in the story, reinforcing the presence of the archetype—the frightening idea of a dominant, desiring female, out of place, displaced, and laying waste the vulnerable, impotent male. Having forced Ivan Ilyich to lie with "her," "she" pushes him into a narrow, deep, black sack—an obvious womb motif. He struggles, fearing he can't push through. As Jung points out, containment (for Ivan, the spiritual travail of dying) "symbolizes the latent state preceding regeneration." (SMR:234) Since Ivan has lived only for material pleasures, he does not see the light of the spirit at the end of the sack until his last moment. It is, needless to say, the same light that brightens his dying memories of his childhood when he was "his mother's little Vanya." When Ivan finally passes through the hole at the bottom of the sack, his soul emerges "all at once," not merely from "two sides" (as his body did at birth), but, in a kind of cosmic parturition, "from ten sides, from all sides." Ivan's newborn eternal self, engendered in loving without sex, through a gesture of nurturing compassion for his son, conquers the anima

and nullifies death: "There was no fear because there was no death. In place of death there was light. 'Death is finished,' he said to himself, 'She is no more.'" (PSS:XXVI/113) *"Končena smert'"* (Death is finished)—the rapacious "she" who once "penetrated through everything" has finally **been** pacified/passivized/ finished—by whom? The implied agent is the light (Ivan's psychic force, libi- do). He has "finished" (come, finally, into new life) and his "light" has finished her. Surely the "most devoutly to be wished" of Tolstoyan "consummations," the very antithesis to/antidote for the sexual ones that "kill." No wonder Ivan Ilyich's face in death wears an expression which "said that what was necessary had been accomplished, and accomplished rightly."

[17]Jungian analysis of Tolstoy's treatment of death shows to what degree the writer's creative "meditations on death" (see Pasternak, *Dr. Zhivago*, Signet Books, 1958,78 where Yuri speaks of all great art as a meditation on death and thus a continuation of the Revelation of St. John) derive from a "primitive idea: self-reproduction via entrance into the mother's body." Yet, Tolstoy strove for transcendence not only through conquering his appetites, but through the more spiritual act of self-sacrifice. Although he rejected Christ as a symbol of the crucified god, spiritual archetype of rebirth, he hailed Him, in "On Life," as the model of self-renunciation in life that dispelled fear of death and insured the eternal continuance of the "I." In his entire opus Tolstoy gives only one example of a death that could be called Christ-like (in his terms) and transfigur- ing—the death of Vasily Andreyich in "Master and Man." An act of the spirit conveyed through concrete physical gesture, Vasily Andreyich's conquest of death reveals both Tolstoy's desire and his failure not to think carnally about death. Sacrificing his life for his servant by covering the latter's half-frozen body with his own, Vasily neither fears nor struggles against death when it actually comes. His immobilized body (he can't get up, can't move his arms or legs, can't turn his head) offers no resistance, yet he feels himself in motion. The more frozen his body becomes, the harder it is for him to restrain his rush to freedom: he wants, realizes, remembers, strains his ears, hears, talks, thinks, and finally, knows: "He [Vasily's former self] didn't know, but now I do. Now I know for sure. Now I know." The final emphasis on KNOWING contrasts strikingly to the initial repetition of NOT BEING ABLE, and the contrast underscores the superiority of mental to physical effort for conquering INIQUI- TOUS DEATH and coming to ULTIMATE LIFE. "'I'm coming, I'm coming!' says his whole being joyfully and humbly" to a "Someone" he has seen in a pre-death dream and who seems to be beckoning to him (PSS:XXIX/44). The Someone is God, as Tolstoy's use of the pronoun, "kto-to," in the *Confession* indicates ("I can't hide from myself that in loving, someone engendered me"), yet one cannot help but be amazed at how stubbornly Tolstoy resisted naming the divinity. One recalls Jung's comment that the fight of the hero for rebirth is with the father. (DM:331) In dying Vasily Andreyich more than accomplishes what is necessary, and what is necessary, in Tolstoy, is the conquest of death and achievement of "family happiness." Thus, the Master merges fully into the Servant/Other, two become one in a moment of self-realizing, perfect love, similar in symbolic/symbiotic terms to the mother's giving of her body to nur-

ture her child, and in Tolstoy's visual representation, to the sexual act. The
Master exceeds mere emulation of the Mother: he becomes her, and at the same
time regenerates himself by engendering his servant-child's "new" life. His
experience of real love, effected through the physical gesture of its false, sexual
reflection, renders him changed, "unlike his former self," who appears in his
last memories as alien to him. The Master conquers the death he once feared by
attaining to God, the Father, and full knowledge, the Mother. His is Tolstoy's
version of the "marriage of the Lamb" through which the son is united with the
mother-bride and "the ultimate bliss is attained" (SMR:223). Jung would note
that the totality of Vasily's experience is indicated by the absent presence in his
death-scene of a symbolic quaternity/archetypal Family: Father/Mother/Son/
Holy Spirit—the former master; the transfigured master-servant; the revived
servant-man; and the Someone who beckons to "indisputable truth." The truth
moves us, but where? Closer, I think, to the knowledge that family happiness
is hard of accomplishment, especially for wives and daughters.

University of Massachusetts at Boston

VERBS OF 'TEACHING' IN RUSSIAN:
ON CROSS-LINGUISTIC LEXICAL EQUIVALENCE

Patricia R. Chaput

A recurring problem for linguists and students of Russian alike is the question of lexical equivalence—the determination of when words and expressions in these two languages are close enough in meaning to be considered more or less equivalent and therefore analyzable in similar terms and usable in similar linguistic contexts. Apparently straightforward concepts often turn out to be deceptive, with unsuspected restrictions on combination or limitations in denotation. Such is the case with the Russian verbs that convey the meaning of 'teaching,' which are the focus of the following analysis. The conclusions presented here are the result of an examination of dozens of examples, some taken from handbooks and dictionaries,[1] but most collected from original literature, followed by a series of speaker tests to try to determine the limits of acceptability. The resulting "definitions" show considerable overlap with English "teach," but also unexpected areas of divergence.

In general terms, and in both English and Russian, the subject of the teach verb is responsible for some potential transfer of knowledge (the teach object, hereafter Object) to a learner or learners. There seem to be no restrictions on how this transfer can be accomplished, and any number of different actions (showing, explaining, demonstrating, guiding, correcting, etc.) can be subsumed under a general notion of teaching. The English uses (meanings) of "teach" range from teaching as an occupation ("She teaches history.") to a conscious instructional process ("She taught him to read.") to an unintentional or even avolitional converse of learning ("His answer taught me something."). The English verb "teach" is also a high frequency cover term which may informally substitute for an entire series of more specific instructional verbs, including, among others, "instruct," "train," "educate," "school," "drill."[2] Green identifies two 'teach' verbs for English, distinguished by means of word order and the use of the dative preposition "to":[3]

> I want to teach English to the sophomores.
> I want to teach the sophomores English.

According to Green, the first expresses only that the teacher is teaching, with the second marked with an additional element of intent. Although it is not clear whether intent is the crucial element here, as opposed to some kind of intentless causative, it will be seen that there is at least some parallelism between these constructions in English and the usage of the Russian teach verbs. In Russian, teaching is expressed primarily by two verbs, *prepodavat'* and *učit'*, and by a third verb, *obučat'*,[4] which is lower in frequency, but for a particular set of common contexts is the preferred choice. *Prepodavat'* is closest to the first "teach" in the examples above; it identifies the agent as a member of the teaching profession with the Object usually an academic subject. *Učit'* is used to refer to the teaching process itself, and implies student learning. *Obučat'* is used when the Object is a technical skill and the agent trains the student in mastering it.

Prepodavat' is the least complex of the 'teach' verbs. It is used to denote that the agent is a professional teacher in some accepted academic situation (location). The Object is typically an academic subject,[5] the location usually some kind of school.

> Марусина мать преподавала русский язык в школе красных курсантов. (Панова: *Листок с подписью Ленина*)
>
> Надежда Егоровна в молодости тоже была учительницей — преподавала в школе для взрослых. (Эренбург: *Оттепель*)

In effect, *prepodavat'* is a verbal statement of the phrase "to be a (professional) teacher". (Compare: *On prepodaet anglijskij jazyk* and *On prepodavatel' anglijskogo jazyka*.) The primary function of *prepodavat'* (that of communicating the agent's profession) is reflected in the possibility of intransitive use without Object: *on prepodaet*. Hierarchically, the Object is second in importance and the student third, but since both are implied by the nature of the profession, neither will be stated unless they are specific in nature, for example:

> *Она преподает предмет в школе.
> Она преподает самые трудные предметы в школе.
>
> *Она преподает студентам английскую литературу.
> Она преподает слепым студентам английскую литературу.

As a statement of profession *prepodavat'* is an abstract state; it is not normally used to refer simply to concrete teaching activity. Compare English: "Where is Anna?" "She is teaching (i.e. that which she is off doing)."

> Где Анна?
> Она сейчас на уроке (английского языка).
> Она сейчас ведет занятия (по английскому языку).

but not

*Она сейчас преподает (английский язык).[6]

Finally, since the focus is on the subject, evaluation reflects the agent's teaching ability exclusive of its effect on the student:

> Она хорошо преподает.
> Она хорошо предподает, но ученики неспособны, многому не учатся.

Semantically, *učiť* (Pf. *naučiť*) is the broadest of the 'teach' verbs. It denotes the complex process by which the student learns and, with an animate agent, may also function to express the activity of teaching. The agent need not be a professional or even an authority on his subject, and the activities which constitute the teaching process are limited only by the imagination. It is the Object, however, which is restricted. Gruber analyzes the objects of both "teach" and "learn" in English as falling into a general category of "information," as in "John taught Bill a story" or "John taught Bill that the earth was flat."[7] It is interesting that he chose this particular designation, since it is precisely informational Objects which are prohibited in combination with *učiť*. In Russian, informational Objects can be told, explained, communicated, etc., but not taught. Compare,

> *Билл научил меня, что земля плоская.
> Билл объяснил мне, что земля плоская.

> *Билл научил маленького Даню его номеру телефона.
> Билл заставил Даню запомнить его номер телефона.

The restriction on the Object of Russian *učiť* is that it be viewed as an acquired ability to perform, something the student learns **to do**. It is not surprising, therefore, that the Object is expressed most frequently as an infinitive complement. This infinitive is imperfective, since what is being taught is how to perform the action (not a single action and no reference to completion).

> Он научил меня плавать и скоро плавание стало моим любимым летним увлечением.

> Во-первых, он научил жителей города играть в винт; . . . во-вторых он научил обывателей пить пиво, которое тоже здесь не было ивестно; . . . (Чехов: *Дуэль*)

An animate agent usually implies intent, but it is not necessary that the teaching be intentional, so that *učiť* might be more strictly defined as a kind of avolitional or resultative causative, "to cause to learn." Such a definition would account for use with inanimate subjects:

> Леса украшают землю . . . Они учат человека понимать прекрасное
> . . . (Чехов: *Дядя Ваня*)

> Его рассказы, даже грустные, оставляют ощущение полноты и счастья
> жизни. Они учат любить жизнь, любить человека. (Anonymous, in sto-
> ries by Ju. Kazakov)[8]

Učiť is frequently found reporting verbal instructions, but note that what is
being taught must still be viewed as an ability to perform:

> Главное, поцелуй—и молчи! — учил он. — Потом можешь и гово-
> рить, несколько спустя, а когда поцелуешь, то молчи. Не говори сразу
> после поцелуя, понимаешь? (Андреев: *Рассказ о семи повешенных*)

> Няня, передавая тебе единственный известный ей признак благовос-
> питанности, когда-то учила тебя: «Шаркни ножкой!» (Бунин: *Цифры*)

It is not that noun Objects are prohibited with *učiť*; they are acceptable as
long as they express a performable skill. There is, however, a difference in
aspectual use in the matrix verb. With infinitive complements both perfective *naučiť* and imperfective *učiť* are common; with noun objects perfective
naučiť is rare, as if mastery of the whole of a skill represented in a noun is
exceptional.

> Мать учила (научила) свою дочь шитью.

> Он учил меня всему: гальванопластике, французскому языку . . ., за-
> вязыванию морских узлов, распознаванию насекомых и птиц, пред-
> сказанию погоды, плаванию, ловле тарантулов . . . (К. Чуковский:
> *Борис Житков*)

With indefinite pronoun objects, however, perfective *naučiť* is common:

> Футбол меня многому научил. (Евтушенко: *Автобиография*)

> Для учителя, может быть самое важное — не принимать себя всерьез,
> понимать, что он может научить совсем немногому. (Распутин: *Уроки
> французского*)

Sometimes the distinction between performability and information may be
very subtle. Personal qualities which one learns to act upon or demonstrate
are considered performable and are acceptable.

> Всю неделю Макар ходил по домам и обстоятельно, въедливо учил
> людей добру и терпению. Учил жить — по возможности весело, но
> благоразумно, с «пониманием многомиллионного народа». (Шукшин:
> *Непротивленец Макар Жеребцов*)

So, apparently, are linguistic constructions or words which one must learn
to use properly to incorporate into one's speech:

> Она научила нас новым словам и конструкциям.

However, the "rules," by which one performs an action, were judged informational by speakers tested and therefore unacceptable:

> *Она научила нас правилам уличного движения.

Although Russian *učit'*, like English "teach," is not one specific activity but an abstraction referring to a number of concrete teaching activities, it can, as in English, be used non-abstractly. However, it is strongly transitive and cannot be used in this concrete sense without mention of the Object and the student:

> Посмотри, она учит детей плавать!
>
> Что я делаю? Я учу Бориса готовить борщ.
> > *Я учу.
> > *Я учу Бориса.
> > *Я учу готовить борщ.
>
> Где Анна? Она учит мальчиков печатать.
> > *Она учит.
> > *Она учит печатать.
> > *Она учит мальчиков.

Of course, the literal answer to this question would be the location where Anna is teaching. This type of ellipsis is permitted with *učit'*, whereas it would not be with *prepodavat'*. Interestingly, on a more abstract level *učit'* can be used without an Object to focus specifically on the activity of teaching. The student must be included unless it is generalized to all relevant students:

> Я учу, но мои ученики ничего не запоминают.
>
> Иногда надоедает быть только учительницей, учить и учить без конца. (Распутин: *Уроки французского*)
>
> Все дети талантливы/Можно учить без двоек? (Headline, *Литературная газета*)
>
> Пешехода надо учить. (Headline, *Русский язык за рубежом*)
>
> —А нам Ольга Николаевна ничего не объясняет. Все только спрашивает и спрашивает.
> —Не понимаю, как вас учат!
> —Вот так, —говорю, —и учат. (Носов: *Витя Малеев в школе и дома*)
>
> Нет, я не собирался учить Алену на своем горестном опыте. Просто я хотела этим опытом утешить ее. (Алексин: *Третий в пятом ряду*)

> Ваня же сам мог если не научить, то уж во всяком случае п р о у ч и т ь
> меня. (Алексин: *Третий в пятом ряду*) (Note use of perfective in this
> function.)

The meaning of *obučat'* is closer to English "train" than to "teach." The
agent, a master of a skill, transmits the knowledge and ability to perform
that skill to another person, who is then able to perform it. This verb is
very high in frequency in vocational/technical educational literature and is
often associated with types of manual training. It is also common outside
of vocational situations when the Object can be characterized as a technical
skill, or when the teaching process can be seen as training, something
which the student learns to perform through repetition. The specific skill is
most often expressed by a noun, reflecting the totality of mastery. *Obučat'*
is the only 'teach' verb for which mastery is generally implied.

> Когда мы говорим — «обучить грамоте», это значит дать более или
> менее настоящую грамотность . . . А это значит, чтобы учащиеся
> умели читать и понимать книги, умели понимать вообще прочитан-
> ное. (Калинин: Speech 16 August 1931)
>
> Он обучил его столярному ремеслу, обращению со станком.
>
> Старшие обучают детей всему, что умеют сами. (Note the use of
> уметь, the "skill" verb, as opposed to знать.)

Nouns which are not traditionally thought of as skills may appear as the
Object, but the verb retains the element of training. This most often occurs
with school subjects, but any noun conceived as a skill can appear, often
for special effect, as in the last example below. The combination *obučat'*
gramote appears to be a fixed phrase, or cliché.

> Несколько лет назад в качестве эксперимента . . . стали обучать
> иностранному языку, главным образом английскому, детей в воз-
> расте с 5 до 7 лет в детских садах. (Рассудова и Степанова, *Интен-*
> *сивный курс русского языка*)
>
> Тренер обучал нас новым методам.
>
> «Премудростям» профессии монтажницы электровакуумных приборов
> меня обучала Р. С. Кабирова. (Иванова: «В час работы и после»,
> *Правда*, 8 марта 1978 г.)
>
> Священник за жалованье обучал детей крестьянских и дворовых гра-
> моте. (Толстой: *Война и мир*)

The skill may be, but is less frequently expressed by a verb (always imperfective). Speakers sometimes choose a verb for non-abstract reference, but
this is relatively rare; more commonly a verb is chosen when the noun is
not commonly used as a skill name or has other stylistic associations.

Каждый день с рассвета и дотемна Комариков обучал свою роту бросать гранаты, ходить в атаку, незаметно подползать к условному противнику, стрелять из винтовок и пулеметов, уничтожать танки. (Ильенков: *Большая дорога*)

In the above sentence nouns are technically acceptable, but the resulting high-sounding *xoždenie*, or *podpolzanie*, sound clumsy and strange in the context of military training. A general stylistic prohibition for Russian forbids mixing nouns and verbs, so verbs must be chosen throughout. In the example below the skill feature is played on for special effect when Tvardovskij insults a poet proposed as a recipient of a Stalin prize by implying that his poetry is not art but only a skill to which anyone could be trained:

Я помню, как вдруг поднялся с места Твардовский и с раздраженностью пристыдил ораторов, славословящих по адресу одного поэта.
—Да на что вы время тратите! Такие стихи я могу любого деревенского теленка обучить писать! (Евтушенко: *Автобиография*)

Interestingly, *obučat'* appears to represent a higher level of abstraction than *učit'*. It is only rarely used in reference to concrete teaching activity and, unlike *učit'* cannot accept a shift to activity usage without objects. It can, however, like *prepodavat'*, be used to denote the agent's profession.

Посмотри, он обучает их чинить телевизоры.

*Я обучаю, но они ничего не запоминают.

Кто он по профессии? Он обучает столярному делу. (Presupposes: Он мастер столярного дела.)

It might seem at first that the usage of these three verbs is fairly distinct. *Prepodavat'* is used to designate the agent as professional teacher; it combines with Objects which are academic subjects, and also with students (when specified). It is an abstract state and so cannot be used in reference to concrete activities. *Učit'* refers to a process (= activities) by which students learn, and except for a restriction on the Object that it be an acquired ability, is relatively unrestricted. Morphologically related *obučat'* (root: UK) similarly refers to a process by which students learn, but is restricted to kinds of technical training. Selection might be roughly envisioned as a kind of tree diagram with a first criterion of choice being the focus on the teacher's teaching vs. student learning. (See next page.)

Differentiation between *prepodavat'* and *učit'* is relatively easy because of the difference in focus. Overlap might occur when conditions for both are met, as in "Petr Ivanovič taught me math." The selection of *prepodavat'* would be more or less equivalent to "Petr Ivanovič was my math teacher,"

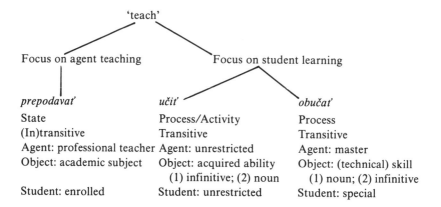

with no reference to learning. If the teaching occurred outside of a school situation or if emphasis is on the success of the learning (= "I learned math from Petr Ivanovič"), then *učit'* is the appropriate choice:

>   Мне преподавал математику Петр Иванович.

>   Меня учил математике Петр Иванович.

Note that the case government of these verbs conforms to the focus. With *prepodavat'* the primary (accusative case) relationship is between the teacher and the Object, the focus of his profession. With *učit'* the primary relationship is between the teacher and the student, reflecting the importance of the student's learning within the teacher-student relationship.

In selecting between *učit'* and *obučat'*, speakers seem influenced by both the semantics and syntax of the verbs. Although the primary distinction remains non-technical vs. technical training, the selection of a verbal complement, even within a technical field, tended to sway speakers toward choosing *učit'*, as was also true for contexts in which the message concerned *how* the teaching took place. Conversely, when the Object was a noun (technical) skill, especially in the situational context of manual or on-the-job training, *obučat'* was felt to be the appropriate choice, although there was no clear prohibition against *učit'*.

Although speakers are unlikely to be choosing between *prepodavat'* and *obučat'*, these two verbs do share a feature in common in that they are both capable of denoting the profession of teaching. In fact speakers asked to give the Russian equivalent of "He teaches carpentry" in reference to an American high school teacher often first suggested *prepodavat'* before discarding it for some other means.

Of course, not all instances of questionable usage can be attributed to purely linguistic restrictions, and especially for these verbs, a complicating factor is the influence of cultural expectations which impose additional constraints on usage. As might be expected, actual usage of these verbs reflects the structure and terminology of the Soviet educational system. Uniformity in job titles, duties, and the educational curriculum cannot but encourage uniformity in describing these phenomena. The Soviet educational system is distinguished by greater specialization in schools and stricter compartmentalization, with academic and vocational training clearly separated. For example, a teacher in a trade school is professionally referred to not as a *prepodavatel'*, but as a *master*, and what he does is *obučat'* or *učit'*. Therefore a sentence such as *On prepodaet stoljarnoe delo* sounds strange in the USSR, since carpentry is not an academic subject. Another example is the education of handicappped or exceptional children, who, in the Soviet educational system are isolated in special schools where they are trained (*obučat'*). However, if the focus is on the teacher's profession, then *prepodavat'* is the natural choice:

> Она преподает в специальной школе для отсталых детей.

Clearly selection is the result of a combination of factors with many situations open to more than one interpretation. Compared to English "teach," *prepodavat'* and *učit'* must be considered the most basic, corresponding to the meanings of "teach" cited earlier. *Obučat'* might be considered comparable to English "train," yet in some contexts (e.g. "He teaches carpentry.") *obučat'* is the only natural choice in Russian, while "train" would be odd in English.

Harvard University

NOTES

[1]For example, see *Slovar'-Spravočnik po russkomu jazyku dlja inostrancev*, vol. 1, ed. E. I. Amiantova, Moskva, 1970; *Sbornik upražnenij po leksike russkogo jazyka*, ed. E. I. Amiantova, Moskva, 1975; *Slovar' sinonimov russkogo jazyka v dvux tomax*, Akademija nauk SSSR, Leningrad, 1970. A few of the examples cited here were taken from the *Slovar' sinonimov*.

[2]From *The American Heritage Dictionary of the English Language*, Boston, 1978, p. 1320.

[3]Georgia M. Green, *Semantics and Syntactic Regularity*, Bloomington, 1974, 156-58.

[4]*Prepodavat'* is an unpaired imperfective; *učit'* is treated together with its perfective counterpart *naučit'*; *obučat'* is treated with *obučit'*.

[5]Non-academic Objects are occasionally possible: По субботам она преподает плавание в специальной школе. For more discussion of this point see below.

[6]Not all speakers seem to agree with this prohibition, although those who accepted it were all emigre Russians who had been living in the United States for some time. It is not clear to me whether this is a case of interference from English or simply careless usage.

[7]Jeffery Gruber, *Lexical Structures in Syntax and Semantics*, Amsterdam, 1976, 125-27.

[8]It might be questioned whether *ponimat'* and *ljubit'* in these examples qualify as performable, although they would seem to qualify clearly as acquired abilities, and in a general sense all verbs express something which one "does." Certainly there is the implication that to understand and to love affect one's actions, so that one "performs with understanding," "performs with love." Verbal Objects of this type are no doubt related to the class of noun Objects denoting personal qualities which are also permitted with *učit'* (see below, especially the example from Šukšin).

TRANSLATING ONE POEM FROM A CYCLE: CVETAEVA'S "YOUR NAME IS A BIRD IN MY HAND" FROM "POEMS TO BLOK"*

Catherine V. Chvany

1. Multiple translation strategies. Isolating a poem from a cycle necessarily breaks the associative links within the cycle, along with the cycle's links to the wider context of the poet's œuvre and the literary tradition. Yet, in practice, cycles are rarely translated in full. For instance, Cvetaeva's sixteen-poem *Stixi k Bloku* (*SkB*), addressed to the Symbolist poet Alexander Blok (1880–1921), is represented in three recent collections, the 1966/67 Markov-Sparks anthology, the 1971 translations by Elaine Feinstein, and the 1978 Glad-Weissbort collection, containing respectively two (M-S), eight (EF), and six poems (G-W).[1] Not found in any of them are VII and XI-XVI.

The only poems translated in all three anthologies is I, *Imja tvoe — ptica v ruke* (Your name is a bird in my hand). As I will show, no translation limited to the overt content of that single poem can convey certain significant elements easily recoverable from its neighbors in the cycle. When a poem is removed from its context, distortion is inevitable, but it is also conventionally more readily accepted than other possible distortions such as adding a line to clarify the meaning. Since it is a truism that no single version can recover **all** of the original meaning, it might be better for translators and anthologists to provide access to a foreign poem through several versions, with complementary illuminations compensating for complementary distortions. This paper illustrates two translation strategies and closes with suggestions for the design of anthologies.

2. The original and its context. Of the sixteen poems in *Stixi k Bloku*, eight were written in 1916, the rest in 1920–21. The cycle was completed soon after A. A. Blok's death. The final poem (XVI) *Tak, Gospodi! i moj obol/ Primi na utverždenie xrama.* (So, Lord, take my mite too/ For establishing the temple) sums up a thematically coherent memorial to the beloved poet, whose death is a loss to her (*Tak, serdce, plač' i slavoslov'* (So, heart, weep and glorify)), and to the country (*Poju svoej otčizny ranu* (I sing my country's wound)), the poet who was in a sense her Teacher, a holy man, a bard, whose death must finally be accepted (*pravednik, pevec — i mertvyj*). The whole cycle is thematically linked to the collection *Remeslo* (Trade, Craft), published in 1921–22, particularly to its first cycle, *Učenik* (Pupil, Disciple). As Margaret Troupin has pointed out, the dates of the last seven poems in *SkB* fill a chronological gap in *Remeslo*, and she has argued convincingly that *SkB* belongs in that collection, even if it was published separately.[2] According to Troupin, the relevant thematic poles of *Remeslo* are The Poet and Russia. Cvetaeva's term *remeslo* for the poet's work implies apprenticeship, with earlier poets as masters.[3] Poem XVI also echoes Blok's own words, *Plač', serdce, plač'* . . ., from his famous patriotic poem "*Na pole Kulikovom.*"

The first poem of *SkB* is reproduced here in the original pre-1917 orthography which Cvetaeva favored for the rest of her life. The punctuation is as in the *BBP* version.

1.	Имя твое — птица въ рукѣ,
2.	Имя твое — льдинка на языкѣ.
3.	Одно единственное движенье губъ.
4.	Имя твое — пять буквъ.
5.	Мячикъ, пойманный на лету,
6.	Серебряный бубенець во рту.
7.	Камень, кинутый въ тихій прудъ,
8.	Всхлипнетъ такъ, какъ тебя зовутъ.
9.	Въ легкомъ щелканьѣ ночныхъ копытъ
10.	Громкое имя твое гремитъ.
11.	И назоветъ его намъ въ високъ
12.	Звонко щелкающій курокъ.
13.	Имя твое — ахъ, нельзя! —
14.	Имя твое — поцѣлуй въ глаза,
15.	Въ нѣжную стужу недвижныхъ вѣкъ.
16.	Имя твое — поцѣлуй въ снѣгъ.
17.	Ключевой, ледяной, голубой глотокъ.
18.	Съ именемъ твоимъ — сонъ глубокъ.

Москва, 15-го апрѣля 1916 г.

I now reproduce the poem in phonetic transcription, with a gloss that is linear except for the reversal of lines 11-12, where the word order of the Russian makes no sense in English. Items lacking in Russian, such as articles or copulas, are supplied in parentheses. Capital letters are used for stressed (and redundantly long) vowels; the diaeresis (¨) indicates a fronted variant. Russian "X" is transcribed as [x] (Greek Chi), and "ц" as [ts]. Reduced /a/ or /o/ is [a] if pretonic or under ictus, otherwise [ə]. The

cedilla (ˌ) marks palatalized paired consonants. Prepositions and other clitics are transcribed as part of a phonological word, but other word boundaries and punctuation have been preserved, to facilitate reading.

1.	Im̦ə tvajÖ — pțItsə vruk̦E,	1.	your name [is] a bird in [the/my] hand,
2.	Im̦ə tvajÖ — ļd̦Inkə nəjizik̦E.	2.	your name [is] an ice-chip on [the/my] tongue.
3.	adnO jid̦Instyinnəjə dyižEnji gUp.	3.	one single movement of the lips.
4.	Im̦ə tvajÖ — p̦Äț bUkf.	4.	your name [is] five letters.
5.	m̦Äčik pOjmənij naļitU,	5.	a ball caught in flight,
6.	șir̦Ebr̦inij bUb̦in̦its vartU.	6.	a silver jingle-bell in the mouth.
7.	kAmin̦, k̦Inutij fțIx̦ij prUt,	7.	a stone tossed in a quiet pond
8.	fsxļIpn̦it tak, kak țib̦Ä zavUt.	8.	will gulp what you're called.
9.	vļÖxkom šč̦Ölkənji načnłx kapłt	9.	in the light clip-clop of night hooves
10.	grOmkəjə Im̦ə tvajÖ grimIt.	10.	your thunderous name resounds.
11.	Inəzay̦Öt jivO nAm y̦yisOk	12.	and a loudly clicking trigger
12.	grOmkə šč̦Ölkəjušč̦ij kurOk.	11.	will name it at our temple|side of our head.
13.	Im̦ə tvajÖ — ax, n̦iļz̦Ä! —	13.	your name—ah/oh, [it's/that's] forbidden!
14.	Im̦ə tvajÖ — pətsiłUj vglazA,	14.	your name — a kiss on the eyes,
15.	vn̦Ežnuju stUžu n̦iyłžnłx y̦Ek,	15.	on tender chill of still eyelids.
16.	Im̦ə tvajÖ — pətsiłUj fsn̦Ek.	16.	your name [is] a kiss into snow.
17.	kļučivOj ļid̦inOj gəlubOj glatOk	17.	from a spring an icy blue gulp/
	. . .		
18.	słmin̦im tvaIm — sOn glubOk.	18.	with your name — sleep [is] deep.

The text is built on acoustic and sensory imagery associated with the sound
of the poet's name. But the name itself, after its initial appearance in the
cycle's title, is not mentioned until the ninth poem (IX, 17-18): *Predstalo
nam . . . svjatoe serdce Aleksandra Bloka* (Has appeared before us . . . the
sainted heart of Alexander Blok). And the name disappears again from
X–XVI after this one reference in an oblique case. Primed by the title, the
Russian reader of this first poem has the pleasure of discovering associations
with sounds and movements that echo the syllable [blOk]. But for the
Anglophone reader of "Poems to Blok," that very syllable requires deci-
sions. How open should the /o/ be? How dark the /l/? Should it sound like
the English word *block*—in one regional variant or another—or is it better
in a faint Russian accent? A reader with access to the Russian naturally
tends toward the latter in the neighborhood of broad sounds, as in *caught*,
while assimilation to a nearby *clock* or *knock* brings it closer to a *"block"*

sound. This subconscious effect remains to be tested on reciters and audiences who know no Russian.

The phonetic transcription, a poor substitute for a recording, shows nonetheless that the purely **iconic** sound associations with [blOk], though undeniably important, are relatively few; the masculine rhymes in 3,4,7,8,9,10 lead into two rhymes in [-Ok] in 11,12, while those in 15,16 are followed by the anagrammatical 17,18, where all four sounds of Blok's name appear in *goluboj glotok* and *glubok*. Perhaps the reason each of the anthologists considered the poem translatable, in spite of its focus on sounds, is that the majority of the sound associations are **indexes** to cross-cultural **non-verbal icons**: line 5 recalls the sound of a ball hitting the palm of the hand, 6 the muted sound of a sleigh or carriage bell (a round jingle-bell) held in the mouth, 7 a stone saying "Blok" [plop] as it hits the water, 9 and 10 recall Blok's name (and the reader could approximate the sound of galloping horses in a clip-clop sound effect with the hands); the name echoes again in the click of a trigger (*kurok*) or in the snap of the fingers (*ščelčok*) which imitates it (11-12). The kiss of 14 and 16 approximates not only the sound of "Blok" but the single gesture of pronouncing it, the lip movement of 3; and 17 again associates the sound with a movement in the mouth.

To me, line 1 suggests a live bird, throbbing to get away. Like the other translators, I choose "in my hand," avoiding the misleading associations of "a bird in the hand." In line 2, the image of ice melting on the tongue as quickly as the syllable is pronounced suggests a momentary ephemeral sensation, hence an ice-chip or sliver rather than Merrill Sparks' "icicle on the tongue." Line 3 is variously translated as "One and just one forming of lips" (MS), "A single movement of the lips" (G-W), "One single movement of the lips" (EF). "One" is preferable to "a" because it reproduces the lip movement; "motion" and "movement" are also more iconic than MS's "forming."

Line 4, "Your name — five letters," refers to the old orthography: before 1917 Блок was spelled Блокъ (the soundless "hard sign" ъ was eliminated by the spelling reform of 1917). Elaine Feinstein's "Your name — five signs" packs the line with a gratuitous riddle. The other two translations better capture the intended thrust: "Your name — four letters . . . done" (M-S), and "Your name — so short" (G-W), for "Blok" is indeed strikingly short for a Russian name.

Line 14, *Imja tvoe — ax, nel'zja!*, is variously translated as "Your name, how impossible" (EF), "Your name — oh! — but one can't!" (MS), "Your name — ah no!" (G-W). In my own linear gloss, I choose "Your Name — but that's forbidden!" But **why** should it be "forbidden," or "impossible"?

The answer to that question is also to be uncovered in the sound of Blok's name. The poem's initial *Imja tvoe* is an obvious allusion to the Lord's Prayer's *Da svjatitsja Imja Tvoe* (Hallowed be Thy Name). The phrase is repeated seven times, including the oblique case form in 18; another repetition in 8 is concealed in *kak tebja zovut* (how you're called). Yet, though entirely devoted to images connected with the sound of the name "Blok," this poem omits the most obvious of all. Your name, Blok, rhymes with the Russian word for "God" — *Bog* [bOk, bOkh], which is produced with the same single movement of the lips. *Ax, nel'zja!* means Cvetaeva stops short of blasphemy: she glorifies Blok's otherworldliness, she draws parallels between him and Christ in this poem and throughout the cycle, but such poetic equations do not **identify** Blok with God or Christ.

Cvetaeva's focus on the poet's sacrifice, otherworldliness, rejection by the secular world, is well grounded in Russian poetic tradition since Puškin; nor is she unique among 20th-century poets in comparing the poet's sacrifice with Christ's.[4] Blok's — or rather, the Poet's — Christlike qualities are alluded to throughout the cycle, most obviously in XI's *Bylo tak jasno na like ego/ Carstvo moe ne ot mira sego* (It was so clear from his face [the word *lik*, rather than *lico*, is the term for the face on an icon]/ My kingdom is not of this world [Christ's words from John 18:36]). But the Christlike qualities are juxtaposed with images of angel, swan, broken wing, lone singer and martyr. There is no deification of Blok, or identification of Blok with God or Christ. The allusion in IX to *svjatoe serdce* (sainted heart) suggests holiness but has no connection to the Sacred Heart of Jesus, which is part of Roman Catholic, not Eastern Orthodox doctrine. Though the *SkB* cycle is often characterized as prayerful, it is not uniformly so. The final *Amin'* (Amen) of II *Nežnyj prizrak* (Gentle ghost (G-W)), (Tender spectre (EF)), is closer to an exorcism than to a prayer: *Amin', Amin', ras-syp'sja, Amin'* (33-34) (Amen, Amen, evaporate/Amen (G-W)). Here, *Amin'*, the last step in blessing oneself, *Vo Imja Otca, i Syna, i Svjatogo Duxa, Amin'* (In the Name of the Father, the Son and the Holy Ghost, Amen), means: "I have made the sign of the cross—as one does for protection from a ghost—so you should disappear." The urgently repeated *Amin'*'s indicate the ghost's—Blok's—persisting presence. In V *Ja moljus' tebe do zari* (I pray to you before/ until dawn), the context is not about God, but about an otherworldly love, never to be met or touched.[5]

Several of Cvetaeva's poems allude to Christ's sufferings; for instance, the crown of thorns in VI: *Cepok, cepok venec* (clinging is the crown), whose thorns catch at hair, skin, clothing. But in II *V ruku, blednuju ot lobzanij/ Ne vob'ju svoego gvozdja* (Into your hand, kissed pale/ I won't hammer a nail of my own), she says that she will **not** deal Blok the same wound. In XIII, the folkloric opener *Ne prolomannoe rebro/ Perelomannoe krylo* (Not a pierced side [lit. rib]/ A broken wing), denies another of Christ's wounds, and the Christ is replaced by images of swan, bird, angel, also found elsewhere in the cycle. In XII *Mater', užel' ne uznala syna?* (Mother, don't you recognize your son?), the ambiguously capitalized initial *Mater'* (rather than *mat'*) is an obvious allusion to *Bogomater'* 'Theotokos', as is *Deva* 'Virgin' two lines below, but the son (uncapitalized) is **not** recognized, and the context is of angel, swan song, and **step**son: *Pasynok k materi v dom. Amin'.* (Stepson to mother's house. Amen.)[6] Clearly, Christ is only one of many mythical analogues to the Poet, and the equation is as often denied as it is suggested.

In poem III, the explicit *vo imja* (in the name of), unsaid in the preceding poem's image of exorcism through the sign of the cross, illuminates the image of I, 16 *Imja tvoe — poceluj v sneg* (Your name — a kiss into snow):

Opuščus' na koleni v sneg   (I'll fall on my knees in the snow
I vo imja tvoe svjatoe   And in your hallowed name
Poceluju večernij sneg.   I'll kiss the evening snow.)[7]

The last line of poem IV makes explicit what is only suggested in poem I: *Mne slavit' imja tvoe* (For me to glorify your name). In that poem, the rhyme with *svoe* [svajÖ], cues *tvoe* [tvajÖ] rather than the Church Slavonic *Tvoe* [TvojE], and thus corresponds to "your name" rather than "Thy Name," providing further evidence that—religious imagery notwithstanding—Blok is praised without being deified.

Other echoes from the Orthodox Christian tradition include the third poem's *Svete tixij — svjatyja slavy* (O quiet light — of sacred glory), from an ancient poetic prayer sung in the Orthodox Vesper service.[8] Its vocative forms recall other vocatives surviving in modern Russian—*Bože!* 'God!', *Gospodi!* 'Lord!', and the Lord's Prayer's *Otče naš* 'Our Father'. Also in III, *Vsederžitel' moej duši* 'Monarch of my soul' recalls the Creed's *Veruju v Boga Otca Vsederžitelja* 'I believe in God the Father Almighty'. Both the Creed and the Lord's Prayer, part of the Orthodox liturgy, were familiar to Cvetaeva from childhood, as they were to every Orthodox Russian.

Cvetaeva's religious terms also echo uses of the same terms by Blok, for instance, in:

Ty v polja otošla bez vozvrata   (You went off to the fields not to return
Da svjatitsja Imja Tvoe   *Hallowed be Thy Name*
. . . (Blok, II, 6)   . . .)

Yet Cvetaeva's play on the sounds in *Aleksandr*, Bloks' first name, in VII's *I imja tvoe, zvučaščee slovno — angel* (And your name, sounding like *angel*), explicitly denies a connection with the Lord's Prayer's *Imja Tvoe* as it is used by Blok. In general, Blok seemed more willing to risk blasphemy than Cvetaeva was. Later in the same poem, after a phrase from the Orthodox funeral service (*so svjatymi upokoj*), Blok presents a feminine *Deržaščaja*, from the same root as *Vsederžitel'*:

O istorgni ržavuju dušu	(O tear out the rusted soul,
So svjatymi menja *upokoj*,	Lay me to rest with the saints
Ty, *Deržaščaja* more i sušu	Thou, Holder (f.) of sea and dry
. . . (Blok, II, 6)	land . . .)

3. Two translations. Poem I as it stands alone, and Poem I as representative of the cycle. My own fairly literal translation is reproduced below. I approximate a poetic translation with the closed-syllable effects so characteristic of this poem, and of Cvetaeva's poetry generally.

1.	Your name is a bird in my hand,
2.	A chip of ice on the tongue,
3.	One single motion of the lips.
4.	Your name, just four letters.
5.	A ball caught in flight,
6.	A silver bell in my mouth.
7.	A rock dropped in a quiet pond
8.	Will say your name as it sobs and sinks.
9.	Your thunderous name resounds
10.	In the light clatter of hooves at night.
11.	And a cocked gun will call it out
12.	As it clicks in aim at our head.
13.	Thy Name — oh, but that's wrong!
14.	Your name is a kiss on the eyes,
15.	On the gentle chill of still eyelids.
16.	Your name is a kiss at the snow,
17.	A cold swallow from an ice-blue spring.
18.	With that name — your name — sleep is deep.

Since a close translation cannot capture the sound asociation [blOk-bOkh], line 13 renders the avoidance of blasphemy in another way.

In my second translation, of **Poem I as representative of the cycle**, I approximate a Lettrist device by working in some non-verbal sound-effects and gestures, indicated in [___]*. In an earlier oral version read at the 1978 AATSEEL meeting, these spaces were occupied by repetitions of the name itself, but for a non-Slavist audience it seems best to limit such repetitions to contexts where "Blok" cannot be replaced by codified sound-effects—the sound [blOk] does not have particularly pleasant associations in English. For Cvetaeva's intended Russian reader, Blok's name needs no reintroduction after the title *Stixi k Bloku*; but since neither the poet's name nor his identity is as accessible to the Anglophone reader's memory, the minimal repetitions are a workable compromise. The full effect of the name's conspicuous absence[9] is necessarily lost in translation, whether or not the name is avoided. For an audience without the Russian's familiarity with the poet and his name, a literal translation cannot fully recreate the tension between knowledge and silence.

The metrical pattern is sketched in a parallel column; there is a rest between the last two closed syllables.

1.	Praised be the sound of your name — Blok	/ – – / – – / /
2.	Held in the hand, it's a bird, caught.	/ – – / – – / /
3.	Melt on the tongue, chip of ice, gone.	/ – – / – – / /
4.	Ball in full flight meets the hand — [clap]*	/ – – / – – / /
5.	Spoken, your name moves the lips — once.	/ – – / – – / /
6.	Printed in full it looks brief, stark.	/ – – / – – / /
7.	Hold a round bell in the mouth, hark:	/ – – / – – / /
8.	Muted, internal, a whisper — [Blok]*	/ – – / – – / /
9.	Drop a small rock in a pond — [plop]*	/ – – / – – / /
10.	Hoofs in the night clatter clip, clop,	/ – – / – – / /
11.	Clapping in thunder your name — Blok.	/ – – / – – / /
12.	We hear it again in a dread knock	/ – – / – – / /
13.	Or ominous sound of a gun, cocked.	/ – – / – – / /
14.	Praised be Thy Name . . . but I must not . . .	/ – – / – – / /
15.	Whatever your own hallowed words prompt.	/ – – / – – / /
16.	A kiss on the eyes says your name, soft,	/ – – / – – / /
17.	On chill tender stillness of lids, shut.	/ – – / – – / /
18.	I bow to your name as I kiss — snow.	/ – – / – – / /
19.	[Gulp]* ice-blue drink from a cold spring,	/ – – / – – / /
20.	Blok — with your name is one's sleep deep.	/ – – / – – / /

Recovering the ellipses adds two lines—a major departure from translator's convention. In 12 I have replaced the image of the gun aimed at the temple with one that conveys the meaning of threat while avoiding the English homonym (the target is the side of the head, not a temple to a deity). My use of the word *hark* in line 7 of the translation reflects Cvetaeva's penchant for archaisms (cf. the penultimate line of III: *Svete tixij — svjatyja slavy*, see above in 2 and note 8 above).

The focus on sounds in my second translation competes with the other images in the poem, much as it does in the original, though it necessarily leaves less to be supplied by the reader. In the more literal first version, however, the images of child's play have less competition, enhancing the "child-like" quality of the first two stanzas (mentioned by both Sloane and Hasty, cf. notes 5 and 9). This effect spills over into the first line of the third stanza—the diction of my literal translation of 13: "Thy Name — oh, but that's wrong!" thus seems more childlike than the original Russian.

As David Sloane's article shows, the entire cycle presents a progression from erotic emotion to a more distant worship. The present interpretation-via-translation shows that the cycle's tension between the two poles is already present in this first poem's ambivalent alternations of sacred and profane imagery and diction. The two translations offered here capture different aspects of this tension.

4. A design for translated anthologies. It would be unproductive to strive for uniformity in translations of the *SkB* cycle. Some of the *SkB* poems lend themselves to verse translation, while for others linear prose may be the best we can do.[10] But poems untranslatable as poems should not be arbitrarily excluded from a translated cycle; they should, instead, be approximated in prose, with annotations as needed.

Of course no single translation can capture all of a poem's meaning. Hence, where several wholly or even partly successful translations exist, it would seem best to include them all, so that a reader can "triangulate" from them to an inaccessible original. Readers who know no Russian would also gain if representative items were printed in the original language, for a visual impression. Selected originals might also be juxtaposed with phonetic transcriptions; or, better still, tape recordings. The goal of translation is, after all, to convey the meaning. And this aim should not be sacrificed to conventional views of editorial consistency.

Massachusetts Institute of Technology

NOTES

*My work on problems addressed in this paper has benefited from comments or discussions with Paul Friedrich, Emily Klenin, and David Sloane.

[1]*Modern Russian Poetry,* ed. Vladimir Markov and Merrill Sparks. Indianapolis–New York: Bobbs-Merrill, 1966/67. This is a bilingual collection totaling 839 pages, with verse translations by Merrill Sparks. The volume's 13 Cvetaeva poems include *SkB* I and IV.

Marina Tsvetaeva: Selected Poems. Translated by Elaine Feinstein, London: Oxford, 1971. Feinstein was assisted by translators Angela Livingstone, Valentina Coe and others. The collection (not a bilingual one) contains *SkB* I, II, III, IV, V, V, VIII, IX, X.

Russian Poetry: The Modern Period, edited by John Glad and Daniel Weissbort. University of Iowa Press: Iowa City, 1978. This book contains ten translated Cvetaeva poems (without the originals), including *SkB* I, II, III IV, V, VI. Glad and Weissbort state in their Introduction that their selection was largely determined by the translatability of the poems.

Citations from Cvetaeva's poetry are from *Izbrannye proizvedenija*, ed. V. Orlov, Biblioteka Poèta, Bol'šaja serija. M–L.: "Sovetskij pisatel'," 1965. Abbreviated in the text as "BBP."

Citations from Blok are for Aleksandr Blok, *Sobranie sočinenij v vos'mi tomax*. M–L.: "Xudožestvnenaja literatura," 1960-63.

[2]Margaret Troupin, *Cvetaeva's "Remeslo": A Commentary*. Unpublished Doctoral dissertation, Harvard University, 1974.

[3]In *Krasnoju kist'ju rjabina zažglas'* (The rowan tree lit up with red tassels), (BBP, p. 83), Cvetaeva celebrated her birth on the day of Ioann Bogoslov (St. John the Theologian, the Evangelist, the **Disciple**—according to Church tradition, one and the same person). Of this poem she wrote: "Vot odno iz moix samyx ljubimyx, samyx *moix* stixov . . . (That's one of my favorite, one of the most 'mine', of my poems . . .)" (letter to Ivask, *Russkij Literaturnyj Arxiv*, eds. M. Karpovich and D. Chizhevsky, New York, 1956, 215-16, cited in Troupin, p. 99).

[4]On Puškin and parallels between poet and Christ, cf. David A. Sloane, "Pushkin's 'Lyric Cycle of 1836' and the Lessons of Izmailov's Hypothesis: Some Notes on the Semiotics of Cycles," in press, *Ulbandus Review*. On similar parallels in Pasternak, see Katherine Tiernan (O'Connor), "Pasternak's 'Hamlet' (from *Doctor Zhivago*)," *The Explicator* 24:5, 1966, pp. 45-46.

[5]For textual evidence, see Sloane's article "'Stixi k Bloku': Cvetaeva's Poetic Dialogue with Blok," in this volume, and references therein.

[6]The stepchild, *pasynok*, is another favorite Cvetaeva metaphor for the poet as outcast or social misfit, for example, in the third poem of the cycle "Poèt": *Čto že mne delat', slepcu i pasynku,/ V mire gde každyj i otč i zrjač?* (What can I do, blind and a stepchild/ In a world where every other is both fathered and sighted?), BBP, p. 233.

[7]Though one might suspect allusion to a ritual, I have so far not found any correspondent, either in Orthodox tradition or in Russian folklore.

[8]The source is *"Večernjaja pesn' Synu Božiju svjaščennomučenika Afinogena,"* traditionally known as *Svete tixij* (and so listed on the jackets of choral recordings of Orthodox Vespers). For comment on its use here see A. Saakjanc, "Marina Cvetaeva ob Aleksandre Bloke," in *V mire Bloka: Sbornik statej* (M.: "Sovetskij pisatel'," 1981, 416-40). In annotations in BBP, p. 735, Saakjanc points out the variation on the prayer's first line, *Prišedšie na zapad solnca, videvše svet večernij* (Those who have come at sunset, having seen the evening light) in *Ty proxodiš' na zapad solnca,/ Ty uvidiš' večernij svet* (III, 1-2). In this context, *zapad* should be translated "sunset": "You pass by at sunset, You will see the evening light," rather than Feinstein's "You are going west of the sun now/ You will see there evening light," or Glad-Weissbort's extremely free "You're going by, west of the sun,/ And snow will cover your tracks." The modern word for "sunset" is *zakat*, with iambic stress, and at that point (III, 1), even a reader familiar with the hymn is likely to gloss *zapad* in its common modern meaning, "West"; but a revision of that initial reading is forced by the unmistakably archaic final stanza, with its undistorted quotation from the hymn.

[9]Insights on the role of proper names and their purposeful omission, in this poem and in other Cvetaeva works, are found in Olga Peters Hasty's "'What's in a Name?': Cvetaeva's Onomastic Verse," read at the Yale Colloquium on Marina Tsvetaeva, New Haven, April 12-14, 1984.

[10]Such a distinction is carefully maintained by master translator Walter Arndt, who prints linear prose next to the original, while verse translations stand alone as poems in English; cf. his *Pushkin Threefold. Narrative, Lyric, Polemic, and Ribald Verse. The Originals with Linear and Metric Translations*. New York: E. P. Dutton & Co., Inc., 1972.

THE STRUCTURE AND IMAGERY OF PUŠKIN'S "IMITATIONS OF THE KORAN"

Julian W. Connolly

Aleksandr Puškin wrote the cycle of nine poems entitled *"Podražanija Koranu"* ("Imitations of the Koran") in the autumn of 1824, during his exile in Mixajlovskoe. Since that time the cycle has provoked a diverse range of critical responses, most of which have focused either on Puškin's personal mood at the time of the cycle's creation or on the question of the poet's intentions in the cycle: did he mean the work to make a statement about religion, ethnology, or the mission of the poet? P. V. Annenkov regarded Puškin's introduction of motifs from the Koran as a "banner under which he put forward his own personal religious feelings."[1] N. I. Černjaev wrote that while composing the cycle Puškin "found in his soul a sympathetic response to the mystical pathos of the Koran."[2] An opposing view was asserted by V. I. Filonenko when he wrote that what interested Puškin in the Koran was something "human" and "not at all divine"; the second poem of the cycle, Filonenko claims, contains a realistic description of Arab life.[3] B. V. Tomaševskij espoused a fourth opinion in his discussion of the cycle, which he regards as a reflection of a "new—optimistic—ideal of poetic creation."[4]

Throughout this debate, however, critics have tended to dwell almost exclusively on the apparent message of the cycle, rather than on its aesthetic features, which have largely been ignored. This study, in contrast, will concentrate on the composition and structure of the cycle, and seeks to achieve two goals. It is hoped that an examination of the structure and central imagery will help illuminate the question of Puškin's concerns in composing the cycle as well as delineating the specific character of his artistic accomplishment in the work.

Before turning to an examination of the poems in the cycle, a few preliminary observations about its general character are in order. In the first place, it is important to recognize that Puškin entitled his cycle *"podražanija"*—imitations—not *"perevody"* (translations) or *"pereloženija"* (transpositions). This designation suggests that the poems were not meant to be faithful reproductions or translations of central passages from the Koran. Rather, they are fresh compositions loosely based on ideas or images found in the Koran, but carefully reworked to create an original mosaic of Puškin's own design. In his notes to the cycle he specifically mentions that his poems are "*vol'nye podražanija*" (free imitations). The writer was clearly impressed with the poetic language of the Koran (which he read in a translation from the French by M. I. Verevkin), and by certain incidents and ideals described in the work.[5] Yet whereas the Koran is a discursive text containing a broad range of disparate material gathered together without a clear organizational principle, Puškin imposed a tighter unity and cohesiveness onto the material he selected for poetic treatment. While his work, too, contains much disparate material, he held it together with a conscious scheme of recurring images and rhetorical structures. Puškin thereby transformed a loose prose text into poetry of high quality.

In composing the work Puškin could draw upon several literary antecedents as stylistic models. Tomaševskij has pointed out the affinities between certain of Puškin's "imitations" and the style of the spiritual odes of the eighteenth century, but in the main Puškin's works are quite different in tone and treatment of detail.[6] Somewhat closer to Puškin in time and spirit were the imitations or reworkings of Biblical, ancient, and oriental works and themes by such writers as Byron, Moore, Chénier, Kjukel'beker, and Glinka.[7] Again, however, Puškin did not merely follow a trend, but forged his own path. A comment he made on Moore's poetry is revealing: "And by the way, do you know why I don't like Moore? Because he is already too Eastern. He imitates childishly and in an ugly way the childishness and ugliness of Saadi, Hafiz, and Mohammed. A European, even in the rapture of Eastern opulence, must preserve the taste and vision of a European."[8] With this reference to "taste" and "vision" Puškin signals his own respect for balance and refinement in poetic composition; these qualities are evident in his "Imitations of the Koran."

A final observation to be made about these nine poems is that together they form a cycle. Each poem must therefore be considered both as an individual work with its own internal thematics and structure and as a component of a larger entity. Themes, images, and devices found in one poem often take on a broader resonance when viewed in the context of the cycle as a whole. A comprehensive study of this cycle would include a detailed analysis of each of its poems, but due to limitations of space, it will be impossible to examine them all in depth. Instead, three of the more important poems—the first, fourth, and ninth—will be singled out for particular attention. Discussion of these works will concentrate on their language, structure, and imagery, while briefer remarks will be directed to the other poems, so that the overall design of the cycle emerges. Puškin did not put together a haphazard collection of verse. His cycle is a calculated weaving of subjects and themes that alternates in a general way between views of the prophet's life and role (poems I, III, V, VII) and moral lessons for humanity (poems II, IV, VI, VIII). Over the course of the cycle Puškin moves from the relationship between Allah and the prophet to the people who surround the prophet in his daily life, and finally to the structure of existence in the world at large.

I

Kljanus' četoj i nečetoj,
Kljanus' mečom i pravoj bitvoj,
Kljanus' utrennej zvezdoj,
Kljanus' večerneju molitvoj:

Net, ne pokinul ja tebja.
Kogo že v sen' uspokoen'ja
Ja vvel, glavu ego ljubja,
I skryl ot zorkogo gonen'ja?

Ne ja l' v den' žaždy napoil
Tebja pustynnymi vodami?
Ne ja l' jazyk tvoj odaril
Mogučej vlast'ju nad umami?

Mužajsja ž, preziraj obman,
Stezeeju pravdy bodro sleduj,
Ljubi sirot i moj Koran
Drožaščej tvari propoveduj.

(I swear by the odd and the even, I swear by the sword and just battle, I swear by the morning star, I swear by evening prayer: No, I did not abandon you. Whom did I lead into a bower of tranquility, loving his head, and whom did I hide from sharp-eyed persecution? Was it not I who gave you desert waters to drink during a day of thirst? Was it not I who endowed your tongue with a mighty power over minds? Take courage, despise deceit, follow boldly the path of truth, love orphans and my Koran, preach to the creatures who tremble.)

In this first poem Puškin introduces many of the leading elements, both thematic and stylistic, out of which the entire cycle is molded. His concern for a life of truth and righteousness, his vision of Allah's power and the special relationship of the divinity to the prophet, and his interest in the role given to the prophet as a ruler of people's minds all have counterparts in subsequent poems. By the same token, several of the major stylistic features of the poem—the use of imperatives and vocatives, archaisms and Church Slavonicisms, and the manipulation of images in pairs for antithesis and contrast—introduce the structural and stylistic framework which lends the cycle much of its cohesiveness and unity. Significantly, Puškin has drawn upon just a few lines from the Koran to create an entirely new poem of power and elegance.

As one examines the poem in more detail, one is struck most of all by its dramatic rhetorical drive. Puškin achieves this effect through a series of rhetorical constructions—four oaths followed by three questions and culminating in a string of five imperatives. The poet has greatly intensified the force of Allah's profession of support; the original passage on which the poem is based has only one oath.[9] Here, however, Puškin's entire first stanza is a series of oaths beginning "*Kljanus'*," and the poet does not provide the concluding portion of the oath until the first line of the second stanza: "*Net, ne pokinul ja tebja*" (No, I did not abandon you). This creates a strong link between the first and second stanzas while leaving the first stanza a vivid demonstration of the sincerity of the oath.

The first stanza itself can be broken down into separate but parallel constructions. The first line—"*Kljanus' četoj i nečetoj*"—consists of a verb and a pair of nouns forming a complementary contrast. The latter construction is indicative of much of the imagery in the cycle, since it consists of (1) a pair, and (2) a complementary contrast or antithesis. The binary structure follows again in line two—"*mečom i pravoj bitvoj*"—and the complementary contrast is found in lines three and four—"*utrennej*" and "*večerneju.*" Although the basic contrast of morning and night appears in the Koran, Puškin elaborates on these images to add certain elements prominent in the life of desert Muslims—the morning star and evening prayer. At the same time the imagery he introduces here will recur later in the cycle: the images of the sword and righteous battle appear in poem six; the images of light and morning recur repeatedly; and finally, the last word of the stanza— "*molitvoj*"—stands in a position of emphasis, underscoring the importance of the spiritual experience and communication with the divine, with which the entire cycle is concerned.

The second stanza begins with a strong negative construction that gains force because of its striking contrast with the affirmative oaths which dominate the first stanza. Allah's affirmation of support for the prophet is enhanced by the direct juxtaposition of "*ja*" and "*tebja.*" This clearly indicates the direct, "transitive" relationship between Allah and the prophet. Whereas the original Verevkin translation reads "*gospod' tvoj ne ostavil tebja*" (your lord did not leave you), Puškin has changed the grammatical structure to heighten the immediacy of the personal relationship. The following rhetorical question continues to demonstrate this transitive relationship: "*Kogo . . . / Ja vvel.*"

Perhaps the most controversial element in this poem is the statement about protecting the prophet from persecution. Critics have offered differing interpretations of this statement. N. O. Lerner argues that it refers to a legend about the pursuit of Mohammed by non-believers resulting in his miraculous salvation.[10] N. V. Fridman, on the other hand, sees in this a reference to Puškin's own exile in Mixajlovskoe, citing in support of his view an earlier variant of the phrase *"glavu ego ljuba:"* *"glav/u/ izgnannika ljubja"* (loving the head of the exile).[11] Such an interpretation has much to recommend it, especially since Puškin had identified himself with Mohammed in a letter written to P. A. Vjazemskij on November 29, 1824. There he speaks of being forced to flee from Mecca to Medina, and he refers to his poetry as his Koran. Yet one must be wary of the temptation to interpret every statement in *"Podražanija Koranu"* as a veiled reference to Puškin or his identity as a poet, for in preparing the final drafts of these poems, Puškin deleted or toned down at least two passages in which the identification of Mohammed with a persecuted poet is suggested.[12] Instead of trying to assert that behind the figure of Mohammed in *"Podražanija Koranu"* stands Puškin the poet, one ought rather to speak of a sense of shared experience or modest kinship, not literal identity.

Puškin continues to focus on Allah's concern for Mohammed in stanza three. The rhetorical questions he introduced in the second stanza multiply here, and again one notes a reliance on parallel structures. The first and third lines both begin *"Ne ja l'"* and end with a verb, while the second and fourth lines contain nouns in the instrumental case and conclude the questions. Allah's personal involvement is emphasized by the placement of the pronoun *ja* in a stressed position in lines one and three. Of particular interest are the specific gestures of support mentioned in the stanza. Both the notion of giving the thirsty prophet something to drink and of endowing him with power over other people's minds are Puškin's inventions, and they carry special significance in the context of his other work. The image of the prophet's thirst before divine intercession looks ahead to the concluding poem of the cycle, and it anticipates the famous opening line of the poem *"Prorok"* ("The Prophet" 1826): *"Duxovnoj žaždoju tomim"* (Tormented by spiritual thirst). The concept of thirst may carry both literal and figurative meaning in this first poem of the cycle.

The second gift granted to Mohammed by Allah in stanza three—the power over people's minds through language—also carries major significance. Again this concept is not mentioned in the original Koran passage, but the idea of the elevated status of the word has fundamental meaning for Puškin. Affirmations of the prophet's distinctive gifts recur throughout this cycle and in Puškin's work as a whole, where not only the prophet is a chosen one but the poet too shares his special status when touched by divine inspiration (e.g. "*Poèt*"—"The Poet" 1827). Of seminal import here too is the concept of might introduced by the epithet "*mogučij*." This concept plays a considerable role in the rest of the cycle as Puškin contrasts the power of the divinity with the weakness of ordinary mortals.

The cycle's opening poem reaches a vivid poetic climax in its final stanza. The driving force of the rhetorical structures in the preceding stanzas is now rechanneled, directed toward the prophet and released in a rush of imperatives. Two imperatives open the stanza, and each of the following lines contains a verb in the imperative as well. Moreover, Puškin arranges these imperatives symmetrically in key positions in the stanza. In lines one and three, imperatives stand at the beginning of the line, while in lines two and four, they are in line final position and carry the rhyme. Both the first and last words of the stanza are imperative verbs.

Allah gives the prophet a wide variety of instructions, two of which are Puškin's own inventions: "despise deceit" and "follow boldly the path of truth." This concern for truth and the rejection of deceit has echoes later in the cycle, and it is an important theme elsewhere in Puškin's work too, especially in poems dealing with the poet's role or duty in life. One thinks of the instruction "*Dorogoju svobodnoj / Idi*" (Travel along a free road) in "*Poètu*" ("To the Poet" 1830). Again this suggests a broad affinity between the personality of Mohammed and the personality of the poet at large. Also noteworthy here is the image of the path. This image is linked with the motif of movement toward a goal in the cycle (variously treated as movement toward the Lord, toward light, etc.), and it serves as the opening element of an important image system which runs throughout the cycle and which is not concluded until the final line of the last poem.

The final line of this opening poem contains yet another noteworthy element, the poet's vision of humanity as "creatures who tremble." Once more the concept is Puškin's own, and he sustains the impression of human frailty throughout the cycle. Humanity, Puškin suggests in "*Podražanija Koranu*," is innately weak and insignificant, and needs to draw strength from a higher or external source. The insignificance of ordinary mortals is depicted in several other of Puškin's works, and one thinks of the "*detej ničtožnyx*" (insignificant children) in "*Poèt*" and even "*červ' zemli*" (worms of the earth) in "*Poèt i tolpa*" (The Poet and the Crowd").

Over the course of his opening poem Puškin has introduced the central themes and imagery which he utilizes throughout the next eight poems. Of particular import are the concept of divine power, human weakness, and the need for faith in the divinely inspired word. Having revealed a direct relationship between Allah and the prophet, Puškin concludes his poem with a glimpse of the broader world of humankind. In the following poems he expands his focus first to touch upon the people who immediately surround the prophet and then the community of mankind in general. Throughout these works Puškin explores the kind of behavior people must demonstrate in their lives and the proper attitude people should take toward God and toward the cosmos itself. In the second poem, for example, Puškin follows the Koran in enjoining the wives of the prophet to be respectful of his own modesty and seriousness. The poet then turns to the outside world in the third poem. After recounting an anecdote about the prophet's reluctance to preach merely to anyone, Puškin begins the third stanza by asking "*Počto ž kičitsja čelovek?*" (Why does man strut?). He goes on to expose man's weakness through a series of observations that resonate with incidents mentioned elsewhere in the cycle. His observation that God can slay and resurrect people at will looks forward to the last poem in the cycle, while his observation that God has given man such things as grain, dates, and olives recalls Allah's assertion in poem one that he gave the prophet water to drink when he was thirsty. Yet the idyllic picture of fertile pastures and vineyards created in the three middle stanzas of the poem is suddenly demolished in the last two stanzas by a dramatic depiction of the day of reckoning, when "everyone will stream toward God, / Disfigured with terror: / And the impious will fall / Covered in flame and dust." This apocalyptic scene underscores both the frailty of mortals and the might of Allah himself, and it provides a concise introduction to the fourth poem of the cycle, a simple yet striking statement about the incomparable power of the divinity and the foolish hubris of ordinary man.

IV

S toboju drevle, o vsesiľnyj,
Mogučij sostjazaťsja mnil,
Bezumnoj gordosťju obiľnyj;
No ty, gospoď, ego smiril.
Ty rek: ja miru žizn' daruju,
Ja smerťju zemlju nakazuju,
Na vse pod"jata dlan' moja.
Ja takže, rek on, žizn' daruju
I takže smerťju nakazuju:
S toboju, bože, raven ja.
No smolkla poxvaľba poroka
Ot slova gneva tvoego:
Pod"emlju solnce ja s vostoka;
S zakata podymi ego!

(In ancient times, Almighty One, a powerful man, filled with senseless pride, thought he could compete with you; but you, Lord, subdued him. You said: "I grant life to the world, I punish the earth with death, for all things is my palm upraised." "I too," he said, "grant life, and I too punish with death: I am equal to you, God." But the boasting of vice fell silent at a statement of your wrath: "I raise the sun from the East; raise it now from the West!")

Puškin's transformation of the original Koran account is noteworthy. In the original text (Sura II, 260), the story of an earthly ruler's arrogance is reported as a dialogue between the ruler and Abraham, and it is Abraham who points out God's power. Here, however, Puškin recasts the episode into a direct confrontation between the ruler and God himself. This directness and immediacy is characteristic of the cycle as a whole.

The poet has given the poem an interesting structure. The first four lines provide a general account of the anecdote's plot. The poet directly addresses the Lord and couches his tale in a quatrain with a rhyme scheme of AbAb. In the fifth through the tenth lines, Puškin conveys the confrontation between Allah and the ruler through a series of parallel and counterweighted statements. For three lines Allah defines his power, and Puškin utilizes a rhyme scheme of CCd. Then the ruler's boast follows, also in three lines and again with a rhyme scheme of CCd. Indeed, the rhyme "*daruju—nakazuju*" introduced by Allah is repeated by the ruler. This sytem of parallelism and repetition culminates in the ruler's affirmation: "I am equal to you, God."[13]

Metrically and rhythmically his impression of equality seems to be borne out, but as one looks more closely at the dialogue one realizes that Puškin has created a significant imbalance within the two figures' speeches. To begin with, when the Lord says, "I grant life *to the world*" and "I punish *the earth* with death" (emphasis added), one realizes His direct life-giving (and death-giving) relationship to the world, and this recalls the transitive force of "*ja tebja*" in poem one. The ruler's speech lacks any indication of such a relationship: there is no mention of the world or the earth in his claims. Moreover, the greater majesty of the Lord is underscored by the fact that He uses the personal pronoun *ja* twice in his speech, but the ruler only uses it once—a diminution of personal power. Likewise, the important statement by the Lord—"for all things is my palm upraised"—has no counterpart at all in the boaster's speech; he simply does not have that comprehensive involvement in the life of the world that is characteristic of God. His power is indeed limited when compared with the Lord's, and he is reduced to slavish imitation: "*takže . . . takže*." Even the epithet with which Puškin identifies him—"*mogučij*"—reveals that he has less might than the Lord, who is called "*vsesil'nyj*."

The final section of the poem puts an end to the boaster's foolish egoism as the Lord discloses an ability that truly proves his power: "*Pod''emlju solnce ja s vostoka.*" One notes that the pronoun *ja* is metrically stressed. Then the Lord silences his rival with His injunction to the mortal to raise the sun from the West. Herein lies one of the main characteristics of Allah's might: his rule over the heavens as well as the earth. The sky motif has appeared earlier in the cycle, most prominently in the preceding poem, and the singular attention the Lord gives to the sun anticipates developments in the next poem.

Indeed, the fifth poem seems to begin where the fourth left off, with a description of the universe sustained by the Lord: "*Zemlja nedvižna—neba svody, / Tvorec, podderžany toboj,*" (The earth is immobile, the vaults of heaven are supported by you, Creator). Such a smooth transition is Puškin's accomplishment, since the Koran itself is a disorganized amalgam of themes and images. This particular poem recalls Mixail Lomonosov's philosophical meditations on nature, specifically his "*Utrennee ražmyšlenie*" ("Morning Meditation"), where the image of the sun as an icon lamp, also used by Puškin here, is introduced as proof of God's might. As the central poem of the nine works that make up the cycle, this poem represents the high point of the cycle in terms of its homage to the Lord. For three stanzas the poet attributes to Allah the responsibility of supporting the universe and giving life to the entire cosmos by means of the sun. In the last stanza, though, the poet returns his attention to people on earth, stating that the Lord has revealed the "shining" Koran to Mohammed: "So that we too shall stream toward the light, / And mist shall fall from our eyes." With this conclusion Puškin signals his intention to concentrate in the second half of the cycle on the human race itself, particularly on its need to reject all doubt and to adopt a spirit of faith and courage.

Thus the sixth poem speaks of holy war and the rewards that will come to the faithful and the contempt that will be heaped on those of lesser integrity. Similarly, the seventh poem focuses on a moment of doubt in the prophet's life and summons him to take heart and dispel his fear through humble prayer. It is interesting to note that this poem stands apart from the preceding ones in its meter—unrhymed two-foot amphibrachs—but, as if in compensation, Puškin has filled it with imagery whose significance has been established earlier in the cycle (e.g. an icon lamp, prayer, a posture of humility, reading the "heavenly book"). Most of all the poem hearkens back to the first poem with its solitary focus on the figure of the prophet and its suggestion that he is subject to doubt and despair. The epithet with which Puškin characterizes the prophet here—"*bojazlivyj*" (timorous)—is highly significant, for it connects the prophet to the "creatures who trem-

ble" mentioned in the final line of the first poem. The prophet is still a
select individual chosen by Allah to convey His word, but he is also a man,
fearful and in need of faith. Beyond his immediate interest in the prophet
as the chosen one, then, Puškin is concerned with humanity at large, and
this concern pervades the last two poems of the cycle. After making an
earnest plea for open-hearted generosity and charity toward others in poem
eight, Puškin concludes his cycle with a broad allegorical vision of human
frailty and spiritual renewal.

Due to its considerable length—six stanzas of six lines each—the ninth
poem will not be quoted in its entirety. In content the poem consists of an
anecdote depicting the essential nature of man's spiritual quest and his relationship to the divinity in allegorical terms. Puškin sets the tale in rhymed
couplets of amphibrachic tetrameter. Both the meter and the fact that the
poem tells a story with a fantastic conclusion are somewhat reminiscent of
the ballad genre but the style of the work also recalls the Bible with its
archaisms and Slavonicisms and repeated clauses beginning "*I* . . ." (and).
Even the setting suggests a Biblical influence as well as the Koran model.

In fact, Puškin has made significant changes in the story which originally
appeared in the Koran (cf. Sura II, 261). In the one-paragraph Koran version, a traveller saw a ruined town (Jerusalem) and doubted God's power
to restore it. Allah then killed the man and brought him back to life one
hundred years later, demonstrating to the man that this amount of time
had passed by pointing to his spoiled food and drink and his dead ass. The
traveller then became a believer. Puškin's version is quite different. The
poem depicts a weary traveller wandering in the desert and grumbling at
the Lord for his physical discomfort. Spying a well, he eagerly drinks from
it and falls asleep. Through "the will of the Lord," many years pass while
he sleeps. Finally he awakens and hears a voice which asks him how long
he has been asleep. He answers that it has been one day, but the voice
counters with the statement that it has been much longer: "You lay down
still young, but arose an old man." The well has dried up, the palm has
decayed, and the bones of his animal have been bleached by the sun. The
man is stricken with grief, but then a miracle occurs: the palm revives, the
well becomes full, the ass is brought back to life, and the traveller's youth is
restored. The poem concludes: "*Svjatye vostorgi napolnili grud': / I s bogom
on dale puskaetsja v put'*" (Sacred ecstasies filled his breast: And with God
he set off further on his journey).

In addition to filling out the sparse Koran account, Puškin has made
several noteworthy emendations, beginning with the Middle Eastern desert
setting itself. The image of the desert—*pustynja*—is seminal, and Puškin

underscores its significance by incorporating it into all but the last stanza of the poem. This image not only serves to link the last poem of the cycle with the opening poem, thus providing the work with a cohesive frame, it also serves as a broad emblem of a certain psychological or emotional condition affecting individuals in life. Indeed, all the elements of "local color" in the opening stanza carry a dual significance—as realistic details of a specific physical situation and as metaphoric representations of inner psychological states. This dual significance is readily apparent in the lines depicting the traveller's distress: "*V pustyne bluždaja tri dnja i tri noči*" (Wandering in the desert three days and three nights). The image of wandering in the wilderness recalls the figures of John the Baptist and Moses, and looks forward to Puškin's own poem "The Prophet." Anticipating the latter as well is the description of the traveller's suffering: "*On žaždoj tomilsja i teni alkal*" (He was tormented with thirst and craved shade). One notes that Puškin matches the pair of the traveller's needs with a corresponding pair of potential remedies—a well and a palm tree—but as the poem reveals, these material objects cannot fulfill the man's innermost needs. The picture of suffering painted here hearkens back to the first poem with its image of a "day of thirst," and this resonance suggests a link between the generalized traveller and the figure of the prophet. Moreover, the traveller's state of despair and unrest also recalls the state of doubt experienced by the prophet in poem seven. Puškin thus endows the traveller with traits linking him to the central figure of the prophet treated earlier in the cycle, but he also depicts him in such a way that he carries broader significance as a man languishing with unfulfilled needs and impatient with the Lord because of this.

The second stanza contains the episode of the traveller's sleep. Again Puškin has changed the Koran story somewhat. In the original, God "slew" (*umertvil*) the traveller (a harsher action), and set a term of 100 years for him to lie dead. Puškin alters this term to a more general and suggestive "many years." In expounding upon the event, Puškin returns to the leading concepts and images introduced earlier in the cycle. One notes Puškin's use of the theme of God's might when he writes that many years had passed "*Po vole vladyki nebes i zemli*" (Through the will of the master of heaven and earth). Puškin utilized the phrase "*po vole*" in similar fashion in poem three where he also attributed to God the power of death and resurrection. Also familiar is the image pair of heaven and earth. Used frequently in the cycle, it appears for the final time here.

The third stanza provides further evidence of Puškin's poetic transfiguration of the Koran story. When the voice asks the traveller how long he has

slept, the traveller in the Verevkin translation replies: "*Edinyj den' s polovi-
noju*" (One day and a half). Puškin completely revises this prosaic phrase,
making use of imagery already developed in the cycle to give the answer
new lyric dimensions. The traveller says: "*už solnce vysoko / Na utrennem
nebe sijalo včera: / S utra ja gluboko prospal do utra*" (The sun was already
shining high in the morning sky: I have slept deeply from morning till
morning). All these images—the sun, sky, morning, shining—are familiar
from the previous poems; even in a simple reply Puškin chooses to utilize
the particular system of imagery he has created within the larger cycle.

The traveller's confident reply at the end of the third stanza is sharply
countered at the beginning of the fourth, where the phrase "*No golos . . .*"
(But the voice . . .) tersely and abruptly marks a turning point for the traveller and for the poem itself. "*O putnik*" (Oh, traveller), the voice begins,
and this vocative is followed by a characteristic imperative: "*Vzgljani*"
(Look). Puškin uses a whole series of images to show the passage of time.
First he introduces the contrast between lying down a young man and arising as an old one: "*leg ty molod, a starcem vosstal.*" This contrast is made
more effective by a reversal in word order: verb—predicate adjective becomes predicate noun—verb. Also highlighting the contrast in age is a stylistic contrast between the Russian "*molod*" and the Slavonic forms "*vosstal*"
and "*starec.*" Yet Puškin saves the most gripping proof of time's passage
for the last line of the stanza where he unveils an image of death: "*I kosti
belejut oslicy tvoej*" (And the bones of your donkey are growing white).

This view of decay and destruction overwhelms the man, felicitously
termed a "*mgnovennyj starik*" (an instantaneous old man). The traveller
feels crushed, as Puškin indicates through such details as "*Gorem ob"jatyj*"
(seized with grief) and "*drožaščej glavoju ponik*" (he lowered his trembling
head). The latter description echoes the "*drožaščej tvari*" of poem one. The
traveller belongs to the race of mortals who are weak and dependent in
their natural state. At this desperate juncture, however, a sudden change
occurs, and in the last two lines of stanza five Puškin describes the restoration of the natural objects which had decayed with time. He then presents
the greatest miracles in the final stanza of the poem. In a remarkable scene
of animation the bones of the ass rose up and "clothed themselves with a
body and issued a roar," while the traveller undergoes a revival that is both
physical and emotional. He feels a surge both of "strength" and "gladness,"
and in his blood "resurrected youth began to play." Through this renewal,
God's immense power, which has been described in abstract and general
terms in the cycle, becomes personal and immediate in the traveller's experience. As a consequence, a spiritual renewal follows the physical renewal:

"Sacred ecstasies filled his breast: And with God he set off further on his journey."

With this affirmation of new hope and joy, Puškin brings to a close his "*Podražanija Koranu*." The final poem of the cycle is directly linked with the opening poem in its evocation of a needy individual receiving guidance and care from a higher source. Yet Puškin has not merely come full circle here. Rather, the geometric figure which best describes the movement in the cycle is the spiral. Although his closing poem returns to a situation similar to the one which opened the cycle, it does so on a different level: Puškin's focus is wider and more suggestive here than in the first poem. The center of his attention is not the prophet alone, but a kind of everyman. Similarly, just as the poet has widened the scope of his focus to touch upon a universal human experience, so too does his treatment of such concepts as doubt and faith, despair and hope transcend the limitations of a single narrow interpretation. Puškin's "Imitations of the Koran" are not meant to promote the religious tenets of Islam or to expose certain details of the Muslim's life and world view. Nor should one regard Puškin's treatment of divine inspiration solely as a veiled statement about the mission and identity of the poet. Rather, his cycle seems to encompass the entire spectrum of these concepts. Walter Vickery perceives the general nature of Puškin's intentions when he argues that these poems reflect the poet's desire "for a world in which everything would be clear-cut and recognizable, where everything would be in its appointed place, where the distinction would be clear between good and evil, between friend and foe."[14]

Indeed, through the nine poems that make up the cycle one senses Puškin's understanding of and appreciation for the weakness and doubt that afflict all people, and one realizes that in the cycle the poet articulates a countervailing vision of affirmation and hope. Mindful of the human propensity for error and confusion, Puškin raises the hope that the world can be a just place and that one can make one's way through life secure in the knowledge that integrity and justice will prevail and that arrogance and treachery will be punished. Puškin's "*Podražanija Koranu*" represents a significant accomplishment in the evolution of Puškin's art. Faced with the diverse set of thematic elements that make up the Koran, the poet managed to remold these elements into a carefully crafted set of poems that retains the semblance of diversity and local color of the original but at the same time replaces the looseness of the original with a tightly organized system of cohesive yet suggestive imagery. The intriguing synthesis of elements drawn from the Koran and from Puškin's own imagination make the "*Podražanija Koranu*" a unique work in his *œuvre*. The cycle continues to attract attention both as a work of art in its own right and as an intimation of subsequent developments in the great poet's career.

University of Virginia

NOTES

[1]P. V. Annenkov, *Aleksandr Sergeevič Puškin v Aleksandrovskuju èpoxu* (S.Pb.: Tipografija M. Stasjuleviča, 1874), 304.

[2]N. I. Černjaev, "'Prorok' Puškina v svjazi s ego že 'Podražanija Koranu'," *Russkoe obozrenie*, Nov. 1897, 396.

[3]V. I. Filonenko, "'Podražanija Koranu' Puškina," *Izvestija Tavričeksogo obščestva istorii arxeologii i ètnografii*, t. II (59), 1928, 11.

[4]B. V. Tomaševskij, *Puškin*, II (Moskva: Akademija nauk, 1961), 45.

[5]For a discussion of specific correspondences between Puškin's cycle and his original sources see K. S. Kaštaleva, *"Podražanija Koranu" Puškina i ix pervoistočnik*, Zapiski Kollegii vostokovedov, No. 5 (Leningrad: Akademija nauk, 1930).

[6]Tomaševskij, *Puškin*, 27.

[7]See G. A. Gukovskij, *Puškin i russkie romantiki* (Moskva: "Xudožestvennaja literatura," 1965), 267-273.

[8]From a letter to P. A. Vjazemskij written in the spring of 1825. A. S. Puškin, *Polnoe sobranie sočinenij*, XIII (Moskva: Akademija nauk, 1947), 160.

[9]The oath in Sura XCIII in the Verevkin translation as quoted by Tomaševskij (*Puškin*, p. 20) reads: "Kljanusja lučezarnostiju solnečnogo vosxoda i temnotoju nošči, čto gospoď tvoj ne ostavil tebja" (I swear by the radiance of the rising sun and the darkness of night that your Lord has not forsaken you).

[10]N. O. Lerner, "Podražanija Koranu," in Puškin, *Polnoe sobranie sočinenij*, III (S.Pb.: Brokgauz-Èfron, 1909), 540.

[11]N. V. Fridman, "Obraz poèta-proroka v lirike Puškina," *Učenye zapiski*, Trudy kafedry russkoj litratury, No. 118 (1946), 83.

[12]See Tomaševskij, *Puškin*, 36-37.

[13]One notes that the beginning of the boaster's last line ("*S toboju*"—With you) echoes the beginning of the poem itself, when the poet is addressing the Lord. Here too the contrast concealed by the parallel is revealing. Just as the ruler is shown to be inferior to the Lord in power, so too is he inferior to the poet in displaying a reverential attitude toward the Lord.

[14]Walter N. Vickery, "Toward an Interpretation of Pushkin's '*Podražanija Koranu*'," *Canadian-American Slavic Studies*, 11, No. 1 (Spring 1977), 65.

PETERSBURG AND THE PLIGHT OF RUSSIAN BEAUTY: THE CASE OF MANDEL'ŠTAM'S *TRISTIA*

Anna Lisa Crone

Et comment souffrez-vous que d'horribles discours
D'une si belle vie osent noircir le cours?
Avez-vous de son coeur si peu de connaissance?
Faut-il qu'à vos yeux seuls un nuage odieux
Dérobe sa vertu qui brille à tous les yeux?

(How could you suffer such dishonorable slander
to blacken a life as pure as his?
Are you so ignorant of his good heart?
Can you not distinguish between innocence and crime?
Must you alone be blinded by an odious cloud
That hides his virtue, which shines bright to all others?
Racine, *Phèdre*, Act IV, Scene III.

—Mandel'štam

In Russian literature of the mid-to-late nineteenth century Petersburg was associated in the main with a negative semantic field.[1] Beginning in the 1890s and through the Silver Age, the city-symbol becomes increasingly associated with Russia and "the Beautiful," and the loss or disappearance of Petersburg takes on a tragic meaning. I shall attempt to show here how Mandel'štam's collection *Tristia* contributes significantly to this new, more positive treatment of Petersburg in Russian letters.

In nineteenth-century works, the "non-Rusian" capital was often portrayed as a major factor in the undoing and suffering of the common man; it symbolized the repressiveness of the regime of Nicholas I. In the more positive Silver Age treatment of Petersburg, the city emerges as a model of architectural beauty and as a national cultural treasure, one that is in extreme jeopardy, already partially lost and on the verge of being lost irretrievably. This theme of Petersburg and the plight of Russian beauty as it is embodied in Mandel'štam's poetry is a unifying theme in *Tristia*.

The basic theme of beauty in jeopardy is not new. Many Russian writers attempted in their works to depict the positive elements in Russian life— that which was beautiful and Russian—and to show them vital and flourishing. Gogol' destroyed the end of *Dead Souls* because he thought he had failed to embody a positive hero and vision. Dostoevskij made several attempts to depict a "truly beautiful individual." In his Petersburg novel,

The Idiot, there are two characters exhibiting the kind of beauty that would or could save the world: Prince Myškin and Nastasja Filippovna. Myškin, who is on one level a Christ figure, depicts the plight of a Russian Christ returning to a Petersburg that is in the grips of the Third Horseman of the Apocalypse. The Prince cannot and does not survive in the entanglement of earthly passions into which he falls the moment he arrives on Russian soil. Myškin has boundless compassion for Nastasja (Greek means "resurrection") Baraškova. Religious exegetists of various persuasions, Romano Guardini (Roman Catholic),[2] Konstantin Močuľskij (Russian Orthodox)[3] and Vjačeslav Ivanov (both),[4] interpret Myškin's and Nastasja's mystical meeting and sense of mutual recognition as evidence that they both emanated from a more perfect, ideal (Platonic) realm of Goodness and Beauty. They see in Nastasja a fallen version of the Gnostic Divine Sophia or of Soloveʹv's *Sofija-premudrostʹ*,[5] entrapped in matter. Only an elect can see through appearances to recognize her inner beauty and the meaning of her tragic suffering and entrapment.

Myškin, of course, becomes similarly ensnared in the Petersburg world he enters. Only such penetrating natures as Mrs. Epančina and Aglaja recognize the Prince's saintly qualities and admire him. The majority fail to recognize the "returning Christ" as was foretold in *Revelations*: "If therefore thou shalt not watch, I shall come as a thief at night and thou shalt not know what hour I will come . . ." (*Rev.* 3:3-4). We read further that many will mistake the Beast and the Antichrist for the Son of Man and will not perceive the spiritual beauty that can save the world.

In the Silver Age Blok shares these concerns about contact with the sublimely beautiful. His early work is dominated by the presence and inspiration of the Beautiful Lady, who is *prekrasnaja* (sublime), not merely *krasivaja* (beautiful). Ultimately, he loses her: she changes form.[6] Becoming mired down in the dens of a Babylon-like Petersburg, she becomes "the Stranger" in Blok's cycle "The City," and subsequently appears as a *demimondaine*, utterly fallen from her former ideal realm. In the epigraph to his play *The Stranger* Blok relates this fallen ideal to Nastasja Filippovna:

> In the portrait was depicted a woman of truly unusual beauty. She was photographed in a black silk dress of inordinately simple and elegant style (*The Idiot*, Pt. I,I).
> "How did you recognize me? Where have you seen me before?"
> "What is this, really? It's as if I had seen him somewhere . . ."
> "It's as if I have seen you somewhere, too."
> "But where? Where?"
> "I have certainly seen your eyes somewhere . . . oh, but that's impossible! It's just that . . . I was never here before. Perhaps it was a dream (*The Idiot*, Pt. I, IV).[7]

While Nastasja's physical allure dazzles everyone in the novel, her hidden inner beauty is really understood only by the deeply spritual Myškin and is divined perhaps also by the lost soul, Rogožin, who cannot seem to possess that in her which he desires. The tragic inevitability of Nastasja's murder by Rogožin reminds us of the crime of Blok's vampirish persona in "Song of Hell,"[8] as well as to the destructive persona who defiles his feminine ideal in "To My Double."[9]

Michael Holquist interprets Nastasja's murder as a violence done against Russia and Russian history; Rogožin, after all, first places the murder weapon in Solovev's *History of Russia* and later in Nastasja's breast.[10] Blok associates Nastasja with his Fallen Ideal and apparently sees violence done against her as the defilement of the Good and the Beautiful. Vjačeslav Ivanov in his Gnostic interpretation of the novel, treats the murder as an act of mercy which frees Nastasja's soul from entrapment in matter and allows it to return to its original realm.[11] This may be a solution for Nastasja, just as the Prince's return to derangement at the novel's end may, in some sense, "put him out of his misery," but both are a tragic loss for the world which is even more devoid of the Spirit. These analyses share the following: (1) the *summum bonum* is in a situation of duress, confinement and suffering, unable to express itself effectively and have a beneficial affect on the world; (2) the poet has lost touch with the *summum bonum*, his former more perfect connection with beauty has been interrupted or severed. Often the latter occurs because the poet has misused or abused that Beauty, has made it the object of base passions, sullied it and thereby has become the victim of his own action, been condemned to a hell of his own making. He longs to return his ideal to its former state, but this is impossible: by destroying it he has destroyed himself. He finds himself in a self-imposed exile from the Sublime, from the kingdom of Beauty, a paradise he tries, sometimes frantically, to regain. Exile from Petersburg comes to take on this meaning of separation from the realm of Beauty and art in Mandeľštam's poetry even before the Bolshevik Revolution as we shall see.

*   *   *   *   *   *   *   *

> Ljubov'ju černoju ja solnce zapjatnala . . .
> (With my black love I sullied the sun . . .)
> —Mandeľštam

Mandeľštam's exquisite collection *Tristia*[12] has the same general theme of the sullying of beauty as one of its major unifying *Leitmotive*. In the poem "In the many-voiced song of a girls' choir" he says: ;"Sad longing ate away at me,/ For a Russian name and Russian beauty" (I,58). The poet like Ovid in *Tristia* is isolated from the ideal land of beauty and poetry:

O gde že vy, svjatye ostrova,
Gde ne edjat nadlomlennogo xleba,
Gde tol'ko med, vino i moloko,
Skripučij trud ne omračaet neba,
I koleso vraščaetsja legko? (I, 75).

(Oh, where are you, blessed islands,
 Where they do not eat broken bread,
 Where there is only honey, wine and milk,
 Where creaking work does not darken the sky
 And the wheel turns easily?)

Mandel'štam's exile from Beauty is different from Blok's in that Mandel'štam seems to hold the poet more responsible, to feel the poet is more capable of resisting his fate. For Mandel'štam as for Blok, the Age, Time with its external events partly causes the threat to beauty that pervades *Tristia*, his elegiac collection. Indeed, the threat to art, culture, the poet, to the age-old tradition of achievements of Western culture that he and his fellow Acme- ists so revered is associated by Mandel'štam with a threat to "Petersburg." This beloved tradition, often referred to as the Word of "the blessed, sense- less word" is seen in *Tristia* through the rays of the apocalyptic *black sun*. And this is so in a period when the "last days" had all but come, when a negative answer to the question "Who shall stand"" seems inevitable for St. Petersburg/Russia. Petersburg is plagued by encroaching night in *Tristia* while those nations which will enter the city of God will "Know night no longer":

> And the city hath no need of the sun . . . to shine upon it: for the glory of the
> Lord did lighten it, and the lamp thereof is the Lamb . . . And the gates
> thereof shall in no wise be shut by day for there shall be no night there
> (*Rev.* 21:23-25).

In *Tristia* light and sun clearly belong to a positive semantic field—night and darkness, to a negative one. The basic binary oppositions with respect to our themes of Petersburg/Art/Beauty and the assault upon them are given in the table below. The central column represents ambiguous states, transi- tional towards betterment or worsening in different instances of use. All the concepts/images in a particular column are interrelated among themselves (i.e., sun and color are both positive and both frequently represent flourish- ing art, etc.). Intermediary combinations in the central column are oxymo- ronic and more problematic images; their role must be determined in con- text. Next to each concept/image are the numbers of those poems which contain it in a clear, easy-to-comprehend form.

THE ASSAULT ON BEAUTY IN MANDEL'STAM's *TRISTIA*[13]

Positive Semantic Field +	Intermediary Ambiguous States + or −	Negative Semantic Field −
I. Art Culture Beauty/ Petersburg	Threatened Art, Culture and Beauty	Lost, dead Art, Cult Beauty
World inside the theatre ##102, 114, 118		World outside theatre ##82, 102, 114, 118
Russian name and Russian beauty #84		
Petersburg in ##88, 89, 95, 101, 118	Dying Petersburg ##88, 89, 95	Dead or Lost Petersburg ##95, 118
Golden Fleece, Meganom #93	Sinking Ship of	
Holy islands—Hellas #105	Petersburg #101	
Cool air of Christian grace #106		
Venetian art #110	Dying Venice and its threatened art and beauty #110	World outside the cathedral ##84, 107, 124
World inside cathedrals, Moscow, Siena ##84, 107, 124		
Tender cameo #87		Lost cameo #87
Dear Troy, home of the maiden and king #119	Trojan War (implicitly present in many poems)	Lost Troy #119

II. Sun/Brightness/Light	Fading light, partial light, partial eclipse, twilight	Blackness, darkness, Night
Puškin, sun of Aleksandr ##95, 118		
Sun #82 bright day	Blackened sun ##82, 91	Night, no sun ##82, 95, 118
	Night sun ##95, 118	Puškin lost ##82, 95, 118
		disappeared sun #95
Sun of Ilium/Troy #109	Black yellow light (Judaism) #100	
	Yellow twilight #109	Jewish night #100
	Hidden burning #107	yesterday's sun #108
	buried sun #118	
	invisible sun #103	Soviet night #118
Sun of Epirus #105	twilight of freedom #103	Night waters #103
World of day ##112, 113, 114	descent and ascent	Hades–Underworld ##112, 113, 114
Honey–sun of poetry #116		Palace of shades
Golden sun of Eucharist #117	Burial of sun at night #102	Lethe #103, Styx #113
Eucharist–eternal midday #117	Dionysus/Bacchus ritual celebrations #92	House of the dead #82
		Greek Erebus #104

+	Intermediate States + Ambiguous –	–
III. Pulsating life, vigor resurrection, rebirth, renewal	+ coming alive anew/ + ← dying, – going to land of dead → –	death
#86,2 Ligeia, return to, life, overcoming death		no faith in resurrection #90
Proserpina/Persephone ##88, 89, 93		dead mother, irreparable night #91
return to Petersburg #118		#82 death/curse on
Hippolytus	Phaedra life threat to Hippolytus #82	death of Hippolytus
	ride to be killed #85	funereal torch #82
	body freezing to death dying #85	murder of Tsarevich #85
	Petersburg dying ##88, 89, 101	Salomé/Solominka–cause of death #86.1, #86.2
		hour of death #89
Susanna #110 vindicated	threat of chopping block #110 execution	midnight funeral #102
New life #104	(dying and threat, transitional states towards death →)	Death in battle #104
	opened graves #105	Man dies #110
		black (cypress) stretchers ##108, 110
Green Adriatica, Venetian beauty #110	warm, newly deceased #110	shroud #110
Man is born #110		Everything passes #110
green meadows upper world #114		Death of swallow #114
green branch #113		Death of poets, put out our candless #118
IV. Visibility (zrjačest') —chromatic color	transparency—loss of color (Prozračnost') or insufficient visibility	total black or white invisibility disappearance
#95 Prophetess Cassandra sees the future	transparent shades #113 leafless forest of transparent trees #113	
#113 seeing finger (zrjačij palec)	fleshless thought #113 transparent star #101 transparent spring ##88, 89, 101	
dear eyes of blessed women #118	transparent thickets of night #116 transparent stage barely flickering #114	invisibility of sun #103, of night sun #118
	star flickers #101 fading light fog (tuman) #113	black Neva #102 Outdoors all black darkness snorts #114 Black carriages #114 black snowdrifts #114

+	Intermediate States + Ambiguous –	–
V. Sound, audibility	insufficient or unclear sound (*zvon, šum*)	silence, loss of sound (*zijan'e*)
Sounding music of named instruments	noise and ringing instrument dying out	silent instruments
Poet singing	Poet unable to catch the Word	Poet separated from Word
Muses present and dancing		unfriendly or quiet Muses

+	+ Ambiguous –	–
Your marvelous pronunciation #97 (Axmatova) #98 Nightingale fever grasshopper's song, etc. #90 a name, a wonderful sound		
#123 poet blends with the singing name of the round dance of shades	#123 weak sound	
Sappho's song #105 bee's blind lyreplayers #105	lyre awaiting Terpander #105	silent, sleeping turtle-lyre #105
	poet gropes for word #113	forgotten word #113
	finds approximate words #113	birds silent #113
golubka Evridika (opera singer, Eurydice, perhaps A. Bozio) #114	half-dead word-dead swallow #113	forgotten night son (*zijan'e*) #113
Native language, singing of Italian	#113 ringing (*zvon*)	
#114 spring song à la Fet	song on its way as in Fet's "I came to you with a greeting" #114	Silence like a spinning wheel #92
#118 eternal song of blessed women	#118 prayer (poetry) for achieving of the blessed, senseless word	Muse ripped off
#116 necklace, result of production of honey-sun-poetry	#116 dead bees = dead words weeping Muses #113 a weeping Muse's song #104	Axmatova (kerchief) #95
#106 organ in Siena crystal of high notes grace like song of Palestine #86 blessed names of art (Salomé, Ligeia, Seraphita/us, etc.)	descent of sound #106	pause of Psalm-singer #106 silencing of Cassandra #95
#84 polyphonic chorus of girls' voices singing churches	longing for a Russian name #84	#84 lost Russian name and beauty

+	+ Ambiguous –	–
VI. Remembrance, Recognition of Beauty	Incomplete Memory	Amnesia, oblivion, inability to recognize
the fan of past years opens up #93	ringing of Stygian remembrance #113	#113 forgot the word
joy of recognition ##104, 113		#113 song sings in memoryless state
power of recognition #113	partially forgotten Puškin, sun #118	
	remembering even in the Lethean cold #103	Styx #112
Remembrance of Greek mythical figures throughout		

+	Intermediate States +　Ambiguous　−		−

VII. Freedom (Christian freedom)	Exile		Imprisonment
#124 Christian freedom overcoming fear the slave is free	#103 the twilight of freedom		
	#103 swallow-words have been conscripted into legions = regimentation of the arts		
#103 suggestion that one more free turn of the wheel of time be taken (what Blok desired of a hero in Preface to "Retribution")			
#94 Decembrist's dream of freedom—free act	*Tristia* implies exile from Rome and Mandefštam's exile from the "Petersburg of the spirit"		#94 Decembrist in Siberia
#118 fearlessness before sentries			
#117 freedom from time and worldy restriction "play"			Freedom turned into its opposite #95

VIII. South as land of birth and flowering of culture	+	−	North as land of death of culture
Mediterannean cultures—Hellas, Rome, Italy, creators of culture	Petersburg		Scandinavian culture, Hyperboreans, Scythians barbarian destroyers of culture
			#95 Hyperborean plague
			#95 Scythians in Petersburg
Religious resurrecting South #90			#90 Faithless threatening North
#99 Magic air of the South			#99 Scalds, Germanic tribes
#110 Venice, Venetian painting	Hellas in Petersburg		
#106 Siena #105 Pieria-Hellas-Epirus	##89, 95		#94 Siberian log cabin
#104 Rome	#84 Florence in Moscow		#84 Moscow Kremlin
#93 Meganom	#87 Rome in Petersburg		
#117 Greece	#92 Tavrida = Russian Hellas		
	#94 Decembrists = Europe in Petersburg		
	#83 Europe in Petersburg		
	#102 Rome in Moscow		
	#115 Tiflis = Russian Italy Georgia		
	#117 Greece in Orthodoxy		
	#124 St. Isaac's St. Sophia and St. Peter		

+	Intermediate States + Ambiguous –	–

IX. Gaiety, joy
#117 religious joy
#94 time when "blue punch
  flame burned in the bowl"—
  Petersburg gaiety
Joy in old Pieria #105
 	
#115 Tiflis
#116 gift of poetry for joy
		Melancholy, anguish
		
		#94 nostalgia for Russian
		  beauty
		
		#82 Phaedra'a anguish
		#119 anxiety for lost Troy
		#99 northern ignorance of joy
		  and playfulness

X. Pure sensuality, beautiful
  love and those capable of it
Hippolytus #82
Penelope #92
Tibullus #104
Ligeia #86.1 & 86.2
	Incomplete, partial or
	  inconstant love
	
	Laban for Leah #109
	Poet's love for addressee
	  ##119, 122
		Destructive, defiling
		  sensuality
		Phaedra #82
		
		Delija #104
		Salomé *Tristia* 86.1 & 86.2
		Lorelei #94

XI. Bravery, heroism, rising
  to life's challenges
Bravery of persona #118
Free is he who fears not #124
	Cowardly vacillation	Fear of death/
		  enslavement to fear
		#110 fear of death

In *Tristia* guilt for tarnishing the sublime, for allowing Puškin to die and Petersburg to be "turned into its opposite"[14] is not borne by the poet alone. It is the collective sin of the entire cultural community. He often seems to be an accessory to the crime because he cannot prevent it. He is the creator, the singer and champion of the beautiful, but he has protected it insufficiently. His "sin" is lack of will to oppose the powers of darkness and destruction. This theme is reflected in the elegiac posture of Ovid's *Tristia* which gave the collection its title; like *Ex ponto, Tristia* was written during Ovid's exile in Tomis among the Scythians.[15] Puškin was exiled nearby in 1821 and his "To Ovid" is an important subtext to Mandel'štam's collection. In it Puškin sympathizes wholeheartedly with the exiled Roman bard and blames the State for insensitivity to poetry. He stresses how nature and the wild tribes of Tomis understood and accepted the banished poet, while his friends, his Caesar and his countrymen did not value him highly enough;

all attempts to assuage Caesar's anger failed to bring Ovid back; he died in exile.

In his *Tristia* Ovid complains of the "sad things" that befell him in exile: separation from his native tongue and his beloved Rome as well as his wife and family. Mandel'štam alludes to the first night of Ovid's exile in his poem "Tristia" and in the collection treats of the sad things that have befallen art, culture and their creators in the present age. Ovid importunes his friends and Caesar to lighten his sentence of "relegation" to the most remote end of the Empire. Mandel'štam importunes the Muses, poets, fate and the reader of the future for a return to the "Petersburg of the blessed Word," just as Puškin in his poem to Ovid hopes future readers will return to his poetry as he has returned to Ovid's poetry and place of burial:

> Žertva temnaja, umret moj slabyj genij, . . .
> No esli obo mne potomok pozdnij moj,
> Uznav, prijdet iskat' v strane sej otdalennoj
> Bliz praxa slavnogo moj sled uedinennyj—
> Bregov zabvenija ostavja xladnu sen',
> K nemu sletit moja priznatel'naja ten'
> I budet milo mne ego vospominanie
> Da soxranitsja že zavetnoe predanie . . .[16]

> (A dark victim, my weak genius will die, . . .
> But if my distant progeny
> Having learned of me, comes to seek in this remote land,
> My lonely footstep near the remains of the famous one—
> Then leaving the cold retreat of Oblivion's shores
> My grateful shade will fly up to him
> And his remembrance of me I will hold dear
> And my cherished legend will be preserved . . .)

In Mandel'štam's Phèdre poem #81 which closes *The Stone* and is closely linked to *Tristia* which opens with a second Phèdre poem #82, the poet predicts "I shall not see the famous Phèdre." He goes on to indicate that this is not because he dislikes the theatre, but because art is at present in jeopardy:

> Teatr Rasina! Moščnaja zavesa/Nas otdeljaet ot drugogo mira . . . (The theatre of Racine! A powerful curtain divides us off from another world . . .) (I,50).

His neighbor in the theatre fears that the crowd may destroy that other world, the world of art, and advises him to depart:

> Ujdem pokuda zriteli-šakaly
> Na rasterzanie Muzy ne prišli! (I,51)

> (Let's leave before the jackal-spectators
> Come to tear the Muse limb from limb!)

This image of hordes of barbarians swooping down to destroy the beautiful, the Muse and the poet is reminiscent of Ovid's description of precari-
ousness in Tomis where the raging Scythians and other barbarian tribes
run through killing and plundering on a regular basis. In the Phèdre poem
which opens *Tristia*, we read:

> Kak ètix pokryval i ètogo ubora
> Mne pyšnosť tjažela sreď moego pozora . . .
>
> (How heavy to me is the lavishness of these
> garments and this headpiece amidst my shame . . .) (I,55)

lines reminiscent of passages in Racine's play. We move onto the stage,
inside the theatre and then inside the play, behind the proscenium arch.
The play is interpreted as the tarnishing of beauty and all participants in
the crime are victimized by it. Hippolytus, youthful beauty, vigor and heroism, as well as purity in Euripides' play, is Phèdre's "sun" which she tar-
nishes by her black, incestuous-adulterous and destructive passion. She is
equated with the negative night (1.16), her passion, with a black flame:

> Černym plamenem Fedra gorit/ Sredi belogo dnja
> Pogrebaľnyj fakel čadit/ Sredi belogo dnja (I,55).
>
> (Phèdre burns with a black flame in bright daylight,
> The funeral torch smokes in bright white day).

And Hippolytus falls, tragic victim of this night:

> Ljubovju černoju, ja solnce zapjatnala (I,55)
> (With my black love I sullied the sun . . .)

He is viciously denounced to his returning father, Theseus, and is trampled
to death by his own horses. Phèdre is undone by her passion, by his death
and her shame, and Theseus, who had been victorious over "night" in his
struggle with the Minotaur, returns home only to fall victim to Night/
Phèdre unexpectedly: "Ujazvlennaja Tezeem/ Na nego napala noč'"
(Wounded by Theseus,/ Night attacked him") (I,56). In the disastrous end
of the poem the chorus is helpless to remedy the tragedy of these three and
of art and can only sing a threnody, lamenting the heinous destruction of
pure beauty and heroism. In interpreting this we must remember Mandeľštam's comparison one year earlier (1915) of Russia in her attitude towards
poets as the tragic Phèdre[17] in the essay "Puškin and Skriabin." The Russian poet is the eternal "stepson."

Several poems after the second Phèdre poem, innocence in the person of
the infant son of Ivan IV, Dmitrij, is murdered in "Na rozvaľnyx uložennyx
solomoj" ("On a sledge bestrewn with hay.") The frightening image of
burning someone on straw (murder) and the destructive effect Salomé was

to have on the poet-prophet ("Solominka"), make straw a particularly sinister bedding. We shall see presently that sleds, straw and bast matting are associated with Puškin's death and funeral. In "On a sledge . . ." the tsarevich, who represents innocent purity and at least potential good for Russia, is surrounded by evil forces, be they Boris Godunov, who burns with guilt in Puškin's play no less than Phèdre in poem #82, or someone else. The poem opens from the child's point of view. He is being transported through and out of "huge Moscow," "huge" presumably because he is so tiny. In the line "Vezut menja bez šapki" ("They carry me without my cap") there sounds combined disregard for the child's welfare and the usurpation of his birthright, "the heavy crown of Monomach" ("šapka Monomaxa"), symbol of Muscovite legitimacy. Straw is being prepared to burn the infant by or in the presence of sinister common people (evil women, "zlye baby"), who disinterestedly eat and spit out the hulls of sunflower seeds as the murder takes place, much as people were unaware of the meaning of the passage of the cart bearing Puškin's body away from Petersburg. This was registered most effectively in the diaries of Nikitenko:

> At Puškin's funeral they deceived the folk: they said the funeral would be at St. Isaac's Cathedral, but at night, secretly, they moved his body to Konju-šennaja Church. Benkendorf convinced the Czar that a demonstration was being planned and military men were dispatched to all parts of the city and many detectives sent into the crowd. Puškin's body was carried away into the country in the same manner. *Nikitenko's wife at one of the way stations saw a simple cart with straw on it and a coffin under bast matting.* [Italics mine] Three gendarmes in the courtyard were seeing to it that the post horses be reharnessed speedily that they might rush the coffin on its way. What is this?" she asked one of the peasants who stood nearby. "The Lord only knows! Some Puškin or other has been killed and they're whisking his body away with post horses on bast matting and straw, the Lord forgive me for saying it, like a dog."[18]

It is the bureaucratic "rabble" (*čern'* or *tolpa*) of Puškin's poetry, not the folk that surrounds these tragic events. Blok attacks it in his last public speech on the anniversary of Puškin's death:

> By *čern'* Puškin meant roughly the same thing we do. He often added the epithet *society* to it, giving the name to that born court nobility that had nothing to it but noble titles. Before Puškin's very eyes that nobility was being replaced by the bureaucracy. The bureaucrats are our "rabble" . . . the rabble demands that the poet serve the same thing it does . . . towards the end of Puškin's life more and more obstacles were placed on his path. He grew weak and with him the culture of his day . . . Puškin died, but he was not killed at all by Dantes' bullet. He died of lack of air to breathe and our culture died with him.[19]

The murder-burial ritual occurs in *Tristia* also in "Still faraway the asphodels," (I,93), "When in the dark night" (I,71-2), "Tenderness and heaviness . . ." (I,76-7) and "Of Venetian life . . ." (I,78). These all share the image of the bearing away of a body or its burial in a strange nocturnal procession by people uncomprehending of what they do or else downright evil and sinister.

The two "Solominka" poems, dedicated to Salomeja Andronnikova-Halpern,[20] one of the leading Petersburg beauties of Mandel'štam's youth, present Salomé and Poe's Ligeia. In Mandel'štam's poetry love for a beautiful temptress often has frightening consequences for the poet, for example, decapitation. Here the poet figure is associated with John and that very fate. Herodias' terrible request that Salomé ask for John's head on a platter had been reworked in the Silver Age with considerable eroticism by Oscar Wilde in *Salomé* and Mallarmé in *Herodiade*, as well as Blok.[21] Taranovskij has pointed out that the black sun in Wilde's play: "En ce jour la le soleil deviendra noir comme un sac de poil."[22] It is extremely close to the French rendering of *Revelations* 6:12. The beautiful, "senseless words" in the final lines of the first poem and the first line of the second one are the names of beautiful ladies of literature (Seraphitus/a is androgynous); they are physically beautiful and the sound attributes of the names have exquisite musicality; they are beautiful, moreover, in the ideal love-beauty their proto-Symbolist creator, Poe and the French and Russian Symbolists after him invested them with. The "beautiful Lenore" represents the beauty from which the poet has been severed by "The Raven." In Blok's "There was an autumn wind . . ." the same thing has been done by a gentleman with a dog.[23] The most interesting name listed, however, is Ligeia, the title character of Poe's story, who, as Joan Grossman and Clarence Brown have pointed out,[24] represents the powerful desire to overcome death and return to life. Ligeia's return occurs in a palatial bed-chamber-like setting of "Solominka." Admittedly, Mandel'štam is more playful than his very portentous sources. Brown quotes the all-important epigraph to Poe's tale where the idea of surviving and making culture survive is central:

> Man does not yield him to the Angels, nor unto death utterly, save only through the weakness of his feeble will.[25]

Ligeia, who personfies "gigantic volition" (Poe's words) which allowed her to return from the world of the dead, represents the resurrection of beauty; Salomé—the martyrdom of the poet. It is not Salomé with whom the poet will be united in the "Solominka" poems. Like Rowena, the second wife in Poe's story who is displaced by the returning Ligeia, Solominka will be killed and Ligeia will return, bringing a victory for the Word and Art:

Net, ne Solominka v toržestvennom atlase
Vkušaet medliteľnyj, tomiteľnyj pokoj.
V moej krovi živet oktjabŕskaja Ligeja,
Č'ja v sarkofage spit blažennaja ljubov',
A ta, Solominka, byť možet, Salomeja,
Ubita žalosťju i ne vernetsja vnov' (I,60).

(No, it's not Solominka in solemn satin
Who tastes the slow, wearying tranquillity.
In my blood lives October's Ligeia
Whose blessed love sleeps in the sarcophagus.
But the other one, Solominka, perhaps Salomé,
Is killed by pity and will not return.)

Another poem illustrating the fate of the poet and poetry in the New Age is "To Cassandra" (December, 1917) (I,67). It is closely associated with Axmatova's early prophecies concerning the negative effects of the Bolshevik Revolution on poetry:

Teper' nikto ne stanet slušať pesen,
Predksazannye nastupili dni,
Moja poslednjaja, mir boľše ne čudesen,
Ne razryvaj mne serdca, ne zveni.
Ešče nedavno, lastočkoj svobodnoj,
Sveršala ty svoj utrennij polet,
A nyne staneš' niščenkoj, golodnoj
Ne dostučiš'sja u čužix vorot. (I, 185-6)[26]

(Now no one will listen to songs anymore,
The days foretold have come,
My last song, the world is no longer marvelous
Don't tear at my heart, don't ring.
Not long ago, a free swallow,
You completed your morning flight
But now you'll become a starving beggarwoman
When you knock at other people's doors
They won't let you in.)

Like the Trojan prophetess, Cassandra, who retained her gift of prophecy, Axmatova's was laughed at and her words were scorned as the ravings of a madwoman; as in this poem of 1917 her warnings were not heeded. But these very negative predictions about the sad fate of poetry are evoked and remembered by Mandeľštam in *Tristia*. Poetry for both poets had once been a "free swallow." In this collection poetry's death has not yet come, its exile and travail are underway.

In "Čuť mercaet prizračnaja scena" (The transparent stage barely flickers) (I, 82-3) a theatre image is again employed. The central figure is the great

Italian diva, Angelina Bozio whose death from pneumonia in 1859 is recorded in Nekrasov's famous Petersburg poem "About the Weather."[27] This event and the poem made a substantial impression on Mandel'štam who began a novella entitled "The Death of Bozio" and then incorporated portions of the unfinished work in his *Egyptian Stamp*.[28] The Italian soprano from the Mediterranean South represents the warmth, perfection and fragility of art. There is warmth inside the theatre, but the stage is pale; it barely flickers as if the light may go out forever at any moment. The presence of this modicum of light in the theater, however, contrasts sharply with the darkness of the streets, the dark herd of cabs and cabbies. The oxymoronic "burning snow" is associated with bonfires that were lit so the cabbies could warm themselves while their masters were in the theater, a custom described in the first chapter of *Eugene Onegin*.[29] Out there:

> Xrapit i dyšit t'ma. (Darkness breathes and snorts, [implying the presence of horses])

But the poet-narrator says:

> Ničego, Golubka Èvridika (alluding to a performance of Glück's "Orfeo ed Euridice")
> Čto u nas studenaja zima. (I, 82-3).

> (It's no matter, Dove-Eurydice,
> That we have cold winter here.)

The burning snow in the context is also black, sullied and thus negative and destructive: "Ot sugroba ulica černa . . ." (The street is black from the snowdrift . . .") This "Ničego," as we shall see in other poems such as "We shall gather again in St. Petersburg," is part of an offhanded bravado which the poet exhibits when a death of artists or the defenders of art is about to occur. It is the narrator's way of telling Fate that this death will not bring about the end of art, that art will yet live on:

> Iz blažennogo pevučego pritina
> K nam letit bessmertnaja vesna,
> Čtob večno arija zvučala:
> —Ty verneš'sja na zelenye luga.
> I živaja lastočka upala
> Na gorjačie snega.

> (From its blessed singing refuge
> Deathless spring flies to us,
> In order that the aria might sound eternally:
> "You will return to green meadows"
> And the living swallow fell
> onto the burning snows) (I,83).

The immortal spring of art emanates from a melodious and holy realm. It is no chance that in other poems of *Tristia*, particularly the one most often placed contiguous to this one, "I dreamt of humpbacked Tiflis" (I,83), includes the words "I služiť tebe gotov" (And I am ready to serve you.) "Because I could not hold onto your hands" contains the line "Equally with others, I want to serve you." (I, 86-7). These lines call forth to any Russian Fet's affirmation of the eternal spring of song in "Ja prišel k tebe s privetom" (I came to you with a greeting):

> Rasskazať, čto *solnce vstalo*,
> Čto ono, *gorjačim svetom*
> Po listam zatrepetalo . . .
> Rasskazať, čto *s toj že strasťju* [pure passion]
> Kak včera, prišel ja snova,
> Čto duša vse tak že ščastiju
> *I tebe služiť gotova* [whole line borrowed]
> Rasskazať, čto otovsjudu
> Na menja veseľem veet,
> Čto ne znaju sam, čto budu *peť*
> No toľko *pesnja* zreet.[30]

> (To tell you that the sun has risen,
> That it with its hot light
> Has quivered among the leaves . . .
> To tell you that with the same passion
> As yesterday, I come again,
> That my heart just the same is ready
> To serve you and happiness,
> To tell you that gaiety is wafting
> Upon me from all directions,
> That I do not know what I will sing,
> But a song is welling up in me.)

The underscored images all belong to the positive semantic field of Mandeľštam's *Tristia* and recur in this affirmation of spring love and song in the pre-poetic anxiety (*predpesennaja trevoga*) that both Axmatova and Mandeľštam often write about. In "The transparent stage barely flickers" for that song to sound "So that the aria might sing eternally: You will return to green meadows," a sacrifice to the harsh reality of Petersburg and its weather must occur: the singer, Bozio, must die. If one remembers that the Orpheus legend in the Glück version is changed so that despite the fateful forbidden look backwards, Orpheus still retrieves his wife and returns her successfully to the "green meadows" of the upper realm, the ambiguity in the poem becomes clear: Eurydice-Bozio is lost to death but the Word is retrieved in the opera: *golubka*-Èvridika. Going to the underworld, crossing the Lethe or the Acheron and then returning, a trip made by the poet and the Word in "I forgot the Word I wanted to say," is a recurrent image in this collection. Orpheus's successful execution of this task in Nerval's famous Chimère "El Desdichado" is what links that poem with *Tristia*. "Le soleil noir de la melancholie" there torments the poet-Orpheus figure before he makes his attempts to retrieve Eurydice. When he does so in the second stanza, he succeeds with his lyre and song in crossing the Acheron twice and restoring to himself his lost beloved, just as Orfeo succeeds in Glück's opera. "El Desdichado," thus, presents a positive resolution of the poet's dilemma.[31]

The Persephone poems in *Tristia* have been studied in detail by Anne Iverson and Donald Gillis.[32] The word as a soul and a shade makes trips back and forth to Hades, just as Persephone spends part of the year in the upper realm. The possibilities of renewal of art through memory are implied in the use of this mythological structure. No matter how frightening the spectacle of the loss or death of the Muse, the loss of Puškin, those destructive elements are not shown to be unconditionally victorious—their victories may be reversed in time. The most negative political assessments of poetry's fate in Russia in *Tristia* are found in "To Cassandra" and "Let us praise, my brothers, the twilight of freedom." In the later *sumerki*—which can signify twilight or the mixed chiaroscuro that precedes dawn—is the lighting condition of the present age:

> Proslavim, brat'ja, sumerki svobody
> Velikij sumerečnyj god.
> Proslavim vlasti sumerečnoe bremja
> Ee nevynosimyj gnet/ . . .
> V kom serdce est', tot dolžen slyšat', Vremja,
> Kak tvoj korabl' ko dnu idet (I., 72).

> (Let us praise, my brothers, the twilight of freedom,
> The great twilight year.
> Let us praise the twilight burden of power,
> Its unbearable oppression/
> Whoever has a heart, must hear, O Time,
> Your ship sinking to the bottom)

Here Mandel'štam talks of the regimentation of art, the harnessing of swallow words for the purposes of the State,

> My v boevye legiony
> Svjazali lastoček i vot
> Ne vidno solnca . . .

> (We harnessed swallows into
> battle legions and you see
> The sun has become invisible).

As ominous as this sounds, the threats to the poet and to art have not yet taken full effect. To counteract this negative scenario, Mandelʹštam gives examples of beauty defending itself from the crowd of ill-wishers, from Puškin's *tolpa*. These examples are not unequivocal: they still contain a large admixture of threat and an air of impending tragedy, but, as in the case of Ligeia ("Solominka"), the prognosis is open and a positive outcome for art is not excluded.

In the beautiful poem "The meaning of dark and fruitless Venetian life . . ." the pale intermediate shading appears to be tending towards death and doom. Visual images make the reader recall one of the Venetian masterpieces depicting "Susanna and the Elders" or "Susanna at the Bath."[33] The last candles burning are associated with death, the funeral imagery and the allusion to the inescapability of death, passion and fear: "For there is no salvation from love and terror" (1.13), "Truth is dark . . . man is dying (1.27), "They place each one on cypress stretchers/ and take them out of the shroud, sleepy and warm [newly deceased]" (11.7-8). Despite this death imagery, the choice of the apocryphal tale of "Susanna and the Elders" and the visual conjuring of a beautiful Renaissance painting belie the death tendency. First, Susanna represents pure and innocent beauty, sensual life and vitality. This is subjected to voyeuristic defilement by the Elders who watch Susanna bathe and try to blackmail her into giving herself to them. When she refuses and attempts to save herself, they bear false witness against her; she is sentenced to death for her allegedly lewd behavior. The chopping block is draped in velvet, just as there is ominous black velvet in Blok's Venetian poem,[34] where the poet-persona is John the Baptist. At the last minute a hero comes forth and proves Susanna's innocence and right to live, as a result of which the guilty Elders are beheaded instead. The message here is clear: there will be threats to art always, death threats, but it is possible, as it was for Susanna, that help will come forth and save art.

This brings us to one final case of a positive prognosis for art in *Tristia*. One ideal of Greek womanhood, Penelope, is evoked by Ovid more than once in *Tristia* as a model for his wife's behavior during his long absence. Penelope appears in Mandelʹštam's poem "A stream of golden honey flowed from the bottle" (I, 63-4) where honey, one of Mandelʹštam's preferred metaphors for poetry as treated in Taranovskij's "Bees and Wasps,"[35] and weaving, Penelope's occupation, stand for poetic composition. The metaphor of woven fabric, specifically silk for poetry is seen in Mandelʹštam's "Conversation about Dante" which abounds in metapoetic usage. Weaving as poetic composition is seen in the signature poem of *Tristia*:

A ja ljublju obyknoven'e prjaži,
Snuet čelnok, verteno žužžit.
Smotri navstreču, slovno pux lebjažij
Uže bosaja Delija letit (I,73).

(I love the custom of weaving,
The shuttle moves, the spindle buzzes
And look, barefoot Delia runs hither
As if she were swansdown.)

That poem treats the first night of Ovid's exile, his departure from Rome and there is allusion to his wife's copious weeping. In the section cited, the poet compares himself to Roman poet Tibullus who is weaving a song about his beloved, Delia, who in fact was unfaithful to him. (See Chart.) Here the poet "weaves" and a beautiful Delia is elicited forth from the material, only later to be found on an amphora, another work fashioned by an artisan (11.25-7). In the poem "A stream of golden honey . . ." Penelope is the faithful poet, the weaver. As poet-creator she draws power from her separation from Odysseus (his exile from her). The words in "Tristia" "Who can know at the sound of the word 'parting',/ What sort of separation awaits us?" (11.9-10) describe the fate of few characters as they do Penelope's. In this poem it is Odysseus's absence that provides Penelope with materials—events, water, movement, travel, space, time. Out of these she weaves her father-in-law's shroud. The final stanza evokes the Golden Fleece, another ideal object of quest, a generic metaphor evoking such undertakings as the Trojan War and the attempt to return to Petersburg. The Trojan War was an attempt to rectify the sin of Helen's abduction from Sparta, just as the return to Petersburg attempts to rectify wrong burial of the sun. Sound and silence are woven into Penelope's tapestry. Odysseus's absence contributes silence: "Well, in the room like a distaff stands silence . . ." While away Odysseus produces the waves that enter Penelope's canvas "Odysseus, having worked the canvas full in the seas" gives Penelope time and space of which he returns a full vessel: "And Odysseus returned, full of space and time." (1.24). Like the running Delia who ends up on the amphora, Odysseus's movements have filled the picture Penelope is weaving, have given her poetic substance and preserved her from the defilement of Antinous and other suitors. It appears to be her poetic weaving activity that *makes* Odysseus return, conjuring and recalling him into existence, just as Tibullus's weaving fashioned him a Delia.

In the poem treating the loss and retrieval of Petersburg most directly, "We shall gather again in St. Petersburg," the return to the haven of art culture and creativity, "the Petersburg of the Spirit" is proposed. But Petersburg had, in Axmatova's words, "turned into its opposite." Petersburg had become exiled from itself and the Petersburg poet who remained there was exiled *in situ*.[36] There Mandeľštam makes one of his most hopeful declarations, or sanguine pleas for the salvation of high art, as well as the hope that future achievements in it will surpass those of the past:

> And we will utter the blesed, senseless word
> *For the first time* [Italics mine].

That "blessed word" never achieved before is the Catullus, the Horace, the Puškin that are *better than* the historical Catullus, Horace and Puškin. Mandeľštam spoke of it in "The Word and Culture" and exhorted Russian poets to create such poetry "[it] does not exist in Russian, but it *must* exist in Russian" (Harris, p. 114). This imperative is the "category of obligation." The Muses (blessed women, 11.7 and 23-24) still live and keep vigil in the ominous darkness of Soviet night. The poet is reckless and fearless before the tramplers of culture and before the prospect of his own death:

> I don't need a night pass,
> I am not afraid of sentries,
> I will pray for the blessed, senseless Word,
> In the Soviet night

Puškin in "The Poet and the Crowd" had said that "praying," in this special sense, was the province of the poet, not the mob:

> My roždenny dlja vdoxnoven'ja,
> Dlja zvukov sladkix i molitv.[37]
>
> (We are born for inspiration,
> For sweet sounds and prayers.)

The third stanza of "We shall gather again in St. Petersburg" moves from the street into a theatre where an actress or ballerina is being regaled with roses after a performance. This reminds us of the ballerina Istomina in the first chapter of *Eugene Onegin* where the cabbies are warming themselves from boredom in the street and the image includes Nekrasov's "It's boring and it's cold" ("Skučno," "xolodno") in a Petersburg setting of 1918, just as they are found in Blok's "The Twelve."[38] Even should the dark night of culture last for centuries, Mandeľštam affirms that in the end the poet will be remembered just as Puškin remembered Ovid and visited his grave. The fourth stanza uses the familiar form for disrespect and addresses Puškin's *čern'*, the detractors and enemies of the Word. They will be oblivious to art, will not see the "night sun" buried or resurrected in Petersburg. In variants of this poem we find "In the velvet of a *January* night" which further strengthens the link of the buried sun with Puškin whose body was removed from the capital on a January night. In "Puškin and Skriabin" lies the key to the seminal image of the buried sun which has been noted by Brown, Van der Eng–Liedmeier, Broyde and Axmatova:

> I mention this picture of Puškin's funeral because I wish to call up in your memory the image of the night sun, the image of Euripides' last tragedy—the vision of the ill-fated Phaedra (II, 92).

As we have demonstrated time and again, the broader meaning of Puškin in this twentieth-century Petersburg context is the suffering of art/beauty, the assault upon it. Puškin, Russian culture's golden moment, has been betrayed by Phaedra-Russia, who while loving him, still allows his tragic death to occur. One cannot forget in this context the line

> Vse poterjali my, ljubja.
> (We lost everything, loving)

In "Puškin" Merežkovskij reads out a litany of accusations against Russia of maltreatment and betrayal of A.S. Puškin.[39] Many of the crimes were committed by Russians who claimed to exalt and love Puškin. If Puškin's death was "collective" in the ecclesiastical sense of *sobornost'*[40] (*sobornaja smert'*), all of Russia died in Puškin, bears a collective guilt for the way he was allowed to die, and stands in need of a cleansing, redemption after it. Puškin was stained and besmirched by the State in his lifetime and by those who betrayed his legacy afterwards. The feeling of this mass betrayal is sensed clearly in the widespread opposition to the official Puškin national holiday among Petersburg writers, voiced in *The World of Art* in 1899.[41]

Mandel'štam called all poets, living and dead, to reconvene in "Petersburg" and revive the great spirit of Russian art that has become dormant. Axmatova sheds light on Mandel'štam's understanding of Puškin:

> Towards Puškin Mandel'štam had an unheard of, almost fearful attitude. In it there was a crowning element of superhuman chastity (II,177).[42]

The highest value, Puškin, has been abused in Russia, but those who can still see the night sun must disinter it and make it live again in their works. This is the task facing Russian art at the dawn of the Soviet period: to summon the strength of will needed to vindicate beauty that has been "tainted by a black love," to resist the enslavement of art and the Word:

> Zane svoboden rab, preodolevšij strax . . . (I, 91).
> (Because the slave who has conquered fear is free.)

These are the final words of Mandel'štam's *Tristia*.

University of Chicago

[1]N.P. Anciferov, *Duša Peterburga* (Petrograd, 1923), *passim.*

[2]Romano Guardini, "Dostoevsky's *Idiot*: A Symbol of Christ," tr. Francis X. Quinn, *Cross Currents*, VI (Fall, 1956), 359-82.

[3]Konstantin Mochulsky, *Dostoevsky: His Life and Work*, tr. Michael A. Minihan (Princeton U. Press, 1967).

[4]Vyacheslav Ivanov, *Freedom and the Tragic Life. A Study in Dostoevsky*, tr. Norman Cameron (New York: Noonday Press, 1971), pp. 86-106.

[5]For full elucidation of the concept of the Divine Sophia, see D. Stremoukhoff, *Vladimir Soloviev and His Messianic Work* (Belmont, Mass.: Nordland Books, 1979), pp. 47-74.

[6]Aleksandr Blok, *Sobranie sočinenij v vos'mi tomax*, ed. V.N. Orlov, K.I. Čukovskij (Moscow-Leningrad, 1960-3) I, 94. All quotations from Blok refer to this edition unless otherwise indicated.

[7]Blok, IV, 72.

[8]Blok, "Pesn' ada," III, 14.

[9]Blok, "Dvojniku" I, 152.

[10]Michael Holquist, *Dostoevsky and the Novel* (Princeton U. Press, 1977), pp. 117-18.

[11]Ivanov, p. 105-6.

[12]Osip Mandel'štam, *Tristia*, in *Sobranie sočinenij* (Munich: Interlanguage Literary Associates, 1967) I, 53-91. All page references to poems of Mandel'štam in the text refer to this, the standard edition of Mandel'štam's poetry and prose.

[13]The left column (positive semantic field) and the right one (negative semantic field) represent achieved states. The central column includes images that are in flux between the positive and negative poles. The various images are grouped according to general themes that are numbered in the lefthand column.

[14]Quoted in Sharon Leiter, *Akhmatova's Petersburg* (U. of Pennsylvania Press, 1983), pp. 63-64.

[15]*Tristia* and *Epistulae ex Ponto* were the two works Ovid wrote in exile. See: John C. Thibeault, *The Mystery of Ovid's Exile* (Berkeley, U. of California Press, 1964).

[16]Aleksandr S. Puškin, "K Ovidiju" in *Sočinenija v trex tomax* (Moscow: Xudožestvennaja literature, 1964), pp. 140-1.

[17]Mandel'štam, "Puškin i Skriabin," II, 313-14.

[18]D.S. Merežkovskij, "Bol'naja Rossija," in *Polnoe sobranie sočinenij* (Moscow: Sytin. 1914), XIV-XV, 152ff.

[19]Blok, VI, 164-167.

[20]One of the great beauties of the Petersburg of Mandel'štam's youth.

[21]In Blok this is found in his Italian poem "Venecija," the second of three: "Xolodnyj veter ot laguny," "Italjanskie stixi" are in III.

[22]Oscar Wilde, *Salomé*, quoted in K. Taranovsky, *Essays on Mandelshtam* (Cambridge: Harvard U. Press, 1976), p. 54.

[23]Blok, VII, 42.

[24]See Joan Grossman, *Edgar Allan Poe in Russia* (Würzburg: JAL Verlag, 1973) and Clarence Brown, *Mandelshtam* (Cambridge U. Press, 1973).

[25]Brown, p. 242.

[26]Anna Axmatova, *Sočinenija* (Munich: Interlanguage Literary Associates, 1968), I, 185-6.

[27]See Note in Jane Gary Harris in "Fourth Prose," in Osip Mandelshtam, *The Complete Critical Prose and Letters* (Ann Arbor: Ardis, 1979), p. 665. See also Lidija Ginzburg, "Poètika Osipa Mandel'štama," in *O starom i novom* (Leningrad: Sovetskij pisatel', 1980), pp. 283-4.

[28]Harris, p. 665.

[29]John Malmstad, "A Note on Mandel'štam's "V Peterburge my sojdemsja snova," *Russian Literature* (April, 1977), II, 194-5.

[30]Afanasij Fet, *Stixotvorenija* (Moscow: Izd. "Xudožestvennaja literatura," 1970), p. 95.

[31]Gerard De Nerval, "El Desdichado," in *Les Chimères*. Exégès par Jeanine Moulin (Lille: Giard, 1949), p. 5.

[32]Anne Iverson, "Adaptation of the Hellenic Legacy in the Poetic Art of Osip Mandelstam," Diss., Univ. of Ottawa, 1972. Donald Gillis, "The Persephone Myth in Mandeľštam's *Tristia*," in *California Slavic Studies* (Berkeley: U. of California Press, 1976, IX, 139-59.

[33]The most famous Venetian rendering of this theme is Tintoretto's "Susanna and the Elders" which is in the Vienna Kunsthistorisches Museum. Another is "Susanna ed i vecchoni" by Tintoretto in the Louvre. There are several by Veronese also.

[34]Blok, III, 102-3.

[35]Kiril Taranovskij, "Bees and Wasps," in *Essays on Mandelshtam* (Cambridge: Harvard U. Press, 1976), pp. 83-114.

[36]By this term we mean exile caused by the change of the place where one is located, not by movement in space.

[37]Puškin, p. 273.

[38]Blok, "Dvenadcať," III, 347-59.

[39]Merežkovskij, "Puškin" in *Večnye sputniki*, XVIII, pp. 89-171, *passim.*

[40]*Sobornosť* is defined as an organic conception of ecclesiastical consciousness which internally defined the Church not as a center of authority but as a congregation of "lovers in Christ"; the members are "organically united"—faith is in the collectivity only.

[41]See the first three articles in the journal *Mir iskusstva*, I (1899), all against the Puškin National Celebration.

[42]Axmatova, II, 177.

A REVISED HIERARCHY FOR STEM CLASSIFICATION IN SLAVIC VERBAL SYSTEMS

Mark J. Elson

1. Introduction. Morphological analyses typically begin with a definition of stem structure, following which stem types, or classes, are established on the basis of attributes common to subsets of stem-level units. Such classes reflect phonological, morphological, and/or semantic identities (i.e. identities in segmental structure, constituent structure, and/or meaning). The synchronic justification for stem-level classification is that it permits the formalization of inflectional and derivational regularities assumed to be those with which native speakers operate. Thus, for example, it is usual in descriptions of the nominal system of modern English to assign classificatory significance to certain articulatory attributes of stem final segments in order to formalize regularities in the formation of the plural (i.e. the distribution of -*s* versus -*z* versus -*əz*), regularities which can be stated only with reference to these phonological properties. Stem-level classification is also relevant in historical morphology, where the assumption is that changes in inflectional and/or derivational patterns reflect interaction among stem-level units of a single class. In English, for example, the occurrence of non-standard *brang* is explained as a result of interaction within the class of verbal stems defined, in part at least, by segmental properties reflected orthographically in the sequence *ing* (e.g. in *ring*).

In synchronic descriptions, Slavists frequently follow Jakobson 1948 in recognizing two types of verbal stem: one with the canonical shape CVC-V- or CVC-//CVC-V-, united by the occurrence of a constituent following the lexical morpheme;[1] and another with the canonical shape CVC-, CV-, or CVC-//CV-, united by the absence of this constituent. The latter subsumes all reflexes of Leskien Classes 1a (e.g. *vesti*) and 5 (e.g. *dati*);[2] the former, reflexes of Leskien Class 1b (e.g. *bъrati*), as well as all reflexes of the remaining classes (e.g. *dvignǫti* representing Class 2; *klati, mlěti, dělati, bělěti,* and *rězati* representing Class 3; and *nositi* as well as *viděti* representing Class 4). Reflexes of Class 4a (e.g. *nositi*), however, present a problem within this descriptive framework. They are invariably assigned to the -V- type, presumably on the basis of structural identity (e.g. $CVCV$- in the infinitive) to verbs like *rězati, viděti,* etc. In the imperfect past and the passive participle, however, they, unlike such verbs, are structurally indistinguishable from those which lack -V-; both *nositi* and *vesti* use CVC- in these formations, unlike *rězati, viděti,* etc., which use *CVC-V-* (e.g. *nošaaxъ* from *nositi* like *pečaaxъ* from *pešti* in the first person singular of the imperfect; *nošenъ* from *nositi* like *pečenъ* from *pešti* in the masculine singular passive participle; cf. *rězaxxъ* in the imperfect and *rězanъ* in the passive participle, both with *CVC-V-,* from *rězati*). The purpose of this paper is to argue that, despite the similarity of *nositi* to verbs like *rězati, dělati,* etc., it can reasonably be likened to those like *vesti.*[3] Several claims will be made, the most important of which are:

1. that the presence versus absence of *-V-* is relevant in the classification of verbal stems;
2. that *-V-* determines two attributes, which we term **suffixed** versus **nonsuffixed** and **vocalic** versus **nonvocalic**;
3. that these oppositions can be defined to include *a* and *ě* as realizations of *-V-,* but exlude *i* and;
4. that *nositi* can therefore legitimately be termed nonsuffixed and nonvocalic, making it structurally identical to *vesti,* for which nonsuffixed and nonvocalic status are generally accepted.

2. Evidence. To support these claims, we begin with an examination of the distribution of *-ěa-* versus *-a-* in the imperfect, and *-en-* versus *-n-* in the participle, the assumption being that the distribution of allomorphs in each instance correlates with structural attributes of the stem relevant in its classification.[4] The available evidence, although scant, implies the relevance of two attributes: **suffixed** versus **nonsuffixed** (i.e. *-V-* versus its absence),[5] which is morphological, and **vocalic** versus **nonvocalic** in the stem-final segment, which is phonological. The crucial data are provided by *dati,* a reflex of Leskien Class 5, which attests *dad--ěa-* in the imperfect past and *da--n-* in the passive participle.[6] With regard to the imperfect, it is significant that *dati,* with the stem *dad-//da-,* evolved *dad--ěa-* and not *da--a-* like *rěz-a--a-, děl-a--a-,* etc. (i.e. other stems attesting a variant with final *a*). Assuming systemic motivation for *-ěa-* in this instance, we must conclude that its occurrence versus that of *-a-* was determined morphologically, by the presence versus absence of *-V-,* since *dati* differs from *rězati, dělati,* etc. only in this respect. Hence, **suffixed** versus **nonsuffixed** supplies systemic motivation for the occurrence of *-ěa-* in the imperfect past of *nositi* if we can demonstrate, contrary to the usual assumption, that *i* was not a realization of *-V-.* This would permit us to claim that, despite its appearance, *nositi,* like *vesti,* is *nonsuffixed.* The suffixal status of *-V-,* however, is not relevant in the distribution of *-en-* and *-n-* in the passive participle. Returning to *dati,* we note the occurrence of *-n-* in *da--n-* and in *rěz-a--n-, děl-a--n-,* etc., from which we infer that -*n*- was *not* associated with -*V*- as a suffix, but with a final vowel—in particular with *a*, and also with *ě* (e.g. in *vid-ě--n-*). Hence, verbs were apparently classified not only on the basis of -*V*- versus its absence into *suffixed* versus *nonsuffixed*, but on the basis of the stem-final segment into *vocalic* versus *nonvocalic*. If the occurrence of -*en*- in the passive participle of *nositi* is systemically motivated, therefore, we must demonstrate not only that it is nonsuffixed, but also that it is nonvocalic—like *vesti*, for which nonsuffixed and nonvocalic status are evident.

3. Conclusions. Since the attributes of **suffixed** and **vocalic** are determined by the segments *a* and *ě* (i.e. *a* and *ě* define the opposition suffixed versus nonsuffixed **and** the opposition vocalic versus nonvocalic), we can approach the problem of establishing the systemic basis for unification of *vesti* and *nositi* by asking if there is any charcteristic common to *a* and *ě* which distinguishes them from *i*, and on the basis of which it can reasonably be claimed that verbs with them are suffixed and vocalic but verbs without, represented by *vesti* and *nositi*, are nonsuffixed and nonvocalic. There is one: *a* and *ě* occur **throughout** the conjugational unit (i.e. in all forms of all formations) of at least some verbs (e.g. *dělati*, with *a* throughout; *bělěti*, with *ě* throughout); *i*, in contrast, is not found throughout the conjugational unit of any verb. It is always absent in the first person singular present, third person plural present, the imperfect past, and the passive participle. This difference can be considered significant since, by definition, stems—regardless of part of speech—must occur overtly in all word-level forms expressing their lexical content (i.e. there is no word-level form constituted solely by grammatical morphemes, but either solely by a stem, or by a stem and grammatical morphemes). It is therefore not unreasonable to assume that any string assigned to a stem as an independent unit (i.e. a morpheme) must occur as well in every word-level form of every formation of the conjugational unit, if not of every stem, then at least of one, as a prerequisite to the assignment of stem-level status. Since *a* and *ě* occurred throughout conjugational units, they were eligible for independent stem-level status, and assigned it, not only in verbs like *dělati* and *bělěti*, but, we must assume, in those like *rězati* and *viděti*, which attested them in some, but not all, forms of the conjugational unit. In contrast, *i* of verbs like *nositi* was not eligible and, as a result, such verbs were opposed to verbs like *dělati* and *bělěti* as well as *rězati* and *viděti* with regard to each of the attributes determined by *a* and *ě*. If *a* and *ě* determined the attributes which we have termed **suffixed** and **vocalic**, their absence must have entailed the attributes **nonsuffixed** and **nonvocalic**. They were absent in both *vesti* and *nositi*; hence, nonsuffixed and nonvocalic status for both. Special status for *a* and *ě*, however, does not preclude assignment of *i* to the stem, only assignment as an independent unit. Thus, we assume that the stem of *nositi* is *CVC-//CVCV-*, with no boundary preceding the final vowel of the *CVCV* variant.

A single problem remains. The classification we have proposed motivates the conjugational similarity of *nositi* to *vesti*, but does not motivate its similarity to suffixed verbs as we have defined them (i.e. verbs with underlying *CVC-V-* where *-V-* is *a* or *ě*). The handbooks are not totally incorrect in their assignment of *nositi* to the *-V-* type since, in at least one respect, the formation of the aorist, it is structurally identical to this type (i.e. *nositi*, like *dělati* and other suffixed verbs, exhibits *-x-* in the aorist, not *-ox-* like *vesti*). Yet the dichotomies we have proposed preclude formalization of this identity. Since the structural similarity between the types represented by these verbs is apparently the occurrence of an underlying stem variant in which the root is followed by a vowel regardless of its morphological status (i.e. a *CVCV* variant, which is *CVC-V-* in *dělati, rězati,* etc. but *CVCV-* in *nositi*), and since we have determined that morphological status is a function of the realization of *V* following *CVC*, the solution to the problem lies in a revision of the notion **vocalic**. We must assume that underlying stems are classified at two levels phonologically: a primary one at which vocalicity is a function of *V* regardless of its realization, which may be *i, ě,* or *a,* and a secondary one at which vocalicity is a function of *V* only if its realization is *a* or *ě*. The primary specification can be formalized as [±vocalic]. It unites *nositi* with *rězati, dělati,* etc., which are [+vocalic], and opposes them to *vesti*, which is [−vocalic]. The secondary specification can be formalized as [±a, ±ě]. It unites *rězati, dělati,* etc., which are [+a, +ě], and opposes them to *nositi* and *vesti*, which are [−a, −ě]. The result is intermediate status for *nositi*: it is like *rězati, dělati,* etc. with regard to one of the classificatory features, but like *vesti* with regard to the other. This classification, therefore, accurately reflects its peculiarity.[7]

4. Implications. The interpretation we have suggested is relevant not only for the analysis of *nositi*, but, more generally, for the notion of **stem type**. The implication of our assumption that occurrence throughout the conjugational unit of at least one verb is required for the assignment of independent stem-level status to a string is that verbs which can be analyzed with uniform stem structure (i.e. with a single constituent structure in the stem) have special significance: They determine the stem types in terms of which other verbs (i.e. verbs which are incompatible with uniform stem structure) are analyzed. In Slavic verbal systems, uniform stem structure is defined by the opposition *CV(C)-* represented by *vesti* and *biti* versus *CVC(-)V-* represented by *dělati* and *bělěti*. Nonuniform stem structure is defined by the combination of uniform types, yielding *CVC-//CVC-V-* represented by *rězati, viděti,* etc. and *CVC-//CVCV-* represented by *nositi*. These claims are supported by the fact that, historically, nonuniform stem structures have interacted with uniform, but uniform structures have not interacted with each other. The interaction of nonuniform types with uniform is well attested in the phenomenon of class shift: verbs which inherited *CVC-//CVC-a-* have been reassigned to *CVC-a-* and vice versa in all of the Slavic languages. The implication is that *CVC-a-* in *CVC-//CVC-V-* is structurally equivalent to the same string in *CVC-V-*.[8] The absence of class shift on the basis of *CVC-* is not problematic because this innovation was undoubtedly defined by **underlying** stem variants. In *CVC-//CVCV-* and *CVC-//CVC-V-*, we have assumed underlying status for the vocalic variant, following Jakobson 1948. Thus, we expect class shift between *CVC-//CVC-V-* and *CVC-V-*, not between *CVC-//CVC-V-* or *CVC-//CVCV-* and *CVC-*. The equivalent of *CVC-* in *CVC-//CVC-V-* and *CVC-//CVCV-* to *CVC-* in verbs like *vesti* is nevertheless implied by the extension to *nositi* and *rězati* in Bulgarian and Macedonian of patterns of realization inherited by verbs with *CVC-*; in particular, of desinence initial *ĕ* in the imperative plural (e.g., in Bulgarian, *rěžěte*, which replaced *rěžite* in the imperative plural of *rězati*; *nosěte*, which replaced *nosite* in the imperative plural of *nositi*; cf. *veděte*, the inherited imperative plural of *vesti*), and the imperfect past, where it was the reflex of *-ěa-* (e.g., in Bulgarian, *rěž--ě* . . ., which replaced *rěz-a--a* . . . in the imperfect past of *rězati*; cf. *ved--ě* . . ., in the inherited imperfect past of *vesti*).[9] These extensions were restricted to verbs which inherited *CVC-//CVC-V-* or *CVC-//CVCV-* (i.e. no verb which inherited *CVC-V-* was affected), which tells us that the occurrence of *CVC-* was significant since it was the only structural attribute common to them.[10]

Verbs of Leskien Class 3 like *klati* and *mlěti* require special comment. Synchronically, each has a *CVC-* stem variant: *kolí* for *klati* and *melí* for *mlěti*. The nature of the other variant, however, is not clear. The occurrence of *a* in *klati* and *ě* in *mlěti* suggests, respectively, *kl-a-* and *ml-ě-* (i.e. a suffixed variant). Present tense forms like *mlěju, mlěješ,* etc. are nevertheless attested (e..g in the Upper Sorbian literary language; see Ermakova 1973:244-245), leaving little doubt that nonsuffixed verbs like *biti, čuti, kryti,* etc. have played a role in their evolution. The implication is that *klati* and *mlěti*, in some dialects if not all, were interpreted as nonsuffixed and specifically as *CV*, which apparently has been the basis for their interaction with *biti, čuti, kryti,* etc., also with *CV*.[11] We must therefore assume that stem final *a* or *ě* is necessary but not sufficient to entail suffixed status. Apparently it must be accompanied by a syllabic string—i.e. *CV(C)*—preceding. If either condition is unmet, the result is nonsuffixed status. Within this framework, virtually all verbs with final *a* or *ě* are suffixed. Those like *klati* and *mlěti*—and, after the fall of the jers, *brati* etc. (i.e. reflexes of Leskien Class 1b with a jer root vowel; e.g. *ber-//bъr-a-*)—were nonsuffixed despite *a* or *ě* because the string preceding (e.g. *kl, ml*) was not syllabic. Canonically, therefore, the stem structure of such verbs is *CVC-//CV-*. This structure is combinatorial, uniting, like the stem structure of *nositi*, a nonvocalic (i.e. *CVC-*) variant with a vocalic one (i.e. *CV-*) negatively specified for [a, ě].

5. Summary. We have claimed that, in the underlying form of verbal stems, *a* and *ě* following the root are structurally different from *i* because, unlike *i*, they can occur throughout the conjugational unit. This qualifies them as independent entities morphologically, and provides the basis for establishment of two oppositions significant in the classification of verbal stems: **suffixed** versus **nonsuffixed** and **vocalic** versus **nonvocalic**. The result is a classification defined by the feature [±a, ±ě], which opposes *rězati, dělati, viděti,* and *bělěti* as suffixed and vocalic to *nositi* and *vesti* as nonsuffixed and nonvocalic, and thus provides a paradigmatic organization in which structural attributes common to the latter can be formalized as regularities, not exceptions. To formalize the traditionally recognized affinity of *nositi* to *rězati, dělati,* etc., we added the feature [±vocalic] to the classificatory inventory, claiming in effect that verbs like *rězati, dělati, viděti,* and *bělěti* are doubly vocalic: once because, like *nositi,* they attest a final vowel in the full stem, and a second time because the vowel is *a* or *ě*. We have therefore proposed the following hierarchy for the classification of underlying stem variants:

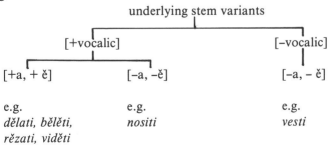

e.g.
dělati, bělěti,
rězati, viděti

e.g.
nositi

e.g.
vesti

University of Virginia

[1]In formulas denoting stem types, $CV(C)$ represents a lexical morpheme which may be prefixed, and $-V-$ represents a vocalic suffix. In $CVC-//CV-$ and $CVC-//CVC-V-$, each component is termed a **variant**.

Of the stem structures we posit, $CVC-//CVC-V-$, $CVC-$, and $CVC-//CV-$ are Jakobsonian. We do not, however, recognize Jakobsonian structures with final j (i.e. $CVj-$ and $CVC-Vj-$). In each such instance, we assign j to the morpheme following the stem, yielding $CV-$ for $CVj-$ and $CVC-V-$ for $CVC-Vj-$. We return briefly to this interpretation below. In $CVC-//CV-$ and $CVC-//CVC-V-$, we follow Jakobson in assigning underlying status to the longer, or full, variant of the stem. The shorter variant is generated from the longer by a rule of truncation. Like Jakobson, we assume that it is the underlying form of the stem which is significant in classification.

[2]Leskien's verbal classification is used in this paper as a neutral point of reference in terms of which to cite verbs. Discussion is restricted to the verbal system of Old Church Slavonic for convenience, but the same argument can be made for those languages (e.g. Russian, Polish) exhibiting the structural attributes with which we are concerned.

Verbs are cited in the infinitive, normalized according to the conventions of Lunt 1974. Following are the verbs, with glosses, to which reference is made: *běléti* 'become white', *bьrati* 'carry', *biti* 'strike', *čuti* 'hear', *dati* 'give', *dělati* 'do', *dvignǫti* 'move', *klati* 'prick', *kryti* 'cover', *mlěti* 'grind', *rězati* 'cut', *nositi* 'carry', *pešti* 'bake', *vesti* 'lead', *viděti* 'see'. Direct reference to Leskien's verbal classes is avoided in favor of representative members: *vesti* (Leskien Class 1a), *bьrati* (Leskien Class 1b), *dvignǫti* (Leskien Class 2), *klati, mlěti, běléti, dělati,* and *rězati* (Leskien Class 3), *nositi* (Leskien Class 4a), *viděti* (Leskien Class 4b), and *dati* (Leskien Class 5).

[3]In principle, it could be claimed that identity in the imperfect past and passive participle are the **basis** for assignment of *nositi* and *vesti* to a single class rather than a **reflection** of it. This paper argues that they can be interpreted as a reflection.

To my knowledge, there has been no previous attempt to establish a classsification which accommodates the peculiarities of *nositi*. Studies of verbal morphology, like Jakobson 1948 and Lunt 1974:71-73, have been devoted primarily to morphophonemic phenomena, not the paradigmatic organization of stems, although an organization is assumed. Micklesen 1972 is concerned with the verbal stem in Russian, but does not discuss problems of classification. The passive participle of *nositi* is considered an exception (269-70). For further discussion of the verbal stem and a list of studies of Slavic verbal systems, see Elson 1980.

[4]The notation *-ěa-* abbreviates *-ěa/-aa-*, which later contracted to *-ě-/-a-*.

[5]Others (e.g. Diels, 1963:242-243; Meillet, 1965:267-271) have assumed the relevance of the opposition **vocalic** versus **nonvocalic** in the formation of the passive participle. We are simply citing evidence to show that it can be motivated systemically **within** Slavic. In this regard, it should be noted that we do not attempt to offer an historical explanation of the facts (i.e. to explain why *nositi* evolved like *vesti*), but simply to argue that, for descriptive purposes, there is evidence to assign the two to a single class. Nevertheless, the evidence adduced may be relevant historically, and deserves investigation.

[6]Morpheme boundary is denoted with the dash. Two dashes mark the boundary between stem and post-stem; a single dash marks other boundaries; e.g. in *rěz-a--n-*, the participial stem of *rězati*, with - separating the root *rěz-* from the suffix *-a-*, which is part of the verbal stem, and -- separating the stem *rěz-a-* from *-n-*, the participial suffix.

[7]It should be noted in this regard that reflexes of Leskien Class 2, represented by *dvignǫti*, also qualify as nonsuffixed and nonvocalic, and, like *vesti* and *nositi*, exhibit *-ěa-* in the imperfect past and *-en-* in the passive participle. The status of *dvignǫti* is implied not only by the absence of *a* or *ě*, but also by the fact that *ǫ*, like *i* in *nositi*, is not attested throughout the conjugational unit. According to our scheme, therefore, *dvignǫti* has the structure $CVC-n-//CVC-nǫ-$, where $-n-//-nǫ-$, with $-n-$ occurring prevocalically and $-nǫ-$ preconsonantally, constitutes a *derivational* suffix structurally different from *a* and *ě*, which may be termed **formatives**.

[8]Interaction between *bělěti* and *viděti* is more complicated because -*ě*- in the former was not only a realization of -*V*-, but conveyed the notion of *becoming*. Nevertheless, there has been interaction; e.g. in Macedonian, where only the type represented by *viděti* is attested in the literary language (see Vaillant 1966).

[9]Interaction between *vesti* and *nositi* is also attested in Polish, where a reflex of iotation (i.e. *Common Slavic consonant* + *j*), historically expected in the passive participle of *nositi*, is now attested in the masculine personal passive participle of *vesti* (e.g. *wiedzeni* instead of *wiedzieni* in the participle of *wieść*). See Elson, to appear, for the details.

[10]Note the implicit assumption that CVC--*ě*- in the imperfect past and imperative of *vesti* does not entail a suffixed stem variant for it (i.e. CVC-*ě*-, identical to CVC-*ě*- in *viděti* and *bělěti*). If we are correct in this assumption, which is the traditional one, the reason is most likely the occurrence of -*ě*- in the infinitive of *viděti* but not in that of *vesti*. The infinitive has minimal grammatical content, and therefore may well determine the segmental extent of the verbal stem. If -*(s)ti* marks the infinitive, the stem of *viděti* is, at its maximum, *vid*-*ě*-; that of *vesti*, however, is *ve(d)*-.

We are also assuming that verbs like *vesti* are noncombinatorial despite their CVC-//CV-structure, which seems to combine CVC- and CV-, since, in this instance, CV is segmentally a part of CVC (cf. the situation in *mel*-//*mlě*-, the stem of *mlěti*, where one of the stem variants is not part of the other) **and** the verbal stem is morphologically a single unit (cf. *rěz*-//*rěz-a*-, where one variant is segmentally a part of the other, but the verbal stem, in one of its variants at least, is morphologically complex). In effect, we are assuming that if the variants of a verbal stem can be interpreted as allomorphs rather than as independent although related units, they will be.

[11]It is here that the decision to assign *j* to the morpheme following the stem is motivated. The attribute common to *mlěti* and *biti* is CV, suggesting that the stem of these verbs terminates in V, not *j*. We have therefore assumed CV- for Jakobsonian CVj- and CVC-V- for Jakobsonian CVC-Vj-.

REFERENCES

Diels, Paul. *Altkirchenslavische Grammatik*, Teil I and II. Heidelberg: Carl Winter (Universitätsverlag). 1963 (2nd edition).

Elson, Mark J. "Morhophonemic Peculiarities of the Passive Participle in Standard Polish," to appear.

Elson, Mark J. "On the Relationship Among Stem Alternants in Slavic Verbal Systems." *Wiener Slawistischer Almanach*, 1980, Band 5, 175-86.

Ermakova, M.I. *Očerk grammatiki verxnelužickogo literaturnogo jazyka.* Moskva: Nauka, 1973.

Jakobson, R.O. "Russian Conjugation." *Word* IV, 1948, 155-57.

Leskien, A. *Handbuch der Altbulgarischen Sprache.* Heidelberg: Carl Winter (Universitätsverlag), 1962.

Lunt, Horace G. *Old Church Slavonic Grammar.* The Hague: Mouton. 1974 (6th revised edition).

Meillet, A. *Le slave commun.* Paris: Champion. 1965 (2nd edition).

Micklesen, Lew R. "The Structure of the Russian Verb Stems." in *The Slavic Word*, ed. Dean S. Worth. The Hague: Mouton, 1972, 261-75.

Vaillant, A. *Grammaire comparée des langues slaves.* Tome III (le verbe). Paris, 1966.

STEM STRUCTURE, HIERARCHY AND
RUSSIAN VERBAL ACCENT

Lawrence E. Feinberg

1. It is axiomatic that the stress of any inflected form falls on a stem or desinence. In working with the Russian verb, however, one begins to suspect that a different division, overlapping the former, is the operative one for verbal accentuation. The object of this paper is twofold. First, I propose to argue for a new accentology of the Russian verb, based on the morphological analysis of stems. Second, I intend to show that the accentual system of the Russian verb is motivated by the phonological shape of the suffixes that define its accent.[1]

1.1 I begin with the assumption that the CSR verb stem consists minimally of a root followed by a verb-forming affix or **stem formant**, which may be real or zero.[2] In "Russian Conjugation," Jakobson, guided chiefly by considerations of descriptive economy, presented the (unprefixed) stem as morphologically simple, even while allowing in principle for a stem formant (see his treatment of specially truncating -nu-, *Selected Writings* II, 25, 2.23).[3] Studies of the Slavic verb in the structuralist line of descent from "Russian Conjugation" have generally adopted Jakobson's presentation of the stem (see most recently Shapiro, "Russian Conjugation" and Stankiewicz, "The Accentuation"). For the most part, to be sure, the rules of conjugation work perfectly well without any reference to stem formants as such. However, the presentation of the verbal stem as morphologically simple has had the unfortunate consequence of masking an important accentual regularity:

(1) Desinential stress and stress on the stem formant are in complementary distribution. While primary (here analyzed as zero-suffixed[4]) and nonsyllabic a-stems (in -a- preceded by a nonsyllabic root) may be stressed or stressless, secondary stems proper (minus nonsyllabic a-) always carry an accent in their basic form, which falls either on the last or only vowel of the formant, or on the preceding portion of the stem. Secondary stems proper become stressless only in case a basically stressed formant becomes nonsyllabic (in the context of vowel truncation).

Taking advantage of the looseness of the term 'affix', which may refer to a desinence as well as a stem suffix, I designate as affixal (A) both the desinential stress of primary and nonsyllabic a-verbs (*neslá, rvalá*) and the formant/desinence stress of the remaining secondary verbs (*govorjú, govoríla*;

čitáju, čitála).[5] I designate as pre-affixal (P) the stem accent of primary and nonsyllabic a-verbs (*krála, ržála*) and the pre-formant accent of the remaining secondary verbs (*pómnju, pómnila*; *délaju, délala*).[6]

By working explicitly with a stem formant and introducing Principle (1), we can account for the non-occurrence of forms like **čitajú, *čitalá* as more than just a random fact of the language. Given the usual analysis in terms of stem and desinence, the absence of aj- and ej-stems with desinence stress must be regarded as an unmotivated gap in the system (see Halle 346 and Stankiewicz, "The Accentuation" 188).

Further, given Principle (1), ova-verbs need no longer be treated as accentually idiosyncratic. Jakobson has a general rule that "in open and broadly closed full-stems the stress moves from their final or only syllable to the first or only syllable of the vocalic desinence." (*Selected Writings* II,127, 2.61). This rule derives the ending stress of the 1st sg. present tense forms *govorjú, kradú* from their respective morphophonemic representations *govor'-í-u, krád-u.* Meanwhile, a separate rule is needed to account for the accentual behavior of finally stressed ova-verbs. Jakobson stipulates here that the final stress of ova-verbs is transferred from *a* to *uj* insofar as the latter occurs in a non-initial syllable, and otherwise shifts to the following vowel (125, 2.24). This rule accounts for the stress pattern of a polysyllabic verb like *arestováť* (1st sg. pres. *arestúju*) and a disyllabic verb like *kováť* (1st sg. pres. *kujú*). It will not, however, generate the correct accent of the disyllabic verb *dneváť* (1st sg. pres. *dnjúju*, not **dnjujú*), which Jakobson gives as an exception (129). Apart from this one case, where *ov/uj* belongs to the formant, the phonological distinction of initial vs. non-initial syllable happens to coincide with the morphological distinction of root vs. suffix; but it is precisely the latter which is crucial for determining the accent of ova-stems, however many syllables they contain. Given Principle (1), the desinence stress of *kujú* and *govorjú* and the stem stress of *arestúju* and *čitáju* turn out to be combinatory variants of one and the same A accent; the variant is conditioned by the fact that the first pair of verbs truncates the suffixal vowel before the vocalic endings of the present tense and the imperative (-a-, resp. -i- ~ -∅-), whereas the second pair of verbs retains a syllabic suffix (-uj-, resp. -aj-) in this context.[7] Note that the ostensible retraction of stress in 'secondary' ova-verbs with A accent (*arestováť* ~ *arestúju*) is not really a retraction at all, but simply the persistence of accent on the last or only affixal vowel. The A accent of *arestováť, čitáť* and *govoríť* contrasts, then, with the P accent of *trébovať, délať* and *pómniť*.[8]

1.2   The unmarked position of stress in the CSR verb is on the affix which defines the stem qua part of speech, enabling it to combine with a particular set of grammatical morphemes: A accent is unmarked, P accent marked.[9] At the same time, fixed accent is unmarked in relation to alternating. The basic suffixal accent has a fixed (A_f) and mobile (A_m) variety, the latter overlapping with P accent and thus attenuating the A/P opposition. The hierarchy of accents is illustrated below in Fig. 1. A_m accent, in turn, has a small number of essentially complementary (exceptions apart) realizations. In secondary stems marked A_m the stress moves one syllable back from the suffix/desinence in the nonpast tense except in the 1st sg. (*prošú ~ prósiš'*). In primary sonorant and nonsyllabic a-stems any basically affixal stress moves to the stem initial syllable in the nonfeminine past; most prefixed sonorant stems have stress on the prefix at least as a stylistic variant of root stress (*perežilá ~ pérežíl*; for details see Stankiewicz, "The Accentuation" 193-94). (Reflexive forms of these stems have an optional pattern with unretracted affixal stress in all the nonmasculine forms: *vpilás', vpilós', vpilís' ~ vpílsja*; compare archaic *vpilsjá*.) Finally, a handful of primary obstruent stems retract their A stress to the root vowel in the past tense and infinitive (*ukradú ~ ukrál, -a, -o, -i; ukrásť*).[10]

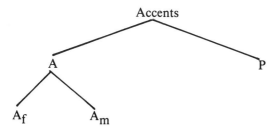

Fig. 1.   The hierarchy of CSR verbal accents. Left branches indicate unmarked and right branches marked categories.

1.3   In the CSR verb interparadigmatic alternation (between the present/imperative and past/infinitive paradigms) is primary, and intraparadigmatic alternation secondary, presupposing the former. This is essentially true of the noun as well, where "number-marking" shifts are prior to "case-marking" from a hierarchical standpoint (see Worth, "Grammatical Function"); however, the second type of alternation does not in every instance imply the first: thus *zub* opposes stem stress in the singular to desinence stress in the plural, with a secondary opposition of stem stess in the nominative-accusative plural to desinence stress in the remaining plural forms; on the other hand, *kon'* has only the intra-number opposition, both singular and plural (minus the nominative) being characterized by desinence stress.

1.4 In the context of stress retraction, A stress is evaluated as marked; accordingly, the forms exempted from retraction are the grammatically marked ones (imperative, 1st sg. nonpast, feminine or nonmasculine past). As I argue below (3.3), the fundamental relation between A and P accent is itself inverted on the periphery of the stem class system, in the primary sonorant stems, where A occurs only to the extent that it intersects with P.[11]

2. In the remainder of this paper I shall try to show that the accentual system of the CSR verb is motivated by the phonological form of the stem suffixes. Elsewhere (Feinberg) I have argued that the conventional "classifying" function of verbal stem suffixes is actually one of motivated stratification. Verbal stem classes are hierarchically ordered, and the suffixes which define these classes at the same time motivate the stem hierarchy through their phonological form. In its stratifying function, the verb-forming affix behaves like a Peircean icon (see Peirce 157-58), specifically, a diagram, in which the relations in the *signans* correspond to those in the *signatum*. Basically, attenuated sonority implies marking.[12] While motivated by phonological form, the stem hierarchy in its turn motivates various features of the verbal system that must otherwise appear arbitrary, including productivity and the capacity for alternation. The morphophonology of CSR verbal suffixes is summarized below.

2.1 In contrast to all other CSR morpheme classes, verbal stem suffixes proper (not counting their expansions) consist exclusively of sonorant phonemes (vowels, glides, nasal consonants). The fullest opposition is between the suffixes which are characterized by a vowel in their weak as well as strong alternants (those with the basic canonical shape VR: -aj- ~ -a∅-, -ej- ~ -e∅-, -ov- ~ -uj-)[13] and those which have a constant zero suffix—the so-called primary stems.[14] This opposition is mediated by those suffixes which contain a basic vowel alternating with zero before vocalic desinences. Of these, the single suffix with the basic canonical shape RV (-nu-) has a constant sonorant (but not vocalic) segment in its weak as well as strong alternant (-nu- ~ -n∅-); it is thus marked in relation to the VR suffixes, but unmarked in relation to the V and ∅ suffixes. Meanwhile, the three suffixes with the basic canonical shape V (-i-, -e/a- and -a/o-) are marked in relation to the VR/RV suffixes but unmarked in relation to the ∅-suffix. I designate those suffixes which contain two segments in their basic forms (and hence at least one sonorant in all their alternants) as strong and those with less than two segments as weak. These two classes exhibit a proportionality which is illustrated in Fig. 2. The full suffixal hierarchy is shown in Fig. 3.

Fig. 2

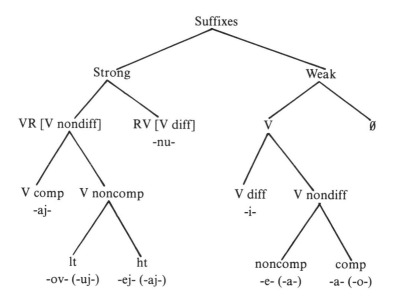

Fig. 3. The hierarchy of CSR verbal suffixes. Left branches represent unmarked, right branches marked classes. V = vowel, R = resonant, comp = compact, noncomp = noncompact, diff = diffuse, nondiff = nondiffuse, lt = low tonality, ht = high tonality. Brackets enclose redundant specifications. Secondary suffixal alternants are in parentheses.

2.2 The strong and weak classes show complementary hierarchies for the vocalic compactness feature. In the strong suffixes, this feature has its normal markedness interpretation: compactness is the unmarked, diffuseness the marked opposite (Jakobson and Halle 38-39). The weak suffixes, however, invert this hierarchy: diffuseness here becomes unmarked and compactness marked. (On markedness reversal in a marked context see Andersen, "Diphthongization" 44-45.) The suffix -aj-, with its steady com-

pact vowel, is the verbal suffix par excellence. In accordance with markedness reversal, the suffix -i-, consisting in its basic form of a diffuse vowel, is
the representative suffix of the weak hierarchy, corresponding to -aj- in the
strong. In both main classes the relatively unmarked subclass (VR and V,
respectively) subsumes, in addition to the representative suffix, a pair of
suffixes which take up an intermediary position between the former and the
most marked suffix (-nu- and -Ø-, respectively). All four intermediary suffixes are characterized by mid (nondiffuse, noncompact) vowels in alternation with high (diffuse) or low (compact).[15] In the strong hierarchy, the
intermediary suffixes both contain basic mid vowels which alternate with a
high and a low vowel, respectively (-ov- ~ -uj-, -ej- ~ -aj-). The weak hierarchy, meanwhile, distinguishes a less marked suffix with a basic mid and
secondary low vowel alternant (-e/a-) and a more marked suffix which
inverts this relation (-a/o-).

2.3 Andersen ("Diphthongization" 24) offers evidence that low-tonality
vowels are closer to the vocalic optimum than corresponding high-tonality
vowels. Given this intersection of tonality with sonority, we may account for
the restriction which the strong and weak hierarchies place, respectively, on
high-tonality (nonflat) and low-tonality (flat) vowels. Of the five CSR vowel
morphophonemes, the strong suffixes omit only the diffuse nonflat *i*, the
weak suffixes only the diffuse flat *u*. In either case, a marked specification
is excluded, with markedness varying acording to context: high tonality in
the (unmarked) strong suffixes, low tonality in the (marked) weak.

Further, we are now in a position to account for the distribution of high
vs. low tonality in the intermediary suffixes. The hierarchy of weak intermediary suffixes is determined by the compactness specification of their
basic vocalic alternants: the less marked suffix has a basic noncompact (*e*),
the more marked suffix a basic compact (*a*) vowel. High tonality here
redundantly characterizes the basic alternant of the unmarked suffix (*e*)
and low tonality the secondary alternant of the marked suffix (*o*). In the
corresponding pair of strong suffixes, where the basic vocalic alternants are
both mid, the tonality feature assumes the stratifying function that elsewhere belongs to sonority: the opposition low vs. high tonality—which here
involves both segments of the suffix, glide as well as vowel (*ov* : *ej*)—is
isomorphic with the higher oppositions V compact vs. V noncompact, VR
vs. RV, and strong vs. weak.

2.4 Productivity is basically a function of suffixal strength, except that
the least marked of the weak stems (in -i-) are productive, while the most
marked strong class (in -nu-) subsumes an unproductive subclass of about
60 verbs which truncate the thematic suffix in the past tense (*soxnut'*).

2.5 The two most marked stem classes, those defined by the suffixes -∅- and -a/o-, are subcategorized according to properties of the root. Two hierarchies are relevant here. On the one hand, nonsyllabic roots are marked in relation to syllabic. On the other, roots ending in a sonorant are marked in relation to roots ending in an obstruent. While the former hierarchy obtains for all root morphemes, the latter is specific to verbal roots, and is dissimilative with the hierarchy for verbal suffixes: the optimal verbal root ends in an obstruent, just as the optimal verbal suffix ends in a sonorant (i.e. has the canonical shape VR).

2.51 In the primary verbs, the opposition obstruent vs. sonorant subsumes the opposition syllabic vs. nonsyllabic, while the reverse is true in the a/o-stems. Thus primary sonorant stems distinguish syllabic roots (*stan-, d'en-, duj-, roj-*) vs. nonsyllabic,[16] with the latter undergoing a further division into glide roots (*p'#j-, živ-*) vs. liquid/nasal (*ž#m-, p'#r-*). In the context of asyllabicity, roots in a basic glide are interpreted as more natural, since they alternate zero with the vowel of minimal sonority (2.3)—high tonality diffuse *i* (*p'#j- ~ p'i-*). Asyllabic glide roots have a combinatory variant in steady *i* where the root ends in *v* and/or begins in a consonant cluster (*živ-, sliv-, gn'ij-*). Nasal and liquid roots, meanwhile, are less natural in the context of asyllabicity, since these alternate zero with a nondiffuse (i.e. high-sonority) vowel in verbal inflection (*a,* resp. *o: ž#m- ~ ža-, p'#r- ~ p'or(e)-*).[17] According to Heffner (74), the most sonorous nonvowels are glides, followed by liquids, nasals and obstruents, in that order. If we accept this gradation, the relation between the vowel alternant of basically nonsyllabic roots and the root final sonorant becomes complementary: the least sonorous vowel occurs where the basic root ends in the most sonorous non-vowel, and vice-versa; roots in *r* are intermediary in this regard.

2.52 Obstruent roots are subdivided, again according to sonority, into compact (= velar) roots (*p'ok-*) vs. noncompact, with the latter subdivided into continuous (*n'os-*) vs. interrupted (*v'od-*). The mutually exclusive specifications of compactness and continuousness—each of which entails a moderation of the vowel/consonant dichotomy (Jakobson and Halle 38-44)—are interpreted as marked. A secondary hierarchy in the obstruent roots opposes morphophonemic *o*—or zero in automatic alternation with *o* (see n. 16)—to the remaining basic vowels, as unmarked to marked. The synchronic motivation for this hierarchy is not apparent.

2.53 The a/o-stems, inverting the subordinate and superordinate hierarchies of the zero-suffix stems, are subdivided primarily into marked nonsyllabic (*r#v-*) and unmarked syllabic roots; the latter in turn distinguish unmarked obstruent (*r'ez-*, *plak-*, *tr'op-*) and marked sonorant roots (*kol-*, *kov-*, *s'ej-*).

3. In light of the foregoing, the distribution of stem vs. suffixal and of fixed vs. alternating accent among different stem classes ceases to be random. It is now motivated, on the one hand, by the hierarchy of accents (1.2), and, on the other, by the hierarchy of stem classes.

3.1 The strong and dominant (-i-) weak classes systematically oppose A_f to P accent. Where the latter occurs in newer verbs, it shows a specificity of function that accords with its marked status. Thus in aj- and ova-verbs, P accent functions as an index of derivation via an enlarged suffix (-iv-aj-, -n'ič-aj-, -ir-ova-, -stv-ova-; cf. *zamoráživat'*, *liberál'ničat'*, *registrírovat'*, *diréktorstvovat'*). (Note, however, that the converse does not hold: ova-verbs with the enlarged suffix -iz-ova- always have A accent (*mobilizovát'*); those in -ir-ova- (without the preceding increment -iz- or -f'ic-) may have A accent, although this is relatively rare—see n. 6.) In a more limited way, P accent in aj-verbs serves as a colloquial/expressive marker (*šámat'*, *ljápat'*, *áxat'*). The productive type of nu-verb has A_f accent (*spekul'nút'*, *psixanút'*), except for the subset of semelfactive verbs with "acoustic" meaning (*áxnut'*: Townsend 105), which have P accent; the latter is characteristic also of the unproductive (mostly inchoative) subclass of nu-verbs (*sóxnut'*). In the i- and ej-stems, which are productive in denominal derivation, P stress in newer items occurs mostly where the underlying noun or adjective has a fixed stem stress and/or syllabic stem suffix (*partizánit'*, *rybáčit'*, *obolvánet'*).

In the strong stem classes, A accent is represented all but exclusively in its unmarked (fixed) variety. Only the weakest strong class (in -nu-) allows A_m accent, which it limits to six items (*tjanút'*, *tonút'*, *vzgljanút'*, *obmanút'*, *minút'*, *pomjanút'*).

Of all the stem classes, only the i-stems systematically oppose both A to P accent, and A_f to A_m. New i-stems entering CSR exclude the latter accent. However, A_m has long been productive among traditional (basically, non-denominative) items. As the statistics of Kiparsky (316) show, close to 90% of the i-stems which are mobile in CSR were originally of the A_f type. The accentual bifurcation of the i-verbs is difficult to understand without taking into account their ambivalent position in the stem hierarchy. As a weak class, they are prone to attentuate accentual opposition and hence to favor alternation. Yet as the **dominant** (hence only productive) weak class, corresponding to the aj-class in the strong hierarchy, they tend to maximize opposition and hence to exclude alternation.

3.2 The remaining weak stem categories, all unproductive, fall into marked/unmarked pairs: -e/a- (unmarked) : -a/o- (marked); primary obstruent (unmarked) : primary sonorant (marked). In each of these classes, the accentual opposition is reduced essentially to alternating (marked) vs. fixed (unmarked), with one of the fixed accents excluded or sharply limited. The two unmarked classes, containing, respectively, about 80 and 40 items (not counting prefixed derivatives), virtually exclude P accent, which in either case is limited to a pair of verbs (*vídet', slýšat'/lézt', sést'*).[18] These classes are dominated by A$_f$ accent (cf. *letét', kričát'/nestí, péč'*), with A$_m$ appearing in a relatively small number of items (cf. *smotrét', deržát'/krást', strič'*). In the two marked classes, meanwhile, it is the basically unmarked A$_f$ accent which is restricted. Out of 60 or so a/o-stems, A$_f$ is found in the irregular obstruent-root stem *sosát'* and otherwise in stems with sonorant roots (2.53): in the eight "primary" ova-verbs (those in which -ov- is radical: e.g., *kovát'*) and in two isolated items, *smeját'sja* and *orát'* 'howl'. It is completely lacking in the nonsyllabic a- and the primary sonorant stems.

3.3 The primary sonorant stems, comprising the most peripheral stem category, reverse the overall accentual hierarchy. P is interpreted as unmarked, and A allowed only to the extent that it intersects with the former, i.e. in its attenuative (A$_m$) variety. Moreover, these opposites tend here toward complementary distribution, with the former favoring a context of full and the latter one of reduced sonority. In syllabic sonorant stems and in nonsyllabic stems which alternate basic zero with a non-high vowel (2.51), P accent is unexceptional, whereas A$_m$ has special status; it is found for the most part in stems which are otherwise unusual in their morphophonemics, exhibiting partial suppletion or irregular alternation (*daj+∅+, poj+∅+, kl'an-∅+, -n'#m-∅+*).[19] The opposite is true in those sonorant stems exhibiting minimal root-vowel sonority, viz., the nonsyllabic j-stems and their combinatory variants with basic *i* followed by *v* and/or preceded by a consonant cluster: here shifting accent is unexceptional, while fixed accent is limited to two stems (*b'#j-∅+, š#j-∅+*).

The most marked subclass of secondary stems, the nonsyllabic a-stems, are identified accentually with nonsyllabic sonorant stems in a glide. Here again the unexceptional accent is A$_m$ and the special accent P, the latter being limited to four of the approximately fifteen items in this class (*s#l-a+, st'#l-a+, p#r-a+, r#ž-a+*).

Throughout the present tense and imperative of nonsyllabic sonorant and a-stems, desinential stress appears in a context of neutralization for the A/P opposition. The A position contrasts with the P only in the feminine (for reflexives, optionally, the nonmasculine: see 1.2) past tense. From this extreme functional limitation of the A position it is a small step to the elimination of accentual opposition in the most marked stem categories. This step has in fact been taken by colloquial Russian, which generalizes the unmarked P stress position in the past tense (*píla, brála*).[20]

University of North Carolina at Chapel Hill

NOTES

[1]Note the following conventions. Morphemes and basic verb stems are given in morphophonemic transcription, with boundaries indicated by hyphens; however, a desinence boundary is indicated by a plus sign (+); Ø represents a zero segment; # stands for a zero-vowel unit, i.e. an abstract morphophonemic unit realized primarily as zero and secondarily as a vowel. Forms are cited in transliteration. CSR = Contemporary Standard Russian.

[2]In denominative verbs the root slot may be filled by a nominal stem, consisting of a root and one or more suffixes (cf. *učitel'stvovat', onemečit'*).

[3]It is important to understand that the stem formant, while endowed with a lexico-grammatical function (defining the stem qua part of speech), lacks any inherent lexical or grammatical meaning narrower than 'verb'. Such meaning may, however, be superimposed on a given formant (e.g., semelfactivity on -nu- or factitivity on -i-; note that in neither case are we speaking of an invariant meaning). As I argue elsewhere (Feinberg), the capacity of a given formant for semantic overlay is motivated by its position in a hierarchy of formants (cf. below 2.-2.4).

[4]I follow Worth ("'Surface Structure'" 413) and Flier (242-43) in treating verbs like *nesti* as having a zero suffix rather than no suffix.

[5]The nonsyllabic a-stems seem to contradict Principle (1) in that most of them exhibit a contrast between desinence stress in the feminine past and formant stress in the nonfeminine past (*zvalá ~ zválo, -i*; see below 1.2). However, the formant -a- preceded by a nonsyllabic root behaves like the zero suffix of primary verbs: it is incapable of carrying a basic A accent, which is therefore realized as desinential except where it undergoes retraction. The stress which falls on the formant vowel represents a stress on the zero-vowel unit of the root, which may be basic (as in the handful of P-accented verbs, e.g., *ržát'*) or result from retraction (*zvát'*). Observe that of all stems in a nonsyllabic root, only a-stems have an accentually inactive formant; other such stems behave accentually like the corresponding stems in a syllabic root (cf. *gnút', mčát', čtít'*, to which Principle (1) applies without qualification, as it does to *tolknút', kričát', prosít'*). At this point we are left with only one CSR verb for which we need to distinguish desinence stress as such, viz., perfective *rodít'* (fem. past *rodilá ~* masc. *rodíl*, neut. *rodílo*). This is the only secondary stem in a syllabic root that exhibits alternation in the past.

[6]The stipulation in Principle (1) that the basic position of A accent is on "the last or only vowel of the formant" is needed for verbs built on the suffix -ova-, which in its basic form presents two syllabic elements: a suffixal nucleus -ov- (in alternation with -uj-) and the obligatory expansion of this nucleus (-a-), the latter appearing before consonantal desinences but automatically truncated before vocalic. P accent is here interpreted as an accent falling anywhere before the last or only suffixal vowel. This pertains not only to root-stressed verbs (*trébovat'*) but also to those with the leftward suffixal enlargement -ir-, which is typically stressed, e.g., *kvalificírovat'* (Zaliznjak gives only 76 verbs out of 1095 of this type which have final accent—e.g., *formiróvát'*).

[7]Principle (1) makes it unnecessary to treat verbs in -avát' as accentually unusual; their peculiarity is now strictly segmental. Assuming a suffix -aj-which undergoes special truncation before the desinences of the nonpast tense (just as -nu- in certain—admittedly more numerous—verbs is truncated before the past tense desinences), the accent of this suffix automatically becomes desinential when it is truncated: $daj\text{-}áj+u \rightarrow daj\text{-}\theta+ú$. To the extent that the suffix remains intact, the root final jod (which itself may alternate with basic n) undergoes a dissimilative "glide-shift" alternation $(j \sim v)$. On glide shift see Flier 247-48.

[8]A description of CSR verb stress in terms of root and post-root syllables is to be found in Levin 91-92 and Bitekhtina et al. 576-77. Such a distinction, while similar to the one proposed here, and workable in the main, still requires separate stress specifications for verbs like *arestovát'*. Further, it leaves out of account the fixed stem stress of verbs in -*írovat'* or of denominatives with stress on a more deeply nested suffix, e.g., *učítel'stvovat'*. It would be equally amiss to describe such verbs as having root or post-root stress.

[9]When I speak of marked/unmarked in relation to morphophonemic categories, I have in mind the relative position of two or more correlated terms in a hierarchy. In this I am following Jakobson, who, particularly in his later writings, sought to extend the notion of markedness beyond the confines of phonology and semantics, e.g., "The entire network of language displays a hierarchical arrangement that within each level of the system follows the same dichotomous principle of marked terms superposed on the corresponding unmarked terms ["Verbal Communication" 76]." Short of adopting an a priori theory of markedness such as that proposed by Shapiro ("Russian Conjugation"), we must, of course, decide in each instance which of two correlated terms is marked and which unmarked. This does not mean, however, that we must fall back on subjective criteria, for granted the accuracy of our analysis, the bias of the system will usually be apparent. Thus once we determine that the operative accentual dichotomy for CSR is A vs. P, we can identify A as the unmarked member of the opposition on the basis of the asymmetrical relation between the two terms (basic P accent is inherently fixed, whereas basic A has a mobile variety that overlaps with the P position) as well as by the greater information carried by P accent in productive formations (see below 3.1). Similarly, for the verbal formants, the marked status of relatively weak sonority is clear once we determine that these suffixes (excluding their enlargements) contain only sonorant phonemes (2.1). Incidentally, one can only agree with Chvany (68) that "unraveling and relating the multiple meanings of 'markedness' in linguistic theory" is one of the more urgent tasks of linguistic research.

[10]While Jakobson treats *krást'* as a basically stressed stem that becomes stressless before vocalic desinences by a general rule (see above 1.1), I regard it as a basically stressless (i.e. A-accented) stem that is specially marked for P-accent in the past tense. I am thus assuming that nonautomatic (grammatically conditioned) stress alternation occurs only from right to left; automatic alternation occurs basically in the opposite direction (cf. the shift of accent from a truncated formant vowel to the desinence), leftward transfer taking place only where a stressed desinence contains a zero-vowel unit $(n'os+\#^{'} \rightarrow n'ós+\#)$. This assumption is diametrically opposed to that made by Stankiewicz (see "The Accent Patterns"/*Studies* 75-77).

[11]The A/P framework presented above is applicable also to the past passive participle, both on the inter- and intraparadigmatic level. The accentuation of the past passive participle will be presented in a separate study.

[12]Shapiro (*Aspects* 12-17) has presented a similar analysis of the CSR substantival case desinences.

[13]Among the VR suffixes, -ov- is unique in that it exhibits its weak alternant not before consonantal, but before vocalic desinences. The suffixal nucleus -ov- is obligatorily extended by -a-, which appears only before consonantal desinences; before vocalic, it truncates automatically, with a concomitant alternation of the nucleus -ov- $\sim$ -uj-. On the treatment of v/v' as a glide, see Andersen, "The Phonological Status."

[14]See n. 4. By "zero suffix" I mean a variant of the verbal stem formant that is segmentally null instead of having one of the basic abstract shapes V, VR or RV. One should not confuse the zero suffix with the zero-vowel unit (#); unlike the latter, the zero suffix neither triggers nor participates in zero/vowel alternation: the basic representations *ž#g-Ø+l-a* and *n'os-Ø+l-#* do not yield *žogla and *nesol. Observe that in so-called zero desinences it is not zero per se that conditions vowel insertion in the stem, but rather the zero-vowel unit that is the sole constituent of the desinence: thus we get *ljubov'* from underlying *l'ub#v'+#*, just as we get *ljubov'ju* from underlying *l'ub#v'+#ju*. Nevertheless, it seems that in certain nonsyllabic a-stems the zero alternant of suffixal -a- may have a vowel-triggering effect similar to that of # (hence *brat'* ~ *beru*; see Worth, "On the Morphophonemics").

[15]The basic suffix -a- alternates with -o- after roots of the shape CoL-, where C = consonant and L = liquid (*pljasat'* ~ *kolot'*). The basic suffix -e- alternates with -a- after root final palatal (*videt'* ~ *slyšat'*), with the single exception of *kišet'*. Under the same conditions, but with considerably less regularity, -ej- is found in alternation with -aj- (*staret'* ~ *dičat'*); note, however, the occurrence of *e* after palatal in *svežet'* (cf. *dorožat'*), *zamšet'* (cf. *obvetšat'*) and (colloquial) *mjagčet'* (cf. *legčat'*).

[16]Only two obstruent stems, -*č#t-Ø*+ and *ž#g-Ø*+ (not counting *š#d-Ø*+, in suppletive alternation with *id-Ø*+) have basically nonsyllabic roots. However, unlike their sonorant counterparts, which make reference to special conditions (e.g., desinence beginning in a consonant), these roots insert a vowel according to general rules valid for CSR nominal as well as verbal inflection: # becomes a vowel when followed in the next syllable by #; the vowel is *e* when following by a sharp consonant, and otherwise *o*.

[17]The r-stems, the only sonorant class without truncation, exhibit an (always stressed) mid-vowel root extension before the infinitive desinence: *p'oré-Ø+t'*. That this is an extension and not a vocalic suffix is shown by the fact that the root becomes syllabic (# ~ o) here, just as it does when followed (across the zero stem suffix) by the consonantal desinence of the past tense (*p'ór-Ø+l-a*); the enlargement occurs, as it were, after vocalization of the zero-vowel unit.

[18]Not counting the suppletive *jéxat'*. Two further idiosyncratic verbs have P accent in the present system alternating with A$_f$ and A$_m$, respectively, in the past, viz., *léč'* and *být'*.

[19]The stem *m'#r-Ø*+ has P accent where it is simplex and A$_m$ accent where it is prefixed. The stem *p'#r-Ø*+ has A$_m$ accent with two prefixes (*za-* and *ot-*).

[20]A further manifestation of markedness reversal in these stems involves the relation between inter- and intraparadigmatic alternation. Basically, the former dominates the latter (1.3). In the primary sonorant and nonsyllabic a-stems, however, the opposite is true: stems like *p'#j-Ø* are interpreted as having alternation between the present and past paradigms only so long as they exhibit alternation within the latter.

REFERENCES

Andersen, Henning. "The Phonological Status of the Russian 'Labial Fricatives'." *Journal of Linguistics* 5, 1969, 121-27.

———. "Diphthongization." *Language* 48, 1972, 11-50.

Bitekhtina, G. et al. *Russian: Stage I.* Moscow: Russian Language Publishers, 1980.

Chvany, Catherine V. "From Jakobson's Cube as *Objet d'Art* to a New Model of the Grammatical Sign." *International Journal of Slavic Linguistics and Poetics* 29, 1984, 43-70.

Feinberg, Lawrence E. "Motivational Design in the Russian Verb: The Hierarchy of Suffixes." Unpublished ms.

Flier, Michael S. "On the Source of Derived Imperfectives in Russian." *The Slavic Word: Proceedings of the International Slavic Colloquium at UCLA.* Ed. Dean S. Worth. The Hague; Mouton, 1972, 236-60.

Halle, Morris. "The Accentuation of Russian Words." *Language* 49, 1973, 312-48.

Heffner, R-M. S. *General Phonetics.* Madison: University of Wisconsin Press, 1960.

Jakobson, Roman. "Russian Conjugation." *Word* 4, 1948, 155-67. Rpt. in R. Jakobson, *Selected Writings,* II: *Word and Language.* The Hague: Mouton, 1971.

⸻. "Verbal Communication." *Scientific American* 227.3, 1972, 72-80.

⸻ and Morris Halle. *Fundamentals of Language.* The Hague: Mouton, 1956.

Kiparsky, Valentin. *Der Wortakzent der russischen Schriftsprache.* Heidelberg: Carl Winter, 1962.

Levin, Maurice I. *Russian Declension and Conjugation: A Structural Description with Exercises.* Columbus: Slavica Publishers, 1978.

Peirce, Charles S. *Collected Papers.* Ed. Charles Hartshorne and Paul Weiss. vol. 2: *Elements of Logic.* Cambridge: Harvard University Press, 1932.

Shapiro, Michael. *Aspects of Russian Morphology. A Semiotic Investigation.* Cambridge: Slavica Publishers, 1969.

⸻. "Russian Conjugation: Theory and Hermeneutic." *Language* 56, 1980, 67-93.

Stankiewicz, Edward. "The Accent Patterns of the Slavic Verb." *American Contributions to the Sixth International Congress of Slavists.* vol. 1: Linguistic Contributions. Ed. Henry Kučera. The Hague: Mouton, 1968, 359-76. Rpt. in Stankiewicz, *Studies* 72-87.

⸻. *Studies in Slavic Morphophonemics and Accentology.* Ann Arbor; Michigan Slavic Publications, 1979.

⸻. "The Accentuation of the Russian Verb." *Studies,* 185-204.

Townsend, Charles E. *Russian Word-Formation.* Corrected rpt. Columbus: Slavica Publishers, 1975.

Worth, Dean S. "Grammatical Function and Russian Stress." *Language* 44, 1968, 784-91.

⸻. "'Surface Structure' and 'Deep Structure' in Slavic Morphology." *American Contributions to the Sixth International Congress of Slavists.* vol. 1: Linguistic Contributions. Ed. Henry Kučera. The Hague, Mouton, 1968, 395-427.

⸻. "On the Morphophonemics of the Slavic Verb." *Slavia* 39, 1970, 1-9.

Zaliznjak, A.A. *Grammatičeskij slovar' russkogo jazyka. Slovoizmenenie.* Moscow: "Russkij jazyk," 1977.

THE PREPOSITION OF CAUSE *IZ*: ITS SEMANTIC AND SELECTIONAL PROPERTIES

Valentina Gitin

1. Introduction. Although Russian prepositions have been studied for more than two centuries, a number of blank spots remain, especially in the semantics of causal prepositions (CP). There exists so far no satisfactory description of the functional system of CPs in terms of distinctive features for each CP and the conditions for the selection of a particular CP or its interchangeability with others. In this work we establish certain semantic properties of the CP *iz* that account for the behavior of *iz* both in nuclear causal constructions and in larger contexts. We examine selectional properties involving both the governed nouns and the verbs which may or may not present the result of a cause denoted by *iz* NP; cf. the impossibility of **iz soobraženij*, **iz myslej*; the acceptability of *Ona skazala èto iz zavisti* 'She said that out of envy' beside the unacceptable **Ona posedela iz zavisti* 'She turned grey [-haired] out of envy.' (The asterisk (*) will be used throughout this paper to indicate impossible or anomalous collocations; marginally acceptable phrases will be preceded by a question mark instead.) Though our research is limited to a single preposition, we believe that the principles and facts discovered in the course of our analysis will be helpful in further investigations of Russian CPs, as well as in the development of theoretical models of functional systems.

The traditional view of the distribution of the CP *iz* is nicely summarized by Nirenburg (254): "In all phrases with *iz₄* [our CP *iz*], the governed word is regularly chosen from the semantic class of words with the meaning of "property or quality pertaining to a person." Other scholars, among them Peškovskij, Vinogradov, Pavlova, Klyčkova, Leont'eva & Nikitina, Popova, have proposed more detailed subclasses; all of these fall under Nirenburg's definition, which—though it does work in a great number of cases—proves to be inadequate. For instance, some words with the meaning "property or quality pertaining to a person" refuse to combine with *iz* in some contexts, yet are compatible with it in others. For example, (1) and (2) are totally unacceptable:

(1)   *On poexal na celinu iz želanija/iz svoego želanija.
      'He went [to work] on the virgin lands out of desire/out of his own desire.'
(2)   *Ja zaščiščal ee iz čuvstva.
      'I defended her out of (a) feeling.'

but (3) and (4) are well-formed:

(3) On poexal na celinu iz želanija zarabotat' pobol'še deneg.
     'He went [to work] on the virgin lands out of a desire to make more money.'
(4) Ja zaščiščal ee iz čuvstva spravedlivosti.
     'I defended her out of a sense of justice.'

Compare also such nouns as *mysl', razmyšlenie, duma,* and *soobraženie,* which are near-synonyms meaning 'thought', clearly "a property pertaining to a person," yet none of them combine freely with *iz*: **iz myslej, razmyšlenij, dumy, soobraženij.* With *soobraženie,* however, a larger context can save the sentence, as it did in (3) and (4): *iz gumannyx soobraženij* 'out of humanitarian considerations'; *iz svoix soobraženij* 'out of considerations of [my/his/her] own'; *iz soobraženij vygody* 'out of considerations of profit'. But a larger context cannot help the other synonyms: **iz svoej mysli o den'gax* 'out of his/her thought about money; **iz razmyšlenij o žizni* 'out of reflections about life'.

Some other problems of usage of CP *iz* appear in the primed sentences below:

(5) a. Vasja slušal starika iz vežlivosti.
         'Vasja listened to the old man out of politeness.'
     a'. *On slušal starika iz svoej vežlivosti.
         '*He listened to the old man out of his politeness.'
     b. On ubil ee iz revnosti.
         'He killed her out of jealousy.'
     b'. *On ubit' ee byl gotov iz revnosti.
         '?He was ready to kill her out of jealousy.'

But the sentence is fine if *iz* is replaced with another CP, *ot*:

     c. On ubit' ee byl gotov ot revnosti.
         'He was ready to kill her from jealousy.'

In the following sections we attempt to isolate the properties responsible for the distribution of CP *iz*. Some of these are semantic, others are pragmatic, operating, as we will show, on a discourse level.

2. Referential conflicts. Speaker's attribution vs. reference to actant's participation in a specific narrated event.

Let us now insert (5a) into a larger-than-one-sentence context:

(6) Slova Petra Gerasimoviča neskončaemym potokom lilis' na Tanju i Vasju. Nakonec ej udalos' vstavit' frazu o tom, čto ej nado sročno napisat' pis'mo, ona izvinilas' i uselas' v drugom uglu s bloknotom v rukax. Vasja prodolžal slušat' starika **iz vežlivosti.**

'Petr Gerasimovič poured his words at Tanja and Vasja in an endless torrent. At last Tanja managed to stick in a phrase about her need to write an urgent letter, she excused herself and retired into the corner with a notebook in her hands. Vasja continued to listen to the old man out of politeness.'

If the last sentence is read with falling intonation, the sentence is acceptable. But if we continue the story, with a rising intonation on *vežlivosti* indicating continuation, the expanded sentences offered below are at best ill-formed (in our opinion they are completely unacceptable).

(7) a. Vasja prodolžal slušat' starika iz vežlivosti. (cf. 5a, 6)
  a'. . . . *iz vežlivosti, kotoraja proizvela na Tanju bol'šoe vpečatlenie.
   . . . '*out of politeness that greatly impressed Tanja.'
  a". . . . *iz vežlivosti, kotoruju Tanja našla izlišnej.
   . . . '*out of politeness that Tanja found excessive.'

While the English gloss improves somewhat with the addition of an article (*?out of a politeness that greatly impressed Tanja*), there is no simple correlation between the ungrammatical Russian combinations and the presence or absence of a determiner in English, as is clear from the examples below:

(8) a. On vzjal ee v dom iz žalosti.
   'He took her into his home out of pity.'
  a'. . . . *iz žalosti, kotoraja pokazalas' ej oskorbitel'noj.
   . . . '*out of (*a) pity that seemed to her insulting.'
  a". . . . iz žalosti. *Èta/*Ego žalost' pokazalas' ej oskorbitel'noj.
   . . . 'out of pity. This/His pity seemed to her insulting.'

The semantic distinction between indefinite or generic and specific reference seems to play a role (as it does in the distribution of the English determiners, a problem beyond the scope of this paper), but it does not fully account for the behavior of CP *iz* in these sentences.

We propose that the unacceptability of the primed sentences is due to a referential difference between the first and second instances of *vežlivost'/politeness*. The rising intonation of the continued sentences suggests a link, inviting incorrect assignment of coreference. That is, if Vasja in (5a, 7) had experienced a certain specific emotion or psychological state, which had served as a motive for his action and at the same time could be observed by other participants, then (and only then) would the reference to such a state in the continuing clauses have been correct. But how does a person acting politely **experience** politeness? It is clearly neither a state nor an emotion. We can define it rather as a **system of deliberate acts adjudged to be polite/ civil in a particular culture.** Since Vasja cannot possibly experience a **system**, the apparent coreference of the second *vežlivost'/politeness* (affecting other participant-observers, as in the primed sentences), to the first instance of *vežlivost'* is misleading and wrong, for it requires reinterpretation of *vežlivost'* in (7a) as Vasja's experienced emotion and motive. The difference is less obvious in the examples with *revnost'/jealousy/envy* or *žalost'/pity*, since these words **can** refer to emotions of the doer (the actant or participant in the **narrated** event), but they may also have other meanings, such as a label attributed to the action by the speaker (participant in the **speech** event); compare, for instance, *On uexal, kakaja žalost'!* 'He left, what a pity!', which gives the speaker's categorization of the cause of the event rather than a reference to the actual experience of a participant in the narrated event. The referential discrepancy becomes even more evident in variations in (5b) with *ubit' iz revnosti* 'kill out of jealousy' in contexts referring to a specific experience:

(9) a. (=5b) On ubil ee iz revnosti.
    a'. . . . *iz revnosti, ot kotoroj vsja krov' brosilas' emu v golovu.
        . . . '*out of jealousy from which all his blood rushed to his head.'
    a". . . . *iz revnosti, oxvativšej vse ego suščestvo i zastlavšej emu glaza krovavym tumanom
        . . . '*out of jealousy which filled all his being and clouded his eyes with a bloody haze.'
    a"'. . . . *iz revnosti, pri mysli o tom, čto vot tol'ko čto ona obnimala drugogo.
        . . . '*out of jealousy at the thought that just a moment ago she had been embracing another man.'

As with the two senses of *vežlivost'/politeness*, we intuitively recognize that the two senses of *revnost'/jealousy* are not the same.

Again, as in (5c) above, the discrepancy disappears when CP *iz* is replaced with CP *ot*:

    b. On ubil ee ot revnosti, ot kotoroj vsja krov' brosilas' emu v golovu.

The naturalness of the sentence (9b) is slightly strained by the repeated *ot*, a redundancy which may be removed by replacing *ot kotoroj* with *kogda* 'when'. In either case, the identity of *revnost'* as motive and *revnost'* as experienced emotion leaves no doubt, since it resides in the same participant. Substituting *ot* for *iz* saves other contexts as well: *ot revnosti, oxvativšej . . . i zastlavšej . . .; . . . ot revnosti, pri mysli . . . .* Unlike *iz*, the preposition *ot* does not exclude specific reference to an experienced emotion. When *ot* NP is presented in a causal construction as a motive for action, it allows further elaboration of details accompanying such motive-as-experience; none of the sentences with CP *iz* allow such elaboration. As was demonstrated in the examples above, *iz* NP does not describe actual feelings or experiences of the actant at the time of the narrated event.

Another illustration will reinforce this point:

(10)   Vasja zametil u svoix nog pjatak, no ne podnjal ego iz gordosti.
        'Vasja noticed a 5-kopeck coin/nickel at his feet but did not pick it up out of
        pride.'

According to Zasorina (76), "*iz* indicates a cause as internal incentive, of
which the doer is aware [pobuždenie, osoznavaemoe dejatelem]." If we
were to accept this definition, then we would have to assume that the
approximate internal monologue of Vasja (the doer, actant, participant)
was more or less as in (11):

(11) a. *Ja sliškom gord, čtoby naklonjat'sja za ètoj melkoj monetoj.
         'I am too proud to bend over for such a petty coin.'
or   b. *Net, gordost' ne pozvoljaet mne podnjat' ètot pjatak.
         'No, pride does not permit me to pick up this nickel.'

A more likely actual monologue would be something like the following:

     c. Dan nu ego, stoit li naklonjat'sja iz-za takoj meloči!
         'The hell with it . . . it's not worth bending over for such a trifle.'

We can go on making up shorter or longer monologues, but if they are to
be natural, the word *gordost'/pride* must not be mentioned. Similarly, in
the situation referred to in (7) *On slušal starika iz vežlivosti* 'He listened to
the old man out of politeness', it is unlikely that Vasja said to himself:

(12) a. Ja čelovek vežlivyj. Nado vykazat' vežlivost' stariku.
         'I am a polite person. I have to demonstrate my politeness to the old man.'

It is more likely that he said to himself:

     b. Pridetsja poslušat' starika, a to ved' obiditsja.
         'I've got to listen to the old man, or he'll be hurt.'

Here again, the NP with *iz* (*vežlivost'/politeness*) cannot be ascribed to a
natural or plausible monologue. It does not belong to the actant's actual
experience in the narrated situation. The word *vežlivost'/politeness* in (7)—
like *gordost'/pride* in (11)—belongs to the **speaker** rather than to the
doer-actant-participant.

     A careful distinction between participant in the narrated event and par-
ticipant in the speech event, as proposed in Jakobson 1957, accounts for
the discrepancy between motive and actually experienced emotion, which is
noted in the examples (7-12). We can therefore predict that if the motive
attributed to the participant by the speaker is combined with modifiers
referring to an actual narrated situation, the result will be a semantically
anomalous sentence. We have shown that the distinction between attributive

and referential uses, well known in the literature (cf. Rothstein 1980), is related to the distinction between speech event and narrated event—at least in the grammar of CPs.

This distinction proves to be crucial for a better understanding of the role of "the speaker's point of view" in the selection of CPs (which often is treated in the literature as a stylistic embellishment); it also seems to be responsible for organizing the semantic properties (or distinctive features) of CP *iz* into a hierarchical system.

We will return to this and other problems of reference in section 4 below.

3. Spatial analogies based on Schooneveld's theory of prepositions. In order to understand the way *iz* operates in context, we must make a short theoretical digression, on the basis of three premises:

A. It is universally recognized that many Russian prepositions with causal meaning have spatial origin referring to the source of the action.
B. Certain spatial fetures of *iz* can be treated if we accept van Schooneveld's view that a preposition has the same distinctive features in all its meanings (Schooneveld 1978).
C. We also accept Schooneveld's definition: "Prepositions refer deictically to a reference to extra-linguistic reality that is made in the utterance" (ibid., 220).

With these points in mind, we will try to establish the features of extra-linguistic reality which determine the perception of the spatial situation described by *iz* in its spatial meaning. Since the spatial preposition *iz* presupposes the question *otkuda?* 'where from?', we can imagine the situation described in a sentence with *iz* as a set of certain possible or known sources and the answer as the act of making a choice among them. Let us examine the following situation:

A detective wants to find a criminal's connections. He suspects that the criminal might appear at a certain time from one of the houses either in District I or District II. Watching the suspected houses, the detective missed the moment when the criminal exited. Now he asks himself: "Otkuda/ iz kakogo doma/ vyšel prestupnik? 'From where/ From which house/ did the criminal exit?'"

(13)

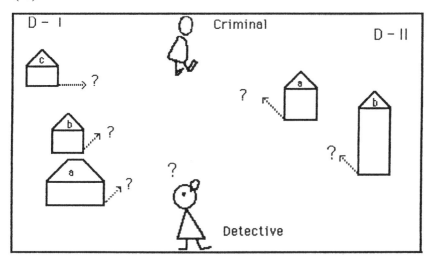

A casual passer-by who can determine the point of departure of the criminal might give a hand and share his observations with our detective:

(14)

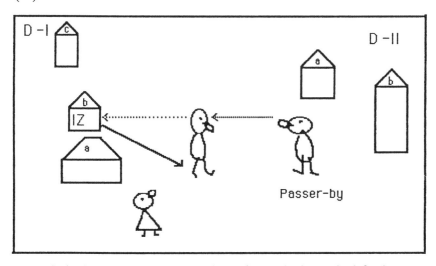

The criminal, when cornered, can also point at the house he left, thus combining the positions of observer and doer.

(15)

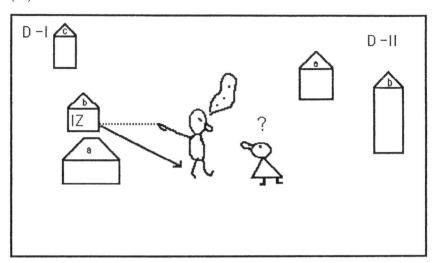

Or he might say which of the houses he came out of, thus combining all three roles (doer, observer, and speaker).

When reporting this information to the chief of police, the detective describing where the criminal came out of would refer to the set of suspected houses known in advance, and then specify the point of departure (message, referring to a code—"District I" in our situation—Jakobson 1957).

The speaker occupying the position of "omniscient author" can have all the information on extra-linguistic reality independently from any set of observers (Schooneveld 1978).

One final presupposition of a well-known type can be inferred from this situation: the question *otkuda* presupposes that the doer was previously in the house. We can draw a parallel with the similar presupposition in the usage of the CP *iz* (see (16) on next page).

The fact that all three roles (speaker, actant-doer, and observer) often coalesce tends to obscure the distinction. But even in first person narratives, what is presented is not so much the actual experience of **I the doer**, as **I the speaker**'s names or labels for the experiences of **I the observer**. The actual experience of the doer cannot be automatically equated with the observation of the experience by the same or other participants, or with the speaker's description.

4.   The semantics and pragmatics of CP *iz* vs. CPs *po* and *ot*. The NP governed by *iz*, whether in its spatial or causal meaning, must denote something internal to a larger source, as illustrated in the drawing (16). The NP

(16)

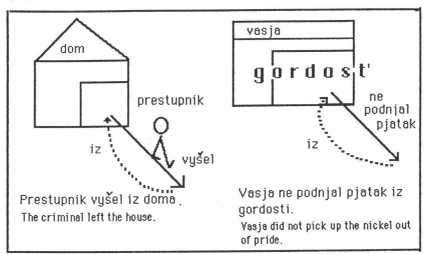

Prestupnik vyšel iz doma.
The criminal left the house.

Vasja ne podnjal pjatak iz gordosti.
Vasja did not pick up the nickel out of pride.

governed by *iz* is tentatively assigned the semantic feature [+ internal], while *ot* governs noun phrases marked as [± internal].

The preceding excursus into the spatial meaning of *iz* can help us to draw further conclusions about its causal meaning. The NP given as the cause of the action cannot be a constant personal quality of the doer; though [+ internal] to the doer, it is [+ alienable]. This feature discriminates between the CPs *iz* and *po* (which is [– alienable]). This property explains the impossibility of such combinations as *iz molodosti* 'because of being young', *iz dobroty* 'out of kindness', *iz svoej vežlivosti* 'out of his politeness', in spite of the fact that youth and kindness and politeness belong to the semantic class of qualities pertaining to a person. *Po molodosti, po dobrote, po svoej vežlivosti*, by contrast, are grammatical, since *po* collocates with nouns denoting inalienable qualities or properties.

Besides the semantic distinctive features isolated above, the compatibility of *iz* with noun phrases is sensitive to pragmatic and stylistic factors. In discussing these, we will use feature notation for expository purposes only; the optimal labels of the features or their markedness values are byeond the scope of this study. The spatial analogy drawn in the context (16) should help us to clarify another signficant point which is connected with the causal meaning of *iz* as well.

As we mentioned in section 3, such words as "District 1" represent a code, non-specific term, which is known in advance to both the speaker and the hearer, and as code words they do not describe the narrated event (i.e., "District 1" does not describe specifically any of the houses of that district). In its causal meaning, *iz* works the same way. As we showed in section 2, the distinction between attribution and specific reference is relatable to the distinction between the speaker's and participant's points of view. When the speaker names or labels the incentive actually experienced by the doer-actant, he assigns it to a certain generally known category of incentives, making it a fact of the abstract **speech situation**, while divorcing it from its actuality in a **specific narrated event**. We claim that this distinction is based on certain semantic properties of lexical items chosen for causal NPs.

Some words (for example, *jarost'* 'rage') allow contextual interpretation only as lexical items designating an actual experience of a doer, in which case we call it [+specific] or [+referential]; some (like *vežlivost'* 'politeness') could be used only in a context with reference made by the speaker to a code, to a member of the well-known category of incentives/motives, in which case we label it [−specific]. There is also a large group of words (such as *želanie* 'desire', *žalost'* 'pity', *strax* 'fear', *len'* 'laziness', etc.) which potentially can participate in both types of contexts, that is, have the marking [±specific].

If *želanie* 'desire' is marked [+specific], it can be used only in the meaning of "actual experience of longing for something," while [−specific] marking brings forth another meaning of this word, which is close to the meaning of setting a goal, rather than to the meaning of experiencing an emotional state. In fact, when marked [−specific], *želanie* is easily replaced by *čtoby* 'in order to' construction Cf. (3): *Poexal na celinu, čtoby zarabotat' deneg.*

As we showed in section 2, the CP *ot* is not as restricted as CP *iz*. The differences are important for understanding the different behavior of semantically similar nouns with respect to interchangeability of these prepositions. We claim that the near-synonyms *mysl'* 'thought', *razmyšlenie* 'meditation, reflection', and *duma* 'thought' are marked [+specific], while *soobraženie* 'consideration' is [±specific], that is, open to contextual modification.

Since CP *iz* requires that the word it governs be at least potentially [−specific], words which are exclusively [+specific] will not participate in *iz*-constructions. *Ot* does not carry this restriction, hence the sentences (5c) and (9b) were free of semantic conflict between the values for the [±specific] feature. When a dependent noun has only the [+specific] meaning, only *ot* is possible:

(17)   On zadyxalsja ot volnenija /*iz volnenija.
       'He was panting with emotion/*out of emotion.'

The contrast is beautifully illustrated by a passage in Dostoevskij's *Notes from the Underground*:

(18) Ne dumajte, vpročem, čto ja strusil oficeru ot trusosti. Strusil ja tut ne iz trusosti, a iz bezgraničnogo tščeslavija.
'And by the way, don't think that I chickened out before the officer out of cowardice. I chickened out, not out of cowardice, but out of boundless vanity.'

In the first sentence of (18), *trusost'* is presented as [+specific], a mark emphasized by the quite irregular government of *oficeru*. This unusual use of the dative is justified by the underlying semantic relationship of yielding, giving up an abandoned object to a recipient usually represented on the surface level by the dative case. The second sentence contains two *iz*-constructions. The "I" of the sentence combines the roles of speaker, observer and doer. As observer, he uses the *iz*-construction of the second sentence to put a label "vanity" on the actual situation described in the first sentence. As is especially characteristic of Dostoevksij's prose, the second sentence contains reported speech. The first *iz*-construction of the second sentence represents an imaginary speaker's view of the situation: "*strusil oficeru ot trusosti*" (where *trusost'* is potentially [+specific]); "*iz trusosti*" [–specific] thus denies the actual experience of fear, confronting the wrong labeling. The interchange of *iz* and *ot* reflects a change in point of view: when *trusost'/cowardice* was regarded as a narrated event marked [+specific], the CP *ot* was used; when the same word was treated as a [–specific] label giving the speaker's categorization of the incentive, the CP *iz* was chosen instead.

5.   The semantics of verbs selecting CP *iz*. The choice of CP *iz* from among other CPs has to do with presuppositions (or invited inferences) of the governing verb or verbal noun. Thus, even out of context, many lexical verbs suggest a generally known or naturally expected cause for the action denoted by the verb. For example, *slušat'* 'listen to' implies as its cause an interest on the part of the listener. To tell someone "I am listening to you (only) out of politeness" is to insult one's addressee, or at least break his or her natural expectations concerning the origin of the other party's listening. With a verb like *slušat'*, the presupposition is self-evident, but other verbs can have several naturally expected causes, hence their presupposition (or invited inference) is clear only in context.

The action denoted by *molčat'* 'be silent', for example, could originate from a) lack of desire to speak, b) not knowing what to say, or c) violation of the norms of cooperative conversation. With *ubit'* 'kill', a naturally expected cause for the action is that the victim does not deserve to live. Compare: *They killed many innocent people*, where, to show that the action was aimed at the wrong people who actually did not deserve death we had to use the adjective *innocent*. A context containing reported speech can establish more specific or detailed expectations, as in (19):

(19)   My vot imenno iz žalosti bez promaxu b'em raznuju pakost' — xot' ob dvux, xot' ob četyrex nogax — kakaja drugim žizni ne daet. (Šoloxov)
'It's in fact out of pity that we kill without a miss all sorts of slime, whether this slime has two or four legs — the slime which harms other people's lives.'

Vot imenno iz/ That's the reason indicates that the immediately following word *žalost/ pity* is an indirect quotation, a report of the subject's alleged ruthlessness as the cause of killing. Thus the CP *iz* is used when a generic cause suggested by the speaker conflicts with or deviates from the standard expectation suggested by the verb; the same phenomenon was seen in the *slušat'* example (7), where the cause-label *vežlivost'/politeness* deviates from the expected cause, that of interest on the part of the listener. In (3) *On poexal na celinu iz želanija zarabotat' pobol'še deneg*, the *iz*-phrase provides information deviating from the standard cultural implication that the Soviet people are driven to the virgin lands by their enthusiastic desire to help the state. The more the context prepares one for the standard expectation, the more apparent is the deviation expressed in the *iz*-construction. Most obvious in this respect are the contexts where people's actions are described as if they conform to the standard expectations and then are unmasked by the speaker who gives their real motives in an *iz*-construction.

The frequency of such contexts must not lead to the conclusion that the speaker is judging the motives of the participant. The deviation from the expected standard is signaled by the *iz*-construction, without evaluation of the motive as positive or negative. For example:

(20)   On iz blagorodstva možet otdat' vse den'gi pervomu kto ix poprosit.
'He could give away all his money out of nobility, to the first person who asks him for it.'

At first sight it looks quite natural to presuppose noble motives for giving away one's money. However, there may be other reasons: the label *blagorodstvo/nobility* may be the speaker's label for the doer's compassion in recognizing the need of the person asking. In any case, the speaker of the sentence may choose to point out that the motive, which in itself is positive, was inappropriate for the situation described. The selection of *iz* thus seems to require some deviation from the standard context presupposed by the verb. This property, which is tentatively assigned to a feature [+conflict], accounts for the ungrammaticality of *Slušat' iz interesa* or *slušat' iz ljuboznatel'nosti* 'to listen out of interest' or 'out of a love of knowledge'—the normal reasons for listening. On the other hand, such near-synonym for *ljuboznatel'nost'* as *ljubopytstvo* 'curiosity' does combine with CP *iz*: *Slušat' iz ljubopytstva* 'to listen out of curiosity'. Since *lyubopytstvo* in some contexts can have the additional meaning 'poking in other people's business', 'doing something which is not directly connected with one's affairs or interest' (cf.: *prazdnaja ljuboznatel'nost'* *'idle love of knowledge' but: *prazdnoe ljubopytstvo* 'idle curiosity'), it represents a deviation from the verb's presupposition, which accounts for its acceptability.

A last property of the verb selecting CP *iz* we call [+controllable]. This term replaces the traditional but misleading "purposeful action," which excludes non-volitional verbs. We find, however, that some non-volitional verbs can denote controllable actions in appropriate context, and can select *iz* NP:

(21)   Žirov iz straxa pered Mamontom spal v vannoj.
        'Out of fear of Mamont, Žirov slept in the bathroom.' (A. Tolstoj)

Spat' in the sense of 'sleep' is a non-volitional verb (cf. *mne ne spitsja* 'I can't sleep [though I wish I could]'); but in the context (22), Žirov intentionally chose the bathroom as his sleeping place. Compare also *Gde ty segodnja budeš' spat'? Na divane, ili na polu?* 'Where are you going to sleep tonight? On the couch or on the floor?' The possibility of choice shows the verb is [+controllable].

(22)   No vse otlično ponimali [. . .], čto plakala ona ne iz zavisti, a iz grustnogo
        soznanija, čto vremja ee uxodit i, byt' možet, uže ušlo. (Čexov)
        'Everyone understood perfectly that it was not envy that she cried from but
        rather from a sad awareness of the fact that her time was passing by, and,
        perhaps, had already gone.'

Here the weeping is not "purposeful or deliberate action" but is controllable, since the doer does not choose to control her emotion. (Cf. *K gorlu pristupili slezy, no ona sderžalas', ne zaplakala.* 'She felt the tears rise, but she controlled herself and didn't cry.')

6.   **Summary and conclusion.** The selection of CPs in context operates at a much subtler level than has been recognized. Our analysis has shown that the meaning of the CP *iz* predetermines the choice of components of nuclear constructions (verb + *iz* + NP), as well as larger contexts. All the features posited for the CP are connected with the speaker's judgment.

Some are semantically distinctive, others refer to more elusive pragmatic factors which affect the selection of *iz* with particular NPs or verbs.

The governed noun must not only denote a "quality or property pertaining to a person," but that quality must be internal to the person. The feature pair [±internal] distinguishes CP *iz* from *ot* and *po*, which are neutral to the distinction, as well as from some other CPs not discussed here. The quality denoted by the NP governed by *iz* must be alienable. Inalienable properties such as *talant, sposobnost', molodost'* resp. 'talent, ability, youth', or qualities presented as inalienable by the speaker's choice of modifiers (*ego žestokost'* 'his cruelty') cannot combine with the CP *iz*. The feature pair [±alienable] distinguishes the contexts of *iz* from those of *po*, which governs NPs denoting inalienable qualities.

The verb denoting an action of which *iz* NP is the motive is not necessarily volitional, but it must be [+controllable]. This feature accounts for the ungrammaticality of **Ona posedela iz revnosti* 'She turned grey from envy.' The CP *ot* is not so restricted.

The choice of *iz* is possible only if the human property is not limited to a specific narrated event; the NP with *iz* labels the speaker's categorization of a motive, while *ot*-constructions refer to narrated events. We tentatively ascribe this difference to a feature pair [±specific]. It accounts for the impossibility of **iz jarosti, *iz zlosti* 'out of anger [on a specific occasion]'; *jarost'* and *zlost'* are [+specific]; *zavist'* 'envy', on the other hand, is [±specific], allowing a [−specific] interpretation in context, hence *iz zavisti* is acceptable.

Finally, the feature we have tentatively called [+conflict] is required for a felicitous use of *iz*. *Iz* is not used when the governed NP would redundantly express the standard presupposition of the verb: **Slušat' iz interesa* 'to listen out of interest' is bad, since *slušat'* presupposes the listener's interest. This pragmatic property of CP *iz* is often exploited for literary effect.

We can now account for the ungrammatical collocations in (1–5). The combinations **iz želanija, *iz čuvstva, *iz soobraženij* are unacceptable because these governed nouns without their modifiers denote actual experience and refer to a narrated event, hence are marked [+specific]. **Iz svoego želanija*, on the other hand, is ungrammatical for the same reason as **Iz ego žestokosti* is—a modifier which forces a [+specific] interpretation makes the noun incompatible with *iz*. Only when such words have a modifier which testifies that they belong to a general category rather than a specific experience do they become compatible with CP *iz*: *čuvstvo spravedlivosti, želanie zarabotat', soobraženie vygody*.

The features we have proposed distinguish CP *iz* from other CPs. They belong to different semantic domains—the feature [+conflict] being clearly more in the realm of pragmatics than of lexical semantics. The challenging problem of defining their interrelations in the system of all CPs will require further detailed study.

Harvard University

REFERENCES

Jakobson, R. *Shifters, Verbal Categories and the Russian Verb,* (1957). In *Selected Writings* II, The Hague: Mouton, 1971.

Klyčkova, Z. *Pričinno-sledstvennye otnošenija i ix vyraženie v jazyke.* Učen. Zap. MGPI, 1954.

Leont'eva, N. and S. Nikitina. *Smyslovye otnošenija, peredavaemye russkimi predlogami.* Slavica IX, Drezden, 1969.

Nirenburg, S. "Sposob opisanija semantiki predložnyx sočetanij." *Russian Linguistics,* v. 5, no. 3 (1981).

Pavlova, R. *Pričinnye otnošenija v sovremennom russkom jazyke v sopostavlenii s bolgarksim jazykom.* Sofija, 1978.

Peškovskij, A. *Russkij sintaksis v naučnom osveščenii.* Moskva, 1956.

Popova, L. *Pričinnye otnošenija nekotoryx predlogov v russkom jazyke.* Učen. Zap. LGU, no. 310, vyp. 60, 1961.

Rothstein, Robert A. "Gender and Reference in Polish and Russian," in C. V. Chvany and R. D. Brecht, eds., *Morphosyntax in Slavic.* Columbus: Slavica. 1980.

Schooneveld, C.H. van. *Semantic Transmutations,* vol. 1. *The Cardinal Semantic Structure of Prepositions, Cases and Paratactic Conjunctions in Contemporary Standard Russian.* Bloomington, Physsardt, 1978.

Vinogradov, V. *Russkij jazyk.* Moskva–Leningrad, Učpedgiz, 1947.

Zasorina, L. "Opyt sistemnogo analiza predlogov sovremennogo russkogo jazyka (Predlogi so značeniem pričiny)." *Problemy jazykoznanija,* LGPU (1961).

TOWARDS A POETICS OF THE GOGOLIAN ANECDOTE: "THE CARRIAGE"

Vladimir Gitin

Gogol''s "The Carriage," written in 1836, arose out of an anecdote, as did "The Nose," a work written shortly before this but published in the same year. While the latter work followed in the literary tradition of Sterne, Hoffmann, and the fantastic, as well as exploiting the tradition of the "Petersburg tale" as its key, "The Carriage" remained entirely in the realm of the insignificant anecdote of everyday life. This explains why Belinskij ignored it, inasmuch as he could not place it within the framework of his image of Gogol'. The story had no greater success among later critics. It has at times been considered a bridge between "Nevskij Prospect" and Nozdrev's estate, at times something along the lines of a comedy of characters, especially in light of the fact that it was composed so close to the time of "The Inspector General."

Gogol' had a predilection for the anecdote: already in the Dikanka stories the character of his story-teller, Rudyj Pan'ko, and his interlocutors are given as speech "masks," and any potential plot developments are already inherent in these masks. Later, this attraction for the anecdote was realized in a tendency towards plots which depend entirely upon language.

In the 1830s the anecdote once again was brought to the attention of literature. Puškin, for example, employed it with relish as a vehicle for parodying the "novella" (in its Renaissance and Romantic meaning) and within its own structure, namely by redistributing weight between the details and the whole. While the significance of the "novella" is based on the significance of the whole, especially of the plot, the anecdote emphasizes the importance of each detail separately and minimizes the importance of the whole. In Puškin, however, the short story was still trying to break loose from the bounds of the anecdote. Though the "incident" (i.e. the occurrence which in the traditional "novella" could drastically change the order of presented reality) had the tendency to appear in the end as the familiar "norm," still they were both given as different levels of narration between which there could be artistic play and competition.

In Gogol' reality is homogeneous, and "incident" is only a matter of appearance.[1] Unlike Puškin, he parodies the very possibility of plot itself. Gogol' also bases his anecdotes on the redistribution of weight among the parts and the whole. In "The Nose," for example, there is no single point of view on events that can unite all the diverse shifts in the plot. On the other hand, each separate part lives, as it were, by means of its own significance. In "The Carriage," this principle is elaborated even further. From the standpoint of narrative structure, the reality of the whole remains intact. The plot itself, however, is so buried in the story's "texture" that if the reader has the same expectations of the plot as the general in the story has of the carriage—said to be worth four thousand roubles—then the same disappointment awaits him: "What do you mean, four thousand! It isn't worth two thousand! Why, there's nothing to it at all." "The Carriage" treats the inconsequentiality of that which is promised (namely, the plot) in comparison with the promise itself (that is, speech). Speech, the material out of which the plot is constructed, is accorded primary significance.[2]

If the discontinuity between fragments in "The Nose" exists on the level of the plot, in "The Carriage" it is the level of speech which is marked by this discontinuity. Speech takes on a function in the plot. By eliminating "plot" and injecting it into the story's "texture," Gogol' substitutes the principle of demonstration or exhibition for that of narration.[3] This principle is connected, in Gogol', with the idea of pure corporeality as the essence of the world described in "The Carriage." Corporeality announces its presence through demonstration. It is therefore the major feature of the story's texture. An example of this feature on the level of language can be seen in the following passage:

> "'Puff, puff, puu, puu. . .uu. .uu. .ff here,' the general said and disappeared completely into a cloud." (p. 181)[4]

In the first version of the story, the word "puff" was given as an object of speech ("The general looked at him and let out a long puff from his pipe," p. 469). In the final version it is difficult to distinguish speech from object—the general who disappears into a puff of smoke is in its own way a representation of the character disappearing into speech. Speech as an object of demonstration has replaced the character.

The plot-line of "The Carriage" can be reduced to the following: the landowner Čertokutskij boasts about his carriage to some officers at a party and invites everyone to his home for dinner under the pretext of showing them the carriage. As a result of this drinking at the party, however, he forgets about the dinner. When the guests arrive, he hides in the very carriage he had meant to show them, where he is discovered. The plot is a pure anecdote, both in the character of the objects treated and in the behavior of the main character.

According to memoirs, the inspiration for Gogol's story came from an account of absentmindedness he had heard about Count Viel'gorskij who had once invited the entire diplomatic corps to dinner and then gone visiting on the night the dinner was to be held. This incident is almost a paraphrase of Gogol's story. Here, however the similarity between the source and its artistic reinterpretation ends, a fact which reflects a change in the conception of incident as the dominant constructive element in the anecdote. The distillation of the plot from "The Carriage" says nothing essential about that story. The most that can be derived from it are two edifying principles: don't boast and don't drink.[5]

The composition of the tale divides neatly into two parts: the introduction, which is given in one long, unbroken paragraph, and the story itself. Everything that occurs in animated form in the latter appears in the descriptive introduction as a play of speech. The description contains the event-in-itself as potential, but event which is not necessarily realized in the plot. The dinner Čertokutskij promises is present as an object of description, but it does not happen as a plot-event. There are two dinners in the tale: the one given by the general, for which no *Vorgeschichte* is given ("it is very much a pity that I cannot recall . . .") and the one that Čertokutskij fails to give, from which only the *Vorgeschichte* remains. The carriage embodied in the description (cf., "such carriages as no one had ever seen, even in dreams . . ." or Čertokutskij's description of his carriage) is never actually incarnated in the plot.

The plot itself starts with a scene which is decisive for understanding the tale's artistic structure, namely, the examination of the general's horse. The bay mare is called Agrafena Ivanovna, and the phrase applied to her, "strong and wild, like a Southern beauty" underscores the feminine principle in her:

> The general lowered his pipe and began with a satisified air to look at Agrafena Ivanovna. The colonel himself went down the steps and took Agrafena Ivanovna by the nose, the major patted Agrafena Ivanovna on the leg, the others made a clicking sound with their tongues.
> Čertokutskij went down and approached her from behind; the soldier, drawn up to attention and holding the bridle, looked straight into the visitor's eyes as though he wanted to jump into them." (p. 182)

The situation is constructed according to a pattern Gogol' frequently employs, namely that of the "kartinka"—trite pictures, whether from advertisement, store-front displays, or banal examples of popular art. Among the pictures characteristic of Gogol's poetics there is one kind which bears a direct relation to the scene described above—the depiction of a beautiful woman.

(. . .) paint me a beautiful girl. She must be a real beauty. Her eyebrows should be black and eyes as big as olives; and let me be lying next to her smoking my pipe—do you hear? She must be beautiful! ("Nevskij Prospect," p .29)

(. . .) to his great indignation he saw in the shop window (. . .) a lithograph depicting a girl pulling up her stocking while a foppish young man, with a cutaway waistcoat and a small beard, looked at her from behind the tree; a picture which had been hanging in the same place for more than ten years. ("The Nose," p .72)

He stopped with curiosity before a lighted shop window to look at a picture in which a beautiful woman was represented, taking off her shoe and display-ing a bare leg, a very shapely leg, too; and behind her back a gentleman with whiskers and a handsome imperial on his chin stuck his head through the door of another room. ("The Overcoat," pp. 158-59)

All of these "pictures" have one distinctive feature: either in the back-ground or alongside the woman there is always "some man" present. This man is the key to the image—he is her symbolic spectator in the picture. It is as though a picture were given within a picture. The woman appears visible, embodied through such a "visual approach."[6]

Gogol' himself gives a commentary to this. The idea of beauty was con-nected in his mind with the image of a woman. Moreover, he gave this idea a romantic interpretation in the article "Woman" (1831), where one can sense the influence of Plato reworked by Schelling. Gogol' described the idea of "beauty as a woman" in his own terms: "What is a woman? The language of the gods!" It is interesting there that it is not beauty, but rather "woman" that Gogol' calls the language of the gods. Objects constitute lin-guistic signs for him. The question is, signs from precisely what language?

Any condensation of language, any "matter" is already "speech." "The idea of the artist is boundless, infinite, incorporeal." (VIII, p. 146) The dis-tance between the conception and the incarnation is the distance between "language" and "speech." "Language" to a great extent approaches the notions of "idea" and "incorporeality," while movement towards the narra-tor brings us nearer to "speech," to object-depiction.

Following Schelling, Gogol' identifies beauty and the "idea" from the aesthetic point of view. Beauty-idea is the object of "language" (as he puts it the language of the gods), and not the object of "speech." Upon entering speech, that is, upon "crossing into the realm of matter," beauty loses its ideality and becomes debased, corporeal:

> As long as the picture is still in the mind of the artist, arising and taking
> shape incorporeally—it is a woman; when it crosses into the realm of matter
> and clothes itself in tangibility—it is a man. (VIII, p. 146)

Returning to the above-described type of the "beautiful woman" depicted in a banal picture, we can add that the "man" present in the picture functions not only as a special means of "seeing" the woman, making her still more visible for others, but also as her double, the corporeal counterpart of ideal beauty. In other words, using Gogol's means of expression, we see the man in the woman, beauty transformed into substance.

The scene in which the officers examine the general's horse is built on the same principle. Gogol' stresses the nature of the gathered company: "The society consisted exclusively of men." (p. 179) Agrafena Ivanovna is likewise surrounded only by men, and the very character of the inspection, with such phrases as "he took her by the nose" and "he patted her on the leg," underscores the extent to which the horse has been reified into a mere object. In the context of this objective world the idea itself has been hypostatized so much that it loses any connection with the original feminine aspect of beauty and can be transformed into any object, for instance, a horse. Here Gogol' travesties his own idea in the spirit of romantic irony. On provincial soil ideal beauty has been incarnated as a horse, a bay mare. The only thing that connects her with her Platonic fatherland is her "southern" beauty and her Greek name, Agrafena.

This scene is a model of demonstration, and it could be said of "The Carriage" as a whole that the tale is built on such artistic models. Let us consider this thesis. First the description of the town B., which opens the tale, is pure demonstration. The central place in the description is occupied by the "market place," which serves not as a functional place for trade, but as a reason for exhibiting objects. In this sense, characters such as the "peasant woman in a red kerchief" lost between bunches of bagels and a pood (35 pounds) of soap and the governor who, along with his biography, has been incorporated in the town's architectural layout (time rendered as space) are of the same order: they are objects of demonstration. The central location of the market square in the town of B. corresponds to the centrality of the fair in the spatial image of Russia.

The description of the dinner at the general's, given as a series of listings and details, continues the exhibit of the market ("the whole market was taken for the dinner"). It is noteworthy that Gogol' removes any motivations that could prevent such a perception: "It is very much a pity that I cannot recall the circumstance under which the general came to give a big dinner." (p. 179) The space of the market moves into the interior of the general's apartment. Now the wares appear as dishes. From the point of view of demonstration, the fair, the market, and the dinner constitute one paradigm manifesting the same principle: demonstration.

The plot itself starts with a display of "noble suspenders of silk." Then follows an entire series of demonstrations: the general's horse; the carriage which Čertokutskij strives to present as a picture: "cushions, springs—it all appeared as if drawn on a picture" (p. 182); the group of officers demonstrating the concept of hierarchy in quite a picturesque way:

> The general stepped out and shook himself; after him the colonel, smoothing the plumes of his hat. Then the fat major jumped out of the chaise, holding this saber under his arm. Then the slim sublieutenants skipped out of the bon-voyage with the lieutenant who had been sitting on the other's laps; finally the officers who had been showing off on their horses alighted from their mounts. (p. 188)

The series can be extended to include Čertokutskij's "pretty wife." The detailed way in which she is described can be reduced to her sitting in front of the mirror for nearly two hours and contemplating the image which shows her "with a white night dress draped about her like flowing water." (p. 186) Finally, the main protagonist himself is demonstrated "curled in an unusual position" in the carriage.

There are special details which bring the reader into this poetics of demonstration. Among the dinner guests is a "landowner who had served in the campaign of 1812." He tells the story of some battle "which never took place." At the same time, "for no apparent reason, he took the cork from the carafe and thrust it into a piece of pastry." (p. 185) His reasons for doing so are completely incomprehensible in terms of narration. But they are self-evident from the point of view of demonstration. The motivations for the exhibition do arise from the plane of narration. This becomes clear if the narrative situation described above is presented in terms of opposition: event-demonstration. An event which, in fact, never took place, can be demonstrated (cf. Čertokutskij's attempts to draw a picture of the nonexistent carriage). Nothing can be shown as something. Hence the demonstration itself guarantees neither the occurrence nor the relevance of what has been exhibited. On the contrary, the former can be inversely proportional to the latter.

Developing this point further, we find that demonstration as a dominating image in narrative reflects a reality in which ideas become objects and there is no longer any connection between those objects and their initial ideas. For Gogol there are undoubtedly higher and lower realities. He always proceeds from the higher one (i.e., from the ideal), and in this sense it can be said that the premises of his writing are metaphysical. The corporeality of the world, which Gogoľ presents in his "realistic" works is only one side of the whole, behind which there exits a reality of ideas which has no connections with the world of objects. (In this lies the tragedy of Gogoľ's creation.)

Corporeality (the world of objects) must first of all be seen. Hence its direct connection to demonstration and to a picture. Take for an example of such a connection Gogoľ's description-exhibition of town B.: "Kogda, byvalo, proezžaeš' ego i vzgljaneš' na nizin'kie mazanye domiki, kotorye smotrjat na ulicy do neverojatnosti kislo, to . . . nevozmožno vyraziť, čto delaetsja togda na serdce: toska takaja kak budto by ili proigralsja ili otpustil nekstati kakuju-nibuď gluposť, odnim slovom: nexorošo." (p. 177)

> When you drove through it and glanced at the low-pitched, painted houses which looked into the street with a terribly sour expression . . . well, it is impossible to put into words what is going on inside you: You feel such ennui as though you had lost money at cards, or just uttered some inappropriate nonsense; in a word: depressing." (p. 177)

At first glance it might seem that the given description contains nothing more than what is said. The sour expressions of the low-pitched houses which evoke a sensation of inappropriately uttered nonsense are a sort of "landscape of the soul," a backwoods elegy hummed to the tune of "In a word: depressing." Yet there is something suspicious in the elegiac parallelism in which objects and emotional states contemplate one another, as in a mirror ("you take a look"—"they see"). The psychological picture hardens, and it is difficult to make a choice between emotion and object. The sentence, if one takes a closer look, breaks down into two parallel periods (the *caesura* being marked by graphic dots) which "rhyme" two adverbs: "sourly" to "depressing" ("kislo" to "nexorošo"). The feeling experienced after uttering some inappropriate nonsense is reflected in the sour expressions on the houses. "Nonsense," to a certain extent, appears as its own objective double. In this description, we see the process of an idea becoming an object.

As Gogoľ subsequently develops this description, the feeling caused by the inappropriate uttering of nonsense is demonstrated simply as an architectural absurdity:

> The tailor's shop is foolishly located, not facing the street but meeting it sideways . . .[7]

Continuing the narrative story of "inappropriately uttered nonsense," one can observe that it is realized in the plot itself on the level of the hero's act of speech. Čertokutskij quite "inappropriately" goes from a conversation about the saddle horse to one about a carriage. At this point, scholars generally look for a psychological motivation for Čertokutskij's statement (Hulanicki 1975). In our opinion, psychological reality has nothing whatsoever to do with it. We are dealing here with nothing other than plot-demonstration of a reified concept.

In this respect one cannot even talk about the personality of Čertokutskij.[8] He can barely be distinguished from the world of objects surrounding him. Gogol' underlines one particularly crucial feature in his representation: this character lives not in time but in space. His biography is constructed as a spatial series (balls, regions, fairs) and a listing of objects. Čertokutskij's age is not even mentioned.

Some details describing Čertokutskij synthesize the substitution of space for time. It is said, for instance, that "he wore a high-waisted dress coat, . . . spurs on his boots, and a mustache under his nose." (pp. 179-180) One cannot suspect that Gogol' "did not know Russian reality" to such extent that he would combine a dresscoat and spurs. In the description, another element explains these two details—namely the "mustache under his nose," (Where else?). The unnecessary information is a "clarification" of speech, which interpets the hero's face in terms of space. Now the combination of the dress coat and spurs can be explained as a combination of different times in one space (i.e., different stages of his career). It is one more "picture" in which Gogol' tries to present an aesthetic of temporal art as a spatial one for his own ends.

The key word in Čertokutskij's description is "vidnyj" (distinguished, notable): "[he] was one of a number of significant and notable officers." Speech through punning specifies the notion "vidnyj" as "uvidennyj" (seen, visible): "At least he was seen at many balls and gatherings." (p. 179) To be seen is the fate of Čertokutskij (cf. the fair as a part of his biography). When he wants to become invisible he hides in the carriage, which had supposedly been intended for show. It is an irony of fate he cannot escape and which reveals, on the level of the plot, the text's deep symbolism: the understanding of depicted reality as an object for demonstration.

Speaking of this symbolism, we should analyze the central object in the tale—the carriage. This carriage undergoes a visible transformation from an ideal concept to an objective embodiment. As subject of a dream, it is an ideal carriage, from the inventory of Platonic "realia," and being such, it is connected in the tale with the distant names of Petersburg and Vienna. These names are suggestive for Čertokutskij; they also feed a collective dream image of a carriage: "It seems to me, Your Excellency, there are no better carriages than the Viennese." (p. 182) At the same time, in showing this idea prototype, Čertokutskij furnishes it with objects that trivialize it. The initial lightness and beauty in the image acquires a brutal character. In fact, the objective demonstration of a carriage already takes place in Čertokutskij's speech, and there is no need to actualize it in the plot as the general insists.

The image of the carriage is a metonymical sign of space, for which it is both a representation and a generalized formula. The central events of the provincial cosmos depicted correspond to a "provincial space." The preparations for dinner in the town of B. are described as follows: "Stuk povarennyx nožej na general'skoj kuxne byl slyšen ešče bliz gorodskoj zastavy." (p. 179)

> The clatter of the cook's knives in the general's kitchen could *still* be heard by the town gate.

Or take as another example the space of Russia: "On byval na vsex mnogoljudnyx jarmarkax, kuda vnutrennost' Rossii . . . naezžala veselit'sja. . . . (p. 180)

> He visited all crowded fairs, to which the innards of Russia . . . flocked to enjoy themselves. . . .

Within this "homogeneous" space, Gogol' does not make any distinctions between people and objects. A person can be presented in terms of space:

> . . . facing it, a brick building with two windows has been under construction for fifteen years; a little further, standing all by itself, there is a fashionable wooden fence, painted gray to match the mud, and erected as a model for other buildings by the mayor, in the days of his youth, before he had formed the habit of sleeping immediately after dinner and drinking before night time some kind of beverage with dry gooseberries. (p. 178)

Gogol''s sentences are unstable; the focus of their information constantly shifts. In the quotation above, the architecture competes with the mayor's habits. The sentence is structured according to the rule of maximum significance of speech at any given moment.[9] Thus, the mayor's biography and architectural space cannot exist without each other.

As already mentioned, Čertokutskij's life is described in terms of space. In the first draft of the story, Gogol' emphasized this even more explicitly: ". . . one can ask ladies and unmarried women about this in the provinces of Saratov, Penza, Tambov, Vologda, Simbirsk, Podol'sk, Xerson, and others." (p. 464) These provinces constitute a sort of chronological outline of the hero's life. Such a biography is necessarily connected with the carriage as a means of covering these spaces. It is for this reason that a carriage accompanies the hero everywhere: he always comes to the elections "in a foppish carriage" (p. 179); he is introduced to the officers "nimbly leaning out of his light carriage or droshky." (p. 180) In the first draft, it was mentioned that Čertokutskij's capital was invested in a "carriage, coach." (p. 465). In the final version, Gogol' changed it to a "team of six really first-class horses," which is a metonymical shift. The carriage, although not mentioned, is nevertheless kept in mind because a team of six horses can only be used for a carriage. This is the same kind of metonymical shift employed when Čertokutskij asks about Agrafena Ivanovna, "Very fine horse, very; and have you a suitable carriage, Your Excellency?" (p. 182), in spite of the absurdity of such a supposition. A horse, to Čertokutskij, is a permanent metonym for a carriage. As a result, an ideal relationship is established between them in that a carriage becomes for the hero much more than an object. It is a way of describing the hero's life in the framework of biography-space, and in that capacity it is an archetype in relation to which all other carriages in the tale are only a realization of their ideal pattern. The carriage in question has an entire prehistory in the story, which is teeming with different means of transportation—carriages, traps, britzkas, cabriolets, tarantasses, gigs, coaches, carts, and even half-britzkas and half-carts. The quantitative accumulation of vehicles creates the illusion of motion in a "motionless" plot.

When the dinner conversation turns to a carriage of "genuine Viennese craftsmanship," which Čertokutskij claims to possess, the general asks:

> Which one? The one you came here in?"
> Oh no, that one is for everyday needs, just for my excursions, but the other. . . . It is wonderful; light as a feather, and when you sit in it, it is simply, if Your Excellency will permit me to say so, as though your nurse were rocking you in a cradle! . . . Very comfortable, indeed, cushions, springs—all as if it were drawn in a picture. (p. 182)

From Čertokutskij's statement, it literally follows that he does not travel around in this carriage. The object does not serve its original purpose; it exists as an aesthetic object. Secondly, in the description of the carriage, a speech situation arises which foreshadows a later plot development: ". . . and when you sit in it, . . . it is . . . as though your nurse were rocking you in a cradle." At the end of the tale, the hero is discovered in the carriage in exactly this position. Earlier, when Čertokutskij is awakened by his wife, Gogol' writes, "[he] uttered a slight grunt such as a calf gives when it is looking for its mother's udder." (p. 187) The implication of a "cradle," a "mother's udder," and "comfort" shifts the semantic sign of an ideal carriage from the function of transportation to that of a quiet shelter, a cradle, giving it an added maternal connotation. The semantics of "shelter" is suggested through a strange series of images of capaciousness (*ukladistost'*) which ends with a typically Gogolian cadence: "You could put an entire bull in the glove compartment." (p. 183) The reader's initial perception of a pragmatic description of the carriage's inner space—"ten bottles of rum and twenty pounds of tobacco"—vanishes at the mention of "six uniforms" and especially "an entire bull." These final images present the carriage's inner space as special, not consonant with real-life space. Thus when Čertokutskij "places" himself in the carriage, his "shelter" is perceived in more than just a literal way.

It should be briefly noted that time, in relation to the ideal carriage, also has a symbolic meaning. While describing the carriage, Čertokutskij mentions the distant past: "When I was in the service" "in the old days." At the same time, the general speaks of the carriage as a recent acquisition: "Well, show us the new carriage, which your master got recently. (p. 189) Here we are no longer dealing with our forgetful Čertokutskij; nobody in this story remembers. In this generalized state of forgetfulness, a collective myth about the carriage is created.

The time frame of the hero's life is conveyed by "reducing space": from a list of provinces, where he was "seen," to the inner space of a carriage where he tries to be unseen. The categories of being seen-unseen, visible-invisible are introduced in the tale as categories of existence. Čertokutskij's attempt to become invisible is identical with the wish to cease existing (cf. the expression: provalit'sja skvoz' zemlju ot styda—"to fall through a crack in the earth from shame.") The reduction of biographical space to the interior of the carriage is a reduction of biography to the point of death, which, on the superficial level of plot, equals the loss of reputation in the eyes of his fellow-officers.

The loss of reputation as a motif has already been mentioned in the hero's *Vorgeschichte*: "either he had given someone a slap in the face in the old days, or was given one." (p. 179) It was this motif which forced Čertokutskij to give up his military career and become a civilian. In other words, it was this motif which caused the transformation or rebirth of the hero who was resurrected in a new capacity.

The concept of the soul and its incarnations, a kind of metempsychosis, is seen in the tale from what would appear to be very insignificant details. The town is described as follows:

> There is never a soul to be met with on the streets; at most a rooster crosses
> the road, which is soft as a pillow from the dust that lies on it eight inches

thick and at the slighest drop of rain is transformed into mud, and then the streets of the town of B. are filled with those fat animals which the local mayor calls Frenchmen. . . . (p. 177)

"The soul" is given here a whole series of expressions: "rooster," "fat animal," and "Frenchmen." These "Frenchmen" come to life from a speech theme: "francuzy—porjadočnye svin'i." ("Frenchmen are real pigs.")[10] In the first version it is even more obvious that the rooster is subjected to yet another transformation: "There strolled across the street, no longer a rooster but an officer in a tricorne hat with feathers." (p. 463) "Feathers" are an atavism which connect the officer to his previous life. The same kind of atavism can be seen in Čertokutskij's transformation; his spurs and mustache are remnants of his previous military existence. (Spurs, "špory" in Russian, by the way, are also an attribute of a rooster.) Thus, a chain of transformations (rooster - officer - landowner) can be seen as the deep structure of Gogol''s reality in the plot. To this can be added "pig," "horse," "landowner dressed in a full nankeen coat," as speech themes embodied in a mythological structure of the world where everything is subject to metamorphosis. This chain leads to the last reincarnation of the hero.

The next (in this case, civic) death of Čertokutskij occurs at the same time as his rebirth, which is presented in the plot as his awakening. Of his sleep, we read: "He slept like a dead man" (p. 187). If one remembers that the speech theme in Gogol' is a reality of his artistic world, the expression "slept like a dead man" interprets sleep as death. Consequently, his awakening is likened to that of a newborn baby (cf. analysis above). The hero's conversation with his wife is colored with the vocabulary of baby talk: "mon'munja." The ideal corporeality of the carriage, identified by the hero with a cradle, in the context of "birth" receives new semantics: that of the womb. When the interior of the carriage is revealed, "what met the officers' eyes was Čertokutskij sitting in his dressing gown curled up in an unusual way." (p. 189) His pose more than hints at the symbolic sense of the occurrence.

The symbolism of the hero's "birth" appears in direct connection with the ideal corporeality of the carriage. The latter being "archetypical" and connoting the womb, reveals the ultimate incarnation of Čertokutskij as the soul of an object—"Perhaps there is something unusual inside." In terms of Gogol''s axiology, the contrast of internal versus external ultimately goes back to the concept of soul and body. In this system, Čertokutskij is revealed as the soul of a carriage. Thus a person in Gogol''s reality manifests himself as the soul of an object, and there is no other way

for him to make a statement about himself in this world (cf. "The Overcoat"). What makes a person interesting is the object. From this point of
view, the superficial plot tells us the same thing. The general reacts to the
praise given his horse as if it were an evaluation of his personal qualities.
Čertokutskij's boasting demonstrates his desire to raise his own value
through an object. The latter displaces the person: it becomes an engendering substance for this objective world. Objects give birth to objects. Therefore the concept of space is the most relevant and characteristic of this
reality.

The idea of metempsychosis constitutes a symbolic plot which turns the
provincial anecdote into a myth, or parable about a man who is the soul of
objects and about the corporeality of the world.[12] The traces of this plot
can be found from the very beginning of the tale in the changes which the
town B. undergoes, of which so much is said as background to the plot.
The name of the hero—Pifagor Pifagorovič Čertokutskij—reflects the
same idea. Originally he had a different name—Krapuškin—, and the horse
was called Mar'ja Ivanovna. Gogol' changed the names after the narrative
plot of "The Carriage" was formed in all its details. Therefore it would be
logical to assume that the new names were intended to give final shape to
what was already expressed in the text. By doing this, Gogol' also brought
together the names of the hero and the mare, making the connection
between them more visible in that they ultimately both bear Greek names.

Usually, the surname Čertokutskij has been interpreted only in connection with the devil: i.e., "čert v uglu" ("devil in the corner"), or "kucyj čert"
("docktailed devil"). This interpretation, although well founded, is also
overdone, especially since the appearance of Merežkovskij's *Gogol' and the
Devil*. Yet, taking into consideration the full name, Pifagor Pifagorovič, it
can be read differently: i.e., "čerta" ("line") + the Ukrainian "kut" ("angle").
To support such a reading in the framework of Gogol''s context, we can
recall as an example Gogol''s tendency to use monosemantic Russian-
Ukrainian doubles in surnames, for example the name in *Inspector General*,
Skvoznik-Dmuxanovskij. Here, the Russian "skvoznik" ("draft") and the
Ukrainian "dmuxaty" ("to blow") create an image of wind blowing through
both parts of his name. This word play realizes a speech theme built upon a
pun: "produvnoj plut" (an out-and-out scoundrel).

Underlining "geometrical" semantics in the name of the hero introduces
us into a poetics of the name, in this particular case of the Greek Pythagoras. Within the framework of Gogol''s onomasticon, the name of Pythagoras corresponds to names like Schiller and Hoffmann from "Nevsky Prospect." We will not discuss its meaning as travesty, since this has already

been done. At the same time, the name of Pythagoras contains specific semantic implications.

In the Russian cultural consciousness in the first third of the nineteenth century, there were two ways of perceiving Pythagoras: as a half-legendary founder of the Pythagorean brotherhood, and as a mathematician and philosopher. Different literature, translated into Russian, supported each of these perceptions.[13] Pythagoras, in his first hypostasis, was surrounded by legendary myths which not only ascribed to him various miracles—three journeys to the underworld, the gift of prophecy, and the ability to appear in several places at the same time—but also directly identified him on occasion with the son of Apollo or Apollo himself. The same legendary aspect of Pythagoras was connected to a "knowledge" of the Pythagorean brotherhood, not as a philosophical circle, but as a religious and moral society. Its existence was also surrounded by legends which in a certain cultural context were easily translated into anecdotes.

It is this aspect of the perception of Pythagoras—especially his teaching on the reincarnation of the soul—which most likely brought him into Gogol's tale. Indeed, this teaching brought Pythagoras the greatest fame.[14] At the same time, the popularity of this teaching was accompanied by a certain aura of anecdote, made possible by the ease with which it was "democratized" and acquired a "literary" character.

Finally, if we wanted to define the artistic function of "The Carriage" in the poetic world of Gogol' in general and to examine it as a key to his writing, we should speak of this tale in connection with his elaboration of the poetics of the external versus internal worlds. The ultimate limit of Gogol's word is the object, gesture (Belyj 1934). It is a quintessentially visual reality. Let us take as an example the image from "The Nose" of the old ladies in the cathedral with wrapped faces and holes for eyes. Here the plot suggests by means of an image the idea that this world is sufficient in its visibility, that it exists for the eyes alone.

The Russian Romantics were elaborating a poetics of intimation, trying to avoid close contiguity between the word and the object. Unlike them, Gogol' was perfecting the poetics of ambiguity and lack of convergence: ". . . and then the streets of the town of B. are filled with those fat animals which the local mayor calls Frenchmen." (p. 177) As if out of delicacy Gogol' does not name the pigs, but simply depicts them. As for the name "Frenchmen," it contains nothing peculiar to the object in question. The object pulls the name into the sphere of its figurativeness. The object becomes a context for a name, for a word.

This polysemic quality of the Gogolian word lies at the basis of the metamorphosis of reality that we often encounter in his work. The object possesses an uncertainty, it is a word-changeling. It is always an anonym of another object. All Gogolian tropes and objects, which often remain ambiguous in terms of the plot, are constructed according to this principle.

Yet, in Gogol's world, the object itself receives a peculiar life, a special quality. His reality is to a great extent a reality of devices more than a reality of objects as such. Details in his world cannot deceive us as to their "realism":

> However, it is difficult to meet a traveler in the town of B. On rare, very rare occasions, some landowner, owning eleven serfs and dressed in a full nankeen coat, rattles over the cobblestones in some half-carriage or half-cart, peeping out from among piled-up sacks of flour, and lashing his bay mare, beside which runs a colt. (pp. 177-8)

The details of speech divert attention from the initial description of the town with its uninhabited and neglected "architecture." A contrast is created between the details and their absolute randomness for the plot.

Realism of detail is not motivated by the whole. It is a "wandering" device which is shown under the guise of an object. From plot to plot, the device remains the same, underscoring the incompatibility of the details with the whole. This is what creates, in terms of poetics, a special mythology in Gogolian texts: the fact that images in them constantly bring us back to the device underlying the total context of Gogol's works.

Harvard University

NOTES

[1]In the last scene of "The Nose," when the actual plot of transformations has already come back to a familiar reality with no tricks; when the nose has been reestablished in its place, and the "norm" has regained its normal status, Gogol' writes:

> Kovalev sat down. Ivan Jakovlevič put a napkin round him, and in one instant, with the aid of his brush, transformed his whole beard and part of his cheek into a cream that is served at merchants' name-day parties. (p. 73)

Reasonable reality, once again put to the test for its solidity, turns out to be the same reality in which the mayor's nose was planning to run away to Riga. Although in the plot, Kovalev received full satisfaction with respect to his nose, the language of narration still seems somehow suspicious:

> And his nose, too, as though nothing had happened, was sitting on his face, not giving even the slightest indication that it had been playing hooky.

> I nos tože kak ni v čem ne byvalo, sidel na ego lice, ne pokazyvaja daže vida, čtoby otlučalsja po storonam. (p. 75)

Reality retains the same characteristics that allowed it to play jokes on the major. What happened to Kovalev is only a condensation which easily dissolves in the plot, but is always present there as the permanent potential for the fantastic. In this constant possibility of the fantastic, the romantic correlation between two realities becomes apparent. For romantics, there is, on the one hand, the familiar, finished world. On the other hand, beneath this crystallized reality, exists the world of vital potential that manifests itself through phenomena incomprehensible to the familiar world. The latter is always treated by romantics as a positive principle. In Gogol', the correlation is a subject for romantic irony. The vital potential exists as the nose's constant readiness to "play hooky"

[2]The second sentence in the tale serves as the first example. The sentence provides no new information, but merely repeats what has already been said. However, the word *strax* (meaning in this case "very"), being a *skaz* word, indicates that the information is presented on a different level of language. Thus, the opening sentences establish the correlation between what is said and how it is said. The focus of the narration shifts sharply towards the mode of expression and away from the content.

[3]"Gogol' emphasizes this invidiously, by making his language eventful as his material is not." (Fanger 1979, p. 123)

[4]All references to Gogol''s texts are given from the edition: N.V. Gogol', PSS, AN SSSR, 1938, Vol. 3 (Gogol' 1938). References to different volumes of the same edition are specified in the text.

[5]The Russian word *kartinka* (the diminutive of "kartina," picture) might also have a diminutive semantic meaning. As such, Gogol' uses *kartinka* for the expression of two correlated realities as he understood them: the world of initial meanings and that of reflected, travestied meanings. A picture (*kartinka*), being a realium of Gogol''s artistic world, has a peculiar connotation, serving the function of an object-device, an object-term. The significance of this term reveals itself through the juxtaposition of the two Russian words—*kartinka* and *kartina*—as they appear within the Platonic concept of Gogol''s artistic universe. If the latter is an expression of a true reality (cf. the description of Brjullov's picture "The Last Day of Pompei" in Gogol''s article of the same title from *Arabesques*), the former is a grotesque reflection by the world of objects of this ideal-artistic reality. Gogol' presents certain of his actual scenes as if they were *kartinki*. These vitalized *kartinki* that are part of the action are also an integral part of Gogol''s poetics of *kartinki*. A *kartinka*, which reflects the reality of a *kartina*, is sometimes taken out of the context of familiar execution and is superimposed onto a depiction of live human scenes, though with the same unchangeable meaning:

> All this would not have surprised Pirogov; what did surprise him was the extraordinary attitudes of the two figures. Schiller was sitting with his head raised and his rather thick nose thrust out; while Hoffmann was holding him by this nose with two fingers and was flourishing the blade of his cobbler's knife over its very surface. (p. 37)

[6]Cf. "The Carriage," in which one such "picture" depicts the "pretty wife" of Čertokutskij "lying in a most charming way, in a snow-white night dress" (p. 185) and next to her sprawling hero.

[7]In the image of "nonsense" uttered "out of place," we have the same principle: a *kartinka* (picture) without a motivation, a pure demonstration.

[8]If Gogol' had wanted to present Čertokutskij as a personality he would not have missed the chance to make use of the episode of the slap. Instead, the episode is deliberately belittled to such an extent that the narrator does not remember who slapped whom.

[9]Theoretically, a sentence of Gogol''s can be imagined as capable of extending endlessly. To illustrate this, extended segments of Gogol''s text that he chose not to break into paragraphs can be cited: cf. the first part of "The Carriage" and the several-page-long "paragraph" in "The Overcoat." In "The Overcoat," Gogol''s divisions between paragraphs could easily be identified as breaks between chapters.

[10]By turning speech themes into plot themes, Gogol' endows speech with the characteristics of substantial reality, which cannot be controlled by the objective logic of narration. This is the basis on which he creates a special mythological world where everything is subject to metamorphosis.

> K nim esli priedet kakoj-nibud' gus'-pomeščik, tak i valit, medved', prjamo v gosti-nuju. (vol. 4, p. 30) This passage is almost impossible to translate and preserve Gogol''s intentions. Quite literally, it reads:

> > If some goose-landowner comes to visit, then, this bear, [i.e., the man pre-viously mentioned as the goose-landowner] pushes straight into the living room.

Two speech themes—"goose-landowner" and "bear"—constitute the plot by mechanical connection. There is no sense in ascribing both qualities simultaneously to the same person. Instead, the plot comes into existence through the literal interpretation of speech meaning, which renders it a sequence of metamorphoses—from landowner to goose, from goose to bear.

[11]Two versions of a biographical fragment about Čertokutskij could serve as an example of Gogol''s tendencies in his poetics:

> He traveled around the most crowded fairs, to which the internal parts of the prov-inces, consisting of hives of aunts, daughters, mothers, nurses and king bachelors called landowners, flocked to enjoy themselves in brakes, large coaches, wagonettes and carts. In a word, he experienced the changeability of the wheel of fortune in all its strength. (p. 465)

> He visited all crowded fairs, to which the innards of Russia, consisting of the nurses, children, daughters, and stout landowners, flocked to enjoy themselves on chaises with hoods, gigs, wagonettes, and carriages such as have never been seen in the wildest dream. (p. 180)

In the first version, speech has not yet established the precise relationships of expressions connected with the symbolic meaning. It would be sufficient to examine the "flock of pleasure-seekers," which is still rather amorphous from the point of view of speech. In the second version, the speech relations of meanings are brought to the foreground more strikingly. The list that includes both "children" and "daughters" offers an example in which specifying "daughters" separately from "children" has no logical motivation. The same could be said for the list of vehicles. Gogol' dynamizes the increasing flow of modes of transport and builds this accumulation around the sound "p." He underlines the prevailing character of this series within the sentence by stressing the cadence—"and carriages such as have never been seen in the wildest dream." The narrative composition of the sentence turns out to be redistributed in such a way that the emphasis placed on all these wagonettes and carts suppresses the signifi-cance of the daughters and fat landowners.

[12]It would be natural to compare such an interpretation with the elucidation of an object reality in "The Nose," in which the coporeality is, in a way, canonized. There is one detail in the text that can in no way be called accidental. It is said that the event on Voznesenskij Prospekt occurred on the morning of March 25. Gogol' initially tried different dates before he came finally to this one. March 25 is the day of Annunciation. According to the Gospels of Matthew and Luke, an angel announced to Mary that she would give birth to a child whose kingdom would be eternal. The discovery of a nose baked into the bread in the very beginning of Gogol''s tale unexpectedly correlates to the announcement. Following this scene, a series of details hints at the plot of the New Testament, albeit ambiguously. There are hints concerning the holy family, the non-participation of the husband in the birth of a child (such an offensive treatment by Praskovija Jakovlevna). Finally, the bread baked in the house of the barber is implied to be "sacred." This bread was once used for temptation in the scriptures. Ivan Jako-vlevič is also tempted by it. He even refuses his morning coffee for the bread with onion.

Another scene worth mentioning is the one in the Kazan Cathedral. Gogoľ writes that the nose goes about with the visits and, on the way, stops in at the cathedral. It is one of the visits. Those at prayer are referred to as "moleľščiki" (a special morphological adaptation of the word "moljaščiesja," meaning "those who are praying"). "Moleľščiki" is a bureaucratic transcription, resembling "prositeli" (petitioner). Here the chancellary pun slips through. The whole scene plays on the ambivalence of the word "služba" (service), which can refer both to a church service and to service in the government bureaucracy. The spiritual world is conceived of within the table of ranks.

Gogoľ presents us with a kind of New Testament of the external world, an apocrypha of the reality of objects. In light of this interpretation, we turn to the final scene of "The Carriage." The officer's arrival and discovery of Čertokutskij, curled up in the carriage (with the implied semantics of a child in a cradle), presents a travestied version of the Adoration. Generally speaking, it should be noted that Gogoľ had a predilection for such travesties of biblical episodes. One could approach the appearance of Xlestakov in *The Inspector General* as a false coming, whereas the appearance of a real inspector in the end is a true coming. The mute scene in the comedy could also be perceived in this light. Another example is the scene of Ostap's execution in "Taras Buľba." Here, the allusion to Jesus praying in the Garden of Gethsemane is rather obvious (this time as a direct, serious analogy): "And the strength had left him and he cried out in natural infirmity—'Father! Where are you? Do you hear?'" (vol. 2, p. 165)

[13]From the middle of the nineteenth century, the name of Pythagoras appears in the corpus of translated texts of Greek philosophers ("Nravoučenija drevnix filosofov." M., 1769; "Kabinet ljubomurdija," 1782; "Zlatye ostatki drevnosti, soderžaščie drevnix grečeskix filosofov dragocennye nravoučenija," M. 1783; "Kratkoe opisanie žizni drevnix filosofov," M., 1788) as well as in the works dedicated to Pythagoras ("Dux Pifagorov, ili nravoučenie sego filosofa," SPb., 1767: Viland "Pifagorovy učenicy," SPb., 1797). Starting at the end of the eighteenth century and continuing into the first decade of the nineteenth, special attention and popularity was gained by Pierre Sylvain Maréchal's book, *Voyages de Pythagore*, published in France, in 1799, in nine volumes. The complete translation of this book into six volumes in Russian was begun in 1804 and completed in 1810 ("Putešestvija Pifagora znamenitogo samosskogo filosofa, ili kartina drevnix slavnejšix narodov, izobražajuščaja ix proisxoždenie, tainstva i dostopamjatnosti"). We should assume that the translators were not very well acquainted even with the name of the author, because in the translation he is called "g. Marešaľ de Siľven'." This forces us to think that it was not the name of the author (who incidentally had published his "Histoire de la Russie" in 1802) but rather the genre of the book which first interested the Russian translators. This is also suggested by the fact that they changed the title in such a way as to stress "the picture of ancient, famous nations." Apparently, the travel genre, which was introduced into literary practice by the school of Karamzin, was not the least factor in their choice of what to translate. Simultaneously with the issuing of this book, the translations of separate parts of it by different translators were being published in various magazines. The very selection of translated parts allows us to judge the interest behind it. It is now not only the "travel" itself (as, for example, "Pifagorovo putešestvie"—"Severnyj Merkurij," 1809, part 3), but rather the Pythagorean teaching which is of interest, especially in connection with the set of moral rules and mystical beliefs of the Pythagorean school ("Pifagorovy nravoučiteľnye pravila"—"Ljubiteľ slovesnosti," 1806, c. 2, 4; "Nravoučenie Pifagorovo"—"Novosti russkoj literatury na 1804 g.," c. 10. 1) In 1808 in Petersburg the new translation of Maréchal's book was published as an abridged version under the title "Pifagorovy zakony i nravstvennye pravila." Here one can already see the attempt to shift the focus of interest even as the work was being translated by others.

[14]Mention of this teaching in Russian philosophical treatises (of a rationalistic, not masonic nature) was no longer interpreted seriously in the eighteenth century and was almost always presented with anecdotal inflection (Kozeľskij 1952; "Russkie prosvetiteli" 1966).

BIBLIOGRAPHY

Belyj 1934
  Belyj, A. *Masterstvo Gogol'ja.* Moskva: 1934.
Fanger 1979
  Fanger, Donald. *The Creation of Nikolai Gogol.* Cambridge: Harvard University Press, 1979.
Gogoľ 1938
  Gogoľ, N.V. *Polnoe sobranie sočinenij.* Vol. 3. Moskva: Akademija Nauk SSSR, 1938.
Hulanicki 1975
  Hulanicki, Leon. " 'The Carriage' by N.V. Gogoľ." *Russian Literature.* Vol. 12. 1975.
Kozeľskij 1952
  Kozeľskij, Jakov. "Rassuždenie dvux indejcev o čelovečeskom poznanii." *Izbrannye proizvedenija russkix myslitelej vtoroj poloviny 18 v.* Moskva: 1952.
Russkie prosvetiteli 1966
  "O mire, načale ego i drevnosti." (1785). *Russkie prosvetiteli.* Vol. 2. Moskva: 1966.

BULGAKOV AND ŠKLOVSKIJ: NOTES ON A LITERARY ANTAGONISM

Edythe C. Haber

"Mixail Bulgakov is not my kind of writer."
Viktor Šklovskij[1]

In the playful introduction to his book, *The Hamburg Reckoning* (1928), Viktor Šklovskij ranks some contemporary writers, including Mixail Bulgakov, according to the standards of a Hamburg wrestling match:

> By the Hamburg reckoning, Serafimovič and Veresaev do not exist.
> They don't reach the city.
> In Hamburg—Bulgakov is on the carpet.
> Babel' is a lightweight.
> Gor'kij is doubtful (often not in form).
> Xlebnikov was champion.[2]

Several good reasons can be found for Bulgakov's poor showing in this literary sporting event. It is, first of all, entirely appropriate that the formalist Šklovskij award the title to Xlebnikov, as creator of a self-contained, "trans-sense" poetic universe, rather than to one of his more realist competitors. Moreover, Šklovskij's particular distate for Bulgakov can at least in part be attributed to the literary polemics of the day. These pitted the futurists and their allies (including Šklovskij) against Bulgakov, whom they regarded—especially after the Moscow Art Theater success in 1926 of his "white guard" play, *Days of the Turbins*—as a retrograde, both in politics and art. One need only recall a similar jab at Bulgakov in Vladimir Majakovskij's *The Bedbug*, in which Bulgakov's name is listed among the obsolete words in the Communist utopia of the future.[3]

While literary taste and literary polemics might thus have provided reason enough for Šklovskij's slighting remark, there is strong evidence of yet another, personal motive for his antagonism. Its origin can, in fact, be traced to a period before Bulgakov had become a professional writer, but which is reflected in important literary works of both men: Šklovskij's memoirs, *A Sentimental Journey* (1923), and Bulgakov's first novel, *The White Guard* (1925).[4] Both books describe events which occurred during the Civil War in Kiev. A comparison of the two accounts reveals some surprising and—for Šklovskij, at least—disturbing correspondences.

A Sentimental Journey is actually a much broader work, chronologically and geographically, at least, than *The White Guard.* The Kiev of late 1918 and early 1919 which forms the setting of Bulgakov's novel represents but one stop in Šklovskij's "journey," which began in Petrograd in February 1917 and ended only with his temporary exile to Berlin in 1922. The book begins with Šklovskij, an instructor in an armored division in Petrograd at the time, jubilantly greeting the February Revolution. A supporter of revolution but not a Bolshevik, he describes his participation in demonstrations, his driving an armored car through the festive, noisy crowds. The reader then accompanies Šklovskij on his journey to the front, to Persia, then back to Petrograd, which in his absence had been taken over by the Bolsheviks. A staunch advocate of the Constituent Assembly, he joined a group sharing his convictions. When, however, their activities were unmasked and many of the group's members were arrested, some executed, Šklovskij fled from Petrograd, finally ending up in Kiev.

When he arrived in the Ukrainian capital in late 1918, Šklovskij found the city filled with the artistic, financial, and aristocratic elite of Russia, which had also escaped the terror and famine of Russia for the relative abundance of this Bolshevik-free region. The definitely *ancien régime* atmosphere he encountered in Kiev can be explained by the odd and complex political situation in the Ukraine at the time. Throughout most of 1918 the area was ruled by a conservative Ukrainian government headed by Pavel Skoropadskij, who had adopted the obsolete royal title of hetman. In fact, Skoropadskij's regime was created and propped up by occupying German forces, dissatisfied with the more leftist Ukrainian coalition that had preceded it. By the time Šklovskij arrived in Kiev, however, the hetmanate, which had never won the allegiance of the Ukrainian masses, was on the verge of collapse—a collapse made all the more inevitable by the Germans' imminent defeat in the World War. The forces of more populist Ukrainian elements, led by Simon Petljura, were already massing outside the city, with the threat of the Bolsheviks also looming in the background.[5]

Perhaps due to this confusing and unstable political situation, Šklovskij's behavior in Kiev, as he describes it, is by no means easy to understand either. Rather surprisingly, given his leftist proclivities, he enlisted in an armored division in the service of the hetman. He adds, however, that the Fourth Armored Division, which he joined, "didn't serve Skoropadskij directly" and that many in the unit were leaning to the Bolsheviks.[6] Simultaneously, moreover, Šklovskij had some ties with the local Social Revolutionaries who, to make things still more confusing, "were connected with the Union for the Rebirth of Russia" (p. 157), a moderately leftist, anti-Bolshevik coalition.[7]

For reasons that remain unclear, on the night when Petljura's forces were entering Kiev (Skoropadskij, unbeknownst to his troops, had already fled to Berlin with the Germans), Šklovskij performed an act of sabotage against the hetman's forces:

> I put sugar in the hetman's cars.
> Here's how it's done: the sugar, either granular or in chunks, is put in the gas tank; it melts and it goes along with the gas into the carburetor . . .
> Because of the drop in temperature caused by evaporation, the sugar congeals and plugs up the opening.
> You can blow out the carburetor with an air pump, but it will clog up again. (p. 161)

Šklovskij also tried to subvert his unit, but only fifteen men followed him. He then commandeered a truck and machine guns and, when he found no one at the military branch of the Union, ultimately went over to the workers at the Greter plant. Šklovskij does not say here to which faction these workers belonged, but elsewhere, in a digression, he gives a clearer, although somewhat different, version of events: "In December or at the end of November 1918, I was in Kiev serving with Hetman Skoropadskij's troops, which ended by my taking an armored car and a machine-gun truck over to the Red Army" (p. 123).

After the Petljura takeover, Šklovskij notes, many members of his party became more and more sympathetic to the Bolsheviks. He himself once made a speech at a meeting: "I said: 'Let's recognize the triple-damned Soviet regime: Like at the judgment of Solomon, let's not demand half the baby. Let's give up the baby to strangers; only let him live!'" (p. 165). These sentiments, while hardly an encomium to the Bolsheviks, might explain why the writer, at considerable risk to himself, decided to return to Russia. Once in Moscow, he made at least temporary peace with the Bolsheviks and, with the aid of Gor'kij, arranged for his case to be closed. Indeed, he even agreed to carry out an invasion of the Revel prison for the Bolsheviks: "I was used to being in motion and I had no quarrel with the Bolsheviks, so I agreed to attack Revel with armored cars and attempt to take the prison" (p. 173).

To readers of Bulgakov's *The White Guard*, Šklovskij's account of his activities in Kiev sounds strangely familiar; they are, in fact, strikingly similar to those of the diabolical Mixail Semenovič Špoljanskij in the novel. Špoljanskij, like Šklovskij, is a literary personage who has come to Kiev from Petersburg. He too joins the hetman's armored division. And the narrator comments:

> The hetman's City perished three hours earlier than it should have, and precisely because, on the evening of December 2, 1918, Mixail Semenovič

announced the following . . . [to his literary associates]:
"They're all scoundrels. Both the hetman and Petljura. But besides that Petljura is a *pogromščik*. That's not the most important thing, however. I've become bored because I haven't thrown any bombs for a long time."[8]

One should note, parenthetically, that Šklovskij did actually engage in throwing bombs at one point during the Civil War, and gives boredom as his reason. He writes: "I was terribly bored. I wrote out a statement to the effect that I knew nothing about the infantry, but I did know armored cars and, if worse came to worst, demolition work" (p. 207). Later he comments, "We threw bombs . . . An explosion is a wonderful thing. . . . As beautiful as a horse's neigh" (p. 213).

A few days after Špoljanskij's remark to his literary circle, he makes an eloquent speech to his armored division, derogating the hetman and pointing to the Bolsheviks as perhaps the historically necessary alternative. Then, after one more speech to the division, on December 13, he performs an act which precisely duplicates Šklovskij's. He arrives at the armored car shed with a large package wrapped in paper. "Sugar?," queries a colleague, to which Mixail Semenovič responds, "Uhuh" (p. 220). As the narrator comments ironically, the subsequent efforts of Špoljanskij and the mechanic to prepare the cars for battle have a strange result:

The three cars, which the day before had still been entirely healthy . . ., couldn't move from the spot on the morning of December 14, as if they had been struck by paralysis. Nobody could understand what had happened to them. Some kind of rubbish had settled in the carburetor jets and, however much they tried to blow them out with tire pumps, nothing helped. (p. 221)

After this it is discovered that both the mechanic and Špoljanskij have disappeared. It is known only that at four in the morning Špoljanskij, together with a driver, left the armored car shed by motorcycle. The driver later reports that, once they reached the railroad embankment (the railroad is largely associated with the Bolsheviks in the novel), Špoljanskij set out alone on reconnaissance. When the driver hears a shot, he assumes Špoljanskij has been killed. This assumption proves to be erroneous, however, for we later catch a glimpse of the writer in the company of Bolsheviks. And in the third part of the novel it is reported that he has left for Moscow to join forces with the Bolsheviks.

Bulgakov also describes concisely, but in concrete detail, Špoljanskij's literary activities in Kiev. These include reading his works at the literary club "Dust" (its Russian name, *Prax*, formed from the initials of *"poèty -režissery - artisty - xudožniki"* [p. 150]). Šklovskij tells us virtually nothing about his literary involvements in Kiev. From another source, however, Il'ja Èrenburg, who was also in Kiev at that time, we discover that Šklovskij did indeed read his work at a literary club analogous to Bulgakov's, its name, *Xlam* (rubbish), derived from "'Painters, literary men, actors, musicians (*Xudožniki, literatory, aktery, muzykanty*).[9] According to Èrenburg, Šklovskij arrived there and "gave a brilliant involved lecture . . ., smiled slyly, and criticized absolutely everyone mercilessly, but with affection."[10]

In addition to this rather inconclusive parallel (a great many writers passing through Kiev read their works at *Xlam*) Bulgakov also offers a more specific allusion to Šklovskij by naming the poetic group Špoljanskij heads the "Magnetic Triolet" (p. 216). This is a quite transparent reference to Elsa Triolet, the object of Viktor Šklovskij's unrequited love, celebrated in his epistolary work, *Zoo*, published shortly before *The White Guard*.[11] *Zoo* is dedicated to Triolet, and she contributed seven letters to it.

Thus, the parallels between Šklovskij and Špoljanskij are abundant. Both are literary men from Petersburg who join the hetman's division. Both try to subvert the troops and sabotage the efforts of the hetman's supporters by pouring sugar into the armored cars' carburetors the night of Petljura's invasion. That same night they both disappear, going over to the Bolsheviks, and eventually depart for Moscow to the Bolsheviks. The literary allusions to *Prax/Xlam* and, especially, to the Magnetic Triolet/Elsa Triolet lead unavoidably to the conclusion that Šklovskij served as the prototype for the sinister Špoljanskij.

Once this is said, however, it must be conceded that the description of Špoljanskij's literary activities, as well as of his appearance and life style, diverges in some ways from what is known of Šklovskij. Špoljanskij's luxuriant side-whiskers, reminiscent of Evgenij Onegin's, his expensive, dandified attire and sybaritic habits, could hardly be more different from the description Šklovskij provides of his already rapidly balding head, his tattered clothes, and makeshift living arrangements.[12] Of more importance, Špoljanskij, while he does write literary criticism, is primarily a poet, author of *Drops of Saturn* and principal contributor to a miscellany, *Phantomists-Futurists* (pp. 215, 218).

While these details might be interpreted as mere fictional camouflage, there is one small hint—the name of the Bilboquet Café where Špoljanskij spends his mornings (p. 216)—of a second literary prototype, and one with family ties to the Bulgakovs. This is the Kievan poet, Vladimir Makkavejskij (1893-1920?), son of a friend and colleague of Bulgakov's father, Nikola Kornilievič Makkavejskij, whose archeological work on Jesus Christ might have been used as a source for *The Master and Margarita*.[13] Makkavejskij

was a well-known literary figure in Kiev in the late teens, a playwright and
literary theorist, as well as poet. He was prominent enough in the activities
of *Xlam* to warrant special mention in Èrenburg's memoirs, written over
thirty years later.[14] Among his many activities, he edited a literary miscellany, *Hermes*, published in Kiev in 1919, whose contributors included,
among others, Osip Mandel'štam, Il'ja Èrenburg—and Viktor Šklovskij.[15]
One of Makkavejskij's own lengthy entries is a play entitled *About Pierrot
the Murderer*, a variant of the Pierrot-Harlequin-Columbine story. Figuring
very prominently in the work is an object Harlequin constantly carries
around, a *bilboquet*[16]—which is also, surely not coincidentally, the name of
the café Špoljanskij frequents.

Another of the contributors to *Hermes*, the poet Jurij Terapiano, has left
a description of Makkavejskij which in some regards fits Špoljanskij well.
Terapiano recalls that the poet was "elegantly dressed, with the most
refined, even somewhat old-fashioned manners, . . . and liked to play the
dandy."[17] He was an excellent speaker, known by all of Kiev for his "verses
and lectures on questions of art." But, although endowed with truly
impressive gifts, Makkavejskij, according to Terapiano, lacked in simple
humanity. He was incapable of "experiencing simple human feelings" and
"considered any 'heart-felt emotions' [*duševnost'*] superfluous."[18]—a description which would certainly fit Špoljanskij.

Thus it appears that, in his depiction of Špoljanskij, Bulgakov borrowed
the most essential features from Šklovskij, but created a more generalized
portrait by adding negative traits he observed in Makkavejskij and possibly
other members of the literary *avant-garde*: dandyism, excessive aestheti-
cism, and cold egoism. This portrayal clearly would have given Šklovskij
an added motive—and one more compelling than the rest—for summarily
eliminating Bulgakov with a knockout in his *Hamburg Reckoning*.

The identification of Bulgakov's Špoljanskij with Viktor Šklovskij raises
many questions, both biographical and literary, which lie beyond the scope
of this paper. It is worth commenting in conclusion, however, on Špoljanskij's pivotal role in Bulgakov's artistic evolution. While in his earlier writings, beginning with *Notes on Cuffs* (1922-23), Bulgakov did occasionally
engage in the art of the literary lampoon,[19] Špoljanskij is the first negatively
portrayed writer to be given large thematic significance in the writer's
works and, near the end of the novel, where he is characterized as "precur-
sor of the Anti-Christ" (p. 337), to be associated with the devil.[20] He thus
foreshadows the central role the literary sphere is to play in Bulgakov's
later works and, in the most important of them, *A Theatrical Novel* and,
especially, *The Master and Margarita*, its association with the devil.

That the eminent literary critic, Viktor Šklovskij, should have served as principal prototype for the first of Bulgakov's diabolical literary men is an oddity of Russian literary history—an oddity that Šklovskij himself must surely not have savored.

University of Massachusetts at Boston

NOTES

[1] Quoted from a conversation with Leonard Gendlin in 1961. See Gendlin, "Podvig mastera," *Novoe russkoe slovo*, 16 Sept., 1981, p. 6.

[2] Viktor Šklovskij, *Gamburgskij ščet* (L.: Izd. pisatelej v Leningrade, 1928), p. 5.

[3] Vladimir Majakovskij, *Klop, Polnoe sobranie sočinenij* XI (M.: Xudožestvennaja literatura, 1958), p. 250. See also Majakovskij's remarks attacking *Days of the Turbins*: "Vystuplenie po dokladu A.V. Lunačarskogo 'Teatral'naja politika sovetskoj vlasti'," *Polnoe sobranie* XII (1959), pp. 301-5.

While particular attention has been paid to Majakovskij's polemic with Bulgakov (see, for example, Ellendea Proffer, *Bulgakov* [Ann Arbor: Ardis, 1984], pp. 193-97; 250-53), A.M. Al'tšuler, in his unpublished dissertation, *"Dni Turbinyx" i "Beg" M.A. Bulgakova v istorii sovetskogo teatra 20-x godov* (M., 1972), notes that several of Majakovskij's associates, including Šklovskij, also opposed Bulgakov (p. 10). Moreover, he includes in his bibliography an article by Šklovskij on Bulgakov which I have not, unfortunately, been able to locate: "Mixail Bulgakov," *Naša gazeta*, 30 May, 1926.

[4] The publishing history of both works is very complicated. *A Sentimental Journey* first appeared jointly in Berlin and Moscow in 1923: *Sentimental'noe putešestvie: Vospominanija 1918-1922* (Moscow–Berlin: Helikon, 1923). Cut versions were subsequently issued in the Soviet Union in 1924 and 1929, after which it has not been republished there. For this reason one is particularly grateful to Richard Sheldon for his fine English translation, based upon the 1923 edition: *A Sentimental Journey: Memoirs, 1917-1922* (Ithaca & London: Cornell Univ. Press, 1970).

The first two parts of *The White Guard* were published in 1925 in the journal *Rossija: Belaja gvardija, Rossija,* No. 4 (1925), pp. 3-100; No. 5 (1925), pp. 1-82. After this the journal was shut down, and Part 3 of the novel did not appear in the Soviet Union in Bulgakov's lifetime. The entire novel was, however, published in Paris, under the name *Dni Turbinyx*, I (Paris: Concorde, 1927); II (1929). The work appeared in full for the first time in the Soviet Union in: Mixail Bulgakov, *Izbrannaja proza* (M.: Xudožestvennaja literatura, 1966). Since then it has been republished several times.

[5] See John S. Reshetar, Jr., *The Ukrainian Revolution, 1917-1920* (Princeton, N.J.: Princeton Univ. Press, 1952), pp. 3-4.

[6] *A Sentimental Journey*, trans. Richard Sheldon, p. 159. All further references to this work appear in the text.

[7] See George A. Brinkley, *Allied Intervention in South Russia, 1917-1921* (Notre Dame, Ind.: Univ. of Notre Dame Press, 1966), p. 41.

[8] *Belaja gvardija, Izbrannaja proza*, p. 216. The translation is mine. All further references to this work appear in the text.

[9] Ilya Ehrenburg, *People and Life: 1891-1921*, trans. Anna Bostock & Yvonne Kapp (N.Y.: Alfred A. Knopf, 1962), p. 314.

[10] *Ibid.*, p. 320.

[11]*Zoo* was first published in 1923 by the Helikon Publishing House in Berlin, and was again issued in 1924 by the Athens Publishing House in Leningrad. (See Richard Sheldon, "Translator's Preface," Viktor Šklovskij, *Zoo, or Letters Not about Love*, trans. Richard Sheldon [Ithaca & London: Cornell Univ. Press, 1971], p. v.)

[12]Šklovskij's distinctive bald head plays a key role in one episode, almost resulting in his arrest by a Cheka agent (pp. 171-72). The shameful state of his clothes and living quarters is mentioned frequently.

[13]See I.F. Bèlza, "Genealogija 'Mastera i Margarity'," *Kontekst* 1978 (Mosow: Nauka, 1978), pp. 161-62. The hypothetical date of Makkavejskij's death and some other information are taken from Bèlza.

[14]Èrenburg, pp. 319-20.

[15]*Germes: Ežegodnik iskusstva i gumanitarnogo znanija* I (Kiev, 1919).

[16]Vladimir Makkavejskij, "O P'ero ubijce. Psevdotragedija v četyrex aktax s prologom," *Germes*, pp. 23-102. A *bilboquet* is a French toy, called in English a *cup-and-ball*.

[17]Jurij Terapiano, *Vstreči* (N.Y.: Chekhov Publishing House, 1953), p. 11.

[18]*Ibid.*, p. 12.

[19]In addition to some of the literary portraits in *Notes on Cuffs*, see Bulgakov's biting description of Mejerxol'd's biomechanical production of *The Magnanimous Cuckold* in "Stolica v bloknote" (1922). (M.A. Bulgakov, *Sobranie sočinenij* I [Ann Arbor, Mich.: Ardis, 1982], pp. 284-86.)

[20]While *diablerie* certainly plays a role in Bulgakov's earlier works (as the title of his collection, *D'javoliada* [1925] attests), it is not anywhere associated with writers. In its most serious manifestation, in "Fatal Eggs" and "Heart of a Dog," it is connected instead with the scientist who, in tampering with nature, tries to play God. See Proffer, *Bulgakov*, p. 113; pp. 127-28.

"BY THE WILL OF OUR LORD GOD AND SAVIOR"

Norman W. Ingham

It is natural that editors of the seventeenth-century narrative poem *Povest'*
o Gore i Zločastii (The Tale of Misery and Ill Fortune; hereafter: PGZ)
have followed the indications of the sole existing manuscript with respect to
the title. The scribe of the manuscript, which is from the eighteenth century, wrote in half-uncials and red ink what he believed to be the heading:
Povest' o Gore i Zločastii, kak Gore-Zločastie dovelo molodca vo inočeskij
čin (The Tale of Misery and Ill Fortune: How Misery-Ill Fortune Brought a
Young Man into the Monastic Order). Then he copied out the rest of the
poem in cursive script. That he thought the text proper began with the next
words, "Izvoleniem Gospoda Boga i Spasa Našego" ("By the will of Our
Lord God and Savior"), is evident too from the fact that he introduced that
phrase with a decorative initial.[1] There is reason to suppose, however, that
he was mistaken and that the words he took to be the first three verses of
the poem were actually a part of the title. When we restore the heading we
also obtain an insight into the author's intended meaning.

According to the usual division, the poem begins with an instrumental
phrase which extends over the first three lines and makes little evident sense
in the context:

> Изволением Господа Бога и Спаса Нашего
> Иисуса Христа Вседержителя
> От начала века человеческого
> А в начале века сего тленного
> Сотворил [Бог] небо и землю,
> Сотворил Бог Адама и Евву. . . .

By the will of Our Lord God and Savior/ Jesus Christ Almighty/ From the
beginning of the human age/ And in the beginning of this perishable age/
[God] created heaven and earth,/ God created Adam and Eve. . . .)

I have temporarily omitted punctuation from the first three lines. At least
one editor placed a comma at the end of the third, apparently on the
assumption that the construction forms part of the following sentence.[2]
This is highly unlikely, however, since to say that God created heaven and
earth by the will of God would be pointlessly tautological. And what are
we to suppose would be the logical and grammatical connection between
lines 3 and 4? The latter partly mimics 3 but seems, with its contrastive

conjunction and its significant change of preposition and adjective, to begin a new sentence and a new though related thought. Obviously, lines 1–3 cannot be an introductory phrase to the following sentence.

Most editors appear to acknowledge that as a fact, because they put a period or other end-punctuation at the close of lines 1–3, treating them as independent.[3] But if the verses are complete in themselves, what should we suppose are their meaning and function? Two possibilities come to mind. They might be a prefatory statement (or an "epigraph") about the theme, or else they might be an invocation for the poet's task. Although it is evident they have something to do with the theme, lacking a verb they do not make a complete and coherent statement by themselves; and we have already noted that the transition from line 3 to 4 would be awkward.[4]

Can they be an invocation? Formulas asking for God's blessing or assistance at the outset of writing were common in medieval works, and one here would nicely balance the brief prayer that closes PGZ. But the form and diction are not those of an invocation. The opening does not implore God at all, while the prayer at the end has the customary appeal couched in imperative verbs:

> Избави [нас], Господи, вечныя муки,
> А дай нам, Господи, светлы рай,
> Во веки веков, аминь.

Spare [us], Lord, from eternal torment,/ And give us, Lord, bright paradise [heaven],/ Forever and ever. Amen.

Furthermore, "izvoleniem Gospoda Boga" (by the will of the Lord God) is quite the wrong phrase for an invocation or prayer, as we will see later. One might possibly expect "blagosloveniem Božiim" (with God's blessing), or the like.

Metrical considerations—while not decisive—tend to confirm our suspicions about the first three "verses." The supposed opening line is unusually long, and F. E. Korš when reconstructing the rhythmical pattern of the poem was compelled to treat "i Spasa Našego" (and of Our Savior) as a separate part-line (Simoni, p. 49). Granted, there are other cases of apparent part-lines in the poem, e.g., "ot zemnyx plodov" (from the fruits of the earth) and "otečeskija dočeri" (fathers' daughters); but the textological and prosodic status of all of them is uncertain. The problem in line 1 is that removing the phrase "i Spasa Našego" leaves the verse without its dactylic clausula. Evidently for that reason, Korš very tentatively suggested emending it to: "Izvoleniem Boga Výšnego" (By the will of God on high); but his change has no justification beyond a scholar's wish to make the line fit the expected pattern.

Next we should notice the exceptional degree of enjambement in these lines. Following the practice of the Russian folk epos (the *bylina*), whose accentual verse form he was imitating, the poet ended nearly all lines of his tale with a syntactic pause—a sentence or phrase boundary that clearly marks the end of the verse. Exceptions are few, and none quite as striking as we have here.[5] There is no such boundary between "Spasa Našego" (Our Savior) and "Iisusa Xrista" (Jesus Christ). And if "ot načala veka čelo-večeskogo" (from the beginning of the human age) qualifies "Vsederžitelja" (the Almighty, the Pantocrator)—as I think it must—then there is no syntactic and little intonational break between these either. True, the whole passage can, with some effort, be divided into three verses. As usually printed, each verse has an acceptable clausula (the hyperdactylic *čelovéčeskogo* is not unique in the poem); and line 3 comes out very similar to the line 4 which I do not challenge as a verse. However, the least that must be said is that these supposed opening lines, with their enjambement and their bookish phraseology, serve poorly to introduce the folkloric verse pattern of the poem. I would maintain that they are in fact prose and continue the prosaic rhythm of the title.[6]

What is their meaning, and to what do they refer? In writings of the Muscovite period the expression "izvoleniem Gospoda Boga" or "izvoleniem Božiim" (by the wish or will of God) was applied to momentous events, most often but not always misfortunes. God was said to have willed or vouchsafed them. "Bogu izvolivšu" (God having willed/deigned it) was a common phrase to explain calamities.[7] A similar expression was "po Božiju popuščeniju" (approximately, "by God's leave"; that is, God permitted it to happen). In these cases it was sometimes added that God did so because of the people's sins ("grex radi našix"). An account of the disastrous sack of Novgorod in 1570 contains introductory words very much like those of our passage: "Poseščeniem i izvoleniem i nakazaniem Vsederžitelja Gospoda Boga i Spasa Našego Iisusa Xrista . . ." (By the visitation and will and chastisement of the Almighty, Our Lord God and Savior Jesus Christ . . .).[8]

Expressions of this sort are especially frequent in historical writings about the turbulent Smuta (Time of Troubles) at the beginning of the seventeenth century. The so-called *Inoe skazanie* (Another Relation) opens with: "Božiim izvoleniem, pače že Ego čelovekoljubivym xoteniem, byst' v lěto 7092, v neže prestavisja [car' Ivan Vasil'evič] . . ." (By the will of God, and further by His philanthropic wish, [this] happened in the year 7092 [1584], in which [Tsar Ivan Vasil'evič] passed away . . ." [PSV, col. 1]). The *Povest' kako vosxiti nepravdoju na Moskve carskij prestol Boris Godunov* (Story of How Boris Godunov Unjustly Seized the Throne in Moscow) has the same opening as *Inoe skazanie* (PSV, col. 145). Referring to the invasion by the

Polish king, *Novaja povest'* (A New Story) says: "I paki nadejasja na to okajannyj, čto Božiim izvoleniem carskij koren' u nas izvedesja" (And moreover the accursed [king] depended on the fact that by the will of God our dynasty of tsars had died out; PSV, col. 194).

The instances from literature about the Time of Troubles show that it was entirely possible for a work to open with the words "Izvoleniem Božiim" or the like, as does PGZ in the conventional interpretation. However, the examples also confirm that these phrases are unlikely to occur alone. Merely expressing attendant conditions, they cannot form a complete statement; they require a verb and subject. Reading the opening of PGZ, we are impelled to ask: What is the misfortune that happened "by the will of Our Lord God and Savior"? Since, as we have seen, the thought is not completed by the following lines, only two possibilities remain: Either there is a lacuna following the three "lines" in the manuscript, or else they belong with what precedes—the title.

Sound philological principle tells us to avoid positing lacunae where simpler explanations, not involving hypothetical readings, are available. Furthermore, it is hard to imagine what could have been in the line or lines that might be missing after verse 3. The event which happened "by the will of Our Lord God and Savior" is surely not the creation of the world—the immediate subject of the text. More probably it could be the fall of Adam or the ruination of the young Russian protagonist. But the context for such a statement is already provided by the title, and we need not suppose a lacuna.

My solution is precisely that in the author's text of PGZ these three "lines" were not verses but a continuation of the title (more exactly, the subtitle). The full heading read: *Povest' o Gore i Zločastii, kak Gore-Zločastie dovelo molodca vo inočeskij čin izvoleniem Gospoda Boga i Spasa Našego Iisusa Xrista Vsederžitelja ot načala veka čelovečeskogo* (The Tale of Misery and Ill Fortune: How Misery-Ill Fortune Brought a Young Man into the Monastic Order by the Will of Our Lord God and Savior Jesus Christ, Almighty since the Beginning of the Human Age). Lengthy and discursive titles of this sort were common in the seventeenth century and earlier.[9] The very next work after PGZ in the same manuscript has a similar heading.[10]

The copyist's error is plausible if we suppose that he worked from an original that did not clearly separate heading from text. The fact that there were writings in circulation which began with "Izvoleniem Božiim," and the like, can support my argument as easily as undercut it, since the scribe might wrongly take this familiar phrase to be the opening of the text. He might also be misled by the obvious parallelism between the end of the title and the first line, that is, between what he evidently assumed were lines 3 and 4 (his manuscript, of course, does not indicate line divisions).

The poem itself now begins logically, going straight to the first topic:

> А в начале века сего тленного
> Сотворил [Бог] небо и землю,
> Сотворил Бог Адама и Евву,
> Повелел им жити во святом раю,
> Дал им заповедь божественну. . . .

(And in the beginning of this perishable age/ [God] created heaven and earth,/ God created Adam and Eve,/ Ordered them to live in holy paradise,/ Gave them a divine commandment. . . .)

Starting a sentence with a conjunction ("*a*") was a common stylistic feature of epic verse, and there are transitions marked with the same conjunction below in the poem.[11]

As it happens, we have supporting evidence that makes exactly this opening very plausible for PGZ. In the important eighteenth-century collection of Russian folklore known as *Sbornik Kirši Danilova* there is a transcription of the spiritual song "Golubinaja kniga" (The Book of the Dove) which begins with an account of Adam and Eve's fall in paradise so similar in wording to the first section of PGZ that scholars recognize there must have been some genetic connection between the two works (it is unclear which came first).[12] This version begins:

> Да с начала века животленнова
> Сотворил Бог небо со землею,
> Сотворил Бог Адама с Еввою. . . .

(And at the beginning of the moral age/ God created heaven and earth,/ God created Adam and Eve. . . .)

The three lines are almost verbatim the same as my reconstructed beginning of PGZ, even including an initial conjunction, "da."

The words which seemed awkward and inappropriate as the first three verses of PGZ makes perfect grammatical and thematic sense as part of the title. We now see that the long instrumental phrase beginning "izvoleniem" is not syntactically isolated but qualifies the verb "dovelo" (brought, led to). Such a construction after the verb was possible in the poet's language, as is shown by this key passage later in the text:

Срядил молодец честен пир,
Отечеством и вежеством,
Любовным своим гостем и другом бил челом.
И по грехом молодцу [учинилося,]
И по Божию попущению,
А по действу дияволю—
Пред любовными своими гостьми и други
И названными браты похвалился.

(The youth arranged an honor banquet/ According to paternal rank and etiquette./ He invited his beloved guests and friends./ And [it befell] the youth
by chance/ And by God's leave/ And by the devil's action/ [That] in front of
his beloved guests and friends/ And sworn brothers—he boasted.)

The instrumental "otečestvom i vežestvom" (roughly, "according to paternal
rank and etiquette") follows and modifies the verb. A closer similarity to
the title—because of their meaning and despite their being in the dative
case—is found in the phrases "po Božiju popuščeniju, | A po dejstvu dija-
volju" (by God's leave | And by the devil's action). They come after the
verb ("učinilosja" [it befell] has to be restored to the defective line; the
whole verse is a commonplace of epic songs[13]) and motivate the disaster
that is visited on the protagonist, just as does "izvoleniem Gospoda Boga"
(by the will of the Lord God) in the title. Indeed, the parallel tends to
confirm that "izvoleniem Gospoda Boga," etc., goes with "Gore-Zločastie
dovelo molodca vo inočeskij čin" (Misery-Ill Fortune Brought the Youth
into the Monastic Order). The relationship is the same; God wills or allows
a misfortune, and an evil agent brings it about.[14] The sufferings of the
young protagonist could not happen without the acquiescence of the Lord
and Savior who has had power over all human destiny since the beginning
of the race ("Vsederžitelja ot načala veka čelovečeskogo").[15]

The full title, thus restored, anticipates two central ideas of the poem. By
mentioning the role of God through the ages, it prepares for the thematic
connection between Adam and Eve at one end of the time axis and our
anonymous seventeenth-century Russian youth at the other. The lad is a
contemporary instance of the age-old problem of filial disobedience and its
consequences. That much only confirms an interpretation obvious to most
modern readers of PGZ. But the title helps to clarify a second and perhaps
more controversial point: The author expressly says that Gore-Zločastie
acts by the will of God. Misery-Ill Fortune figures in the divine scheme of
things as God's instrument (although possibly an unknowing one). The title
itself integrates this mythic figure from folklore into a broader, Christian
framework.

Nonetheless, we must not jump to the easy conclusion that our poet's theme is a traditional one of sin and redemption. The young man's story is almost devoid of spiritual considerations, despite mentions of "spasennyj put'" (the path of salvation). He is guilty less of sin than of breaking his materialistic parents' code of social behavior, and the monastery is depicted as a refuge from poverty and crime rather than a place for penitence and Christian redemption. Being forced to enter the monastic order seems to be a punishment brought about "by God's will" for disobedience of his merchant parents. Significantly, the title itself omits the customary reference to God's love of mankind (čelovekoljubie) which causes Him to chastize and correct sinners for the sake of their salvation. At the same time, Gore-Zločastie remains an enigmatic figure whose conscious motive apparently is to debase and destroy men.[16] If the full title of the poem helpfully states that Gore was turned loose by God's will, it still does not solve for us our difficult problems of interpretation.

The University of Chicago

NOTES

[1]See a facsimile of the manuscript in P. K. Simoni, *Povest' o Gore i Zločastii . . . (Sbornik ORJaS*, vol. 83, no. 1; SPb., 1907), between pp. 26 and 27. A facsimile of the opening is also given in N. K. Gudzij, comp., *Xrestomatija po drevnej russkoj literature*, 8th ed. (M.: Prosveščenie, 1973), p. 385. The scribe (most parts of this collection were copied in one hand) followed the practice throughout of writing titles in *poluustav* with red ink and beginning each work with an ornamental initial in red (see Simoni's description of the manuscript, p. 13). I quote the poem using present standards for citing Russian of the period, and I make some use of the normalized edition in *Demokratičeskaja poèzija XVII veka* (M.-L.: Sov. pisatel', 1962), pp. 33-44 (hereafter cited as: Dem. poèzija).

[2]V. P. Adrianova-Peretc, in Dem. poèzija, p. 33. However, her colleague D. S. Lixačev changed the comma to a period when he reprinted her text in *"Izbornik": Sbornik proizvedenij literatury drevnej Rusi* (M.: Goslitizdat, 1969) p. 597.

[3]Simoni's reconstruction (p. 74) and Korš's rhythmical version (Simoni, p. 49) place a period and then indent the fourth line as the beginning of a new section. Gudzij in his *Xrestomatija* (p. 383) used a period; but when he quoted these same lines in his *Istorija drevnej russkoj literatury* (7th ed. rev.; M.: Prosveščenie, 1966; p. 403) he put three dots (suspension points), seeming to indicate an even greater break. (N. Kostomarov had used suspension points as long ago as his *Pamjatniki starinnoj russkoj literatury*, pub. by G. Kušelev-Bezborodko, I [SPb., 1860; rpt. The Hague: Mouton, 1970], 1; and V. V. Sipovskij used the three dots in his *Russkie povesti XVII–XVIII vv.* [SPb., 1905], p. 1.) As noted, a full stop ends the third line in the edition prepared by D. S. Lixačev for *"Izbornik."* Recent Soviet anthologies follow the text established in Gudzij or *"Izbornik."* The English translation in *Medieval Russia's Epics, Chronicles, and Tales*, ed. by Serge A. Zenkovsky (rev. ed.; N.Y.: Dutton, 1974; p. 490) uses a period. I have concentrated on current practice and not tried to examine all editions.

[4]An example of an introductory statement (after the title) is Avraamij Palicyn's in his *Skazanie*: "I nyne vsjak vozrast da razumeet i vsjak da priložit uxo slyšat', kiix radi grex popusti Gospod' Bog Naš pravednoe svoe nakazanie i ot konec do konec vseja Rosija, i kako ves' slovenskij jazyk vozmutisja i vsja mesta po Rosii ognem i mečem pojadeny byša. Semu že Skazaniju načalo sicevo: . . ." Quoted from *Pamjatniki drevnej russkoj pis'mennosti, otnosjaščiesja k Smutnomu vremeni*, 3rd ed. (Russaja istoričeskaja biblioteka, 13/1; L., 1925), col. 473 (hereafter: PSV).

[5]Most instances have at least a logical break between lines, indicated by a conjunction separating word groups ("k svoemu otcu i materi | i k svoemu rodu i plemjani | i k svoim prežnim milym drugom") or a prepositional phrase boundary ("ot velikogo razuma | nažival on života bol'še starogo"). Full enjambement seems to occur in: "pred ljubovnymi svoimi gost'mi i drugi | i nazvannymi braty poxvalilsja."

[6]A. Stender-Petersen, in his *Anthology of Old Russian Literature* (N.Y.: Columbia Univ. Press, 1954), p. 426, did print "Izvoleniem . . . veka čelovečeskogo" as prose, placing a exclamation point at the end. In this he was preceded by Fedor Buslaev, who set these words off from the verse and in his introduction called them "prozaičeskoe izrečenie" (*Russkaja xrestomatija: Pamjatniki drevnej russkoj literatury i narodnoj slovesnosti* [9th ed. rev.; M., 1904; rpt. The Hague: Mouton, 1969] p. 332). Unfortunately, Buslaev did not attempt to explain the meaning and purpose of this "prose apothegm" or "dictum." He only remarked that it corresponds to another "prose" passage at the end of the prologue: "Tako roždenie čelovečeskoe | ot otca i ot materi" (literally, "Thus is human birth from father and mother"). He was partly right but did not see that the first passage belongs to the prose title and that the second—while certainly a pithy saying—is in verse.

[7]Related expressions are: "Božiim promyslom" (by God's providence), "po smotreniju Božiju" (by God's oversight), "poveleniem Božiim" (by God's command), and others. Most of these applied also to happy events; in historical writings "by God's command" sometimes announced the accession of a legitimate tsar. "By the will of God," too, could, though more seldom, accompany a fortunate outcome—for example, when Marfa and Marija encountered each other in the tale announced for them: "I po Božiju izvoleniju snidostasja na puti" (*Russkaja povest' XVII veka* [M.: Goslitizdat, 1954] p. 49).

[8]*"Izbornik,"* p. 477. The sentence's continuation makes clear that God's punishment is visited on the people because of their sins. A humorous example occurs in one version of the satirical tale *Erš Eršovič*: "Eto po Bogu i po nesčastiju, i po Božeskomu izvoleniju i po Božiju prognevan'ju bylo na Rostovskoe ozero požarnoj slučaj. . . . I gorelo Rostovskoe ozero četyre gody" (by misfortune and divine will and God's anger a fire took place on Rostov Lake. . . . And Rostov Lake burned for four years!) (*Russkaja demokratičeskaja satira XVII veka*, prepared by V. P. Adrianova-Peretc [2nd ed. rev.; M.: Nauka, 1977] p. 14 [hereafter: Dem. satira]).

[9]Examples in Dem. satira especially similar to PGZ: *Povest' izrjadnaja o kure i lisice, kako ego prelstila lisica* (p. 62); *Skazanie o kure i o lisice, kak sedel na dreve, a lisica kura k sebe z dreva manila* (p. 160). From dem. poèzija: *Skazanie o kievskix bogatyrex, kak xodili vo Car'grad i kak pobili caregradskix bogatyrej, učinili sebe čest'* (p. 50).

[10]*Povest' izrjadnaja o Apollone, care kiprskom, i o slučaex i bedax i pečalex v mire sem, i jako čelovekoljubie Božie nikoliže ostavljaet do konca pogibnuti—načasja seže Antioxom carem* (Simoni, p. 21). The tale proper beings with the last thing mentioned in the title, King Antioch, much as the first line of PGZ (in my interpretation) echoes the end of the heading.

[11]Examples in PGZ: "A se rodi pošli slaby"; "A semu žitiju konec my vedaem." In *Sbornik Kirši Danilova* (see next note) several songs begin similarly with a meaningless monosyllable that helps create the customary anapestic anacrusis.

[12]*Drevnie rossijskie stixotvorenija, sobrannye Kiršeju Danilovym*, 2nd ed. rev., prepared by A. P. Evgen'eva and B. N. Putilov (M.: Nauka, 1977), p. 457 and references there (hereafter: *Sbornik Kirši Danilova*). The text of "Golubinaja kniga" (here, "Golubina kniga soroka pjaden'") begins on p. 208.

[13]Dobrynja misses his aim with an arrow when his foot accidentally slips: "Po grexam nad Dobryneju učinilasja: | Levaja noga evo pokól'znula" (*Dobrynja Nikitič i Aleša Popovič* [M.: Nauka, 1974], p. 160; variant, p. 155).

[14]This was another commonplace. Cf. "bogu popuščajušču, a Satane dejstvujušču" (*Trudy Otdela drevnerusskoj literatury*, 28 [1974], 241); "Bogu popuščajušču, vragu že dejstvujušču" (*Drevnerusskaja literatura i ee svjazi s novym vremenem* [M.: Nauka, 1967], p. 332).

[15]If "ot načala veka čelovečeskogo" were the opening of the text proper, or part of the opening, it would not only duplicate needlessly the following line but would be illogical. God created the world *in* the beginning, not *from* the beginning. "Ot načala" indicates duration and goes more logically with "Vsederžitel'" (Almighty, Pantocrator). If the concept of the eternally Almighty were not obvious enough, Rev. 1:8 would lend it authority: "'I am the Alpha and the Omega,' says the Lord God, who is and who was and who is to come, the Almighty [*ho pantokrátōr*]."

[16]See my articles, "Irony in *Povest' o Gore i Zločastii*," *Slavic and East European Journal*, 24 (1980), 333-48; and "Parody in *Povest' o Gore i Zločastii*," *ibid.*, 27 (1983), 141-57. I have also discussed my interpretation in conference papers ("*The Tale of Misery and Ill Fortune* in the Light of Muscovite Law and Society," AAASS convention, 1978; "*Povest' o Gore i Zločastii*: Parable or Cautionary Tale?" AAASS, 1980) and will write about the theme of the poem in the future.

THE RHETORIC OF NADEZHDA MANDELSTAM'S
HOPE AGAINST HOPE

Charles Isenberg

Despite the critical and popular acclaim accorded Nadezhda Mandelstam's two volumes of memoirs, not much attention has been paid to her qualities as a writer.[1] Owing to a combination of her own genius and a congeries of historical accidents, her writings have tended to merge with those of her husband. A contrast may clarify this point: If we are arguing about the meaning of some passage in Dostoevsky, most of us are unlikely to make our first move an appeal to the authority of Anna Snitkina-Dostoevskaja. Nadezhda Mandelstam's work, on the other hand, has become the enabling condition, the virtual horizon, of Osip Mandelstam's. Her commentaries align her husband's writings into a lyrical biography, or a history of consciousness. She becomes his co-author, first, by restructuring his texts, establishing connections between one piece and another and between text and world, and second, by rethinking Mandelstam, partly as a representative figure and partly as the exemplar of his own philosophy. Thus her volumes do not just aim at preservation but at canon formation, and she constructs a canonical image of the poet to go along with the canonical ordering of his work. In all this she has been so spectacularly successful that we do not even need to read her. Take up any edition of Mandelstam's work, begining with the four-volume *Collected Works*, and you will be sure to find at least a digest of Nadezhda Mandelstam's glosses.

But Nadezhda Mandelstam is a writer worthy of consideration for her own achievement and not simply in her capacity as the most privileged interpreter of Osip Mandelstam. Jonathan Culler has argued that every reading of a text entails the story of a reading.[2] Briefly, the story of my reading of her *Vospominanija* (translated as *Hope Against Hope*) comprises an initial reading in search of information about Osip Mandelstam's life and work, a second reading in which I saw them as primarily a meditation upon the fate of the Russian intelligentsia, and subsequent re-readings in which my attention has been increasingly drawn to the rhetorical strategies that subserve—and occasionally subvert—her themes. This essay will attempt to situate Nadezhda Mandelstam as a writer by focusing on two qualities in *Vospominanija*,[3] her first volume of memoirs: her representation of her marriage, and her rhetoric—and by rhetoric I intend both the traditional meaning, that is, those uses of language that seek to persuade us as

to the authority of a writer's point of view, and also the more recent definition proposed by the Liege rhetoricians in their *General Rhetoric*; all the
uses of language proper to literature.[4] As far as possible then, this study
will be concerned with the intersection of power (i.e., of textualized authority) and poetics, and it will use feminist theory and rhetorical criticism as
sources of questions to put to the text.

Phyllis Rose's *Parallel Lives*, a study of five Victorian marriages in which
at least one member of each couple was a writer, can clarify what is at
stake in Nadezhda Mandelstam's representation of her marriage. The main
lesson I draw from Prof. Rose's work is the usefulness of considering a
marriage as a narrative construct; as she puts it, "a subjectivist fiction with
two points of view often deeply in conflict, sometimes fortuitously congruent."[5] Two further considerations follow: first, the story of a marriage will
turn to the clash of assumptions about power and authority. This we find
in great detail in the *Vtoraja kniga* (*Hope Abandoned*), which is more openly
concerned with the story of the Mandelstams' marriage. In the memoirs, on
the other hand, the thematics of the marital power struggle are present but
submerged. Here the titles are instructive: *Vtoraja kniga*, literally the
Second Book, a title that suggests the secondary or supplementary value
placed by Nadezhda Mandelstam on the story of her marriage.

A second consideration that follows from the treatment of a marriage as
a narrative is simply the exceptional narrative interest that attaches to an
unusual marriage. Prof. Rose argues that "the 'plots' of our loves and marriages tend to banality and sterility."[6] Thus it is remarkable when an exception appears. The Mandelstams were not only extraordinary writers but
had an exceptionally interesting relationship. There is the casually under-
taken commitment, the testing through extramarital affairs, the refusal of
children, the long separations with their letters and telegrams, the perpetual
homelessness, the wrenching poverty and constant, grinding scutwork,[7] the
utter subservience of Nadezhda to Osip's gift,—and then, decades later the
revelation of her own gift, and finally, the will evident in Nadezhda Mandelstam's prose to make the marriage, in retrospect, both a countersociety and
a laboratory for understanding the spouses' own social formation.

There is something exemplary or emblematic in the Mandelstams' relationship that calls to mind another famous couple, Jean Paul Sartre and
Simone de Beauvoir. Of course this is an uncomfortable comparison in
many ways. Sartre's and Beauvoir's writings scarcely intertwine to the same
extent as the Mandelstams' do; Nadezhda Mandelstam was contemptuous
of Sartre's Marxism, and I suspect that Beauvoir's feminism would have
been equally alien to her. Nevertheless, these partnerships do share some

common ground. In each case it is the writings of the female partner that create the relationship as a literary phenomenon, and both the Russian and the Frenchwoman represent their primary relationships as a critique of, and counterexample to, the ideology of marriage in its Stalinist-bourgeois and French bourgeois forms. And both women portray couples that are morally exemplary in their determination to live their values.

Other concerns of feminist criticism can be brought to bear upon the memoirs. On the most general level, it hardly needs to be argued by now that it pays to attend to an artist's sense of "gender arrangements," the engendering of social roles and functions as masculine or feminine, as a key to his or her poetic universe. In Osip Mandelstam's verse from the *Tristia* period on, gender, in this sense, plays a totalizing role. For our purposes one famous example should suffice:

> Да будет так: прозрачная фигурка
> На чистом блюде глиняном лежит,
> Как беличья распластанная шкурка,
> Склонясь над воском, девушка глядит.
> Не нам гадать о греческом Эребе,
> Для женщин воск, что для мужчины медь.
> Нам только в битвах выпадает жребий,
> А им дано гадая умереть.

(So be it: the transparent shape/ Is lying on the clean clay dish,/ Like a splayed-out squirrel hide;/ A maiden peers, bent over the wax./ It's not for us to guess about the Greek Erebus:/ Wax is for women what bronze is for a man./ Our lot is cast only in battles/ While to them it is given to die telling fortunes.)

If we read Osip Mandelstam's fate as a metaphorical death in battle, and if we read the verb *gadat'* 'to guess, prophesy, tell fortunes' metaphorically as 'to interpret', this final stanza of "Tristia" sounds uncannily like the poet allocating his own fate and that of his wife/widow. It is of no import that Osip Mandelstam and Nadezhda Mandelstam hadn't even met when "Tristia" was written, since the roles are universalized: men perish in struggle, and women interpret their struggle, commemorate them—and, as other lyrics of this and later periods suggest, resurrect them.

Hence the first inference to be drawn from a gender-based criticism is that Nadezhda Mandelstam shares her husband's view concerning the division of the work of the world between men and women. She represents her writing as a posthumous continuation of her marriage role: Unable to save Osip Mandelstam's life, she is determined to save his writings, and her own prose becomes a part of that magnificent effort.

A more radical feminism would raise different questions. It would acknowledge that the role Nadezhda Mandelstam is representing is what Barbara Dane Clement calls "the suffering servant" of the Russian patriarchal tradition, and that this role sets the criterion according to which the many daughters, wives, and mothers portrayed in the memoirs are to be praised or blamed.[8] It would also acknowledge that gaps and silences about the authorial self are built into the project; after all the memoirs are not primarily autobiography or even biography. But it would still seek to discover tensions arising from the situation of the female writer, along with attendant strategies of indirection that would serve to authenticate her claims to speak. The canonical Classic Russian literature is, after all, largely a male preserve. And in view of this last circumstance, the kind of inquiry for which Elaine Showalter has proposed the term "gynocritics" would also look for connections in a tradition of female writing.

To take the last point first, in addition to her unflagging sense of her own mission, Nadezhda Mandelstam does seem to be empowered by several strands of a Russian woman's culture. First of all, there are the heroines-in-adversity of the "Suffering Servant" tradition, and Nadezhda Mandelstam is aware of predecessors in the wife of the Archpriest Avvakum and the Decembrists' wives, following their hubands to prison and exile. Second, from the time of Princess Dashkova, memorializing (in French) the history of her friendship with Catherine the Great, the memoir is **the** central genre of female writing in Russia. In the 20th century one thinks not only of Nadezhda Mandelstam but of writers like Evgenija Ginzburg and Lidija Chukovskaja. Third, beginning with the generation preceding Nadezhda Mandelstam's, women were claiming a place in Russian poetry. In the age of Gippius, Akhmatova, Tsvetaeva, and Petrovyx, a serious literary artist would not necessarily find being female such an isolating circumstance.

Yet the tensions inherent in the situation of the female writer do figure in the memoirs, albeit in a slightly transposed form. Nadezhda Mandelstam's writing addresses an anxiety that comes not so much from her status as a woman writing as from her status as a nonpoet—more specifically, her status as a poet's **wife**. This anxiety is very close to the surface in the portrayal of her relations with Anna Akhmatova. There is, in my view, a kind of shadow narrative here, one which proceeds by indirection, its unfolding suggested by scattered hints. And one of the thematic centers of this shadow narrative is the implicit triangle with Osip at its apex and Nadezhda and Anna Akhmatova at its corners.

Whatever the scenes portraying Akhmatova may evoke, e.g., admiration for her poetic gift, gratitude for her moral solidarity with Osip and with

Osip's memory, they do not suggest an affection for Akhmatova independent of Osip. In fact, for all the tributes to Akhmatova, there is nothing remotely approaching Nadezhda's words about Vasilisa Shklovskaja: ". . . and Vasilisa greeted us joyfully and tearfully. Even then I understood that the only real thing in the world was this woman's blue eyes. And that is what I think even now (p. 369)."

When she writes about Akmatova, Nadezhda often implies a certain discomfort, giving the reader to understand that she is not writing about a friendship between two women but about the somewhat edgy relations between the poet's wife and the poet's friend. In an oddly self-effacing passage, Nadezhda speaks of the friendship linking the two poets as their "sole reward for all the bitter labor and the bitter path each of them traveled (196)." She also claims that Akhmatova could not stand poets' wives but made an exception for her (247). Hence, along with her insistence on the role played by Anna Akhmatova in Osip's life and in her own, there is also at least the suggestion of a threat to the writer's wifely status, of being the odd one out, there on sufferance, an awareness of being the exception.

I would go further, connecting these hints with a larger but more diffuse pattern, one which emphasizes the exemplary quality of Nadezhda Mandelstam's marriage by alluding to another story, which she represents as the far more typical one: the story of the writer's wife whose lot it is to be rejected and abandoned by her husband. This nightmare surfaces early in *Hope Against Hope*, when Nadezhda Mandelstam comments on the irony of her having been the would-be rescuer of the poems of Vladimir Pjast, which Osip admired, "perhaps because lawful wives were cursed (*zaklinalis'*) in them (p. 22)." This leads into a reflection on what will become a leitmotif of the book, the idea of "broken hearts, scandals, and divorces" as the essence of the "normal" life barred to the Mandelstams; a fate to be envied, like Pjast's good fortune in dying from cancer before his second arrest. Nadezhda Mandelstam is unrelentingly ironic about the stuff of the bourgeois family romance, claiming that Freud's interpretive categories are only relevant to the "dobrodushnye zverstva" (genial atrocities, 142) of those with a settled address. Within the context of Stalin's Russia, "normal life" would have meant joining the privileged caste of the Writers' Union. The "normal" denouement to that kind of marital history can be gathered from Nadezhda's jibe at her friend Sonja Vishnevskaja for failing to recognize how lucky she was in that her playwright husband "died a timely death, without having managed to transfer his earthly goods (*nasledstvo*) to some rival of Sonja's (p. 280)." Valentin Kataev is another exemplar of "normal life," with his "new wife, new baby, new money, and new furniture (p. 296)."

The upshot of all this is that the rhetoric of the memoirs has to manage two varieties of terror. The Stalinist terror is of such magnitude that it reduces the everyday terror of marital abandonment to an object of irony. But the danger from without does not entirely eliminate the danger from within. The situation is a paradoxical one: the writer arraigns Stalinism for its destruction of the possibility of an ordinary life, yet her text risks the implication that the special pressure exerted by the State upon the Mandelstams has the effect of saving their marriage from the usual fate of such marriages.

Both the feminist and the rhetorical orientations lead to a concern with what the one would term strategies of empowerment, the other, strategies of authentication; that is, with the writer's claims to authority. And, since I propose to treat Nadezhda Mandelstam as a literary artist, this concern must allow for an emphasis upon the fictionality of her work. With the appearance of other accounts that treat Mandelstam and his circle, Nadezhda Mandelstam's version of particular events is being called into question in large and small ways. Consider, for example, the alternative interpretations to be found in the memoirs of Ol'ga Vaksel', Boris Kuzin, Lidija Chukovskaja and in G. Freidin's study of the Stalin Ode, not to mention the mass of archival materials that will eventually be unearthed. How could it be otherwise? Nadezhda Mandelstam wrote her books decades after the death of their central figure, she did not witness every episode she describes, and under these conditions there is bound to be considerable amplification of a dynamic observed by Freud, namely, that our beliefs tend to follow our desires. We put an impossible burden on the memoirist if we demand an objective record of what happened rather than her version of events. Of course Nadezhda Mandelstam's writings are not fictions in the sense of some ideal imaginative fiction, appealing chiefly to a semantic coherence. But if she does not want to be read as *literatura* (p. 44), neither should we read her as a chronicler of facts.

I suppose that it must be true of memoirs in general that they display a tension between the heuristic and the reportorial, that is, between an authority based on rhetoric and an authority based on accuracy. Thus in Nadezhda Mandelstam's *Hope Against Hope* many passages seek to set the record straight, to refute the testimony of others—of Georgij Ivanov, for example; not the least of Ivanov's services to Russian literature is his role in stimulating memoirs of Mandelstam, including not only Nadezhda Mandelstam's but also Akhmatova's and Tsvetaeva's. But Nadezhda Mandelstam is also obsessed throughout her narrative by the unreliability of **all** witnesses—not only those who, like Ivanov, are writing from the emigration but also the survivors of Stalinism. She wonders how historians will ever be able to reconstruct the truth about an age in which deliberate lying on a massive scale is the central mode of discourse (p. 26), and she does not exempt herself from the symptoms of the crisis of humanism and the Stalinist terror: "Все мы стали психически сдвинутыми . . . годятся ли такие, как мы в свидителей? . . ." (All of us became psychologially unhinged . . . Can such as we serve as witnesses? . . . 94). No one, she concludes, escaped the Terror without psychic damage (p. 317).

Reflecting on Viktor Shklovskij's determination to survive as an eyewitness, she observes that "by the time the Stalinist era came to an end, we had already managed to grow old and to lose that which makes a person a "witness," that is, an understanding of things and a point of view. That's what happened with Shklovskij (p. 319)." If Shklovskij is the target, still, that "We" must also include the writer, Nadezhda Mandelstam. In such passages she at the same time undercuts and authenticates her own account, inviting us to believe her because she admits the inevitability of error while strongly implying that we should also disbelieve her. In an attack on her contemporaries who want to remember the 20s as the Golden Age of Soviet culture, she seems to offer a rhetoric that undermines her general stance in a similar manner. Memory, she says, is not a direct reflection of events but a representation of the legends that form around events. In order to get at the truth, you must first demolish the legend, and to do that you must first establish what social circles gave rise to the legend (p. 176). This strikes me as a sophisticated formulation of the inseparability of fact and interpretation but also as an invitation to read Nadezhda Mandelstam in this way.

What is at stake, then, is not so much "Truth" as whose version shall prevail. Nadezhda Mandelstam believes, at least in her first volume, that the poet's friends will always have the final say as to how he will be remembered, because theirs is the only body of opinion that does not shift with every new ideological current. However, this hardly privileges the poet's circle with respect to some objective truth. It is striking that such a moral absolutist as Nadezhda Mandelstam should, in effect, so complicate her own claims to be setting the record straight, but then no honest writer tells the truth; unilinear truths are incompatible with the polyvalence of literary discourse. Besides, the habit of conflating fact and interpretation in the concept of an ostensibly value-free truth is weaker in Russian culture; *pravda* and *istina* are always produced by some moral vision. And—fortunately for those of us who teach fiction—what is not true is not necessarily a lie. When a writer interprets her experience, she narrativizes it, turning it into a *legenda*, a fiction, or less pejoratively, a story.

The quality of *Hope Against Hope* as sheer narrativity is underlined by the absence of documentation. Except for the final two chapters, in which Nadezhda Yakovlevna attempts to reconstruct the story of Osip Mandelstam's last days in the camps, she functions more like an omniscient narrator than a memoirist of the type of, say, Lidija Chukovskaja, who takes great pains to inform us as to the circumstances that condition each entry in her reminiscences of Akhmatova. The virtual absence of a documentary apparatus in the memoirs increases their immediacy; there is one less layer of modality to get through. But it also endows Nadezhda Mandelstam's account with a distinctly *rhetorical* authority: there is no appeal beyond the word of the author.[9]

These remarks may serve as a transition to Nadezhda Mandelstam's poetics more generally. Contiguity figures, i.e., synecdoche and metonymy, offer a key to the manner in which her language embodies a worldview. From another perspective, that of logic (or metalogic) the main figure is irony. Readers familiar with the book will probably agree that it has one of the most effective hooks in Russian literature: ". . . Дав пощечину Алексею Толстому, О. М. немедленно вернулся в Москву и оттуда каждый день звонил по телефону Анне Андреевне и умолял ее приехать" ("After slapping Aleksej Tolstoj in the face, O. M. at once returned to Moscow, and from there he telephoned Anna Akhmatova daily and implored her to come," p. 7). Certainly an *in medias res* beginning if ever there was one, this opening evokes the epic tradition—ironically, perhaps, if we recall Osip Mandelstam's claim in the 20s that the epic couldn't be a resource for him and his contemporaries. However, Nadezhda Mandelstam's hero doesn't articulate the origin and destiny of a people but of a social formation: the Russian intelligentsia, or at least its creative wing, viewed from the perspective of a period of crisis and collapse.

The very first sentence establishes the tie between Mandelstam and Akhmatova, and the durability of this friendship is one of the first themes to enter the book:

> Встречаясь они становились веселыми и беззаботными, как мальчишка и девчонка, встретившиеся в Цехе Поэтов. «Цыц,— кричала я,—не могу жить с попугаями!» Но в мае 1934 года они не успели развеселиться.

> (Upon meeting each other, they would become as gay and carefree as the boy and girl who had met at the Poet's Guild, "Stop it!" I would shout, "I can't live with a couple of parrots!" But in May of 1934 they were unable to enter into a giddy mood.)

Nadezhda Mandelstam's first quotation of her own speech presents her as a third party, annoyed at the "boy" and "girl" poets (Along the same lines, later in her narrative she will recall them teasing her as their "mama," p. 237). but in the space of two sentences she also shuttles us from the heyday of the Guild in the 1910s to May 1934, the time of Mandelstam's first arrest, which is what the story is building toward. Because these two time levels are viewed from the perspective of the late 50s and early 60s, the time of writing, a tripartite temporal frame is established, one in which everything earlier and later will be related to Mandelstam's final years, 1934–38. If we think of chronology as the neutral principle of narrative structure in a memoir, the main figure of narration in Nadezhda Mandelstam's first volume is disclosed as a particularizing synecdoche: a slice of roughly five years condenses the drama of half a century. Everything outside this culminating phase of Mandelstam's life, which coincides with the Great Terror, becomes in effect a flashback or flash forward. Her husband's last years are placed at the center in part because Osip's death gives Nadezhda her aim in life from midlife on and thus empowers her as an artist. To put it another way, the death of the poet Mandelstam is represented as the originary act that brings the writer Nadezhda Mandelstam into being.

Beyond the establishing of a line of succession, Nadezhda Mandelstam requires a temporal recursiveness because during these pivotal years, she was in no position either to formulate what was happening to her and to Osip, or to speculate about the thirties as a culmination of earlier developments. She tends in general to place thematic culminations in a chain of anticipation and aftermath, which tendency is often associated with an acute sense of drama and of those ritually significant moments that initiate or end some phase of life.[10] For example, in connection with the strategem used to set up Osip in 1938, Nadezhda recalls his reaction to a story told by Georgian party boss Nestor Lakoba during an earlier stay at a rest home, in 1931. The story concerned one of Lakoba's ancestors, who invited an enemy to his home and then murdered him. According to Nadezhda Mandelstam, "Lakoba's story made a big impression upon Osip Mandelstam; he sensed that it had some second level of meaning (p. 344)." Here we have Nadezhda, looking back from a post-Stalinist perspective, portraying Osip in 1931, experiencing a murky premonition of his fate, which is to be seized in violation of guest-right, rather like the victim in Lakoba's story.

The foregrounding of Mandelstam's last years undoubtedly also has an ideological motive. Rightly or wrongly, Nadezhda Mandelstam portrays her husband as a man largely constrained by what he has written. In this connection, it is Mandelstam's youthful lecture and essay, "Pushkin and Scriabin," that authorizes the narrative strategy of the memoirs. Nadezhda

Mandelstam recalls this essay in the opening lines of the chapter entitled "Gibel'nyj put'" ("The road to Destruction"), "The artist's death is not a matter of contingency but is his final creative act, illuminating his life's course as if with a cluster of rays" (p. 165; cf. also pp. 182, 270-71). If this is to be the standard, then it makes sense to tell the story outwards from the chain of events leading up to the poet's death.

This retrospective illumination can be construed as essentially a form of dramatic irony: the author (and audience) enjoy an understanding of the implications of the interplay of actors, actions, and motives that is not shared by the actors—including the younger Nadezhda Mandelstam—in the time of the narrated events. Yet if the author's irony is a reflex of hindsight, as it is, for example, in her bitter comment as to how a double suicide in 1934 would have spared them the agonies of Osip's second arrest and Nadezhda's widowhood, it is not a general and undifferentiated reflex. Rather, the writer's irony is a rich field for the study of how rhetorical effects can be moves in a contest for authority. To begin with, the writer holds a set of beliefs—in the ineradicability of kindness and its subsistence in the Russian people, in the self-extinguishing quality of evil—that are *not* treated ironically. These are points of reference for her critique of her principal target, the postrevolutionary intelligentsia, which has preserved its traditional pieties but has emptied them of their moral content.

The writer's ironic stance is already evident in her choice of chapter titles, whose ironic relationship to the chapters they head parodies the Stalinist "transvaluation of values" Nadezhda Mandelstam is exploring. Consider, for example, the first and third chapters, "Majskaja noch'" ("A May Night") and "Utrennie razmyshlenija" ("Morning Reflections"), titles which give a fix on the night of Mandelstam's first arrest by stressing its tremendous distance from the world of Gogol's Dikanka or Lomonosov's spiritual ode. Or consider the multiple ironies in "Nasha literatura" ("Our Literature"). The shifter "*nasha*" (our) has never been shiftier; there are at least three pronominal referents involved: those who share Nadezhda Mandelstam's values, those who share the values of the Old Bolshevik who heads the Office of Marxism-Leninism at Tashkent University, and a referent that actually has no existence, based as it is on the false presupposition of the old Marxist that she and Nadezhda are kindred spirits. By the same token, while each has her own "literature," they have none in common.

As examples of sustained ironic discourse, consider the portraits of Larisa Rejsner, fascinated by the cult of force (pp. 115-19); of Nikolaj Bukharin, a kind man who struggles to suppress his awareness of the deadly consequences of his own theorizing (pp. 119-25); or of Tanja Grigor'eva,

Nadezhda's sister-in-law, skewered by one of the author's most telling
ripostes:

> . . . Leaving, I said: "If one night Fascists are substituted for the Bolsheviks
> on you, you won't even notice." Tanja responded that this couldn't happen
> (p. 331).

The memoirs allow the reader to surmise that the quality of the sarcasm
directed at Tanja Grigor'eva is influenced by the respective positions of the
two women in the Mandelstam family system as much as it is by Tanja's
Stalinism. Osip and Nadezhda were in conflict with Evgenij and Tanja over
who should have the responsibility of caring for the brothers' father, over
Evgenij's failure to aid Osip in 1934 and later, and over Tanja's treatment
of her stepdaughter Tat'ka, Osip and Nadezhda's beloved niece. While
most of the writer's irony has a retaliatory quality, serving as a symbolic
summoning unto judgment, there is also a preemptive variety, aimed at
potential challenge to Nadezhda Mandelstam's authority. A good example
is her attack upon "some bright editor,"[11] a hypothetical representative of
the Soviet variety of the species, who would explain to her "with perfect
clarity" why the poet's wishes concerning the selection and ordering of his
verses for publication should be ignored as a matter of principle (p. 209).

The deviation from chronological history entails other figures of narration, most strikingly, what seems to the reader like a refusal to get on with
the story. A number of currents in the text yield this quality of indirection.
For instance, if everything must be anchored to a five-year period, there are
bound to be lots of satellite episodes that will have to be threaded in. On a
less formal level, the author clearly seeks to make both herself and her
husband representative figures, capable of instancing the crisis of the intelligentsia. At the same time, she wants to distance Osip Mandelstam and
herself, in order to underline their uniqueness. Both these drives locate
Nadezhda Mandelstam's discourse with respect to the values of Stalinism.
And both, again, can be construed as synecdoche. Thus the poet becomes
just another intelligent caught up by the Terror, his representative quality
enhanced by his wife's belief that a love of poetry is **the** distinctive feature
of an authentic intelligentsia. Her own fate she depicts as a particulariza-
tion of the fate of the women of her generation (p. 142), the widows
"repeating in the night the words of husbands who have perished (p. 295)."

It is a common enough poetic device to substitute one synecdoche for
another; Nadezhda can tell Osip's story by writing instead about Mikhail
Zenkevich. By the same token she can generalize her own widowhood by
talking about her friend Alisa Usova instead of herself. This particular sub-

stitution is also a device for handling the delicate issue of emphasis on one's own heroism. But the same rhetorical device is at work in her characterizations of the worst capitulationists. To portray what a Nikolaj Tixonov or a Tanja Grigor'eva is like is a way of showing what Osip and Nadezhda Mandelstam are **not** like.

This substitutability of images drawn from the same paradigm makes motif structure an important source of coherence. The reader must always be producing the intersections of meaning that bridge the gap from kernel to satellite episodes. The motif-structure of *Hope Against Hope* depends not only upon synecdoche but upon metonymy, that is, upon figures that evoke a pattern because they stand in some existential relationship to the whole, rather than an attributive or distributive relationship. The logic of metonymy is a way of getting at the poetic effects associated with the author's predilection for capturing a complex condition in a bare statement or even a single detail.

The more obvious of these two techniques is the tendency of a normally unadorned prose to become, if anything, even more spare at moments of the greatest emotional or dramatic intensity. The opening sentence is a good example of this process. Another comes at the very end of the chapter "Sbory i provody," (Collections and Leavetakings) where the merest trace summons up a world of thought and feeling. The Mandelstams are looking out the window as the train taking them into exile leaves the station:

Между нами и тем миром образовалась перегородка. Еще стеклянная, еще прозрачная, но уже непроницаемая. И поезд ушел на Свердловск.

(A barrier was taking shape between us and that world. As yet a glass one, as yet transparent, but already impenetrable. And the train left for Sverdlovsk, p. 44.)

Why is this so effective? I suspect that it is partly a matter of the management of rhythmic sequences, reminiscent of Pushkin's prose, with the final brief phrase serving as a cadence. There may also be something in the *aktual'noe chlenenie*, the functional word order, creating an ominous linkage between the final elements in each rheme: *peregorodka—nepronicaemaja—Sverdlovsk* ("barrier—impenetrable—Sverdlovsk"). The three stressed o's of the third sentence add their own negative overtones. There is also the elliptical quality of the second sentence, which is set off by being a *nazyvnoe predlozhenie* (nominative sentence) and also by the balance and contrast of its three nominative singular feminine adjectives, the third of which is semantically opposed to the first two. And then there are the echoes of word-signals from Osip Mandelstam's early verse: *steklo, prozrachnaja* (glass, transparent). But most of all there is the sense for the ritual moment and the writerly use of the mundane as a way of making connections so that the view from the train becomes a valedictory experience.[12]

The same metonymic impulse operates on the level of individual images. Consider, for example, Nadezhda Mandelstam's use of foods that serve as a kind of shorthand for the experience of arrest, imprisonment, and exile: An egg, mentioned twice, is the only food in the house at the time of Mandelstam's first arrest. During the search of their apartment that accompanies the arrest, a young Chekist offers them hard candies (*ledency*). Nadezhda Mandelstam generalizes this gesture as, first, a ritual of the arrest procedure and second, when she sees it repeated in the 50's by a former Chekist turned writer, as part of an expressive totality that, as she comments, makes itself felt in every trivial detail (p. 110). There is also the opposite of the *ledenec*, the *shokoladka* (chocolate). Tossed into a prison-train car by the writer's working-class landlady in Strunino, the chocolate candy evokes the tradition of popular compassion for all prisoners and is part of a pronounced democratic pathos.

A richer pattern, one which penetrates the whole text, is connected with the motif of masks and masking. An odd conjunction on the second page initiates the development. Describing the unfinished kitchen that becomes Akhmatova's domain during her visits from Leningrad, Nadezhda Mandelstam mentions the disconnected gas stove, which, out of deference to their guest, is covered wth an oil cloth (*kleenka*) and disguised as a table (*maskirovalas' pod stol*). A few sentences later, apropos of the agents who have come for her husband, she says that their civilian coats "served as a uniform, only a disguised one" (*maskirovochnaja forma*). This juxtaposition of the "masked" stove and the "masked" uniforms may appear so unmotivated as to escape notice, yet as the pattern crystallizes over hundreds of pages, the two images acquire, upon rereading, the power to bracket a whole world where survival depends upon a language and a decorum that function as a mask which renders private feeling invisible and almost inexpressible. Nadezhda Mandelstam is an acute field anthropologist describing a discursive system in which the rulers have their code, the victims theirs, and decorum becomes largely a system for regulating social intercourse between these two groups, with terror as the constructive factor in what the writer calls "the peculiar codex of Soviet polite behavior" (*osobyj kodeks sovetskix priličij*, p. 305). The field of "masked utterances" (*zamaskirovannye vyskazyvanija*) is suffocatingly inauthentic, but, at least in public, the mask is mandatory. Recalling the episode of her expulsion from the Ul'janovsk Pedagogical Institute in 1953, Nadezhda Mandelstam uses the institute's director, whose remarkable resemblance to Chekhov facilitates his work as a leader of antisemitic pogroms, to illustrate a more general perception:

Есть степень одичания, *когда с людей слезают все покровы,* придуман-ные лицемерным обществом, чтобы скрыть истинную сущность вещей. Но мы отличались тем, *что никогда не снимали своей красивой и лас-ковой гражданской маски.*

In this instance the use of the first plural pronoun is dictated by the fact that the agents of evil obliged their victims and potential victims to adopt masks also. The wives of those who vanished, for example, had to go on smiling to their neighbors and coworkers. Speaking of the roughly twenty years from the time she received the news of Mandelstam's death to the time she decided to begin the work of resurrecting him, Nadezhda Mandelstam says: "I was someone else, and I wore, so to say, an iron mask" (*železnaja maska*, p. 233). Viewed in this light, *Hope Against Hope* becomes an act of radical unmasking. By calling things by what she considers to be their proper names (cf. p. 64), by restoring her husband's work and memory, she is also restoring herself to herself.

Reed College

NOTES

[1]Richard Pevear's "On the Memoirs of Nadezhda Mandelstam," *Hudson Review*, Vol. XXIV (1971), No. 3, which begins with a brilliant appreciation of Nadezhda Jakovlevna's qualities as a literary artist, is a notable exception.

[2]Jonathan Culler, *On Deconstruction: Theory and Criticism After Structuralism* (Ithaca, New York: Cornell University Press, 1982), pp. 64-83.

[3]Nadežda Jakovlevna Mandel'štam, *Vospominanija* (New York: Chekhov Press, 1970). All page references will be given in the text.

[4]Group μ, *A General Rhetoric*, tr. Paul B. Burrell and Edgar M. Slotkin (Baltimore and London: The Johns Hopkins Univrsity Press, 1981), p. 19: ". . . rhetoric is the knowledge of the techniques of language characteristic of literature."

[5]Phyllis Rose, *Parallel Lives* (New York: A. Knopf, 1983). p. 7.

[6]*Ibid.*, p. 8.

[7]In "O. Mandel'štam—Materialy k biografii" (*Russian Literature* XV-I January 1984, pp. 1-27), A. Grigor'ev and N. Petrova give a bibliography of the Mandelstams' translations that substantiates the impression, implicit in the couple's own writings, of the sheer mass of work they undertook and accomplished as translators.

[8]Anna Akhmatova, the most problematic female character in *Hope Against Hope*, is the partial exception here.

[9]The novelistic vantage point is present already in the first paragraph. It enters when the writer describes how Anna Akhmatova, in far-off Leningrad, hesitates to come to Moscow in response to Osip Mandelstam's urgent summons:

... Уже собравшись и купив билет, она задумалась, стоя у окна. «Моли-
тесь, чтобы вас миновала эта чаша?»— спросил Пунин, умный, желчный и
блестящий человек.

(. . . With the preparations for the trip already made and the ticket already
bought, she lost herself in thought, standing in front of the window. "Are you
praying that this cup should pass you by?" asked Punin, an intelligent, irascible,
and brilliant man.)

[10]Other examples include the writer's many observations on the time-honored rituals of
arrest and on the elements of the "ritual for the restoration of life to writers who perished in
the camps" (p. 397).

[11]"*Kakoj-nibud' umnyj redaktor*," perhaps an echo of "*kakoj-nibud' čestnyj predatel'*" (some
honorable traitor), a phrase from Mandelstam's bitter lyric "*Kvartira*" ("The Apartment").
The allusion would suggest that for Nadezhda a "bright editor" is as much a contradiction in
adjectio as "an honorable traitor."

[12]The quoted pasage also sets up the metaphor of the past as the world behind the mirror
(*zazerkal'e*, p. 44), a figure that links *Hope Against Hope* with Akhmatova's *Poem Without A
Hero*.

THE WONDER OF NATURE AND ART: BELLA AXMADULINA'S *SECRET**

Sonia Ketchian

The latest collection of verse by Bella Axmadulina *Tajna: novye stixi* (*Secret: New Poems*), typifies the artistic development of this poet, both in terms of presenting her most cohesive collection to date and in terms of unveiling the arena for the second stage of her lyric persona's artistic creation. Observing a degree of continuity with the preceding poetry, the collection features at least fifteen poems from previous collections. Fourteen of the poems are found in the collection *Sny o Gruzii* (*Dreams of Georgia*), the most extensive collection of Axmadulina's work. While the opening poem in *Secret* expounds on the secret, the illumination of which occupies a great deal of the collection, it, like the remaining pieces, bears no such title.

As it stands, the collection is intricately interwoven thematically. Some poems are linked openly and sequentially, with their titles clustering around a given theme, such as the moon, space, or the bird-cherry tree. In others the coda of one poem frequently anticipates the subject of a subsequent one, and often the theme enters following its appearance as a motif, as in the final stanza of "Kofejnyj čertik" ("The Coffee Demon") where the speaker says, "Pojdu, spuščus' k Oke dlja pervogo poklona." (I will go down to pay my first respects to the Oka; 22), and the next poem "Prepiratel'stva i primirenija" ("Squabblings and Reconciliation") which begins with: "Vniz, k Oke, upadaja skvoz' les,/ pervocvet upasaja ot sleda." (Down toward the Oka, falling through the forest,/ saving the *pervocvet* from trampling; 23).[1]

In still other poems a fleeting image, as it were, foreshadows an imminent motif, not to be fully developed in the collection, such as "višu, kak stajka novostej" (I hang like a flock of news; 16). The image reappears from another facet in a subsequent poem "Luna v Taruse" ("The Moon over Tarusa"; 19), where a figurative name for bats appears: ". . . v toj niše, gde ja i krylatye myši" (in the niche where bats and I). The normal name is "letučaja myš'." Another example of an isolated echo sounds in the poem "Rod zanjatij" ("Profession"; 41)—"neponjaten rod moix zanjatij" (my occupation is unclear)—to be followed up in the concluding poem, "My načali vmeste: rabočie, ja i zima" (We began together: the workers, winter and I; 123), while, in effect, the entire collection exemplifies the speaker's occupation.

The collection centers on poetic creation, a leitmotif which is no novelty for Axmadulina; however, in her first stage (the period preceding *Secret*), studied in my article "Poetic Creation in Bella Axmadulina," only certain poems focused on it. Now an entire collection scarcely departs from it. Still, the real newness lies in the direction of the leitmotif's development. Previously, in poems of poetic creation the garnered impressions, experiences, and observations from the energetic, multicolored summer ambience were contemplated with the onset of autumnal rain and the flu. This helped the poet to withdraw temporarily from her friends and obligations to absorb summer impressions. In winter all the colors of nature merged into their all-encompassing color—white—through the arrival of frost, the freezing of water and the restriction of mobility in winter. The color white harbored within itself all the possible colors of the rainbow, which made available their intense exploration. The persona-poet crafted her poetic images, encased, as in a cocoon, in a warm snowbound house with a cricket for "artistic" company, as well as for literary continuity with Puškin, and a candle for tangible continuity with the heritage of the past. Love lyrics were conspicuously absent in the early thematic cycle of poems on poetic creation, and what had been a trend for a specific cycle now encompasses the entire volume. Exceptions are minor.

The purpose here is to study the poetic persona of Axmadulina on the writing of poetry first as expressed in the collection as a whole and then in the programmatic opening poem "I have the secret of wondrous blooming."

Two-thirds of the collection addresses the theme of Tarusa; this town on the Oka River serves as the site for the speaker's artistic creativity. After Tarusa the speaker moves briefly to other places, Moscow, Gagra, Riga and Leningrad, before returning home to Peredelkino where her best creative efforts result, ironically, in writer's block in the concluding poem. The persona is not pluralistic; yet she remains very close to the artistic interests of Axmadulina, unlike the numerous personas of Anna Axmatova or even the varying personas of Axmadulina's earlier poems. Still, where personal interests are concerned, the speaker focuses sharply on her art without touching the private aspects of the person Axmadulina. Indeed, there is no mention of parents, siblings, husband (even in the poem dedicated to Boris Messerer's studio; 111), children, or dogs. Humor continues, although it is not as boisterous as before (cf. the earlier "Oznob"—"Chills"); instead it graduates to a forceful irony. While the opening untitled poem presents in capsular form the highlights of the creative process that will unfold in the collection, Tarusa is not mentioned in it. The poet works toward her theme of Tarusa through the following poems, "Sad" ("The Garden"), "Noč' upadan'ja jablok" ("The Night of the Falling Apples"), and "Glubokij než-nyj sad, vpadajuščij v Oku" ("A deep gentle garden falling to the Oka"), and enters it in "Tarusa," a cycle of six poems. With Tarusa develops the theme of the poet Marina Cvetaeva. Poems to her include both old and new ones; however, only those former poems to Cvetaeva are included here which comprise an integral whole with the present themes of Tarusa and poetic creation. Significantly, the cycle "Tarusa" has been enlarged by three poems.[2] Through Tarusa, then, Axmadulina retains in her verse an awareness of Cvetaeva and draws from it inspiration for work.

Tarusa is more than a literary symbol for Axmadulina. In private conversation she told me that she really could not compose at home in Moscow or in Peredelkino (hence the writer's block there), and that she was soon to leave for Tarusa following readings in Leningrad, Riga (with the poet Bulat Okudžava) and in Moscow early that January. In fact, creation in Tarusa merely continues the line of writing evolved in Axmadulina's previous verse, where the speaker consistently creates in a home away from family ties: her earlier "snowbound house" is replaced here by encasement in nature and in the past.

The connection with Cvetaeva is made explicit through a dedication to her in the "Tarusa" cycle and through an epigraph from her poem "Sad" ("Garden"), used in Axmadulina's poem "Sad-vsadnik" ("The Rider-Garden"; 79).[3] It is the only epigraph in the collection. Tarusa is the place where for twenty years the Cvetaev family rented the Pesočnoe Estate. It figures in Cvetaeva's prose and in two poems, "Parom" ("The Ferry") and "Osen' v Taruse" ("Autumn in Tarusa"); they capture the ambience of the place and the time as well as the relationship between Marina and her sister Asja.[4] But Cvetaeva describes Tarusa extensively only in a biographical prose work, on the neighboring sisters "Kirillovny" ("The Kirillovnas"). These sisters, called only by their patronymic in the familiar peasant fashion, lived on the very edge of Tarusa. Since in summer they were always working in their graden, they seemed to live only in their garden and orchard, hidden by willows and elderberry bushes. Cvetaeva clarifies the impression, "The garden gobbled up the house."[5] Above all, Tarusa represents a place of emotional stability for Cvetaeva, one closely connected with family and childhood. It was the place where she would have liked to have been buried:

I would like to lie in the Xlystian Cemetery of the Flagellants of Tarusa, under an elderberry bush, in one of those graves with a silver dove, where the reddest and largest strawberries in our parts grow.

But if this is unrealizable, if not only can I not lie there, but even the cemetery no longer exists, then I would like to have placed on one of the hills
which the Kirillovnas used to climb to visit us in Pesočnoe and which we
climbed to visit them in Tarusa a stone from the Tarusa quarry:

here, would like to lie

MARINA CVETAEVA   (II, 84)

Axmadulina echoes this sentiment in her poem "Palec na gubax" ("A Finger to the Lips"): "Zdes' TA xotela spat'" ("Here SHE wanted to sleep";
75). Tarusa, then, constituted a place of imagined future rest for Cvetaeva,
if conditions permitted a real return—and they did not.

Tarusa has yet another attraction for Axmadulina—it is a place colored
by Cvetaeva's green eyes. Thrice repeated is the opening line of the first
poem in the "Tarusa" cycle:

> Какая зелень глаз вам свойственна, однако.
> И тьмы подошв—такой травы не изомнут.
> С откоса на Оку вы глянули когда-то:
> На дне Оки лежит и смотрит изумруд.

(What a greenness of eyes is typical of you, however./ Even a myriad of
soles—cannot trample such grass./ From the slope onto the Oka you once
gazed:/ on the bed of the Oka lies and looks an emerald.)

Cvetaeva's emerald eyes have impressed themselves on the brilliant greenery.

Further, as noted in my early study on Axmadulina, there is no figure of
the Muse in her verse. With the conspicuous absence of a classical Muse
and the persona's probe into nature on the Oka, the simple life there and
art the collection comes close in attitude to that of Boris Pasternak toward
nature as defined by Anna Axmtaova: "All his life long, nature was his
full-fledged Muse, his secret interlocutor, his Bride and Beloved, his Wife
and Widow—it was to him what Russia was to Blok."[6] In other words, in
this collection, and in the theme of creation specifically, Axmadulina comes
close to Pasternak's art as understood by Axmatova, with the exception of
the reference to youth: "I just now understood the most frightening thing
about Pasternak: he never reminisces. In the entire cycle "Kogda razgulja-
etsja" ("When it clears up") he, already an old man, does not once remi-
nisce about anything: neither his family, love, nor youth . . ." (III, 152).
Moreover, Pasternak seems obsessed with specific current time. Indeed, in
Stixotvorenija i poèmy (Poems and Narratives in Verse) his first poem begins
with the name of a month and concerns writing: "February. To get ink and
to cry!" He seems to use the months to convey his feelings: "to write violently about February." Axmadulina, who never dates her poems by the
year (Cvetaeva always does, Axmatova often does, Pasternak sometimes

does), is, nonetheless, like Cvetaeva and Axmatova through her acute awareness of time as months or the date, which she takes as a topic for her verse. She not only titles certain poems, using the day of the month, "Vosled 27 dnju fevralja" ("Following the 27th Day of February"), "Den' 12 marta" ("The Twelfth Day of March"), "Vosled 27 dnju marta" ("Following the 27th Day of March"), in succession, but she makes the days of the month the main topic of some poems.

Nature, the plants, the moon, space, even days suffuse the verse writing process. Like Axmatova, Axmadulina distinguishes the process of creating, giving birth, as it were, to verse and writing down the verse on paper. The difference is that Axmatova's persona receives ready verse through the medium of the Muse and the various stages of creation preceding it, before writing the verse on paper and firing it to immortalize it and to individualize it, as if to free herself of her own creation.[7] Axmadulina's persona, conversely, must write down in verse form through effort the ineffable poetry produced on the basis of daytime impressions by nature in the night to which this vigilant speaker was a witness. There is, then, some effort on Axmadulina's part, unlike Axmatova who can say in "Tvorčestvo" ("Creation"): "I prosto prodiktovannye stročki/ Ložatsja v belosnežnuju tetrad'" (And simply dictated lines/ Lie in a snow-white notebook; 201). So a poem that Axmadulina wants to write down can elude her for days, at which time she may reluctantly abandon her quest to articulate a given piece (36). Throughout her efforts at creating verse, nature remains close by; an apple falls on a line of poetry in "The Night of the Falling Apples": "And I wince: an apple has fallen, on the 'NOT'—having placed a stress extrinsically" (7). Also, a bee alights on a line of poetry; but first it appears and takes life through a simile: "The verse falls like a bee on the stalks and branches." So the bee in the simile's vehicle turns into a real bee—a way of overcoming the dichotomy of the simile by passing through the metaphor stage into reality: "a bee flew into my line."[8] Petals from a bird-cherry tree (*čeremuxa*) fall on the poem in "Čeremuxa predposlednjaja" ("Bird-Cherry Tree the Last but One"):

> Как трогательно лепестки
> в твой день предсмертный,
> в твой четвертый
> на эти падают стихи. (70)

(How touchingly the petals/ on your dying day,/ on your fourth one/ fall on these poems.)

Axmadulina thus maintains a strong interaction between nature in bloom and flourishing poetry; in other words, nature produces fruit, and poetry in creation will also bear fruit.

Notwithstanding all the reverential intertextuality with Cvetaeva and similarities with Pasternak as well as reminiscences of Russian classical writers (Puškin and Lermontov), Axmadulina has in this collection raised her poetic voice to a most original note. While the themes in her point of departure—Tarusa, the orchard, the moon, the snowstorm—have been nurtured by important literary predecessors, her development and enlargement of her legacy through her wondrous secret is innovative. The key to much of the secret lies in the collection's opening poem.

The poem "Est' tajna u menja ot čudnogo cvetenija" ("I have the secret of wondrous blooming") and, indeed, the entire collection, are geared toward the past, toward perceiving the present through the past. Such an intense and intrusive past must of necessity obfuscate some other, traditional aspects of poetry. Hence love for a human falls victim here—there are no love poems, nor is there romantic love in the poems or in the speaker's life within the period covered by the collection. The absence of love for a man is touched upon in the poem "Luna do utra" ("The Moon until Morning"; 27);

> Что опыт? Вздор! Нет опыта любви.
> Любовь и есть отсутствие былого.
> О, как неопытно я жду луны
> на склоне дня весны двадцать второго.

(What is experience? Nonsense! There is no experience for love./ Love *is* the absence of the past./ Oh, how naively I await the moon/ on the wane of the twenty-second day of spring.)

If love is construed as the absence of that which is past, it stands to reason that love will have little place in a collection strongly laudatory of the past. For while love differs each time, according to the persona, nature repeats itself exactly in its renewal, thereby maintaining a powerful continuity in its link to the past. (If any love is lavished in the collection, it is on Axmadulina's unique conception of the moon.) Through this connection both nature and the past become vital to the persona's sensibility. If earlier Axmadulina showed her persona's process of assessing and translating impressions of nature and life into her art, she now centers largely on the initial impetus for all her impressions and thoughts: namely, on the budding and growth of nature, the ties with previous art and culture, the very possibility of transmutation into poetry up to the exact moment of committing the poem to writing.

Concealment of the wondrous secret is further augmented by deletion of a stanza during publication which Axmadulina wrote in the copy that she inscribed to me. Thus through deletion the message has been twice obscured in the published version. The poem's opaque message equates nature and life with speech, letters, writing and literature. The Oka River distinguishes a live person and living creatures from inanimate nature in a retort to the speaker in "Squabblings and Reconciliation":

> —Ты не ведаешь, что говоришь
> Ты жива и еще не природа.

(You do not know what you are saying./ You are alive and not yet nature; 23)

A live person-poet can in no way affect inanimate nature but can reflect the beauty of fields and of forests, inculcating it through his aorta and turning it into speech, which is the equal of spoken verse, in preparation for its eventual transformation into written poetry. This creates a second world, which works well enough through reflection. The complete poem[9] reads:

> Есть тайна у меня от чудного цветенья,
> здесь было б: чуднАГО—уместней написать.
> Не зная новостей, на старый лад желтея,
> цветок себе всегда выпрашивает «ять».
>
> Где для него возьму услад правописанья,
> хоть первороден он, как речи приворот?
> Что—речь, краса полей и ты, краса лесная,
> как не ответный труд вобравших вас аорт?

Лишь грамота и вы—других не видно родин.
Коль вытоптан язык—и вам не сдобровать.
Светает, садовод. Светает, огородник.
Что ж, потянусь и я возделывать тетрадь.

> Я этою весной все встретила растенья.
> Из-под земли их ждал мой повивальный взор.
> Есть тайна у меня от чудного цветенья.
> И как же ей не быть? Все, что не тайна,—вздор.
>
> Отраден первоцвет для зренья и для слуха.
> —Эй, ключики!—скажи—он будет тут как тут.
> Не взыщет, коль дразнить: баранчики! желтуха!
> А грамотеи—чтут и буквицей зовут.
>
> Ах, буквица моя, все твой букварь читаю.
> Как азбука проста, которой невдомек,
> что даже от тебя я охраняю тайну,
> твой ключик золотой ее не отомкнет.

Фиалки прожила и проводила в старость
уменье медуниц изображать закат.
Черемухе моей—и той не проболталась,
под пыткой божества и под его диктант.

Уж вишня расцвела, а яблоня на завтра
оставила расцвесть . . . и тут же, вопреки
пустым словам, в окне, так близко и внезапно
прозрел ее цветок в конце моей строки.

Стих падает пчелой на стебли и на ветви,
чтобы цветочный мед названий целовать.
Уже не знаю я: где слово, где соцветье?
Но весь цветник земной—не гуще, чем словарь.

В отместку мне—пчела в мою строку влетела.
В чужую сласть впилась ошибка жадных уст.
Есть тайна у меня от чудного цветенья.
Но ландыш расцветет—и я проговорюсь.

(I have the secret of wondrous blooming,/ here it would have been more suitable to write: [in the old spelling] wonder-filled./ Ignorant of novelty, yellowing in the old way,/ This flower always cries out for a "jat'."

Where will I get for it the pleasure of spelling,/ Although it is primordial as the magic of speech?/ What is speech, beauty of fields and you, sylvan beauty,/ if not the responsive labor of aortas that have imbibed you?

Only reading-and-writing and you—no other homelands are to be seen./ If language is trampled—neither will all be well with you./ It's growing light, horticulturist. It's growing light, gardener./ Well, I too will reach out to cultivate my notebook.

This spring I greeted all the plants./ From inside the earth my midwife's gaze awaited them./ I have the secret of wondrous blooming./ And how could it not be? All that is not secret is—nonsense.

A joy is the *pervocvet* to the sight and hearing./ Say, "Hey, *ključik*'s!" and it will show up right away./ It will not blame you if you tease it: *barančik*'s! *želtuxa*!/ And the would-be learned do honor and call it a *bukvica*.

O my *bukvica*, I keep reading your primer./ How simple is the alphabet which does not comprehend/ that even from you I guard the secret;/ your gold key will not unlock it.

I outlived the violets and saw off to old age/ the ability of the lungworts to portray the sunset./ Even to my bird-cherry tree I did not disclose the secret,/ under torture of the divinity and to his dictation.

The cherry tree has already blossomed, and the apple tree till tomorrow/ has left its blossoming . . . and right here, contrary to/ empty words, in the window, so close and suddenly/ has ripened its blossom at the end of my line.

The verse falls like a bee on the stalks and branches/ in order to kiss the floral nectar of names./ I no longer know: which is word and which is floret./ But the whole flowerbed of earth is no denser than a dictionary.

In retaliation—a bee flew into my line./ The error of greedy lips has bitten into someone else's sweetness./ I have the secret of wondrous blooming./ But the lily of the valley will bloom—and I will blurt it out.)

The mood in the poem is that of the final commitment of verse to paper as day breaks; however, the added, third stanza undercuts the assurance.

Whereas the verdant grass and plants were connected with the green eyes of Cvetaeva, the leitmotif of flowering and flowers in the poem is grounded in Cvetaeva's surname. (So she is present in the collection before obvious mention of her name.) Indeed, her name is comprised of the root *-cvet-*, spelled with the letter "jat'" in the old orthography (*cvět*). It will be recalled that in her poems Cvetaeva called attention to names, specifically, of Blok, Axmatova and her own.[10] The flower imagery of the surname found subtle expression in such poems of Cvetaeva as "Ljubov'! Ljubov'! I v sudorogax i v grobe . . ." ("Love! Love! Both in convulsions and in the grave") and "Znaju, umru na zare!" ("I know I will die at dawn!"), but it is less obvious than for her first name. Axmadulina again goes beyond her predecessor in this collection. While underscoring the image of blooming in Cvetaeva's name, she develops it to connote flowering and flowers as the equivalent of letters and verse, and possibly of learning. Her speaker evidently moves toward an understanding of the world as comprised of letters and writing, with their interdependence and interchangeability (compare the bee, bird-cherry tree and the apple tree). Such a notion appears to embrace the philosophy of the Talmud as presented by Isaac Bashevis Singer in his short piece "Of Providence, Free Will and the Future of Learning": "Judaism is one religion based entirely on learning. Its very essence is the Torah, a scroll, a book. According to the Talmud, God has created the world with the letters of the Torah."[11] Inasmuch as nature, despite its cyclical change and renewal, is old, so too are writing and script to the extent that the letters were seemingly dictated to man by nature (without the divine intervention propagated in Old Russian Literature or in Classical Armenian Literature). Whether the parallel of nature and letters was conscious on Axmadulina's part, cannot be ascertained at this point. Put simply, the introductory poem clearly reflects notions that poetry and script stem from nature and are tantamount to blooming and development. Hence the mis-construing of the original deleted stanza. Language as nature and litera-ture, the land, its plants and people comprises the speaker's fatherland.

In this first poem, where flowers demand in their spelling, through their yellowing in the old way and their adherence to the old without knowledge of the new, the letter "jat'," the persona is at a loss in securing for the flower the pleasure (*uslad*) of the old orthography. In the poem the dual concepts of plants growing in a garden and words growing within the capa-cious word *sad* (garden, orchard) evolve as closely meshed activities: "Pro-stornej slovo [sad], čem okrestnost'" (The word is more spacious than the environs; 5). Further, the striking image of the "Deep gentle garden falling to the Oka" enlarges through the spilling over of the garden on the river banks to the water the world of change and inspiration to all of Tarusa and, implicitly, to the world and *œuvre* of Cvetaeva. The use of this specific locus evokes the Russian past through the line "Ostanemsja v sadu minuv-šego stoletija" (Let's remain in the garden of the past century; 9). With *sad* as the specific environment for cultivating poetry (since the muses lived there) and the nineteenth century as the artistic ambience in which Axma-dulina now has her strongest roots, there emerges a sense of the importance of all the land and its history. Thus is Axmadulina's poetry of this stage grounded in her visualization of the intermingling of nature and letters as the essence of life and art.

Like most poems in the collection, the opening piece, "I have the secret of wondrous blooming," is written in quatrains. There are nine published stanzas plus the added third one. The meter is iambic hexameter, the Rus-sian equivalent of the classical Alexandrine. In this collection's new poems Axmadulina eschews novelty in meter and stanzaic form in favor of tradi-tion and uniformity. This poem marshals the prime themes, motifs and images to be developed and revealed throughout. It inaugurates the title of the persona's artistic secret, which is fairly well guarded, despite measured release of certain aspects in an effort to tease and to spur on the reader's imagination.

Axmadulina's cherished secret concerns wondrous blooming, not in a new-fangled way, but as of old with all the religious awe for something holy; hence the appropriateness of the old Russian orthography for the verses. This blossoming of nature and life, which is translated into verse, knows no novelty, no drastic change other than the inevitable winter hiber-nation; it knows only continuity with an illustrious past: hence the perso-na's inclination to spell *čudnago* using the -*ago* ending of the old orthogra-phy as well as to use the old letter "jat'" for the word "flower" in the old way. Its color in turn evokes the yellowed pages of a manuscript or, a yellowed book which uses the "jat'." The message here is that a flower remains a flower throughout the ages in spite of the newness of each individual flower that appears each new season. The secret of nature being old stimulates the persona's wish to use the old orthography. According to the poem, speech, which equals verse (even in early Axmadulina) obtained through the crucible of poetic talent, is interdependent on the beauty of fields and woods. The reflection of this beauty results in speech, following its assimilation in the speaker's aortas and, indeed, in her very being. The writing down is another matter, it is treated in Axmadulina's later poems and is a topic for future discussion.

The added stanza (number 3) equates the fatherland with reading and writing and the sources of beauty introduced earlier: speech equals verse, which stems from fields and forests; hence the people, the land with its nature and the culture through writing and learning. If the language, which probably equals writing, is trampled, then the situation bodes ill for the all-important trinity—speech and the beauties of field and woods. As darkness fades and light grows, the persona reminds the tillers of the land, the *sadovnik* (horticulturist) and the *ogorodnik* (gardener) to set to work. She too is impelled to cultivate, or work at, her notebook to create written verse. Accordingly, through metaphor the paper (formerly the parchment) performs the role of her land, or soil, for cultivation—an image not at all new to literature—hence "no other homelands are to be seen." A horticulturist should probably work in the forest, which, due to its trees, is an uncultivated form of orchard, while a gardener should till the open fields to grow certain plants. Their efforts will turn part of these places into cultured areas.

The first flower to be mentioned is appropriately *pervocvet*, "a joy to sight and hearing." This word can denote either the first early blossoming of plants or a low plant with pretty flowers of various colors.[12] The ambiguity in name directs the poem's profile. The *pervocvet* is the flower which gladdens the persona who greets all the plants sprouting from the earth. Metaphorically, she performs the role of a midwife to facilitate the timid emergence of the plants, all of which are blooming ones. Other persons, less conversant with the natural origins of poetry, may call forth the same flower by using the name *ključiki*. Dal's dictionary defines the word as "a floral bunch or cluster, in which small bellflowers hang on long stalks." Further, the word in Russian sounds like a key, possibly the key to the secret. The *pervocvet*, surprisingly, will not mind if it is teased as *baránčiki* or *želtuxa*. In Dal's dictionary *baránčik* is defined as "Primula veris, kuritina, gasnik?, gorlupa, skorospelka, bot'i ručki, kudel', *ključiki*, white *buk-*

vica; the plant Nepeta Glechoma, ground ivy, budra, podbiruxa, kotovnik, košečnik, rasxodnik, košač'ja-sobačja-mjata" (my italics; I, 47). *Želtuxa* is listed in dictionaries only as "yellow jaundice," but it could well have the meaning of a yellow flower (one educated native speaker of Russian uses it in the meaning of "dandelion") in some local parlances, as shown in Daľ where a close variant, a diminutive *želtuška* has, among other definitions, the meaning "The plant Anthemis tinctoria, pupki, pupavka, pupavni, želtyj-cvet, žetlyj-pugovnik, šafran-polevoj, dikaja-rjabinka?, cvetuxa, polevaja-jagodka, želtorod'e" (I, 531).

Now the speaker turns ironic toward would-be learned people who will revere the plant and call it *bukvica*. The meaning of a letter or characters peeks out of the plant. In Daľ's dictionary the word is listed as "old alphabet, primer; currently the old Slavic letters are called so to distinguish them from Glagolitic and from other most recent ones; . . . white *bukvica*, . . . *ključiki, barančiki*" . . . (I, 139). Addressing the flower *bukvica*, the speaker avers that she continues perusing its primer, i.e. each flower contains sufficient information to instruct in the basics of life and art, particularly this specific flower. However, the speaker keeps to herself the secret of the simple alphabet—a secret not revealed even to the plant *bukvica* itself, a secret that the *bukvica*'s gold key will not open (a reference to *ključiki* is evident here). I will later attempt to unravel the mystery with which the speaker is taunting the plant and her readers.

Thus the principal secret is the blossoming of plants, probably as viewed by a poet. Other aspects of the secret will unfold with the progression of the collection, but in the first poem the wondrous blossoming initially focuses on a single yellow flower. With the image of the yellow flower figures the yellowed paper or parchment and use of the old orthography. Axmadulina employs the masculine of *uslada*, which according to Ušakov's dictionary is bookish and poetic, if indeed the form is not the genitive plural form of the common feminine gender word. It would then mean "orthographies of delight," a less likely rendition than the meaning of "the pleasure of orthography is as primary as the enchantment of speech." By rendering as simultaneous the pleasure of orthography and speech, Axmadulina equates them more firmly with nature, the two beauties of fields and woods—and the responsive work of the human body and mind. They impress themselves on the speaker. In effect, she converts visual images into phonetic ones that depict reflected visual images before converting to visual symbolic images of script, which are letters that in turn equal nature. A full cycle is achieved.

Thus a joy to sight and hearing is *pervocvet*, which denotes the first early blossoming of flowers as well as a plant with pretty flowers of various colors. It is probably the first flower to be noticed by the speaker in the early spring. Through the phrase "ej, ključiki" the speaker hopes the beauty of the woods will induce the appearance of the flowers. She prays the *pervocvet* will forgive her for mocking it as *barančiki* and *želtuxa*. By contrast, would-be literate men will call the plant *bukvica* out of respect, its name alone elevating it to the pinnacle of learning. So these flowering plants that sound like letters or the alphabet, a key to reading and learning, or conjure up the form of letters—*barančik* in form might be said to equal on "o" (cf. *baranka*, a small *bublik*, or bagel)—all designate a flower. In fact, they all denote the same flower, as expected from the translations in Daľ. Segal's *Russian-English Dictionary* likewise supports the premise of one flower. It lists *pervocvet* as "primrose," *barančik* as "officinal primrose, cowslip" (a common British primrose), *belaja bukvica* as "primrose, cowslip." *Želtuxa* does not have this definition anywhere; it is, however, connected at least visually with the flowers through a definition in Daľ of *barančiki* as "kotovnik" and "košač'ja mjata" which is "catnip, catmint," a plant with yellow flowers. Thus in my translation of this poem into English it would have been correct to use "primrose" instead of *pervocvet*, but then one part of Axmadulina's secret would have been revealed without explanation and the poet's play on words and nuances would have been lost in the English translation. Specifically, the use of "primrose" in stanza five (four in the published version) would have obfuscated the meaning of "first bloom." Moreover, the *želtuxa* reflects the yellow flower image at the beginning of the poem.[13]

Mining esthetic riches may well not be for anyone other than a poet. Only one close to art and nature, as the persona in Tarusa, can keep perusing the primer with its essentials of life in one flower, which through its many names reaches out to various subtleties of meaning. The gold key to the poet's secret is the plants and life, the observation that only a poet can transform through artistic cultivation into written words and verse.

A poem in progress evokes the process of a bee culling nectar from the flowers as shown in the simile in poem one. In literary terms the image evokes Osip Mandel'štam (whose poetry figures later as a tome; 60), which, in turn hails back to classical literature.[14] Words and floscules (*socvet'e*) merge, as in a simile, but the entire earthly flower garden is no more rich than a dictionary. So soil equals a flower garden ready for the poet to cultivate in preparation for making available the information through the instrument of her verse. While Axmadulina parallels the classic image of the poet-bee and honey-poetry, the bee is not the verse since now the persona develops her simile into an extended metaphor, making both the bee and the verse tangible. The bee bites into someone else's sweetness (nectar, honey). At this point the speaker stops abruptly, despite the soothing structural encircling of line one, lest the lily of the valley bloom before she is prepared for it and she involuntarily make a lapse of the tongue. A somewhat ironical, even ominous ending to a serene beginning.

Thus *pervocvet* gladdens the eye and ear as would the delicate sounds of gentle new plants, stirring in the air and in the wind, as well as chirping birds, animals and insects; it also conjures up a specific plant whose image is underscored through the other names for it to follow. Playing on the ambiguity of polysemy in the words, Axmadulina crafts her dual, though comparable imagery. What seems like teasing or sophistry is the name for the plants—all of them flowering ones—that actually signify the same plant—*pervocvet, barančik, želtuxa, bukvica*—a primrose. the last one is probably the most "literary" name, since it sounds like a letter of the alphabet. An early flowering cultured plant, it lends itself to being a primer, as it were, of plants and nature. It underpins the philosophy of the Talmud that the world is created of letters.

More familiar flowers follow in the poem. Their presence underpins flower semantics for the previous panoply of plant names (but actually one plant, although each plant can also signify several others locally): violet, lungwort,[15] the bird-cherry tree that has blossomed, and the apple tree that will blossom later, and the lily of the valley whose blooming threatens disclosure of the secret. The flowers in nature with their sweet nectar mingle with the written poetic line: "where the word is or where the floret is." The names, i.e. the words of the flowers, contain nectar to which the verse, like a bee, can apply itself. As revenge for her verse falling upon the branches like a bee to kiss the flowery nectar of names, a real bee flies into the persona's line of verse. Reality, it would seem, forces entry. Ostensibly, the persona resists, possibly, because as possessor of the secret of wondrous blooming, she fears a lapse of tongue with the flowering of the herald of spring, the pure lily of the valley.

In conclusion, it can be said that Axmadulina's latest collection of verse, *Secret*, marks a new stage in the development of her verse through concentration and intensification of the theme of poetic creation. Nature, comprised of letters, assumes a leading role through its alter ego—verse, the multifarious artistic refraction of speech, learning and culture.

Russian Research Center, Harvard University

NOTES

*This work was made possible through participation in the Senior Research Scholar/Soviet Ministry of Education Exchange, sponsored by the International Research and Exchanges Board in the fall of 1983, which I gratefully acknowledge.

[1]All translations into English are mine. I retain certain Russian words, like *pervocvet*, because their translation before the proper explanations would hamper the analysis. The pertinent pages from the collection (Bella Axmadulina, *Tajna: novye stixi*. Moscow: Sov. pisatel', 1983) are marked in the text.

[2]The three new poems are: "Morskaja—tak idi v svoi morja" (Sea-ling/sea thing—then go to your seas"; 12), "Rastaet sneg. Ja v zoopark sxožu" ("The snow will thaw. I will to the zoo"; 13), "Kak znat', vdrug—malo, a ne mnogo" ("How can one know, what if little, and not much"; 13).

Among the deleted poems to Cvetaeva are "Uroki muzyki" ("Music Lessons"), "Biografičeskaja spravka" ("Biographical Information"), "Četvert' veka, Marina, tomu" ("It has been a quarter of a century, Marina" (*Sny o Gruzii*; 96-101).

[3]The epigraph, as pointed out to me by Axmadulina, had been misprinted. It should read:

> For this hell, [not "year"]
>
> for this delirium
>
> send me a garden
>
> in my old age.

In previous publication in *Sny o Gruzii* (206-07) the Tarusa cycle bore no dedication to Cvetaeva.

[4]I am indebted to Dr. Janet Marin King for locating these poems for me. *Volšebnyj fonar', Vtoraja kniga stixov*. Moscow: Ole-Ljukoje. 1912, 42-43.

[5]Cvetaeva, *Sočinenija*, II, 78.

[6]Axmatova, *Sočinenija*, III, 151.

[7]See my entry on Axmatova in Terras, ed., *Handbook of Russian Literature*, 14-16.

[8]On the dichotomy inherent in a simile see my article, "Vehicles for Duality in Puškin's *The Bronze Horseman*: Similes and Period Lexicon."

[9]The third stanza of the poem was omitted in publication. It was written in for me by the poet on November 13, 1983. It is marked here by printing without indentation.

[10]Her own first name, Marina (*morskaja*), found reflection in several poems; among the best is "Kto sozdan iz kamnja, kto sozdan iz gliny":

> Some are created of stone, some are created of clay,—
>
> But I shimmer like silver and glitter!
>
> My business is faithlessness, my name, Marina.
>
> I am the perishable foam of the sea.

Axmadulina picks up the sea images in her poem from the Tarusa cycle, "Sea-ling—then go to your seas." For the poems on Blok and Axmatova see Cvetaeva, *Sočinenija*, II, 72, 85-86.

[11]*The New York Times Book Review*, June 17, 1984.

[12]Axmadulina showed me pots of this plant with its narrow oval leaves and red-pink flowers.

[13]It must be noted that Dr. Peter Stevens of Harvard University, an expert on flowers, assures me that the flowers on Axmadulina's windowsill, which I photographed, are not the botanical primrose. He believes that the names Bella Axmadulina uses are a folk misnomer, if not a regional appellation. I am inclined toward accepting the poet's knowledge of regional flowers with the assumption that the Russian primrose is probably wild and not cultured as in Western Europe. Due to the imperfections of an amateur photograph, Dr. Stevens was unable to name the flower on the windowsill; a primrose, he assured me, cannot be forced to bloom in the fall.

[14]Kiril Taranovsky, "Bees and Wasps: Mandel'štam and Vjačeslav Ivanov" in *Essays on Mandel'štam*, 86-7.

[15]*Medunica* (lungwort) conjures up Mandel'štam's "Na radost' osam paxnet medunica" (The lungwort's fragrance is for the joy of the wasps), while the bird-cherry is reminiscent of Pasternak.

REFERENCES

Axmadulina, B., *Sny o Gruzii*. Tbilisi: Merani. 1979.

————, *Tajna: novye stixi*. M.: Sovetskij pisatel'. 1983.

Axmatova, A., *Sočinenija*. Eds. G. P. Struve and B. A. Filippov. 3 vols. 2nd ed. N.Y.: Inter-language Literary Associates; Paris: YMCA. 1967-83.

Cvetaeva, M., *Sočinenija v dvux tomax*. M.: Khud. lit. 1980.

Dal', V., *Tolkovyj slovar' živogo velikorusskogo jazyka*. SPb.: M. O. Vol'f. 1880-82.

Ketchian, S., "Vehicles for Duality in Pushkin's *The Bronze Horseman*: Similes and Period Lexicon." *Semiotica* 25, 1/2, 1979.

————, "Poetic Creation in Bella Axmadulina." *Slavic and East European Journal*, 28, 1, 1984.

Pasternak, B., *Stixotvorenija i poèmy*. Biblioteka poèta, Bol'šaja serija. M.: Sov. pisatel', 1965.

Segal, L., *New Complete Russian-English Dictionary*. 3rd ed., rev. and enl. London: Lund Humphries. 1946.

Slovar' sovremennogo russkogo jazyka v semnadcati tomax. M.: AN SSSR. 1950-65.

Smirnickij, A. I., *Russko-anglijskij slovar'*. 10th ed. M.: Russkaja mysl'. 1975.

Terras, V., *Handbook of Russian Literature*. New Haven: Yale U. Press. 1985.

Ušakov, D. N., ed., *Tolkovyj slovar' russkogo jazyka*. M.: Sov. Ènciklopedija. 1934-40.

ON THE PHONETIC STRUCTURE OF ALEXANDER BLOK'S "PETER"

George N. Kostich

1.	Он спит, пока закат румян.
2.	И сонно розовеют латы.
3.	И с тихим свистом сквозь туман
4.	Глядится Змей копытом сжатый.
	—
5.	Сойдут глухие вечеры,
6.	Змей расклубится над домами.
7.	В руке протянутой Петра
8.	Запляшет факельное пламя.
	—
9.	Зажгутся нити фонарей,
10.	Блеснут витрины и тротуары.
11.	В мерцаньи тусклых площадей
12.	Потянутся рядами пары.
	—
13.	Плащами всех укроет мгла,
14.	Потонет взгляд в манящем взгляде.
15.	Пускай невинность из угла
16.	Протяжно молит о пощаде!
	—
17.	Там на скале, весёлый царь
18.	Взмахнул зловонное кадило,
19.	И ризой городская гарь
20.	Фонарь манящий облачила!
	—
21.	Бегите все на лов! На зов!
22.	На перекрёстки улиц лунных!
23.	Весь город полон голосов
24.	Мужских — крикливых, женских — струнных!
	—
25.	Он будет город свой беречь,
26.	И, заалев перед денницей,
27.	В руке простёртой вспыхнет мечь
28.	Над затихающей столицей.[1]
	—

(He sleeps while the sunset is red and his armor is slowly turning pink. With a quiet hiss through the fog the Dragon, nailed down by a hoof, threateningly raises his head.

Night falls and the Dragon will spread his wings above the houses. In Peter's extended hand the torch flame will begin its dance.

Бѣлы Ночи 1907 5

П. Петербургская поэма.

посвящается Е. П. ИВАНОВУ

Той твою блюсти будетъ главу,
и ты блюсти будеши его пяту.
БЫТІА. Г. Еі.

1. Петръ

Городъ _____

Онъ спитъ,
___, пока закатъ румянъ,
И сонъ _____ розовымъ.
_____ Петра _____ латы.

____ _____ вечернюю ____
и съ тихимъ свистомъ сквозь туманъ
_____ _____ _____
Глядецъ Змѣй, коптитъ _____ семьи.

_____ Сойдутъ глухіе вечера,
Но _____ _____ и до утра
_____ Змѣй, _____ надъ _____
Въ рукахъ простянутой Петра
Запляшетъ _____ пламя.

                   чугуннаго
Проснусь и я въ _____ (царя
_____ проклятые завиты.
_____

Rows of lanterns will light, shop windows and sidewalks will begin to glitter. In the glimmer of dimly lit squares lovers will begin their promenade.

The fog will cover them all and a timid glance will sink in the alluring gaze. Let innocence hiding in the corner pray for mercy!

There, on the cliff, the cheerful Tsar raised his fetid censer, and the city soot, like a frock, dressed the luring lantern.

Gather you all to the catch! Obey the call! Come to the moonlit crossroads! The whole city is full of voices: men's — clamorous, and ladies' — harmonious!

He will protect his city. Having started glowing in the early dawn the sword will shine in the extended hand above the calming city.)

This poem of Blok was written on February 22, 1904, and was first published together with the poem "Single Combat" (Poedinok) under the common title "A Petersburg Poem." The work was dedicated to E. P. Ivanov and bore this epigraph:[2]

Той твою блюсти будет главу,	He shall keep an eye on thy head,
и ты блюсти будеши его пяту.	And thou shalt keep an eye on his heel.

The title of the manuscript was "The City Speaks," and, instead of the first two stanzas of the final text here, it contained these three stanzas:

1.   Я сплю пока закат румян,
2.   Пока Петра алеют латы,
3.   Пока я сном вечерним пьян,
4.   Ночной потехою чреватый.
   —
5.   Но конь шагнёт — и до утра
6.   Свободен змей играть над нами:
7.   В руке протянутой Петра
8.   Запляшет факельное пламя.
   —
9.   Проснусь и я. В глазах царя
10.   Прочту проклятые заветы.
11.   Ты, Петербургская заря!
12.   Буди в иных сердцах ответы![3]

(I sleep while the sunset is red and Peter's armor is getting pink, while I am still under the spell of evening nap and fraught with the merriment of night.

But the horse will step forward and the Dragon will be free to play with us until the early morning. In Peter's extended hand the torch will begin its dance.

I will also wake up. I will read out in Peter's eyes his damned behests. You, the Petersburg's sunset! Wake the answers from some other hearts!)

In the manuscript the poem ended in this couplet:

27.   Как встарь, заставит смолкнуть речь
28.   Рукой, простёртой над столицей.[4]

(As in the old times, he will force the argument to die with his hand
extended over the capital.)

Blok himself said that "Peter" was inspired by the famous Falconet
monument to Peter I. The poet did not value the poem highly, considering
it to be "artificial and naive."[5]

This poem is closely related to E. P. Ivanov's article "The Horseman"
(*Vsadnik*) in which the author gives a gloomy apocalyptic vision of the city,
an anxiety-ridden Petersburg, nearing a mysterious cataclysm.[6] Blok spoke
of Ivanov's article and of his conversations with Ivanov, acknowledging
that they influenced him to write this poem.[7] His "Petersburg poem" was
even published together with Ivanov's article in the almanac "White
Nights."

The "Petersburg Poem" or, to be more precise, "Peter" since I am analyz-
ing it alone, is close to Puškin's *The Bronze Horseman*, though all of Blok's
symbolism here is diametrially opposed to Puškin's.

The most interesting and the most basic artistic device in this poem,
which is in iambic tetrameter with masculine and feminine cross rhyme, is
undoubtedly the consonant instrumentation. In the very title "Peter" itself,
the reader receives a definite auditory signal in the combination of the
sonorant R and the occlusives P and T. This signal, given in the title, continues to reverberate following the theme to the very end of the poem.

The consonants P, T, and R are distributed in the poem as our chart
shows:

	1	PT - P - T - R		5	T - R
I	2	PT - T	II	6	T′
	3	T′ - T - T		7	R - PRT′T - P′TR
	4	T′ - PT - T		8	PT - P
		- - - - - -			- - - - - -
	9	T′ - T′ - R′		13	P - RT
III	10	T - TR′ - TRTR	IV	14	PTT - T
	11	R - T - P		15	P - T′
	12	PT′T′ - R′ - PR		16	PRT′ - T - P
		- - - - - -			- - - - - -

	17	T - R′		21	T′
V	18	----	VI	22	P′R′R′T
	19	R′ - RT - R′		23	RT - P
	20	R′		24	R′ - TR

‒ ‒ ‒ ‒ ‒ ‒ ‒   ‒ ‒ ‒ ‒ ‒ ‒ ‒

	25	T - RT - R′
VII	26	P′R′
	27	R - PRT′RT - PT
	28	T - T′ - T

‒ ‒ ‒ ‒ ‒ ‒ ‒

As our chart indicates, all but one of 28 lines contain at least one combination of the consonants P, T, and R. It is interesting to note that the fourth, the central stanza of the poem, contains alliteration and that every line begins with the consonant P. It is interesting also to trace the distribution of P, T, and R in the first three stanzas of the manuscript. It is as if Blok pursued his aim to encipher Peter's name in the poem there even more consistently.

In the three stanzas of the first manuscript, the distribution of P, T, and R is the following:

	1	P - P - T - R		5	T - TR
I	2	P - P′TR - T - T	II	6	RT′ - T
	3	P - R - P′		7	R PRT′T - P′TR
	4	PT′ - R′T		8	PT - P

‒ ‒ ‒ ‒ ‒ ‒ ‒   ‒ ‒ ‒ ‒ ‒ ‒ ‒

	9	PR - R′
III	10	PRT - PRT - T
	11	T - P′T′RR - R′
	12	R - TT

‒ ‒ ‒ ‒ ‒ ‒ ‒

In the final couplet of the manuscript P, T, and R occur in this order:

27	TR′ - TT - T′ - R′
28	R - PRT′T - T - T

The distribution of stressed vowels is likewise very striking. Of 92 stressed vowels in the text, one can tabulate the following:

A - 34, O - 16, I - 15, E - 14, U - 10, Y - 2

There are 27 diffuse I, U, and Y, narrow phonemes, under stress. Most of these are in the sixth stanza and this conveys a sense of alarm and disorder. The smallest number of stressed diffuse phonemes is found in the central fourth stanza, just one I.

The phoneme A occurs in the poem 34 times. Out of these it is repeated 9 times in the fourth stanza, 18 in the first three original stanzas, and only 6 times in the final three stanzas.

The phoneme A, representing "the pole of compactness and related to volume and weightiness," is used mostly in the fourth stanza, the central one.[8] In it A occurs 9 times and with almost total absence of bright high tone vowels (there is only one I) the stanza ring with tragic premonitions for the future.

The phoneme A is distributed in the several stanzas thus:

1	stanza 6A			5	stanza 6A
2	stanza 7A	4	stanza 9A	6	stanza --
3	stanza 5A			7	stanza 1A

Synesthetically, this distribution of the compact phoneme A corresponds fully with the text of the poem. To provide a better idea of the distribution of the vowel A across stanzas, and to emphasize its synesthetic role, I have tabulated this chart:

I.	I A A A	II.	U I - A	III.	U I - E	IV.	A E O A
	O - E A		E I - A		U I - A		O A A A
	I I O A		E A - A		A U - E		A I - A
	I E Y A		A A - A		A - A A		A O - A

V.	A E O A	VI.	I E O O	VII.	U O O E
	U O - I		- O U U		- E - I
	I - A A		O O - O		E O Y E
	A A - I		I I E U		- A - I

The first two verses contain 4 A's and sound solemn and triumphant.

1.   Он спит, покА закАт румЯн
2.   И сонно розовеют лАты.

The impression of solemnity is emphasized by 4 rhymes on A in a row. In the second couplet of the second stanza there are 5 A's and this sound conveys Peter's symbolic power and might.

7.   В руке протЯнутой ПетрА
8.   ЗаплЯшет фАкельное плАмя.

As in the preceding stanza, there are 4 rhymes on A in a row, and this solemn sound gives the necessary coloration to the symbolism of the second couplet. The sonorous, trilled R undoubtedly strengthens this impression.

I have already treated the fourth stanza, but it is worthwhile to emphasize the all-encompassing impression and sense of completeness conveyed in the first couplet.

> 13. ПлащАми всех укроет мглА
>
> 14. Потонет взглЯд в манЯщем взглЯде.

and the tragic quality of the last two lines:

> 15. ПускАй невинность из углА
>
> 16. ПротЯжно молит о пощАде!

The verses of the fifth stanza exude power and inexorability.

> 19. И ризой городскАя гАрь
>
> 20. ФонАрь манЯщий облачила!

The phonemes, mutually opposed in high and low tonality, are distributed in the following order. The high tonality, bright E and I, dominate in the first three stanzas: 14 bright versus 6 dark, while in the last three stanzas the low tonality, dark O and U, exceed the number of high tonality vowels: 15 bright versus 16 dark.

The dominance of the high tonality vowels in the first three stanzas is achieved by four I's, and the absence of U in the first stanza, and the absence of O in the second and third. The excessive number of low tonality vowels in the last three stanzas is achieved by the sharp increase of this type of vowel in the sixth and seventh stanzas: 6 - O, 3 - U, 3 - O, 1 - U. The maximal accumulation of E and I, which is 6 high tonality vowels, is found in the first stanza and the last.

The accumulation of low tonality vowels in the sixth stanza is undoubtedly associated with the frightening, pale moonlight. Thus the theme of alarm and the theme of nocturnal terror reverberates among themselves in the stanza and are phonetically completely justified: 6 alarming, diffuse ones, and 8 frightening, dark ones, the complete absence of the vowel A.

The action of Blok's poem begins with ". . . the sunset is red," and ends with "started glowing in the early dawn." This light frames the poem at both ends, enclosing it in a ring.

The daylight in the first and the last stanzas appears with a maximal accumulation of bright vowels: 4 I's and 2 E's in the first stanza, and 2 I's and 4 E's in the final one. Moreover, it is interesting that the first and last stressed vowels of the poem are one and the same: bright I. And it is further interesting that both of them are accompanied by the compact A!

This combination of vowel groupings, E - A, A - I, is a phonetic linking of the beginning and the end of the poem. It makes a closed chainlink emphasizing the infinity of time, the uninterrupted struggle of light and darkness, of tranquility and alarm, of order and chaos.

To this must be added that the first and last stanzas begin with the pronoun "he" in reference to Peter. "He" explains the symbolism of the poem and of the ringshape thereof. Everything becomes much clearer: Petersburg and Peter's project are eternal, indestructible creations, and no changes or alarms can break the chain of their existence.

In these stanzas there are only two tenses—the present and the future. In the fifth stanza the past tense is used, but only as a narrative device. The same is true of the imperatives which occur in the fourth and sixth stanzas. The present tense in the first stanza is connected with the poet's anxiety caused by the alarming present: "He sleeps while the sunset is red." The future tense of the final stanza: "He will guard his city" and "The sword will flame in his outstretched hand," conveys faith in the consolidation of the present in a peaceful and bright future.

The entire poem is filled with the prophetic motif of imminent change. Blok foresaw the alarming events of 1905 and was aware of the unavoidability of the approaching tumult. He expressed his premonitions by confronting two irreconcilable principles: Peter, the symbol of will, force, might, and order is portrayed in the solemn compact A and energetic trilling sonorant R, and the Dragon, the symbol and incarnation of evil is portrayed in the alliteration of the sibilant S, suggestive of the rustling sound and hissing of a snake.

The last lines of "Peter" express unshaking faith in the victory of the legacy of the past, the symbol of which was and is "He," the last lines ring with optimism and confidence in the future:

> He will guard his city,
> And, having started glowing in the early dawn,
> The sword will flame in his outstretched hand
> above the calming-down city.

College of the Holy Cross

NOTES

[1]Aleksandr Blok, *Sobrannye stixi*, II. Gos. izd. xud. literatury. Moskva-Leningrad, 1960, 141-43.

[2]The epigraph (as shown in the photographic reproduction of Blok's draft), cites Genesis 3:15, using Old Church Slavonic letter symbols for the chapter and verse numbers. The verb *bljusti* 'watch, keep an eye on' in this citation is absent from the Synodal version of the Russian Bible, where the verb *poražat'* corresponds to the English *bruise* in the Revised Standard Version.

[3]See reference in note 1, 414-15.

[4]*Ibid.*

[5]*Ibid.*

[6]E. P. Ivanov, "Vsadnik (Nečto o gorode Peterburge)," *Belye noči*. Peterburg, 1907.

[7]*Pis'ma Al. Bloka k E. P. Ivanovu.* Moskva-Leningrad, 1936.

[8]R. O. Jakobson, "Stixi Maxi o zove gorlicy," *International Journal of Slavic Linguistics and Poetics*, 3, 1960.

A CONTRIBUTION TO ÉMIGRÉ LITERATURE: THE LIFE AND WORK OF GERTRUDE CLAFTON VAKAR

Nicholas Lee

Gertrude Clafton was born September 16, 1904 in Revel, now Tallinn, Estonia, and grew up in Arxangel'sk, where her paternal great-great grandfather had set up a rope factory in 1799.[1] Her father was descended from eighteenth-century English settlers who had retained their British citizenship. Her mother, Avgusta Mixajlovna Kaunisaari, of Finnish and German origin, had grown up in Estonia. Gertrude, and her four younger sisters (a brother died in infancy) were taught by foreign governesses in the sort of cultivated multilingual milieu that nurtured Vladimir Nabokov. Her native language was Russian, but her poems also contain occasional sprinklings of English, French, and German, in which she kept a lifelong fluency.

When the British government offered to evacuate its subjects from Russia after the signing of the Brest-Litovsk treaty in March, 1918, the Claftons left Arxangel'sk and moved to England, while Gertrude, after a year at a Swedish school, went to Paris on a scholarhsip to the Russian Lycée, where she graduated with highest honors in 1923. She continued her education in London, where she also worked for a time as secretary-translator in London's Savoy Hotel, then in 1926 moved back to Paris as the wife of former cavalry officer Nikolaj Platonovič Vakar. He wrote for the Paris Russian émigré daily *Poslednie novosti*, while she concerned herself with bringing up their two daughters. As the wife of an employed alien she had no right to earn money, but in the course of the 1930s she did anonymous Russian translations of 37 English and two French novels for *Poslednie novosti*.

When France was invaded, *Poslednie novosti* closed, and the Vakars eventually found their way to southern France, where their daughters had been evacuated from a summer camp. Nikolaj Platonovič had no steady income, and Gertruda Pavlovna worked as a seamstress in an underground atelier. In December 1940, the girls were sent to the United States under the auspices of the Unitarian Service Committee. The family was reunited in America in July 1941, and in his fifties Nikolaj Platonovič resumed his studies in preparation for a third career as an academician. His wife helped him with his English while he was working on his doctorate from Harvard University, and when he became a professor she assisted with his research, published in books on Byelorussia, Russian language, and Russian civiliza-tion. At this time she was still raising her family and running a *pension* that catered to Americans studying Russian.

By the beginning of the 1960s the Vakars were able to divide their time between a winter home in Florida and the various Northeastern locations where Nikolaj Platonovič pursued his academic career. Gertrude Vakar gradually acquired the reputation of the leading American translator of Russian texts in the areas of history, psychology, and sociology.[2] The drafts of her first poems date from the late 1950s, the first was published in the New York Russian language daily *Novoe russkoe slovo* on December 18, 1966, and 25 appeared on its pages, the last two a little more than three months before her death on December 3, 1973.

Friedrich remembers Vakar as an avid reader, vivacious, unassuming, with a slightly ironic sense of humor. These personal qualities color her poetry, virtually all of which has been included in the 45 *Stixotvorenija* compiled by her daughter, Catherine V. Chvany, and Sophia Lubensky. This volume begins with 25 original poems, all but one of them previously published. They are followed by Russian renditions of 16 English and four French originals, all but one from each language never before published. Each section contains thematic subdivisions that reveal a different aspect of Vakar's poetic personality.

Six poems comprise the first section, "The Poet Carries on a Game with Language, Language Plays with the Poet." Catherine V. Chvany, the pri-mary compiler of *Stixotvorenija*, has written in unpublished annotations that the very first piece, "Echo" ("*È xo*," p. 1) "is, I believe, the most important poem. It was G.V.'s favorite, the one she felt was her best and most origi-nal." The interaction between the exhausted male persona and a woman driving to a mother's funeral sets off a complex train of auditory and semantic associations, some musical, some magical, some ironical, some nonsensical. The man's somnolent stream of consciousness mixes the poetic devices of refrains to French children's songs (the poem contains two French female names), echoes of Russian trans-sense poetry, and the Chekhov story "Sleepy," as he contemplates desperate means of attaining "Nirvana. Zero." The nine *aBaB* quatrains of iambic pentameter, broken by a single hexameter in line 3, stanza 2, with feminine slant rhymes, have a disquieting density and allusive ambiguity unique in Vakar's poetic canon.

"Days of Our Life" ("*Dni našej žizni*," p. 2) takes a male persona out of his bed in the morning and back into it at night, in one stanza of eight lines and one of four, containing twelve symmetrically arranged iambic tetrame-ters in couplets with masculine rhyme in all but lines 5 and 6. Made up

almost entirely of nouns, it illustrates Vakar's oblique, understated evocation of emotion. Each item specifies a material or psychological parameter
of everyday life that is neutral in itself, evoking an emotional reaction by
arranging data rather than interpreting them.

"A Trivial Incident (A Retelling in Synonymns)" ("*Melkoe proisšestvie
[Pereskaz v sinonimax]*," p. 2) likewise has virtually nothing but nouns in its
14 iambic trimeters, divided into stanzas of two, three, four, and five lines,
with feminine slant rhymes in couplets one, two, five and seven, masculine
rhyme in the others.[3] The concrete nouns of the preceding poem—"Alarm
clock. Slippers. Soap. Razor."—turn into abstractions here—"A secret, a
puzzle, a mystery." The only denotative nouns in the piece, "revolver" and
"knife," merely enhance the melodramatic atmosphere. The ironic final line
again demonstrates Vakar's reserve in alluding to emotion: here the dénouement of a tragic drama is "(a notice in the paper)."

The next few poems could have been written to give Vakar's fictional
Russian-speaking grandchildren their private Russian versions of Lewis
Carroll and Edward Lear. "Russian Spoken Here," ("*Zdes' govorjat po-
russki*," p. 3) spins a preposterous tale of watermelon-bearing palms, sul-
tan, ostrich, and crocodile, assigning incorrect grammatical gender to all
declined parts of speech and throwing in "I guess," in English, at the end.
Iambic pentameters are arranged in five *aBaB* quatrains with an *aa* couplet
between the penultimate and final stanzas.

"Terminology. Chapter I" ("*Terminologija. Glava I*," p. 4) turns the verbal virtuosity of "Echo" to a children's theme. Here the lexical and morphological richness of Russian produces puns based on pseudo-logical
phonetic and morphological analogies: the feminine form of "lion" (*lev*),
plus the suffix that feminizes the masculine word for "secretary," produces
the word "*levša*" (southpaw, lefty). The verses narrate another nonsense
melodrama with the addition of a spuriously scientific postscript featuring
the poet's name to complete the rhyme of the final couplet. The poem is
divided into stanzas of six, thirteen, and four lines. It reveals several characteristics of Vakar's poetry: free alternations of couplets and crossed
rhymes, masculine and feminine rhyme, and stanzas with uneven numbers
of lines because a rhyme has been used thrice instead of twice. Typical also
is the basic poetic foot—iambic—and the free alternation between different
line lengths, here trimeters in lines 11, 13, 15, and 17; pentameters in lines
1, 2, 7, and 20; tetrameters in the others. Vakar expressed a horror of poetic
monotony (p. 40), and avoided it by cultivating slant rhymes, varying
lengths of lines and stanzas, and randomly distributing rhyme patterns.
Rhymes occur frequently in lines of different lengths, less often across
stanzas.

In the eight lines of "With Birdlike Gait" ("*Ptič'ej poxodkoj*," p. 5, without a couplet she deleted after newspaper publication) Vakar tries what she calls "an experiment in irregular anapest" (p. 39), to imitate the endearingly comical hopping of birds she sees in dreams. All the couplets have feminine rhyme, and the fourth, in trochaic pentameter, breaks the otherwise regular accentual pattern of the poem. Another quirk of Vakar's metrics makes its first appearance here: a word with an unstressed penultimate /i/ (more rarely /e/) is treated as if the vowel were a consonantal /j/, thus shortening the word by a syllable to fit it into a metrical pattern. Russian allows for this variation, but indicates it orthographically by replacing the vowel with a soft sign, a convention Vakar usually ignores. The word here is *šestvie*, but elsewhere she does the same thing with words like *liniej, teoriju,* and *reputaciju.*

The last two poems in this section yield some basic insights into Vakar's views on life and art. "Foretokens" (*Predvestija*," p. 5) starts out as close to a conventional lyric poem as she ever wrote, finding in an autumn garden "fall's betrayal of spring." It has three quatrains of *AbAb* iambic tetrameters, the last lengthened by a penultimate line that repeats the *A* rhyme. A landscape most often associated with symbolist Russian poetry is here put into a classical framework by an allusion to an oracle as the mediator of whatever meaning the garden's foretokens may have.

This semi-symbolist, semi-classical, semi-metaphysical poem is followed by an exquisitely wrought sonnet in iambic pentameter, with lines 5 and 6, 11 and 13 hexameters, and line 10 a tetrameter. "About the Preceding Verses" ("*O predyduščix stixax*," p. 6) explains that they have lain "out of favor" (*v opale*) a decade "for their insincerity." She rejects the conventional poetic association of autumn with fading and decay: for her it is "fruits and harvest, the fulfillment of all spring's expectations." Yet the phrase "fall's betrayal of spring" militantly pursues its right to existence, so she finally yields it a place: "Let it sing and prevaricate, a witness of verbal imprisonment" ("*slovesnogo svidetel'nica plena*").

The next section, "Literary Reminiscences, Humorous Verses," begins with a "A True Anglo-Russian Story" ("*Anglo-russkaja byl'*," pp. 6-8). At 90 lines this is one of the two longest poems in Vakar's collected works. It is also the most venturesome. Its 10 stanzas vary in length from two to 24 lines. The first three lines break down into hemistichs with hypercatalectic caesura in the second. The poem has a pararhyme, a trailing slant rhyme, a couple of assonances, trailing rhymes, and unrhymed lines. It is one of the two poems Vakar provides with an epigraph, the first quatrain of Puškin's *Ruslan and Ljudmila.* The magical atmosphere of the fairytale poem colors

Vakar's memories, and in several verse anecdotes, some true, some fictional, she recounts the way some of its images shaped her childhood perceptions. The narrative framework is flexible and relaxed—an *aBaB* rhyme scheme with free alternation between iambic lines ranging in length from dimeters to hexameters, with pentameters and tetrameters predominating. The narrator of events "half a century ago" has much in common with the grandmother who wrote the nonsense verses in the preceding section. Here she recreates the "marvelous world" made "out of cards and songs" revealed when the Clafton children snuck off to the servants' quarters, and offers a glimpse of the way words stimulated her imagination even as a girl. The English elements of the story are generally cultural—the family is Protestant; and specifically philological—the word "pagan" conjures up all sorts of associations in the multilingual children's minds. The cat and the non-Orthodox name of the cook Drasida make the children decide she is a sorceress: her name suggests Druids to them, and the region she comes from, "*Pomor'je*" (the Baltic littoral) sounds like exotic words in Puškin's poem, "*lukomor'e*" and "*Černomor*," which the children associate with Russian "*mor*" (pestilence) and French "*mort*" (death). Drasida also introduces them to the folklore of fortunetelling with playing cards.

The persona of "Old Fashioned Novels" ("*Starinnye romany*," p. 9) also has a weakness for the exaggerations of fantasy. In two iambic tetrameter stanzas, of twenty-two and six lines, rhymes follow an *AbAb* pattern, but two non-contiguous A line pairs do not rhyme, a masculine line is rhymed three times, and enjambement occurs eight times. The first stanza catalogues the conventions of the Gothic novel as calmly, and almost as tersely, as the melodrama of "A Trivial Incident." The second stanza rhetorically laments the decline in the popularity of such fictions.

The apologist for "A Victim of Injustice" ("*Žertva nespravedlivosti*," p. 10) takes her inspiration from the marvelous world of cards and songs in "A True English-Russian Story." Drawing on Puškin and on folk superstition, she addresses unnamed friends in defense of the maligned Queen of Spades against her spoiled sister the Queen of Hearts. In a single stanza of 30 lines, anapestic dimeters and trimeters alternate freely, and rhymed feminine couplets (lines 5 and 6, and the last 16, including a dactylic pair) predominate in a flexible *abab* or *AbAb* rhyme scheme. The diction here is cosily colloquial.

A rhetorical dialogue between a conventional ancient Greek tragic hero and a chorus provides the framework for "On Stage" ("*Na scene*," pp. 10-12). In two *AbAb* stanzas, one of 12 lines, one of 16, iambic trimeter dominates; line 20 is a dimeter, lines 23 and 24 pentameters. The hero fills these lines with a diatribe about how corrupt and unstable (*"poročno i nepročno"*) everything is "around and within." The choir answers this argument in two stanzas, one of eight lines, one of twelve, in straight iambic tetrameters and *AAbb* couplets, except for an extra masculine rhymed couplet in lines 15-16. Not only does the choir reject the tragic hero's accusations, it levels its own indictment against him: "he himself calls down misfortune, talking such nonsense." The verdict is guilty, the sentence an invitation to join in cleaning out the Augean stables: "Let us talk with our unfortunate brother, and he will be able to become a soldier in the Herculean battle, with a prayer and a broom (*s molitvoj i metloj*)." Here Vakar comes as close as anywhere to an open statement of what could be called the philosophy of her serious poems, a combination of positive thinking, faith, and work.

The "Young Woman" (*"Molodaja ženščina,"* p. 12) who gives the next poem its title acts as its persona. In four quatrains of anapestic trimeters, barring one pentameter in line 1 and a tetrameter in line 3, she expresses her exasperation at the "old-fashioned love" of a man who persistently plays her cloying love songs on a silver flute. In the last line Vakar slows the tempo by omitting an unstressed syllable, here in the second anapest, the first instance of a device repeated elsewhere. This poem contains only the sketchiest allusions to character and situation, highlighting instead a narcotically, hypnotically sultry atmosphere that makes lilac and mimosa droop.

This section closes with another glimpse into an imagination nurtured on classical literature. The title, "Wanderings," (*"Bluždanija,"* p. 13), is actually the beginning of the run-on sentence fragment that takes the poem through its first six rhymed couplets of iambic pentameter (excepting the alexandrine of line 6) until the transition of the single disyllable of line thirteen. The next iambic tetrameter couplet is split by an unrhymed iambic pentameter, and the poem closes with an alexandrine couplet repeating the rhyme scheme of lines 9 and 10. Couplets freely alternate between masculine and feminine rhyme. The Russian and foreign landscapes Vakar roams in these lines have all been discovered by other poets—Gumilev, A. K. Tolstoj, Griboedov, and Goethe, who is quoted in German. She keeps her customary benevolent irony as she observes the way "imagination wanders insouciantly from end to end around the countries of poetry, the landscapes of memory, misty refuges."

Vakar begins to give her readers a glimpse into her personal life in the section of "Humorous Verses about Approaching Old Age." "In Front of the Mirror" (*"Pered zerkalom,"* p. 14) has three quatrains of trochaic parameters with the same rhyme on all the stressed even-numbered truncated lines. It gives a wry picture of the way "grandmother" beautifies herself to hide what the years have done to her hair, various parts of her face, and her hands. Vakar is at her most briskly self-confident when she directs her irony towards herself, and she gleefully exposes her own foibles in this piece.

She grows somewhat more tentative and tender in another conventional dialogue, this one unspoken, between a husband and wife married nearly fifty years, in "Old People's Thoughts" ("*Mysli starikov*," pp. 14-15): first his (22 lines), then hers (23 lines), finally theirs (6 lines). In his thoughts iambic tetrameters and trimeters alternate, in a rhyme scheme that starts *ABABAB*, goes to *CC*, then continues to the end in an *AbAb* pattern. His reflections, as he gazes on "my madonna," "my swallow," "poor thing," are full of wistful tenderness, and though he realizes that the woman once universally admired for her piquancy ("*s izjuminkoj*") is now as wrinkled as a raisin ("*kak smorščennyj izjum*"). Her thoughts are less linear than his: four *aBaB* iambic pentameters give way to alternating tetrameters and trimeters in the same rhyme scheme; one feminine rhyme is repeated over three lines, two of them enclosing a couplet with masculine rhymes. She worries about his diet and his health, notices the signs of his diminished physical powers, and appreciates his good points. Their thoughts, beginning with a couplet of masculine rhymed iambic pentameters, and ending with alternating *AbAb* tetrameters and trimeters, resolutely set aside any regrets about the past to concentrate on the joys of the present and their golden wedding aniversary celebration in the near future. The trap of sentimentality inherent in the subject has here been avoided by skillful individualization of character through contrasts in both subject matter and poetic meter, and a final blending of both voices to produce a unity recognizably distinguishable from each of its component parts.

The last poem in this section relates an anecdote told by a husband who, "From Nothing to Do" ("*Ot nečego delat'*," p. 16) looks out his office window at a mousey middle-aged woman entering a beauty shop, then marvels when he chances to see her emerge later totally transformed. After a couple of wry reflections on the deceptiveness of appearances, he decides to send his "little woman" ("*xozjajušku-ženu*") to this "temple of beauty and cosmetics for ladies." The male persona thinks mainly in couplets, 14 of a total 22 ending in masculine rhyme, as does a set of three succesive lines. More varied is the stanzaic and metrical pattern: stanzas of five, four, four, ten, two, two, and two lines, alternating freely betwen iambic tetrameter and hexameter. Some may deplore the male chauvinist attitudes of the persona, but his fantasies at least have a cultivated classical cast, for he compares the transformed mouse to Eve, Venus-Aphrodite, and Primavera.

The last sections of original poems, on "The Theme of Loss, Widow-hood, and Approaching Old Age," reveals a breadth, depth, and nobility of spirit that are muffled in the poems touched with humor. The compilers have here, as elsewhere, disregarded chronological order, perhaps in the interests of consistency, but in poems with a strong autobiographical com-ponent, chronological order would have more clearly revealed where, when, and how Vakar commiserated with others, anticipated her own wid-owhood, and reacted to it in her poetry after the fact. The first two poems belong to the last category. "Afterword" ("*Posleslovie*," p. 17) uses the met-aphor of an avalanche to describe the shock of her husband's death on July 18, 1970. An 8-line stanza follows an introductory quatrain, where trochaic pentameter alternates with hexameters to underline the dramatic impact of lines 2, 8, and 9. The poems consists entirely of couplets in an aB rhyme. This poem, like all the others in this section, is more severe and archaic in several aspects than the humorous pieces. Rhyme is usually true, masculine rhyme more obtrusive, rhetorical repetitions more prominent, diction more solemn and conventional. Vakar chastises herself for being frivolous enough to write poetry when catastrophe was approaching: while the family were laughing at "verses" ("*stiškami*") of the poet-grandmother, the snow on the mountain was picking up mass and speed, nobody suspecting that "the flimsy ceiling wouldn't hold." In the "special, last year" of her husband's life, "I was writing a lot of rubbish," a possible allusion to "Old People's Thoughts," with its anticipation of a golden anniversary celebration: "After-word" ends, "there wouldn't be a golden wedding, there would be a disaster at the foot of the mountain."

"Winter" ("*Zima*," p 17) catches Vakar alone in Florida for the first time after her husband's death. Iambs varying in length from dimeter to hex-ameter are distributed in stanzas of six, four, and ten lines, the first with $AbAbAA$ rhyme, the next with $cdcd$, the last with $EEAAAAbbEE$. The A and b rhymes in the last stanza mirror in content as well as form those in the first, as the widow observing the lovely, familiar Southern scene wonders whether her husband in the Northern grave remembers it, then decides, "No, he remembers nothing." This stanza is pentameter, the quatrain devoted to her husband has three trimeters and a final dimeter, other lines have five and six iambs.

The next two poems, written two years earlier, can be considered either premonitions or simply reactions to advancing age. "It's All the Same" (*Vse ravno*," p. 18) expresses a general sensation of the mad rush of life from the inalterable to the unknowable. Iambic tetrameters are arranged in stanzas of three, five, and two lines, with a rhyme scheme of $AAA\ BBBCC\ BB$. The past is summarized in four vigorous verbs: what has been cannot be returned, changed, erased, or forgotten (*"ne verneš',/Ne peremeneš', ne sotreš'./ I ne zabudeš'"*). Then it is stoically shrugged off: "Well, what of it?" (*"Nu, tak čto ž?"*). Everything in the present is passing, fleeting—calendar sheets, diary pages, tree leaves, clouds, the sounds of music and verse. Vakar noted that these lines were to be declaimed "crescendo, constantly accelerating the tempo (p. 39)," until the moaning transitional line that ends the long stanza and leads into the elegiac final couplet, where the diction changes from colloquial and contemporary to solemn and archaic.

Vakar vicariously shares widowhood yet to be experienced in "In the Cathedral" (*"V sobore,"* p. 18). It is all traditional solemnity, three *aBaB* quatrains of anapestic trimeter, the tempo slowed still more by the omission of a syllable in the second anapest of line 6, the first of line 10, and the second and third of line 12. The poem is a kind of synthetic tribute to the widows of Martin Luther King, John and Robert Kennedy, the last of whom was still alive when it was written (p. 40). Synthetic also is the inclusion, as the last line, of a key phrase from the Russian Orthodox burial service, deliberately truncated in the interests of metrical variety. It vividly recreates visual images like white columns and the faces of the widows "behind the mist of a veil."

"The Widower" (*Vdovec,"* p. 19) was written for a friend (Boston University Professor Hugh Webster Babb) after the death of his wife. Stanza 1 has six iambic pentameters, barring a hexameter in line 1; stanza 2 has trimeters in lines 2 and 3, pentameters elsewhere; rhyme scheme is *aBCCaB dCdCC.* The theme of victory over the departed's death in the memory of the surviving partner takes its inspiration from the epigraph, a line from Nadson: "though the rose has been plucked, it continues to bloom." The poetic persona is the widower, who fuses waking, dream, and recollection to immortalize all he has loved in his wife Persis, to whose beautiful brown eyes Vakar happily applies the adjective "Persian" (*persidskie"*).

Compassion rather than condolence informs the verses "To Agnes the Catholic" (*"Agnesse-Katoličke,"* p. 19), apparently a victim of the prohibition of divorce in her church. Inventive rhythms and rhymes eliminate sentimentality in a poem with a highly charged emotional theme. To the ten anapestic lines of the published variant the compilers have restored three others Vakar omitted from the published original, a slightly altered reprise of the opening couplet and a repetition of the first word in the poem. Lines 3, 8, and 13 consist of a single anapest plus an extrametrical unstressed syllable; lines 2, 5, and 10 have three anapests, the other four. Between the framing *AA* couplets the rhyme scheme is *bAbCCdCd.* In this poem about negative consequences of "thou shall nots" grammatical expressions of negation figure prominently: as the prefix in the adjectives "indissoluble" ("*nerazryvnyj*") and "unremitting" ("*nepreryvnyj*"), in particles, and in impersonal expressions—"It is impossible" ("*Nevozmožno*") occurs three times.

Vakar's customary self-deprecation loses its wry reticence and assumes tragic overtones in "How uncomfortable . . ." ("*Kak neujutno . . .*," p. 20), her last published poem, written just over three months before her death. It is "prophetic," to quote the compilers (p. 40), only in a chronological sense. Although Vakar compares her brain, like every other part of her body, to part of a machine that is wearing out, this poem shows her at the peak of her powers. Iambic pentameters alternate freely in two stanzas, ten and five lines long. The rhyme scheme is among her most varied: *aaBBaCCddC EEffE*. Diction, tempo, and modulation of intonation are most masterfully combined in the last ten lines, where she makes the transition between the image of the "important screw in the head" turning as if "in emptiness . . . [and] in the past" to a haunting evocation of "a remote dawn, a forgotten time, a forgotten country, ever more distant motifs and pictures." In the final lines she likens herself to an old gramophone playing a cracked record, its needle stuck on the word "stu. . .," which is never completed ("*zastrja. . . zastrja. . . zastrja. . .*").

Separated by asterisks from the other pieces in this section is one that could have been grouped with other humorous verses but is perhaps placed here because of the simultaneous illumination it gives of Vakar as poet and wife. In stanzas four to six lines long, she describes ten "Pictures" by N. P. V." ("*Kartiny N.P.V.*," pp. 20-21), that is, by her husband, an amateur artist whose late style the compilers call "primitive-surrealist" (p. 41). She approaches this style verbally in stanzas that never display regular rhyme scheme, true rhyme, metrical consistency, or regular stanzaic pattern all at once, but all do have her usual concise visual clarity. Don Quixote, Patrice Lumumba, Edith Sitwell, pairs of cats, a daughter, a granddaughter, and the Little Humpbacked Horse appear against a variety of more or less fantastic backgrounds in this delightful verbal picture gallery.

Of the twenty poems in the "Translations and Imitations" section, only two were published during Vakar's lifetime, and they reveal nothing new about her artistic manner, so they will here be considered only from the viewpoint of their themes. Catherine V. Chvany has perceptively observed, in an unpublished annotation, that Vakar's "task seemed not so much to translate a particular poet, as to recreate a Russian poem inspired by the original." Those Russian poems were unmistakably Vakar's in form, and sometimes in content, but in theme they show a freewheeling eclecticism that suggests many of them were written for experimental purposes, not with the primary intention of publication.

The section entitled "Americana, Russian Style" begins with her version of an anonymous poem in colloquial language called "Jus' doin' nothin'" (p. 22). Omitting the last two letters of the first word in the Russian title, "*Geroj truda*," yields Vakar's Russian Christian name, Gertruda. Slant rhyme, irregular meter, and lines of varying length only partially compensate for the more formal diction in Vakar's thirteen-line adaptation of this hymn to the joys of idleness. The fourteen-line free adaptation of Ben King's "The Pessimist" ("*Pessimist*," p. 22) restates in more relaxed terms the complaints of the tragic hero in "On Stage." "Good, but Not For Long," (*Xorošo, no ne dolgo*," pp. 23-25) recasts a prose piece entitled "Too Good To Last," by a pseudonymous Uncle Dudley who wrote for *The Boston Globe* newspaper. The world's oil supply runs out, and people rediscover the joys of a world without cars until an atomic-powered engine is invented, in this second of Vakar's longest poems, 90 lines of iambic verse to delight children.

The next section contains three stylizations "In the Literary Manner of Earlier Eras." In the six quatrains of "Before Romanticism" ("*Do romantizma*," p. 25), based on an anonymous untitled 16th-century poem, "O Night, O jealous Night, repugnant to my measures!," a male persona begs the night to hide the light of moon and stars until they can celebrate with him the abduction of his beloved, for which the cover of darkness is essential. The thirteen lines of "From the French" ("*S francuzskogo*," p. 26) translate motifs from an Easter hymn by a Bishop Asterius of Amasée. In two six-line stanzas of accentual verse Vakar translates the doggerel "When the Duke of Leeds shall have made his choice" ("*Kogda gercog Lids vyberet sebe ženu . . .*," p. 26), anonymous verses quoted in Boswell's *Life of Samuel Johnson.*

The section entitled "Free Translation of Charles Baudelaire" begins with his sonnet "*Recueillement*" (p. 27), in which Vakar adds an extra quatrain and curiously domesticates the haunting images of misery in the original. The Russian rendition of "*Viens sur mon cœur, âme cruelle et sourde*" ("*Idi v ob"jatija moi, duša gluxaja*," p. 27), much more successfully captures the evocation in the original two quatrains of love's pain and pleasure. Equally powerful is an extension of another sonnet, this time by two lines, entitled "La mort des amants" ("*Smert' ljubovnikov*," p. 28), where Vakar keeps the vivid original intensity of erotic apotheosis.

Five translated poems deal again with "The Theme of Loss and Widowhood." In two ten-line stanzas Vakar recreates the atmosphere and anguish

of Thomas Hardy's "The Phantom Horsewoman" (*"Prizrak vsadnicy,"* p. 28).
An untitled Mary Coleridge poem of two quatrains beginning "Some hang
above the tombs" (*"Vdova,"* p. 29) is adapted specifically to widowhood in
an otherwise very faithful rendition of the original. The compilers have
provided the apt title "Nostalgia for Scotland" to the three untitled quatrains of Robert Louis Stevenson beginning "Blows the wind today, and the
sun and the moon are flying" (p. 30), which have the same haunting quality
as the Hardy rendition. The thirteen-line fragment from Sidney Dobell's
"Return" (*"Obraščenie k umeršej,"* p. 30) focuses on a male persona who
likens himself to a candle that lives only in the night and is used up lighting
his beloved's way through the darkness. A solitary male in "Long are the
hours the sun is above" (*"Otbyv rabočij den' . . . ,"* p. 31) by Robert Bridges,
tells of his relationship with a purely imaginary woman in Vakar's twenty-
four-line adaptation.

"Translations and Imitations" of assorted American poets make up the
last section. Motifs from Phyllis McGinley's "Journey toward Evening"
(*"Večernij put',"* p. 32) are condensed to twenty-six lines, in a doleful
account of what it means to be a sexagenarian tourist. Vakar gives Russian
renditions of two English poetic miniatures by Babette Deutsch, herself a
prolific translator of Russian poetry into English. "Shapely as violins, the
pears" (*"Vin'etka,"* p.3 3) are sketched impressionistically in a Russian version that adds two lines to the five-line original, along with some extra
rhymes and variations of imagery. The three quatrains of Deutsch's "Dam-
nation" (*"Do ada,"* p. 33) are compressed into ten lines where ambiguous
allusions to self-generated torment become a sharper evocation of an autonomous realm of suffering. Seven lines of free verse by Robinson Jeffers,
beginning "I belive this hurt will be healed" are rhymed in the eleven-line
adaptation (*"Ja dumaju, čto jazva zaživet,"* p. 35) that speculates on the
earth's gradual recovery after civilization has destroyed all life on it. The
nineteen couplets of Stanley Kunitz' "Benediction" become eighteen lines of
hemistichs and a couplet in Vakar's untitled adaptation (*"Puskaj pod našej
kryšej ne budet muxi, myši,"* p. 34), a beautiful house blessing. Vakar maintains creative fidelity to the structure and images of John Updike's "B.W.I."
(*"Britanskaja kolonija,"* p. 35), a purely atmospheric piece of twenty-six
lines, which Vakar considered one of her best.

Viewed in strictly quantitative terms, Vakar belongs in the category of
minor poets, but from the standpoint of skill and integrity she yields to no
one. She remains in the memory and the imagination not only as a con-
summate crafter of words, but as an ultimately enigmatic personality. Perhaps her perfect control over her art is what gives the inescapable impression that there is more to her than meets the eye on the page of poetry. In

the last analysis she is always disinterested: never cold, simply detached, in her original poems from herself, in the others from any consideration beside *le mot juste*. Only the disproportionally large number of poems on the theme of bereavement gives a partial glimpse into her private inner world. Considering the countless words of other people she translated, it is amazing that she should have wanted to have anything to do with words in her spare time, yet poetry was an avocation, simultaneously play and a labor of love in a life filled with many kinds of labor. She obviously decided the game of poetry was worth her very best efforts. In her light verses it enabled her to detach joy from the drudgery of life, and in the more serious verses, meaning from life's tragedies. Her œuvre is an unassuming, but not insignificant monument to the delight and the power of the word.

University of Colorado, Boulder

NOTES

[1]For all information concerning Vakar's life I am indebted to the biographical sketch by Paul Friedrich on pp. 36-38 of Vakar's collected poems: Gertruda Vakar, *Stikhotvoreniia*, eds. Catherine V. Chvany and Sophia Lubensky (East Lansing, MI: *Russian Langauge Journal*, 1984). This volume is the source of all the poetry quoted here; page numbers for cited material will appear in the body of the text. The collection was also published in the archival section of the *RLJ*, Vol. 38 (1984), Nos. 129/130 (double issue), pp. 217-68.

[2]As a translator she is best known, perhaps, as the translator and editor, with Eugenia Hanfmann, of L. S. Vygotsky's *Thought and Language*, Cambridge: MIT Press, 1962. The last books she translated were Eugene N. Trubetskoi's *Icons: Theology in Color*, Crestwood, New York: St. Vladimir's Press, 1973; and *The Mensheviks*, ed. Leopold Haimson, Chicago: University of Chicago Press, 1974.

[3]Free alternation between true masculine and slant feminine rhyme is typical for most of Vakar's poetry, so it will be assumed except as noted.

MERMAIDS (*RUSALKI*) AND RUSSIAN BELIEFS ABOUT WOMEN

Natalie K. Moyle

The *rusalka*, or Russian mermaid, is a wonderful creature. She has served as the inspiration for the *pannočka*-witch in Gogol's "Vij," the lovely lady in white who sings so beautifully and nearly drowns Pečorin in Lermontov's *Hero of our Time*, and other characters of literature who are remembered by generation after generation. This is not to mention more direct reference to her in Puškin, in Lermontov's poetry, in Turgenev, Blok, and Cvetaeva, and in Gogol's "Majskaja noč'" and "Strašnaja mest'."

The *rusalka* has been pictured in the Russian broadside or *lubok*, on lacquered boxes, such as the famous Palex ware, and is a favorite subject for wood carving, such as decorations on window shutters and boards for carding and spinning wool. She appears in modern popular art as well, on candy wrappers, on wall hangings, and in tattoos.

In a culture which does not have native words for eroticism or for sexuality and where the popular belief is that any right-thinking man would be more interested in food and drink than in women, *rusalki* are portrayed as super-seductive women of fantasy whose image, according to Pomeranceva, has persisted from the earliest recordings of folklore, to the present day (68-69). As Pomeranceva points out, she probably significantly predates any recording we have because, even in 18th-century discussions, *rusalki* are presented as creatures of great antiquity (68).

Finally, *rusalki* are not only ancient and evocative of powerful emotions, they themselves are creatures of much greater stature than the nixies, sirens, nymphs and mermaids of the West. They are not pathetic creatures like the little mermaid in Hans Christian Andersen's story of the same name. The little mermaid has no soul and would have dissolved into seafoam had she not been rewarded for her love with a chance to earn a soul by suffering for three hundred years. In Russia, on the contrary, *rusalki* seem to be lost human souls and are thus much more than mere water sprites.

To describe *rusalki* briefly: they may have fish tails, like Western mermaids, but this trait is not obligatory. In fact, *rusalki* are often described as having lovely legs which they use for climbing into trees. In the various memorats about encounters with *rusalki*, the informants as often as not describe seeing these beings in the forest, swinging on tree branches, or in the field, singing and dancing in a circle (Zelenin 140-152, 169-170). While some sources say that *rusalki* are water beings who will perish if they, and especially their hair, ever dry out completely (Afanas'ev 128), other sources make no necessary connection between *rusalki* and water.

Rusalki have long hair which they love to comb. The hair may be green, but it may also be of a more human color, very often strawberry blond (*rusyj*). They almost invariably have large breasts which they either display in all their nakedness or barely conceal under clothes of white, a favorite color for *rusalki* (Pomeranceva 69, 72-75, Zelenin 152-162, Maksimov 116, Afanas'ev III, 126-128, 146). The large breasts appear in a number of sources but seem to be a particular favorite for Zelenin who refers to them again and again and even claims that, in some regions, *rusalki* are believed to have such pendulous breasts that they can toss them over their shoulders (153). The *rusalka*'s final notable physical feature is her voice. She sings beautifully and has a melodious laugh (Pomeranceva 72, Zelenin 168-169).

While they may occasionally be pictured as frightening, as in the description from the Smolensk region which talks about the fearsome glow of their eyes (Pomeranceva 72), *rusalki* are consistently presented as irresistably beautiful. Pomeranceva makes several rather interesting statements about the fascination that the *rusalka* holds for human kind, namely, that she embodies the attraction and horror of the other world and that her ugliness is not that of appearance, for she is gorgeous, but that of sin (81). Zelenin's discussion about the *rusalka*'s beauty is also interesting. The argument of his book is that *rusalki* are the feminine version of the unquiet dead. In his effort to demonstrate that people who die an unnatural death stay around on earth in the form of some kind of supernatural being to complete what would have been their allotted time, he states that *rusalki* can be old and ugly (5-6, 160). Using his breast motif, he gives accounts of old *rusalki* with huge teats of iron and, even more terrifying, ugly *rusalki* who tickle people to death not with their fingers, but with their breasts (180). As hard as he tries to argue for the possibility of old and ugly *rusalki*, however, the supernatural being Zelenin describes comes across as very attractive.

A *rusalka* is usually believed to live in or near a body of water such as a river, a stream, or a lake. Those sources that picture *rusalki* swinging on tree branches or dancing about fields often claim that *rusalki* retreat under the ice of bodies of water to spend the winter (Zelenin 144-145). Partly because the *rusalka* does reside in the out-of-doors, most folklorists class her with spirits such as the *lešij*, or forest spirit, the *vodjanoj*, or water spirit, and the remainder of the pantheon which I shall term "place-spirits."

Of course the *domovoj*, or house spirit, the *bannik*, or bath house spirit, and other supernatural beings of the farmstead belong here as well. The spirits of the farmstead, like the *domovoj*, and the spirits of the out-of-doors, like the *lešij*, are indeed similar beings and this fact does make the "outdoor" feature a somewhat questionable classificatory device.

The classification of the *rusalka* in the category of place-spirits can be found in most major sources. It is true of Pomeranceva for whom the *rusalka* is a "mythological character," along with the *lešij*, the *vodjanoj*, the *domovoj*, and, surprisingly, the devil. It is also true of Maksimov who considers her one of the "unclean forces" (*nečistaja sila, nevedomaja sila*) and of Afanas'ev's *Poètičeskija vozzrenija slavjan na prirodu* (The Slavs' Poetics Perception of Nature). No matter who is doing the description, however, there is always the feeling that the *rusalka* is somehow different from the other place-spirits and, perhaps, does not quite fit in the grouping. Pomeranceva, for example, repeatedly complains of the "fuzziness" of her image by comparison to that of creatures like the *vodjanoj, lešij,* or *domovoj.*

If we take a closer look at the *rusalka*, we can see that she is different indeed. For one thing, she is the only true female East Slavic spirit. All of the others, the *lešij*, or forest spirit, the *vodjanoj*, or water spirit, the *domovoj*, or house spirit, the *dvorovoj*, or barn spirit, the *bannik* or bath house spirit, the *ovinnik*, or drying barn spirit, are male. The various male spirits, the *lešij* and the *vodjanoj* in particular, may have wives, the *lešaja* or *lesačixa* and the *vodjanaja* or *vodjanuxa* respectively, but the latter are not spirits in their own right and are, basically, an extension of the male being who is the primary anthropomorphization of a particular territorial feature.

There is another major female spirit, the *kikimora* or *mara*, a being associated more with fields than with water, and sometimes presented as a fanatical spinner, but she seems to be a multiform of the *rusalka* (Maksimov 64-70). Whether the two were originally distinct spirits who were coalesced on the analogy of their gender is hard to say. Now they are clearly linked and *rusalki* are supposed to behave as field spirits, at least in the summer, beginning with the period of *rusal'e*, and confer the fertility of water to the soil where crops will be planted (Maksimov VII 168-172, Zelenin 140-152).

There are also various minor female beings who are not wives of male place-spirits: the *poludnica* (literally, noon spirit), the *lobasta*, the *semuxa* (from *Semik*, the seventh Thursday after Easter and a time associated with the period of *rusal'e* mentioned above), the *rusavka* (from the hair color), the *xitka* or *loskotuxa* (literally, the tickler), but they are even more clearly multiforms of the *rusalka* (Pomeranceva 84, Zelenin 112-118). Sometimes one name is used for "mermaids" which originate in the souls of people who die as adults and another, often *mavka*, for supernatural beings that come from the souls of children (Zelenin 117-118).

The *rusalka* is distinct from other supernatural beings not only on the basis of her sex, but also because of her origin. The *lešij*, the *vodjanoj*, the *domovoj*, the *bannik*, the *ovinnik*, and so forth are true place-spirits. They are the anthropomorphization of their "place" and seem to be coexistent with it so that every forest has its spirit or *lešij*, every bath house has its spirit, or *bannik*, and so forth. For places that are manmade, such as the buildings of the farmstead, the place-spirits come into being as the place that they inhabit is constructed so that, upon completion of a building and before moving into it, one should test the disposition of its spirit by throwing in a rooster and a cat to see if he is benevolent or if he tears the animals apart (Maksimov 31). While every place has its place-spirit, *rusalki* exist only in those places where someone has died, or, according to Zelenin, where someone who died an unnatural death has been buried (11-14). Every body of water has its *vodjanoj*, for example, but only those bodies of water where someone has drowned have a *rusalka*.

Rusalki are said to originate in the souls of maidens who died untimely and, frequently, unnatural deaths. Most of these are suicides, particularly of maidens pregnant out of wedlock who drowned themselves or, more seldom, hanged themselves from trees in the forest. Some are the souls of women who died accidental deaths. In certain regions, girls who happened to die in the period between betrothal and marriage were considered to become *rusalki* and, in a still smaller number of areas, any woman who did not marry had the potential of becoming a *rusalka* after she died (Pomeranceva 72-73, Zelenin 119-127, Maksimov 119, Afanas'ev III 240-244).

Some East Slavic areas believe that the souls of unbaptized infants, children killed by their own mothers, and miscarriages and stillbirths may become *rusalki* (Pomeranceva 72-73, 76, Zelenin 119-127, Afanas'ev III 240-244). Infant *rusalki*, however, seem to be a peripheral part of mermaid belief. They may have become part of the *rusalka* complex because many adult *rusalki* are supposed to be women carrying an unwanted pregnancy. Since these women must necessarily kill their unborn offspring when they take their own lives and because these unborn children are sometimes believed to be carried to term and delivered under the water, infants have become a subsidiary part of the *rusalka*. Another possibility is that children are so much a part of the Russian idea of women that they are attributed to anything female, including the feminine supernatural.

Children, however, are a subsidiary part of *rusalka* belief only. Child *rusalki* are seldom described in either appearance or behavior and are mentioned mostly when the origins of *rusalki* are discussed. It is especially interesting that Zelenin, who examines various unnatural infant deaths as the source of *rusalki* much more extensively than any other author, says that while, obviously, both sexes of infants can die unbaptized, only female dead become *rusalki* (120, 121). Nothing seems to happen to male infants that die. It appears, therefore, that female gender, rather than something like age or religion, is an essential feature of *rusalka* belief.

The primary activity of the *rusalka* is to lure unsuspecting men into her realm and thus to their deaths. It is not clear that she does this from evil intent or out of a desire to destroy. Her actions seem to be motivated more by a desire for company coupled with the failure to realize that human company in the spirit realm, and especially the watery one, can be permanent only if the human being dies. The *rusalka* is often pictured caressing her human victim and one of the most common ways that she brings about her victim's demise is by tickling him to death (Maksimov 116, 118, Pomeranceva 72, 75, Zelenin 176-182). Zelenin mentions the essentially playful nature of the *rusalka* in virtually those words (168), although, in another section, he states that *rusalki* are much more destructive than male unquiet dead (197). He also quotes a field recording which describes *rusalki* that do no physical harm at all. They tickle their victim until he faints, undress him, have their way with him, and then gently carry him to his own bed and tuck him in. There are dark hints that the victim suffers mentally after this attack, but nothing explicit as in other memorats where men who meet *rusalki* suffer no physical harm but become, nonetheless, withdrawn and melancholy (128-129, 130).

Tickling not only repeats the theme mentioned above, namely that the *rusalka* is essentially playful and brings destruction only inadvertently, it also draws attention again to the *rusalka*'s sexuality and sensuality. The sexual implications of tickling appear in the comments of most folklorists discussing the *rusalka*. As a logical corollary, the victims of the *rusalka* are almost all male and are lured by the beauty of her body and her voice.

Sometimes the *rusalka*'s victims are children and especially infants neglected by their mothers. For Russians at least, children as victims are but an extension of the theme of sexuality that appears in the stories of the *rusalka*'s relationship to her adult male prey. Children have already been mentioned as an extension of womanhood in connection with the origin of *rusalki*. Children are supposed to be very much the desire of any nubile woman. The sex act is supposed to culminate in childbirth. This is institutionalized in the marriage rite where, in kin terminology, a bride (*nevesta*) becomes a daughter-in-law (*snoxa*) when she bears her first child (Stankiewicz). A corollary not related to the sexuality of the *rusalka* is that the particular children to whom the *rusalka* is attracted are the type said to become *rusalki* themselves (Zelenin 131, 175, 179-180).

The relationship of *rusalki* to human beings of their own sex is especially interesting. Needless to say, *rusalki* never try to attract women and caress them to death the way they do men. If anything, *rusalki* are supposed to be jealous of human women; they are supposed to chase women away from any place where they have gathered or that they wish to frequent (Zelenin 131, 183). They may victimize adult women indirectly by stealing the most beautiful of their clothing and embroidery, should they be careless enough to fall asleep while washing clothes at a stream and not cross themselves (Maksimov 118, Zelenin 133, 164, 171-172). Beautiful clothes are easy enough to connect to the idea of sexual attractiveness. In fact, the mischievous acts attributed not only to *rusalki*, but to related female beings are all connected to things that young, marriageable girls are supposed to want for enhancing their sexual appeal. These acts include stealing beads, embroidery floss, yarn, and linen, taking away someone's weaving and doing it, only backwards. The clothing and ornaments are means of attracting the opposite sex that a Westerner can easily understand. The weaving is more particularly Russian. It can be seen, for example, in Russian courtship customs, where ability to produce handiwork, especially things in cloth, was a measure of the desirability of a potential bride (Gura, Maslova 8-29). The *rusalka*'s desire to do some weaving can be seen, therefore, as a desire to perform an action that will make her more valuable as a potential bride, in other words, more attractive to the opposite sex. Her inability to do the weaving correctly merely proves that she is supernatural and essentially not a suitable bride for a human being. The *rusalka*'s desire to be attractive, competing with human women for their men, is also apparent in her preoccupation with her toilet. As Zelenin points out, this is one of her primary activities and, as mentioned earlier, she is frequently pictured combing her hair (170-171).

While most of the interaction between *rusalki* and human women seems like jealous, petty rivalry, some field data report a much more serious event that is analogous to the *rusalka*'s interaction with children. When *rusalki* see a woman like themselvs, one trying to commit suicide because of pregnancy or unrequited love, they are supposed to help her die by tickling and caressing her as they pull her under to drown (Zelenin 138-139).

In the Orlovsk region it is said that naked *rusalki* steal horses and take them for joy-rides which invariably result in the destruction of the horse (Pomeranceva 73). In Freudian terms, this wanton riding is but another expression of the *rusalka*'s unbridled sexuality. In terms of Russian ritual, horse rides have sexual connotations of a milder sort. They are a standard pre-wedding (*devičnik*) entertainment that the groom offers the unmarried girlfriends of his bride-to-be as compensation for his taking his betrothed from amongst them (Zorin 89-91, Gura 83).

The *rusalka*'s orientation toward sex and toward human males appears also in the belief that she can be freed of her destructive potential and actually turned into a bride suitable for a human groom if she is Christened, usually by tying a cross around her neck. Any man who initiates this process must complete it and wed his watery intended because, if he fails to do so, she will become a *rusalka* again, only now one with specific malevolent intent, bent on destroying the man who offered her salvation and then took it away (Pomeranceva 81-83, Afanas'ev III 240-244, Zelenin 182-183). The belief that, because of her origin in a human soul, the *rusalka* can be restored to humanity with the help of Christianity separates her not only from place spirits, but also from all other mythological creatures, whose becoming human is simply out of the question.

The *rusalka*'s origin in a human soul appears perhaps even more clearly in related stories about child *rusalki*. A man who wants to make an adult *rusalka* his bride must go about tying a cross around her neck with great care and stealth. The *rusalka* may want the man as her mate as much as he wants her, but she wants him to be her mate in her watery territory, rather than becoming his mate in his home. She, therefore, resists the cross that puts her under the man's power. Child *rusalki*, on the other hand, go about the forest actively seeking someone to tie a cross about their necks and baptize them. They are said to exact revenge on anyone who hears their plea and refuses them this service and on their own mothers, if the reason that they became *rusalki* was that their mothers neglected to baptize them in the first place (Zelenin 137-138).

The attraction of the *rusalka* to human beings, particularly to males, distinguishes her from the place spirits in yet another way. Of the spirits who dwell outside the farmstead, this is the only creature who actively seeks contact with human beings, the only one that seems actually to want human company in her realm, and the only one that causes harm inadvertently. Creatures like the *lešij* or the *vodjanoj* seem perfectly happy without human company, in fact, they resent human intrusion into their abodes. If they decide to interact with people, their behavior is malevolent and intentionally so. They punish and they mean to harm. They punish misbehavior by a human being who has entered their domain, such as fishing out of season, after the Day of St. Ilja. Sometimes they punish the simple act of trespassing. But they harm only people who have entered the spirit's sphere of their own volition or were sent to them by an inadvertent curse, often that of a thoughtless parent. They do not seek to entice or lure and they have no particular sex preferences when it comes to choice of victim (Maksimov 29-64, 71-114, Pomeranceva 28-67, 92-117, esp. 51, 38-39).

Finally, *rusalki* are distinct from the place-spirits due to their relative freedom of movement. All of the male spirits, because they are the anthropomorphization of a particular place, are attached exclusively to, and are also restricted to, that particular domain, be it a specific forest, body of water, building, or other structure. *Rusalki,* on the other hand, can leave their watery homes and sit on the shore, or on bridges and mill wheels. They can climb up into trees and run about the fields. There is a ritualized passage of *rusalki* into the fields in the spring called *rusal'e*, when they bring to the fields the life-giving power of water, but also the threat of death to unwary young men, whom they are said to tickle so hard that they foam at the mouth (Maksimov 118). Because they are not the spirit of a place, but the spirit of a human being who has died an unnatural death, *rusalki* are not restricted to any geographical feature and have wide mobility. Another way of putting it is as Pomeranceva does, namely, that while the *lešij* is master of his forest, the *vodjanoj* is master of his body of water, and so forth, the *rusalka* is mistress of nothing (81). Pomeranceva's emphasis may be overly negative and it is more useful to see the *rusalka* as unencumbered by a tie to a specific place and thus far less restricted than the place-spirits.

If the *rusalka* does not belong in the same category as the *vodjanoj, lešij, domovoj, bannik,* and the other place-spirits, then what is she and in what category does she belong? Zelenin chooses not to make much of a connection between the *rusalka* and the various place-spirits and examines her rather as a primary manifestation of the unquiet dead. The section of Zelenin's book that is about *rusalki* is probably the single most comprehensive treatment of them and, as Pomeranceva, who wrote subsequently, points out, there is much in Zelenin that cannot be refuted. Nevertheless, Zelenin too has trouble classifying *rusalki* because he finds that they are rather unlike male unquiet dead. Male unquiet dead seem to become the servants of the devil, used by him as anything from laborers to horses (the devil rides on the backs of these men when he needs a means of transportation). At best, male unquiet dead are directed by the devil (197). *Rusalki,* on the other hand, seem to be independent, operating on their own volition. There seems to be something about the *rusalka*, then, something connected to her gender, that puts her outside any larger category and into a category of her own.

Zelenin has pointed out that there is nothing like the East Slavic *rusalka* in the West (209). The discussion above indicates that the *rusalka* is unique in the context of East Slavic belief also. She may be a "mythological character," but she is a different sort of being than the *lešij, vodjanoj,* or *domovoj.* She maybe one of the unquiet dead, but she is rather more than that. It seems possible to explain the male unquiet dead in terms of their untimely or unnatural demise alone, but not the *rusalka.*

The trait of the *rusalka* that appears again and again in the discussion above, the trait that distinguishes her from both the ordinary unquiet dead, if there can be such a thing, and from place-spirits such as the *domovoj* or *lešij,* is her gender. It is my contention that, while it is difficult to understand the *rusalka* by placing her in the context of place-spirit beliefs or beliefs about the unquiet dead alone, examining her in conjunction with beliefs about women is very productive. If we examine ethnographic sources that are contemporary with our sources for the *rusalki* and extract beliefs about women, we will find a system against which our little mermaid does make sense. It is interesting in this regard that Zelenin, whose purpose was rather different, himself pointed out the similarities between *rusalki* and ordinary village women (196-197).

Perhaps the most striking phenomenon having to do with women in Russian folklore is wedding customs. In many senses, Russian women are considered to die at marriage. All rites of passage have death and rebirth symbolism, but the death symbolism in the rites for Russian brides goes far beyond the death and rebirth motifs common to all rites of passage. In fact, there is little rebirth symbolism, while the funerary aspects are extensive indeed. They include the bride's abstaining from food and work and behaving as a non-functioning member of the household, as if she were dead (Zorin 85-86, Šeremet'eva 15, Matossian 26, Gura 77, Sokolov 205). The rites focus on ritual washing and dressing of the bride, as of a corpse (Tokarev 84, Zorin 93-95, Gura 77-78, Zyrjanov 50-66, Mahler 254-267). The most widely recorded part of the wedding rite is a series of laments by the bride and another series for her (Mahler 141, 227, 395, 480, 482, 484, Zyrjanov). In a traditional setting, as in a village, the bride is even taken from the house in the same way that a corpse is removed: through an unusual aperture such as a window (Zorin 108-109, Mahler 125-127, Zyrjanov 131-146, Bajburin and Levinton 89-105). It was believed that the door, which was used for normal human passage, should not be used for brides and corpses. Recent ethnographies describe prophylactic magic, such as throwing water and obliterating the tracks left by the horses, performed when the bridal train left for church (Zorin 108-111, Šeremet'eva 41, 46,

Zyrjanov 146-160, Mahler 207-209). This is almost identical to magic with the same purpose performed when the funeral procession left the home to take the corpse to the church service (Mahler *Totenklage* 654, 655-656).

Further evidence that the woman's wedding was considered akin to death can be found in the fact that women, having once "died" at marriage, were not given elaborate funerals. These were reserved for men, whose wedding rites were, appropriately, negligible. In collections from the classic work of Barsov to the *Biblioteka poèta* volume of chants (*pričitanija*), it is striking how few laments for women there are and how much shorter they are than laments for men. A married woman, having already gone through a funeral-like transition, it seems, needs little lamentation.

Marriage, for a woman, was so much her primary rite of passage and so much like the transition a man made only when he died that it took precedence over all other rites celebrated for her. Elsa Mahler not only gives laments, the way Barsov and Azadovskij and the *Biblioteka poèta* do, she discusses their content, as compared with funeral rites. According to Mahler, if a woman died unmarried, in most cases this would be if a girl died young, before she wed, her funeral was celebrated not as such, but as a wedding. The topic of the laments would be changed appropriately or wedding laments would be sung along with funeral ones. The deceased would be dressed in wedding clothes, and a wedding ring would be placed on her finger (Mahler *Totenklagae* 391-408).

The belief that a woman's marriage was much like a death can be seen not only in the wedding and funeral rites themselves, but in the treatment of married and marriageable women. The former especially, having experienced death in a rite that occurred at the very center of their lives, were treated as liminal beings. They were supposed to conduct ritual activity, especially rites which called for contact with the other world. Thus birth rites, up to baptism, were conducted exclusively by married women (Tokarev 85, *Narody mira* 467-468, Matossian). Funeral rites, which dealt with the other extreme of life, the departure of the soul to the realm beyond rather than its arrival from there, were similarly conducted by women. Men made the coffin and removed the body from the house for its trip to church. Usually the men that did this were not related to the deceased and protected themselves from death additionally by wearing gloves (Barsov 304). Married women, on the other hand, were allowed or obliged, depending on one's point of view, to contact the corpse directly and they were the ones who washed and dressed the deceased and laid him out in his coffin (Barsov 299-313, Mahler *Totenklage* 643-685, Tokarev 85-86, *Narody mira* 472-473). Having gone through a death-like transition themselves at marriage, it was women who lamented the deceased. One of the typical elements in a lament, it should be noted, is a description of the journey to the land of the dead, a description that is supposed to help the deceased make just such a journey (Mahler *Totenklage* 48-54, 244-307, 326-329, 347-416, Sokolov 224-234). If women acted as soul-guides, providing this description to aid the transition of the deceased, this is further evidence that women were believed already to have made a similar transition themselves.

As liminal beings, women were the ones that communicated with true place-spirits such as the *domovoj* and the *bannik*. Pomeranceva, Maksimov and Afanas'ev give numerous accounts of fortune-telling done at New Year and at other transitional points, such as the vernal and autumnal equinoxes. Most of the fortune-telling, as might be expected, revolved around marriage, the primary transition in a woman's life, and the marriage-related event of childbirth. Married women would seek to find out if they would conceive during the coming year. Marriageable women were apparently considered already liminal and they could seek to learn if they would marry, what the groom would be like, which village would be the groom's home and the augurer's future one (Maksimov VII 35-38, VIII 55-56, Pomeranceva 112-113).

The extreme nature of the transition that a woman is believed to undergo at marriage can explain a great deal about *rusalka* beliefs. It can be used to account for the origin of the adult *rusalka* in women of marriageable age. It can help in understanding many of the *rusalka*'s characteristics. It can help explain the relationship of beliefs about children, water, and even the unquiet dead to *rusalki*.

To take the marriage rite itself and its connection to *rusalki* first, *rusalki* originate in the souls of women of marriageable age because the transition of marriage for a woman is so extreme, and women are seen as so liminal at this time in their lives, that they can easily slip outside the human sphere altogether into the other world. Anything that goes wrong in the whole wedding procedure, from betrothal to the final incorporation of the woman into her husband's household when she delivers a child and her kin name is changed from *nevesta* to *snoxa,* can leave a woman permanently in limbo. This explains the association between *rusalki* and women who die between betrothal and the wedding itself. *Rusalki*-suicides who killed themselves because they were pregnant can be seen as women whose wedding transition went wrong because it went in the wrong order. Instead of pregnancy being the final stage, it occurred first.

The association between the origin of *rusalki* and the weddings of real women partially explains the heightened sexuality of the former. As Propp has pointed out, their tickling of their male victims and the orgiastic laughter it produces is a kind of inverted, improper sex act (77-81). This inverted sex act fits well with the idea of the origin of a *rusalka* in a kind of improper, inverted wedding.

There are, in fact, a number of motifs that come directly from Russian wedding ritual and appear in *rusalka* belief, often in inverted form. In the description of *rusalki* given at the beginning of this article, we mentioned weaving as something that occurs in courtship practices and that *rusalki* do backwards, as well as horse rides which are a regular part of the *devičnik* and a favorite mischief for *rusalki*. Even though he was not interested in wedding/*rusalki* links, Zelenin noticed the parallel between the loose hair of the *rusalka* and the loose hair of the bride (161-162). Unmarried women are supposed to wear their hair in a single braid down their backs and married women are supposed to wear double braids coiled around the head. The hair is worn loose only during the actual wedding, from the time the bride leaves her house for church until the end of the church service (Mahler 229-253, Maslova 47-62, Bernštam). As Zelenin notes, the bride's loose hair makes her particularly vulnerable to the supernatural and in need of protection from it.

Children, and particularly infants, were also important in both the wedding and *rusalka* beliefs. As mentioned earlier, they are the culmination of the transition of marriage. It should be noted again that they appear in the fortune-telling discussed above and that they are both companions of adult *rusalki* and a source of adult *rusalki*. Children are associated with *rusalki* not only because of their function in the transition of marriage. They play an important role in mermaid belief because they are beings that are themselves liminal, like women of marriageable age. The peripheral position of children, and especially infants, is institutionalized in a number of ways. The most noticeable is the practice of baptizing an infant forty days after birth (Tokarev, 85, *Narody mira* 467-468). Forty days is the period of a soul journey and, from baptismal practices and the parallel custom of celebrating a major wake forty days after someone's death, it seems that East Slavs believe that this is the time it takes for a soul to travel between the land of souls and this world (Mahler *Totenklage* 672-675). Waiting forty days serves the practical function of assuring the parents, the family and the community that the child will live before they make the emotional commitment of accepting the child through baptism. The problem is that, in the meantime, the child is left in a rather ambiguous, liminal position, as reflected in the proverb, "Korova bez vymja — mjaso; rebenok bez imja — čertenok," (A cow without an udder is meat; a child without a name is a little devil). The analogy between women and children, particularly as regards their liminality, is seen also in the fact that children, like women, can communicate with spirits and are the ones who go caroling, who toss cookie birds into the air at Annunciation to make the crops grow and who perform many other ritual acts. In the case of children, the younger the more liminal, and it is the youngest child who announces the evening star and signals the beginning of the Christmas Eve meal (Maksimov VII 28-33, 94-98, Propp 31-34, 35-348).

Water, too, is a motif that is important in both life cycle ritual and *rusalka* belief. As with children, one of the reasons for the appearance of water in both of these places is its association with transition. It could be argued, in fact, that water is virtually the symbol for the transitional, being neither solid nor gaseous, being tangible, and yet without form. Water, to the East Slavs, is the spirit medium. It is not the other world, but a substance through which the human realm and the supernatural can contact each other. Thus many manifestations of the supernatural on earth are described as living in water. *Besy* and *čerti*, demons and devils, live there. Devils in fairytales live in rivers, in wells, and under the tufts of marsh grass in swamps. *Bylina* and fairytale dragons live in seas, river, and wells. The external souls of demons such as Koščej Bessmertnyj are hidden in the sea. *Čerti* live in water not only in folklore, but also in eighteenth- and nineteenth-century Russian literature as, for example, in Puškin's "Skazka o pope i rabotnike ego Balde" (The Tale about a Priest and his Hired Hand, Balda).

If water is a substance through which man can contact the supernatural, one might expect it to appear prominently in fortune-telling and this is indeed the case. There is an enormous amount of fortune-telling using water, from casting wreaths into streams in the spring to tell whether one's beloved has been true or whether one will marry in the coming year, to pouring wax into water at New Year's (Maksimov 172, Afanas'ev II 192-194, Propp 105-110).

More directly relevant to *rusalki* is the use of water in the two life cycle rituals which we have connected to them, the rites of marriage and death. Water is so much the spirit medium, that any spirit seems to have an irresistable attraction to it. In the Russian funeral, in addition to the usual ritual washing, there was some distinctive water-related behavior. Russians dispose of any water in the house at the time of someone's death. In certain regions. all the water in the household is discarded again on the day of the funeral. The reason given for this is that the souls of the deceased have a natural affinity for water. They will enter any water in the vicinity and, if something is not done about this, the souls will become "stuck," trapped in limbo between the world of the living and the world of the dead (Tokarev 85, Barsov 299-313, Mahler *Totenklage* 643-685). Thus water is not just the element of non-human spirits, but a substance associated with transitions made by the human soul.

At least an unconscious association between women, water and perhaps death can be seen in a practice documented by Zorin. All ethnographers mention a *proščanie*, a farewell, as a regular part of the wedding ritual. Most descriptions deal with the bride's farewell to her home and especially to the hearth, the enormous Russian *peč'*. Zorin states that the bride was supposed to say goodbye to the village and its surroundings as well, particularly to the various bodies of water (Zorin 91-92, 107-109, Mahler 184, 186, 204, 445, 451, Sokolov, 206).

If the transition that a woman undergoes when she marries should be seen as extreme and dangerous, it is not difficult to understand that there would be beliefs about women who did not successfully complete this transition and remained somewhere in limbo. If there is a strong association between Russian wedding rites for a woman and the funeral rites celebrated for a man, it is easy to see why there would be the association between unquiet dead and *rusalki* noted by Zelenin. It is perhaps better to see *rusalki* not as unquiet dead, but as undead, creatures in transition who stayed in limbo and never made it to the other side. If there are beliefs about water as a substance between the human realm and the supernatural, it is easy to see why this limbo where undead *rusalki* reside might frequently be portrayed as a body of water. If *rusalki* are creatures in a limbo resulting from marriage-related events, this would explain their reaching out to human kind, particularly men, in an effort to complete this transition and be incorporated as married women and, therefore, human. This also explains the legends of young men actually rescuing *rusalki* by tying crosses around their necks and taking them as brides.

Finally, the one belief that would at first appear to link *rusalki* to place-spirits can be explained by the fact that our "mermaids" are creatures who somehow did not complete the transition of marriage. *Rusalki* are sometimes pictured as marrying the *vodjanoj* into whose domain they enter when they drown (Zelenin 115, 122, 145, 165-167, 189). This should not be understood as a belief that *rusalki* are beings of the same type as the *vodjanoj* because they can mate. Rather, it should indicate that marriage as a transition and the push for the culmination of this rite of passage is such a dominant motif in the *rusalka* complex that it is articulated in a variety of forms.

The Russian perception of what happens at death, as well as the wedding-funeral link, facilitates the idea that *rusalki* may be more in limbo than irreversibly gone into the other world. As mentioned in connection with Baptism, there is an institutionalized forty-day waiting period both after a birth and after a death which is supposed to accommodate the time it takes for a soul to journey either to or from the human world. As discussed in connection with water rites, there is a belief that a soul leaving the body at death will enter water if all of the water in the house is not discarded. There is also the belief that a soul "stuck" in water in this way will be hindered from making its proper journey into the other world. *Rusalki*, then, are women in the transition of marriage who died in the transitional element of water, a place where souls can so easily become stuck, and who did not have proper funeral rites to help them complete their passage into the other world and their incorporation among the souls of the dead.

Even the territorial mobility of the *rusalka* in comparison with male place-spirits, such as the *lešij* and *vodjanoj*, can be explained by the link between her and the real Slavic bride at marriage. One of the reasons for the death symbolism in the woman's wedding rite was the fact that she crossed territorial boundaries, moving from her household of birth to the household of her husband (Moyle). Men never moved, except in very rare instances, and were then also subjected to something akin to funeral rites. The most obvious example is the set of rites performed for the recruit and the laments that accompanied those rites (Sokolov 235-240, Barsov II). The regular movement in space of the real Russian woman at marriage fits well with the territorial mobility of the *rusalka*.

While most of the characteristics of the *rusalka* can be explained by beliefs about women articulated in Russian ritual, one of her features, her sexuality, cannot. Certainly marriage is the ritualization of the sexual union, but the sexuality of the *rusalka* seems to go beyond the sexuality of the wedding rite. The sexuality that goes beyond ritual is very difficult to discuss because there is little data outside *rusalka* memorats themselves. For the connection to wedding ritual treated above, we have the numerous and relatively dispassionate descriptions of the wedding rite. For the *rusalka*'s sexuality, the best sources are the rather emotional accounts of encounters with her.

Based on the memorats that folklorists and ethnographers have recorded about *rusalki*, it would seem that Russians, and East Slavs in general, have a rather ambivalent attitude toward sexuality. The idea of a sexy woman, as the *rusalka* clearly is, is both tremendously attractive and terribly frightening. The things that make the *rusalka* so appealing are her physical beauty, the beauty of her face and figure, and also certain behavioral characteristics that are supposed to be atypical of good Russian girls. The *rusalka* is uninhibited. she runs around naked. She is carefree and sings and dances (Zelenin 168, 179). Certainly the real-life Russian girl, at least during the betrothal and marriage period, is supposed to be anything but happy and carefree and is supposed to cry and lament. We should add that, unlike the *rusalka*, she is also supposed to be extremely modest, and even during the betrothal rite of the *smotriny*, literally "the looking," she is either presented with a kerchief covering her head and upper body, or presented as is, but expected to plead shyness and hide at every opportunity (Zorin 74-78, Gura 75-77, 18). The behavior of the *rusalka*, then, is the opposite of what a good Russian girl does, but, perhaps, something that people wish were possible. In this regard, it is interesting that one of the physical features deemed so important in a *rusalka*, particularly by male ethnographers, is not characterisitc of the Slavic female physique, namely, large breasts.

The sexuality of the *rusalka* and the particular forms that it embodies are, perhaps, expressions of unconscious wishes. It is noteworthy that, as *rusalki* serve as an expression for things that one might wish were true, they also reaffirm that these wishes cannot be fulfilled because *rusalki* are believed to be very dangerous and to pose the threat of death by tickling to any man who might wish to sample the charms of their bodies or their personalities. Put another way, *rusalka* belief says that uninhibited, beautiful, sexy women are very attractive, but that they are not real. They exist in the supernatural realm only and are, thus, very dangerous. Any normal woman should not want to behave like a *rusalka* and any normal man should not look for these characteristics in the opposite sex.

The *rusalka*, then, while she fits neither into the same category as the mermaids of the West, nor into any category of Russian spirits or "mythological characters" other than her own, exists in East Slavic belief as the embodiment of some very important beliefs about women. She helps encapsulate many of the contradictions inherent in being a woman in the Russian setting. We see in the *rusalka* that a woman should be sensual and seductive, but not excessively so. A woman should easily produce lots of children, but only at a certain time. A woman should die from the point of view of her household of birth and yet continue to live and function as a productive member of her husband's household. Contradictions, anthropologists tell us, are inevitable in any social system (Douglas, 39). Contradictions are also the points of greatest danger and greatest potential for creativity, the points which elicit the strongest emotional response. Thus our *rusalka*, evil seductress and potential tender wife, producer and destroyer of children, bearer of crop fertility, and inspiration for folk and fine art.

University of Virginia

REFERENCES

Afanas'ev, A., *Poètičeskoe vozzrenija slavjan na prirodu* (The Hague, Paris: Mouton, Slavistic Printings and Reprintings, 1970). Originally published Moscow: Vol. I—1865, Vol. II—1868, Vol. III—1869.

Azadovskij, M. K., ed., *Russkie plači Kareli* (Petrozavodsk: Gosudarstvennoe izdatel'stvo karelo-finnskoj SSR, 1940).

Bajburin, A. K. and G. A. Levinton, "K opisaniju organizacii prostranstva v vostočnoslavjanskoj svad'be," *Russkij narodnyj svadebnyj obrjad: Issledovanija i materialy*, ed. K. V. Čistova and T. A. Bernštam (Leningrad: Nauka, Leningradskoe otdelenie, 1978), pp. 89-105.

Barsov, E. V., *Pričitanija severnogo kraja, Čtenija v obščestve istorii i drevnostej rossijskix pri Moskovskom universitete*, Vol. I (1872)—funeral laments, Vol. II (1882)—laments for recruits, Vol. III (1886)—wedding laments.

Bernštam, T. A., "Obrjad rastavanie s krasotoj," *Pamjatniki kul'tury narodov evropy i evropejskoj časti SSSR,* ed. T. V. Stanjukovič (Leningrad: Nauka, 1982).

Douglas, Mary, *Purity and Danger: An Analysis of Concepts of Pollution and Taboo* (New York and Washington: Praeger, 1966).

Gura, A. V., "Opyt vyjavlenija struktury severnorusskogo svadebnogo obrjada (po materialam Vologodskoj gubernij)," *Russkij narodnyj svadebnyj obrjad: Issledovanija i materialy*, ed. K. V. Čistova and T. A. Bernštam (Leningrad: Nauka, Leningradskoe otdelenie, 1978), pp. 72-88.

Mahler, Elsa, *Die Russischen dörflichen Hochzeitbrauche* (Berlin: Veröffentlichungen den Abteilung fur slavische Sprachen und Literaturen des Osteuropa-Instituts, Vol. 20, 1960).

Mahler, Elsa, *Die russische Totenklage: Ihre rituelle und dichterische Deutung* (Leipzig: Veröffentlichungen des slavischen Instituts, 1935).

Maksimov, S. V., *Sobranie sočinenij*, Vol. 18, *Nečistaja sila—Nevedomaja sila* (has the section on the various spirits), Vol. 17, *Krestnaja sila—Rasskazy iz istorii staroobrjadčestva* (has the section on festivals, including *rusal'e*), ed. P. V. Bykov (St. Petersburg: Samoobrazovanie, 1896).

Maslova, G. S., *Narodnaja odežda v vostočnoslavjanskix tradicionnyx obyčajax i obrjadax* (Moscow: Nauka, 1984).

Matosian, Mary, "The Peasant Way of Life," *The Peasant in Nineteenth Century Russia,* ed. Wayne Vucinich (Stanford: Stanford University Press, 1968), pp. 1-40.

Moyle, Natalie K. "Spacey Soviets and the Russian Attitude Toward Territorial Passage," *New York Folklore* (Vol. 7, Nos. 1 and 2, Summer, 1981), pp. 83-96.

Narody mira, Vol. I *Narody evropejskoj časti SSSR,* ed. V. A. Aleksandrov (Moscow: Izdatel'stvo "Nauka," 1964).

Pomeranceva, E. V., *Mifologičeskie personaži v russkom fol'klore* (Moscow: "Nauka," Akademia nauk SSSR, 1975).

Pričitanija Biblioteka poèta, ed. B. N. Putilov (Leningrad: Sovetskij pisatel', 1960).

Propp, V. Ja., *Russkie agrarnye prazdniki (Opyt istoriko-ètnografičeskogo issledovanija)* (Leningrad: Izdatel'stvo leningradskogo universiteta, 1963).

Šeremet'eva, M. E., *Svad'ba v Gamajunščine, Kalužskogo uezda* (Kaluga: Trudy kalužskogo obščestva istorii i drevnostej, 1928).

Sokolov, Y. M., *Russian Folklore*, trans. Catherine Ruth Smith (Detroit: Folklore Associates, 1971).

Stankiewicz, Edward, "Slavic Kinship Terms and the Perils of the Soul," *Journal of American Folklore*, Vol. 59 (1958), pp. 115-122.

Tokarev, S. A., *Ètnografija narodov SSSR, Istoričeskie osnovy byta i kul'tury* (Moscow: Izda-tel'stvo moskovskogo universiteta, 1958).

Zelenin, D. K., *Očerki russkoj mifologii: umeršie neestestvennoju smert'ju i rusalki* (Petrograd: Tipografija A. B. Orlova, 1916).

Zorin, N. V., *Russkaja svad'ba v severnom Povolž'e* (Kazan': Izdatel'stvo kazanskogo univer-siteta, 1981).

Zyrjanov, I., *Čerdynskaja svad'ba* (Perm: Permskoje knižnoe izdatel'stvo, 1969).

CHEKHOV ON CHEKHOV: HIS EPISTOLARY SELF-CRITICISM

Katherine Tiernan O'Connor

Any reader of Chekhov who is even casually familiar with the vast body of critical literature on him that is now available has been exposed to numerous discussions of his views on literature and on the role of the writer. And it is, of course, his considerable correspondence that serves as a direct source of information on these subjects. His rejection of tendentiousness, his hatred of lies and labels of any kind, his celebration of life in all its perfect and imperfect forms, his belief in the necessity of freedom—are often highlighted in the critical literature and are irrevocably associated with the image of Chekhov which we carry around in our heads. It is not my intention, therefore, to belabor what has already received considerable attention. Rather, I wish to explore what Chekhov, the letter-writer, has to say about certain of his own texts and, correspondingly, what he has to say about himself as the author of these texts. The epistolary Chekhov commenting on the authorial Chekhov, as it were. To pursue the subject of Chekhov's epistolary self-criticism is, moreover, to be aware that one is engaged in a kind of balancing act whereby one attempts to distinguish between the various Chekhov-personae that present themselves and yet reconcile them as well. First of all, there is Chekhov the **author**, whose name we associate with a specific *œuvre*. Secondly, there is Chekhov the **correspondent**, the epistolary I, the first-person **narrator** of his own self-criticism. Thirdly, there is Chekhov the authorial **character**, the creation of his epistolary I. Finally, there is Chekhov the **man**, that vague presence who seems familiar to us nonetheless, and who emerges as a kind of composite photo of all of the above. To explore Chekhov's epistolary self-criticism is, moreover, also to take into account the identity and gender of the letter's addressee and the dynamics of his or her relationship with Chekhov.

In order to view some of these complexities **in action,** as it were, let us now turn to two separate examples of Chekhov's epistolary self-commentary, both written about the same work, *Ward No. 6*, but each sent to a different addressee. Both letters manifest certain surface similarities in terms of the information which they provide about the story, but far more interesting are their disparities and the insights which they provide into Chekhov's contrasting motivations as a letter-writer and as a self-critic and complementarily, his different expectations regarding each addressee's response. I am speaking, in particular, of the following two letters: the first sent to Chekhov's literary patron, the publisher Aleksej Suvorin, on March 31, 1892; the second sent to Lidia Avilova a month later, on April 29.[1] Avilova was one of Chekhov's numerous "literary ladies," with whom he had once been romantically involved but probably not so intensely as she later suggested in her modestly entitled memoir, *Chekhov in My Life*.[2]

To Suvorin Chekhov writes about *Ward No. 6* as follows: "the story has a lot of argumentation (*mnogo rassuždenij*) and no love element (*otsutstvuet èlement ljubvi*). There's a plot (*fabula*), with a beginning (*zavjazka*), and a denouement (*razvjazka*). It has a liberal orientation (*upravlenie liberal'-noe*)."[3] Terse and concise as this thumbnail sketch of the story is, it nevertheless conveys some crucial information about the story's narrative structure and its thematics. Chekhov's reference to the **absence** of a love element in the story comes **after** his reference to the large amount of argumentation contained in the story. The fact, moreover, that the phrase *much argumentation* is syntactically linked to the phrase *the love element is missing* by means of the coordinating conjunction *i* rather than the contrastive conjunction *a* presupposes that they share a common ground and are akin in some way. The syntax implies that the presence of argumentation goes hand in hand and is totally consistent with the absence of a love element. Chekhov's assertion that his story has a plot with a beginning and an end is also terse but informative. Had Chekhov been a more conventional storyteller, such an assertion (that the story did indeed possess the basic formal components of traditional narrative) might have seemed self-evident to the point of suspiciousness. Was the writer being cryptic, self-ironic, or even playfully or mockingly manipulative of the addressee? Was he implying something in the order of, 'Naturally my story has a conventional plot but just what that plot is I'm not going to say, or, you'll have to wait 'til you read it to find out for yourself'? For Chekhov, however, who was **anything but** a traditional story-teller, such a communication is indeed revealing. He was, of course, conveying to Suvorin that one of the most distinguishing characteristics of *Ward No. 6* was its more traditionally structured narrative, its **unChekhovian** quality if you will. Its newness or "uniqueness" was its adherence to the principles of traditional narrative, and in that sense the story was a departure from the Chekhovian norm.

When we turn to the letter to Lydia Avilova that also makes reference to *Ward No. 6*, we see that, in contrast to his letter to Suvorin, the conveyance of substantive information about a specific text is probably not the primary motivation for the communication. To Avilova Chekhov writes, a month after the letter to Suvorin (April 29, 1892): "I am finishing a story which is very boring, since a woman and the love element are both absent. I cannot abide such stories (*terpet' ne mogu takix povestej*), I wrote it as if by accident, unintentionally (*nečajanno*), out of frivolousness. I can send you an offprint (*ottisk*) if I learn your address after June."[4]

Although this letter obviously reeks of irony even without comparison to any other text, the ironic possibilities multiply if we superimpose it, as it were, on the earlier letter to Suvorin. The first thing we notice is the intrusion of the adjective *boring* (*skučnyj*), which is, I suggest, a marked form here in contrast to its decidedly unmarked quality in many other letters in which it appears. Any reader of Chekhov's correspondence is immediately struck by the frequency, we might even say the **tedious** frequency, with which the adjective *boring* appears. It is, in fact, so frequent that it serves as a kind of formulaic tell-tale of Chekhov's common epistolary pose of self-deprecatory dismissiveness regarding his stories. This is a pose, moreover, which even Chekhov himself indirectly apologizes for in one of his early letters to Grigorovich (March 28, 1886) when he acknowledges his tendency to express low self-esteem regarding his literary merits and then goes on to provide some explanations as to why he found it so natural to fall into that pose.[5] I would argue, however, that given the earlier letter to Suvorin, which we can use as a kind of contrastive model, the insertion of the adjective *boring* in the letter to Avilova is highly suggestive in a variety of ways. The absence of a love element in *Ward No. 6* was certainly duly noted in Chekhov's letter to Suvorin but without the added assertion that the story was boring. Also, the story was described in terms of what was **present** in it as well as what was **absent**. In the letter to Suvorin the **presence** of a lot of argumentation was syntactically paired with the **absence** of a love element. Contrastingly, in the letter to Avilova the reference to the presence of considerable argumentation is gone and in its place is the noun *woman*, which is, in turn, syntactically paired with the *love element*, both of which are, of course, **absent** from the story. By virtue of the fact that the phrase *much argumentation* has been displaced in the Avilova letter by the noun *woman*, one has the amusing sense that the presence of one precludes the presence of the other, or, stated in another way, necessitates its absence. It appears to be a logical impossibility to have both *woman* and *argumentation* present in the same story. The entrance of woman coincides, then, with the exit of reasoning and ratiocination. Likewise, the fact that *woman* and the *love element* are syntactically paired with each other in the Avilova letter suggests that Chekhov is drawing attention to the stereotypical associations usually drawn between the two: wherever there is a woman present in a story, there is also a love element. You cannot seem to have one without

the other. An example of banal togetherness, as it were, in a certain conventional literary sense

To conclude that Chekhov the author would **label** his own or indeed
anyone's work **boring** solely **because** of the absence of a woman and the
love element is highly improbable, to say the least. What is indeed much
more likely is that in his letter to Avilova Chekhov was predicting what her
initial response to the story would be. **Her** response, moreover, was probably assumed by Chekhov to be indicative of that of other "literary ladies"
of her ilk. "What? No woman, no love? What a bore!" Thus Chekhov is
giving a preview of the story in the voice of an epistolary *I* whose banal
sensibilities and critical reflexes echo those of his addressee.

Meanwhile one imagines that the **real** Chekhov, the author-creator of his
epistolary *I* who is a bemused figure in the background, is thoroughly
enjoying the performance which he has staged for himself. There is total
collusion between his epistolary *I* and his addressee, and as a result, they
have both become part of a joint spectacle for Chekhov himself to behold.
The spectacle, moreover, does not end here, for the entertainment heightens
as the letter to Avilova draws to its heady conclusion: "I cannot abide such
stories, I wrote it unintentionally, accidentally, as it were, out of frivolousness." Does this not sound like a perfect parody-burlesque of a literary
lady's oohing and aahing comments about one of her own recently completed "trifles": 'Oh, its' absolutely awful, I'm not happy with it at all. It
just seemed to fly off my pen. I must have written it out of some kind of
whim.' Chekhov's epistolary *I* now shows himself to be the absolute master
of the sensibilities, the critical reflexes, the manner and idiom of a certain
kind of **lady author**, just as earlier he had shown himself equally conversant
in the ways of a certain kind of **lady reader**. Needless to say, the two probably converged in Lydia Avilova.

The story that Chekhov describes to Avilova as reflecting an accidental
or unintentional impulse, born of frivolousness, is, as we recall, the very
same story that he described to Suvorin as having a lot of argumentation,
namely, that which bespeaks the very opposite of frivolousness and negli-
gence. That a mere literary **trifle** should be the brainchild of brainlessness
nobody quibble with, but that *Ward No. 6* should also be labeled as such is
patently absurd. To allude even to the possibility of such a thing is somehow to unmask its preposterousness. Furthermore, Chekhov's letter to
Suvorin attests to the existence in the work of the basic structural components of a traditional formal narrative, that is, he seems to call attention to
what is the **intentional** narrative design of the work, in contradistinction to
what others might view superficially as the more typically amorphous, i.e.,

Chekhovian structure of his short stories. The kind of story that he has already described in his letter to Suvorin is distinguished by its structure and design, and thus it is precisely the kind of story that would appear to defy any allegations of accidental inspiration and haphazard craftsmanship. Indeed the prominence of ratiocination and argumentation in the thematics of the story is matched by the consciousness of its formal narrative design. Imagine, then, such an aggregate of intentionally contrived phenomena coming from a whimsical and frivolous pen!

In the letter to Grigorovič mentioned earlier (March 28, 1886), Chekhov makes reference to the casualness and frivolousness which had heretofore characterized his attitudes to his literary work: "Until now I treated my literary work extremely frivolously, casually, nonchalantly, I can't remember working on a single story for more than a day, and 'The Huntsman,' which you so enjoyed, I wrote while I was out swimming. I wrote my stories the way reporters write up fires; mechanically, only half-consciously, without the least concern for the reader or myself."[6] The echo, albeit a parodic one, of this earlier self-criticism that we hear once again in the letter to Avilova suggests that Chekhov might be experiencing a kind of self-ironic nostalgia for the sins of his past. He may perhaps also be indulging in some ironic self-pathos as well. By calling attention to his earlier acknowledged "sins of omission," as it were, Chekhov is perhaps whimsically atoning for them one more time. And yet at the same time he may also be reflecting on the total inapplicability of such a self-characterization in regard to a work like *Ward No. 6*. Hence he may be enjoying his assumption of a self-deprecatory mask at precisely the instant when it is most unwarranted, at least when judged by his former standards.

Chekhov concludes his remarks to Avilova on *Ward No. 6* by saying, "I could send you an offprint (*ottisk*), if I knew your summer address." After the barrage of comic self-deprecation and the implied condescension to the addressee which it conveys, how would we comment on the above? To begin with, there is the obvious implication that Chekhov's very reference to the story in the first place was the signal that he would be more than happy to send her a copy, should she be interested. Also, in view of the particular kind of negative advance billing that he has given the story thus far, his subsequent offer to send it along to her if she gives him her summer address, constitutes a kind of challenge in its own right. Although some readers might, as Chekhov anticipated in his letter, be bored and exasperated by a work in which there is no woman and no love element, would Avilova, a writer herself, want to admit her resistance to tackling such fare? Might not Chekhov, in fact, by playfully goading her into a more tolerant

and receptive reading of his work precisely by virtue of his having anticipated so devastatingly the contrary response? Might she not fail to conform
to the role tauntingly assigned to her and rise to the challenge instead? In
either case, whether Avilova conforms to his predicted response or whether
she defies his expectations, Chekhov's letter with its wealth of ironic nuances seems to anticipate the outcome. There is no contingency, as it were,
that the letter appears to have ignored.

By way of conclusion, I should like to turn to some of Chekhov's
remarks regarding another of his stories, namely, *A Boring Story*. Of particular interest is his habit of referring to *A Boring Story* as *boring*.[7] Once
again Chekhov seems to be previewing a critical response which he felt was
inevitable. It is indeed ironic, therefore, that Pleščeev objected to Chekhov's
choice of a title because he felt that it would elicit "cheap witticisms" from
the critics.[8] Pleščeev's naivete to the contrary, that seems to be precisely the
point. Chekhov had, in fact, given a preview of such "cheap witticisms" in
his own epistolary reference to the story. To **court** boredom is not to appear
the victim of it.

Considered independently of Chekhov's sideline comments, the title *A
Boring Story* is tailor-made to fit the mood and sensibilities of the old
professor who is the first-person narrator of his own life. Close to death,
irritable and disillusioned, susceptible to self-doubts and self-questionings,
the professor himself is the kind of man who would be motivated to entitle
his life *a boring story*. In this sense, he demonstrates the same capacity for
self-irony that is charcteristic of his author-creator. Rather than appreciate
the self-irony of his narrator's own probable title, however, Chekhov
chooses to undercut it by referring to *A Boring Story* as *boring*. It is almost
as if Chekhov were saying that his narrator's conscious choice of a title that
reflects the boredom **he** feels to be part of his story is not sufficient to ward
off **external** charges of boredom. Chekhov seems to be joining forces, in
fact, with those who would agree all **too** readily wtih the professor's own
self-evaluation.

Given the elaborate series of detachment maneuvers which Chekhov
engaged in to isolate himself from his narrator, it is, of course, doubly
ironic that many of his critics insisted nonetheless on identifying him with
his narrator.[9] This, in turn, elicited Chekhov's impassioned resentment and
denial and led, in fact, to his maligning his narrator in occasionally extreme
terms, seemingly in an effort to stress his detachment from him.[10] No
wonder indeed that in a letter to Pleščeev (September 24, 1889), in which he
spoke of having completed the story, he described the "final chapter" in the
odyssey of composition as follows: "Get away from me, accursed one (*Izydi*

ot menja, okajannyj) into the fire of boring criticism and reader indifference (*v ogon' skučnoj kritiki i čitatel'skogo ravnodušija*)!"[11] Added to the tedium and annoyance resulting from his anticipation of the readers' and critics' boredom, was the tedium elicited by their insistence on identifying him with his narrator. Such skewed attention must have seemed, from Chekhov's point of view, tantamount to indifference. What the quintessential Chekhov—whoever he might be—thought about his **and** the professor's *boring story* is, of course, the ultimate mystery. Perhaps the professor was an exteriorization of a certain accursed part of Chekhov's own persona which he felt he had exorcised in art. How disturbed he must have been, therefore, to learn that many of his readers failed to see that he was **cured** of his possession.

Boston University

NOTES

[1]The Russian texts of the letters which I cite are contained in Chekhov's *Pis'ma*, 12 vols., Moscow, 1977. Unless otherwise noted, the translations are mine.

[2]Simon Karlinsky refers to Avilova as one of Chekhov's "literary ladies" in his *Letters of Anton Chekhov*, trans. Michael Henry Heim in collaboration with Simon Karlinsky, New York, Harper & Row, 1973.

[3]*Pis'ma*, vol. 5, p. 41.

[4]*Pis'ma*, vol. 5, p. 58.

[5]Karlinsky, *Letters of Anton Chekhov*, pp. 58-59.

[6]Karlinsky, pp. 58-59.

[7]The notes to *A Boring Story* found in Chekhov's *Sočinenija*, Moscow, 1977, vol. 7, pp. 669-80, cite many letters in which Chekhov refers to his story as either *skučnyj* or *skučnovatyj*.

[8]*Sočinenija*, vol. 7, pp. 672-73.

[9]Suvorin was among those who felt that Chekhov himself was reflected in his narrator. *Sočinenija*, vol. 7, p. 673.

[10]A letter to Pleščeev, cited in the notes already referred to (*Sočinenija*, vol. 7, p. 673), seems especially harsh in its judgment of the professor, for it is suggested that Liza and Katja might not have been ruined, had he been less indifferent to their fate. Even more extreme is Chekhov's insistence that the only opinion in the entire story that he shares is that held by the "scoundrel Gnekker," namely, that "the old man has gone off his rocker" (*spjatil starik*).

[11]*Pis'ma*, vol. 3, p. 252.

NABOKOV'S ORANGE NIGHT

Linda Nadine Saputelli

In his treatment of the relationship between art and life Vladimir Nabokov enlists into service talent recognized as that of conventional artistic genius—writers, musicians, sculptors, actors, painters, even chess players. Both in life and in literature, the artist's inevitable cross has traditionally been alienation in varying degrees which, as treated by Nabokov, defines plot and synthesizes the emotional, psychological and narrative lines of a given work.

Ordinary people with banal professions but who manage, nonetheless, to create life out of their imaginations and unfulfilled yearnings are also the subject of these same thematics. So consumed are these protagonists by their unfulfilled yearnings, dreams or fantasies that they conduct themselves like absentee tenants in life, occupying physical space while conducting their spiritual and emotional lives in a world of dreams. In the short story "Katastrofa"[1] ("The Catastrophe") the protagonist, an obscure clerk in a haberdashery, differs little in the end result from Nabokov's more traditional artists. By creating his own paradise out of dreams, the clerk transforms his otherwise shabby existence into something extraordinary and beautiful.

"Katastrofa" first appeared in *Segodnja* (*Today*), a Riga émigré daily, in 1924. In 1930 it was included in the *Vozvraščenie Čorba* (*The Return of Čorb*) collection, but more than half a century intervened before it reappeared in 1976 as the title piece to the English volume, *Details of a Sunset and Other Stories*. Nabokov was evidently dissatisfied with the Russian title which he terms "odious" and for which he disclaims responsibility. The new title, he says, ". . . has the triple advantage of corresponding to the thematic background of the story, of being sure to puzzle such readers as 'skip descriptions,' and of infuriating reviewers."[2]

Nabokov's assessment of the title turned out to be correct on all counts but the last one; his new title did not infuriate reviewers, whose reception to the collection was generally favorable, while the title was reported without comment.[3] At a distance of some fifty years, the Russian title may have appeared to be too clinically precise to Nabokov. "Catastrophe" is, after all, a word whose origin is non-Russian and whose first meaning is *dénouement*, or final action that completes the unraveling of the plot. By his title Nabokov shows his hand at the outset, behavior which was far from typical in his later works.

The story, like most of Nabokov's from this period, is set in Berlin. What distinguishes it from others is that its principal characters are German. It takes place over a two-night period, probably in late spring or summer. The milieu in which Mark Standfuss, the protagonist, establishes himself, however, is similar to that of many of Nabokov's Russian émigré protagonists. The reader is introduced to Mark as he is returning home, very tipsy, from a pub where he has been celebrating his forthcoming marriage to Klara Heise. He is head over heels in love with Klara who, like Nabokov's first heroine, Mašen'ka, never actually appears in the story, but is seen through Mark's eyes as a beautiful, pale redhead in a green dress.

Mark is deliriously happy, the reader is told four times in the first three pages. "Mark . . . prikazčik, polubog, svetlovolosyj Mark, sčastlivec . . . (Mark . . . a salesclerk, a demigod, fair-haired Mark, a lucky fellow . . .)."[4] The narrator's irony is evident from the start, and with each repetition of Mark's happiness the impression is reinforced that, if this is not the happiness of a fool, it is certainly that of an innocent. The day after the celebration, Klara's mother visits Mark's mother. Saying that her daughter has gone mad, she delivers a letter from Klara informing Mark she is leaving him for their former lodger with whom she was once in love and who has suddenly returned. That same evening instead of going straight home from work, Mark stops off for a bite to eat with his friend Adolf, after which he decides to go on to Klara's, blissfully unaware that all is over. In his usual absentminded glow of happiness he misses his tram stop. Impatient to see Klara, he jumps off the moving tram before the next stop and is hit from behind by a bus. He dies on the wet asphalt, still unaware of Klara's defection.

Although this is one of Nabokov's early stories, the complexity of its imagery and symbolism link it to his later ones. The opening image of the tram holds a concrete and allegorical significance for the later events of the tale. The story begins with the words: "V zerkal'nuju mglu ulicy ubegal poslednij tramvaj . . . (The last streetcar was disappearing in the mirrorlike murk of the street)."[5] It is only at the end that the reader learns that this tram, which is an integral part of the romance of the city, is also the instrument of Mark's death. Mark's highly charged emotions are interspersed with rich poetic descriptions of Berlin's buildings which at sunset acquire a gothic splendor. Rain glistening on the torn-up streets of the city reflects the evening light. The orange sunset which bathes Mark and the city in its glow is first mentioned as he leaves on his fatal journey to Klara's. It recurs with the intensity of a movie still until its last rays gleam so vividly that the reader is transported along with the nearly dead protagonist from the tops of the highest chimneys and roofs to the heavens themselves.

... *ognennyj zakat* mlel v prolete kanala, i vlažnyj most vdali byl okajmlen topkoj zolotoju čertoj, po kotoroj proxodili černye figurki.

> (... the flush of a *fiery sunset* filled the vista of the canal, and a rain-streaked bridge in the distance was margined by a narrow rim of gold along which passed tiny black figures.)

Doma byli serye, kak vsegda, no zato, kryši, lepka nad verxnimi ètažami, zolotye gromootvody, kamennye kupola, stolbiki, ... byli teper' omyty *jarkim oxrjanym bleskom*, vozdušnoj teplotoj večernej zari, —i ottogo *volšebnymi* neožidannymi kazalis' èti verxnie vystupy, balkony, karnizy, kolonny,— rezko otdeljajuščiesja želtoj jarkost'ju svoej ot tusklyx fasadov vnizu.

> (The houses were as gray as ever; yet the roofs, the moldings above the upper floors, the gilt-edged lightning rods, the stone cupolas, the colonnettes—which nobody notices during the day, for day-people seldom look up—were now bathed in *rich ochre*, the sunset's airy warmth, and thus they seemed unexpected and *magical*, those upper protrusions, balconies, cornices, pillars, contrasting sharply, because of their tawny brilliance, with the drab façades beneath.)

Polneba oxvatil zakat. Verxnye jarusy i kryši domov byli *divno* ozareny. Tam, v vyšine, Mark različal skvoznye portiki, frizy i freski, spalery oranževyx roz, krylatye statui, podnimajuščie k nebu zolotye, nesterpimo gorjaščie liry. Volnujas' i blistaja, prazdnično i vozdušno uxodila v nebesnuju dal' vsja èta *zodčeskaja prelest'* i Mark ne mog ponjat', kak ran'še ne zamečal on ètix gallerej, ètix xramov, povisšix v vyšine.[6]

> (The colors of the sunset had invaded half of the sky. Upper stories and roofs were bathed in *glorious* light. Up there, Mark could discern translucent porticoes, friezes and frescoes, trellises covered with orange roses, winged statues that lifted skyward golden, unbearably blazing lyres. In bright undulations, ethereally, festively, these *architectonic enchantments* were receding into the heavenly distance, and Mark could not understand how he had never noticed before those galleries, those temples suspended on high.)

The passages just cited occur at different points in the narration and are interrupted by accounts of Mark's happiness. "O, kak ja sčastliv, —dumal Mark, —kak vse čestvuet moe sčast'e." ("Oh, how happy I am," Mark kept musing, "how everything around celebrates my happiness.").[7] The last passage with its orange porticoes, its frescoes, its lyres and temples is Mark's hallucination as he lies dying near the tram tracks. Previous descriptive details of the sunset, however, have so prepared the reader for its recurrence that it is not immediately clear that this is the distorted vision of a semi-conscious mind.

The orange light which washes the city extends itself into Mark's personal realm as well. While the sunset exerts its abstract power over him, the red blaze of Klara's hair, so similar in color to the hues of the sunset which it mirrors, holds a more immediate fascination for him.

> . . . a potom [ona] zakružilas' po komnate, — jubka—zelenyj parus,—i bystro-bystro stala priglaživat' pered zerkalom *jarkie volosy svoi, cveta abrikosovogo varen'ja.*"[8]

> (. . . she began whirling about the room, her skirt like a green sail, and then she started rapidly smoothing her *glossy hair, the color of apricot jam,* in front of the mirror.)

At the very beginning of the story, before the sunset motif is even introduced, Klara's red hair promises to light up Mark's life as the sunset lights up the city.

> A čerez nedelju budet ix svad'ba, i potom do konca žizni—sčast'e i tišina, i noč'ju *ryžij požar,* rassypannyj po poduške . . .[9]

> (and in a week they would be married; then there would be a lifetime of bliss and peace, and of nights with her, the *red blaze* of her hair spreading all over the pillow, . . .)

Aside from the last tram in the opening lines auguring Mark's death, the story is fraught with hidden signs and symbols which pertain to other aspects of his death and marriage. On his way home from the pub the first night, Mark passes in an empty lot several moving vans whose contents are significant.

> A za černym zaborom, v provale meždu domov, byl kvadratnyj pustyr': tam, čto *gromadnye groba,* stojali mebel'nye furgony. . . . *Dubovye bauly,* verno, da ljustry, kak železnye pauki, da tjažkie *kostjaki dvuxspal'noj krovati.* . . . A sleva, na zadnej goloj stene doma, rasplastalis' gigantskie *černye serdca,* —uveličennaja vo mnogo raz ten' lipy, stojavšej bliz fonarja na kraju trotuara.[10]

> (On the other side of the fence, in a gap between the buildings, was a rectangular vacant lot. Several moving vans stood there like *enormous coffins.* They were bloated from their loads. Heaven knows what was piled inside them. *Oakwood trunks,* probably, and chandeliers like iron spiders, and the *heavy skeleton of a double bed.* The moon cast a hard glare on the vans. To the left of the lot, huge *black hearts* were flattened against a bare rear wall—the shadows, many times magnified, of the leaves of a linden tree that stood next to a streetlamp on the edge of the sidewalk.)

The coffin-like moving vans have stored in them the furnishings—oak trunks and the skeletons of double beds—of this marriage which will never take place. The tree leaves whose silhouetted shapes resemble black hearts are the images of Klara's betrayal. Mark is tipsy, so drunk with his love for

Klara and overwhelmed with his own happiness that these symbols hold no meaning for him. He is, in fact, blind to all emotions but his own. Before his celebration he had spoken enthusiastically to Klara of their future life together. Even though her response was to burst into tears, he has no doubt that these are tears of happiness.

Mark is somehow more than a young innocent who has fallen madly in love. He has about him the undefined quality of a dreamer. There are, moreover, thematic elements in this story which link to it Dostoevskij's *Belye noči* (*White Nights*). In the light of this information, Nabokov's choice of a German protagonist together with a clearly non-Russian-sounding title seems to have been his attempt at blurring the thematic borrowing and distancing any possible literary association. Like Mark, the unnamed protagonist of the Dostoevskij story is a dreamer whose happiness becomes totally dependent on his fiancée's (who in this case is called Nastenka) love for him. Like "Katastrofa" ("The Catastrophe"), the story also takes place over a restricted time period, four nights, and ends when Nastenka, like Klara, abandons the dreamer for her family's former lodger. The bridge and canal of Berlin where the fiery sunset makes its first appearance are reminiscent of the canals of St. Petersburg along which Dostoevskij's dreamer wanders for hours on end. Although the function of the sunset in "The Catastrophe" is clearly different, there are overtones in its description which recall certain scenes from the Petersburg tale.

> Neravnodušno smotrit on na večernjuju zarju kotoraja medlenno gasnet na xolodnom peterburgskom nebe . . . *On uže bogat svoej osobennoj žizn'ju*; on kak-to stal bogatym, *i proščal'nyj luč potuxajuščego solnca* ne naprasno tak veselo sverknul pered nim i vyzval iz sogretogo serdca celyj roj upečatlenij.[11]

>> (He looked not at all indifferently at the sunset which was slowly going out in the Petersburg sky . . . *He already had a rich personal life*; he had somehow grown rich *and the farewell ray of the extinguishing sun* did not flash so gaily before him nor did it elicit such a swarm of impressions from his warmed heart in vain.)

In addition to the mysterious lodger who suddenly reappears to spoil another man's happiness, Nabokov demonstrates his debt to the Dostoevskij work in the similarity of mood and atmosphere. The real life of these young men is interiorized. They move along the streets of their cities in self-induced states of ecstasy—ecstasy which renders them vulnerable. Totally nourished by his dreams, Dostoevskij's character could be sustained in any world or any life. The reader suspects that he will continue to live on in his dreams and memories of Nastenka. Nabokov's protagonist, before he can be told about Klara, "ušel, — v kakie sny—neizvestno"[12]

("Mark had departed—whither, into what other dreams, none can tell." By this last sentence, the implication is made that Mark's death, which is the major significant fact in the story, changes little, since his life was built on dreams.

The sunset, which has already been shown to function on a concrete level, also has a symbolic meaning for the protagonist. The Russian title, which Nabokov came to disavow, in fact provides a clue to his own understanding of the story. Mark's catastrophe and the sunset are partners. The sunset which builds to such a flaming crescendo before it dies has in it the same dynamics as those at work in Mark's life. His happiness which mounts and mounts until he is about to burst is arrested by a catastrophe which is at first only threatened by Klara's betrayal, but eventually fulfilled by his sudden death. Happy, fairhaired Mark, Mark the demi-god, does not know that he is in the sunset of his life, that the oranges and reds which promise so much are snuffed out by the night as suddenly and as carelessly as a tram accident erases a human life.

In the opposition of emotions there is, moreover, a perpetuation of the concrete and symbolic levels of the story. *"Takoe sčast'e"* (*What happiness*), which is the refrain throughout the first part of the narration, gives way to "kakaja bol'" ("what pain") as Mark lies dying. The pain, which is as intense as his earlier happiness, appears to kill him, but the question can be legitimately raised as to whether in fact he died of too much happiness. Mark feels and can almost visualize his own life slipping away from him. He experiences a total disembodiment which begins to occur at the moment of impact; he imagines that he sees himself walking away as if nothing had happened. The strange sensations are intensified by the visions he has— visions in the form of those buildings which resemble the vaults of heaven—of things he was never able to appreciate or even perceive in real life. It is the final pages of his tale which hold its meaning. In the moment of Mark's death there is more consequence than in the entire, somewhat foolish pattern of his life. His blissful love affair, which is really rather commonplace, if not downright banal, is totally lacking in the poetry which the narrator reserves for the wonderful sunset which is not only real, but representative of Mark's death and more lyrically rendered.

United Nations

NOTES

[1]This article is adapted from my unpublished doctoral dissertation, Linda Saputelli Zimmermann: *The Russian Short Stories of Vladimir Nabokov: A Thematic and Structural Analysis*, Harvard University, 1978.

[2]"Details of a Sunset" in *Details of a Sunset and other Stories*, New York, McGraw-Hill Book Company, 1976, p. 16. The English translations are Nabokov's own, taken from this edition.

[3]Leonard Michaels, "Details of a Sunset," *The New York Times Book Review*, April 25, 1976, p. 5; Anatole Broyard, "Mr. Nabokov on the Brink," *The New York Times*, May 18, 1976; John Sturrock, "Entertainment for Exiles," *Times Literary Supplement* (London), August 20, 1976, p. 1025.

[4]"Katastrofa" in *Vozvraščenie Čorba*, Berlin, Slovo, 1930, p. 147.

[5]*Ibid.*, p. 147.

[6]*Ibid.*, p. 152 and 153-154 (my italics).

[7]*Ibid.*, p. 152.

[8]*Ibid.*, p. 150 (my italics).

[9]*Ibid.*, p. 147-148 (my italics).

[10]*Ibid.*, p. 148 (my italics).

[11]F. M. Dostoevskij, "Belye noči," *Polnoe sobranie sočinenij v tridcati tomax*, vol. II, Leningrad: Nauka, 1972, p. 114 (my italics).

[12]"Katastrofa," *op. cit.*, p. 156.

ZOŠČENKO'S LENIN STORIES: THE PITFALLS OF HAGIOGRAPHY IN A SECULAR CONTEXT

Linda H. Scatton

In much the same way that American children are regaled with tales of the honesty, bravery and resourcefulness of our founding fathers, Soviet children learn of the saint-like qualities of Vladimir Il'ič Lenin. Mixail Zoščenko published a total of eighteen children's stories about Vladimir Il'ič Lenin, all of which appeared in 1939 and 1940, a period rich in Lenin stories. Three collections by different authors entitled *Tales of Lenin* were published in 1939 alone. Zoščenko's first collection was among these in 1939 (Moscow-Leningrad, Detizdat), and was republished the following year by Učpedgiz in Leningrad. A second collection, which included some new stories, was published by Pravda in Moscow in 1941. All but two of the Lenin stories appeared in *The Star*. Critical responses to these pieces was generally favorable; given the nature and stature of their subject, this was to be expected. The critics did find fault, however, with the means by which Zoščenko sought to portray Lenin, especially in the second group of stories. In order to make Lenin look more like a hero of irreproachable ethics, they claimed, Zoščenko had lowered the moral level of the characters surrounding him. For example, when Lenin exhibits what can only be termed common courtesy in the stories, he is held up as a model of new socialist morals and wisdom, while others in the stories are portrayed as Philistines. However these objections are really beside the point, since the genre to which the Lenin stories belong numbers this device among its most basic.

Zoščenko's stories belong to the general category of hagiographic literature about Lenin and to the specific subclass of works about Lenin for children. The *Tales of Lenin* present the following composite portrait of Lenin: he is truthful ("The Carafe"), fearless ("The Little Gray Goat"), brilliant, well-disciplined in mind and body ("How Lenin Studied"), iron-willed and selfless ("How Lenin Quit Smoking"), clever ("How Lenin Outsmarted the Police"), resourceful ("Sometimes It's OK to Eat Inkwells"), generous ("How Lenin Bought a Boy a Toy"), modest and self-effacing ("At the Barber's" and "How Auntie Fedos'ja Chatted with Lenin"), brave, considerate and solicitous of others ("An Attack on Lenin"), law-abiding and unpretentious ("Lenin and the Sentry"), forgiving ("Lenin and the Stovemaker"), self-critical ("A Mistake"), observant ("The Bees"), and sensitive to beauty ("Hunting").

Although only two of the tales concern Lenin as a child ("The Carafe" and "The Little Gray Goat"), the stories are all couched in the simplest language possible, in order to make them easily accessible to a young audience. The narration proceeds in slow motion, using almost none of the colloquial language which was the well-known Zoščenko trademark. (On the rare occasions when such language is used, it appears in the direct speech of one or more of the characters.) The paragraphs, uniformly short, as remains typical for Zoščenko, start repeatedly with "and," thus lending the narration almost a Biblical air. Many of the stories either begin or end with the moral or point stated directly, in a fashion reminiscent of eighteenth-century fables by Krylov. Unlike Zoščenko's more famous works, these stories exhibit little or no humor or irony. In fact, on the few occasions when these elements were present, they were termed inappropriate by Zoščenko's critics and they were removed from later editions: "Although Lenin's hunter-like turns of phrase show that Comrade Zoščenko intended to write a humorous story, they are hardly acceptable as a device for revealing Lenin's character."[1]

The first group of Zoščenko's Lenin stories appeared in *The Star*, No. 1, 1940: "Lenin and the Stovemaker, An Attack on Lenin, How Lenin Quit Smoking, How Lenin Bought a Boy a Toy, How Lenin Studied, At the Barber's, The Carafe, Sometimes It's OK to Eat Inkwells, The Bees, Hunting." The second group, published in Numbers 7, 8–9 of 1940, includes "Lenin and the Sentry, Lenin and the Firewood, How Lenin Was Given a Fish, A Mistake, How Auntie Fedos'ja Chatted with Lenin." (Two other stories which belong to this series were published separately: "At Age Forty-seven" appeared in *Red Army Soldier,* No. 1, 1941, and "The Little Gray Goat" was included in the 1939 volume of *Tales of Lenin.*) When the critics who attacked the second group of stories accused Zoščenko of lowering the moral qualities of Soviet citizens in order to make Lenin look better by comparison, they did not seem to realize that the writer had few other avenues of portrayal open to him. By depicting Lenin in the execution of his official duties as head of state, Zoščenko placed him in a context fraught with danger for the creative artist. Certainly, there is a mystique about Lenin which the portrayal of him within such a day-to-day context might easily dispel.

Two important factors inherent in the structure and realization of these stories combined to shape a dangerous stumbling block for Zoščenko. The first of these is the character of hagiographic literature itself: it is, by nature, a genre built on contrasts. No person may be made to seem extraordinary without the ordinary as background. The stronger the intended contrast, the greater must be the distance between the exception and the rule. Any subject endowed with superhuman, divine qualities must be seen against the background of the mere mortals among whom he moves. This is the stuff of which high drama is made; Russian *Saints' Lives* are filled with examples. One need only recall the saint who, as a mere infant, refused to suckle at his mother's breast during a fasting period; another who cried out three times in church while still in his mother's womb, ran away from home to join a monastery at age ten, and later lived an ascetic existence in the wilderness, refusing all luxuries and honors offered to him. Indeed, there are many instances in Zoščenko's Lenin stories where the hero fulfills the kenotic ideal, one of the most basic traditions of the Russian saints. He humiliates himself before a sentry; he wears plain and undistinguished clothing so that people do not recognize him as a person of special import; he disciplines his body, does manual labor and scorns all luxuries (e.g., the smoked fish proffered to him in "A Mistake"); he forgives the chronically rude and ill-tempered stovemaker; he "suffers for the faith" in a tsarist prison and as the object of an assassination attempt; he is at one with nature and incapable of destroying any part of it (e.g., "The Bees" and "Hunting"). As a young boy, Lenin shows signs of his future greatness when he reveals his fearlessness in "The Little Gray Goat" and his honesty in "The Carafe." At the risk of carrying this series of analogies too far, one might even point to the story "At The Barber's" as Zoščenko's version of the Tonsure.

As similar to the spirit of hagiography as many of these Lenin stories may be, they still necessarily lack the one element which, in religious literature, distinguishes the saint from other men: the divine, the supernatural. With the religious impetus absent, and the need, nevertheless, to create a saint-like *persona*, Zoščenko was left with only the background, the context. Since the miraculous was inadmissable evidence, it was necessary to show Lenin as more kind, more humane, more honest, more self-sacrificing, more brave than other men, i.e., to readjust the context in order to accommodate the non-miraculous hero who is its subject. One sure way to do this was to alter the context itself, to make the people surrounding the hero less brave than he. As the critics Martynov and Goffenšefer[2] noted in their reviews of the Lenin stories, Zoščenko did just this.

The second factor, which is closely related to the first, concerns Zoščenko's artistic method as such. It was his habit and his *forte* to pit the negative against the positive in his works, frequently blackening the negative excessively in order to make the contrast more striking. For his short stories, he had created a "collective type" of Soviet Philistine, one whose portrayal included the most compromising traits of Zoščenko's contemporaries. In these early stories, the attention is focused on the negative, with the positive assumed and never explicitly stated. In the Lenin stories, however, the attention is set on the positive. Although the basis here is still contained in contrast, the real problem for Zoščenko, as always, was to find a way to convey the positive. He uses the sole method with which he has had success earlier: he blackens the negative to heighten the contrast, although here the negative is at backdrop rather than center stage. This device is one of the few left to him, since it was unacceptable to portray Lenin speaking in the familiar Zoščenkovian style or evincing even the slightest hint of humor. All of Lenin's utterances are marked by gravity, seriousness and completely bland, standard language. The few times that the narrator alludes to the behavioral gulf which lies between Lenin and other Soviet citizens ("Another person, in Lenin's place, would probably have . . .") and, consequently, when he uses language which is more colorful, he comes under attack. It is sobering to note that just these sections have been eliminated from the later editions of the Lenin stories.[3]

When Lenin appears as a child in the stories, his speech is standard, correct, listless and colorless: "But why is he afraid? I don't want him to cry and be afraid. Children should be brave." ("The Little Gray Goat"). Lenin as an adult is a model of correct behavior and normative language. In a word, he is dull. Zoščenko's attempts at least to make interesting the background against which he functions proved dangerous for him both artistically and politically.

In her second volume of *Notes about Anna Axmatova* (Paris, 1980), Lidija Čukovskaja relates a conversation with Zoščenko in which he lays the blame for his political misfortune of 1946 squarely on the shoulders of a secondary character in his story, "Lenin and the Sentry." The tale describes how a Red Army guard at first refuses Lenin permission to enter the Smol'nyj Institute because the sentry does not recognize the leader. It is the person who berates the guard for his ignorance (in spite of the fact that Lenin praises him for doing his duty) whom Zoščenko came to view as the root of all his troubles. In the original version of the story, this person sported a mustache and a goatee. Zoščenko's editor claimed that this description bore too close a resemblance to Kalinin and advised the writer to get rid of the beard: "M.M. agreed: he crossed out the goatee. The mustache and rudeness remained. Stalin imagined that he was the one being described" (p. 108).

Zoščenko's attempt at secular hagiography in the *Tales of Lenin* ultimately fails for the reasons outlined above. Both his creative method and the contrastive nature of the genre were inimical to a successful portrayal of Lenin as a man among men. That a writer of Zoščenko's talents and bent tried his hand at this portrayal at all tells us perhaps more about the political realities of the late thirties/early forties than about the artistic evolution of the writer.

The State University of New York

NOTES

[1] I. Martynov, "Novye rasskazy M. Zoščenko o Lenine," *Literaturnoe obozrenie*, No. 24, 1940, p. 21.

[2] Martynov, *op. cit.*, and V. Goffenšefer, "Zametki o xudožestvennoj proze 1940 g.," *Novyj mir*, No. 2, 1941, pp. 195-196.

[3] Laundered versions of the stories appear in Mixail Zoščenko, *Rasskazy i povesti 1923–1956*, Leningrad, 1960 and Mixail Zoščenko, *Izbrannye proizvedenija v dvux tomax*, Leningrad, 1968.

"STIXI K BLOKU": CVETAEVA'S POETIC DIALOGUE WITH BLOK

David A. Sloane

> After Blok's death I continued meeting him at
> night on all the Moscow bridges. I knew he was
> roaming about here and perhaps was waiting. I
> was his greatest love, although he didn't know
> me—his greatest love, fated but unrealized.
>
> —M. Cvetaeva, letter to Baxrax
> (September 1923)

Marina Cvetaeva never met Aleksandr Blok, though she could have. In May 1920 she attended two of his poetry readings in Moscow, stood next to him in the crowd, but said nothing nor made any effort to introduce herself.[2] Instead she sent her seven-year-old daughter Alja backstage to deliver five poems later included in the cycle "Stixi k Bloku" ("Verses to Blok"). Blok is reported to have read them silently and reacted with "a long, drawn out smile."[3] He did not write Cvetaeva, nor did he reply to her in verse.

A complete communication had occurred—apparently in one direction only. The title of Cvetaeva's cycle, which ultimately grew to sixteen poems, suggests too that the verses form a lyric monologue: one poet addressing another.[4] The interpersonal dynamic within the cycle, however, is quite different; between the two poets there is something resembling a dialogue— both poets are speakers, both poets are addressees. Therefore A. Saakjanc's observation that the cycle is "a conversation with a deity" (421) carries much validity, though from a different perspective it is specifically a conversation **between poets**, since both parties communicate in their own verse— Cvetaeva directly, Blok indirectly via mediation of reminiscences from his poetry in Cvetaeva's voice. The aim of the present paper is to analyze the structure of this dialogue and consider its implications.

To begin with, this is not a conventional dialogue in that the speakers are not in direct proximity, nor do they engage in immediate verbal exchange. Cvetaeva speaks to Blok as if she were praying: (V) "Ja moljus' tebe" (I pray to you), on occasion even using phrasings from the Orthodox liturgy, or the vesper service, as in:

Свете тихий — святыя славы —
Вседержитель моей души. (III)

(O quiet light — of holy glory —/Pantocrator of my soul)[5]

She employs apostrophe and rhetorical questions, devices which suppose an absent or non-responding listener:

Нежный призрак,
Рыцарь без укоризны,
Кем ты призван
В мою молодую жизнь? (II)

(Gentle apparition,/ Knight without fault,/ By whom were you summoned/ Into my young life?)

О, кто мне расскажет,
В какой колыбели лежишь? (XIV)

(Oh, who will tell me,/ In what cradle you lie?)

Her speech may take the form of incantation, which presumes to effect behavior but not elicit verbal reponse:

Сделай милость:
Аминь, аминь, рассыпься! (II)

(Do a favor:/ Out, out, be gone!)

And although Cvetaeva usually addresses Blok as *ty* 'you', she alternates between this designation and the third-person *on* 'he', sometimes even within the same poem. These are strategies uncharacteristic of natural conversation, but quite common in lyric discourse, where the audience is an unstable category and the communication is basically self-addressed. As Northrop Frye writes:

> The lyric is . . . preeminently the utterance that is overheard. The lyric poet normally pretends to be talking to himself or someone else: a spirit of nature, a Muse . . ., a personal friend, a lover, a god, a personified abstraction, or a natural object. . . . The poet, so to speak, turns his back on his listeners, though he may speak for them.[6]

Cvetaeva's view of the lyric is very close: "Verse is for myself, prose is for everyone" (quoted by Troupin, 5). Similarly, Blok, as presented in the cycle, does not converse with Cvetaeva in the literal sense. His speech too is "overheard":

Так, узником с собой наедине
(Или ребенок говорит во сне?) (IX)

(Thus a prisoner [speaks] alone with himself/ (Or is this a child speaking in his sleep?))

His voice may be diffused in the natural elements, not directed to Cvetaeva specifically, or it may be silent:

> Без зова, без слова, —
> Как кровельщик падает с крыш.   (XIV)

(Without a call, without a word/ Like a roof-maker falling from the eaves.)

Generally, Blok is not even aware of Cvetaeva's presence:

> И не знаешь ты, что зарей в Кремле
> Я молюсь тебе — до зари.   (V)

(And you know not that by dusk in the Kremlin/ I pray to you — till dawn.)

At the same time, however, the sound of Blok's voice is ever-present in the cycle and continually inspires Cvetaeva to new lyric utterances. In poem II his singing is heard, and in this instance it is indeed addressed to the poetess: "On **poet mne** . . . On **poet mne** . . . **Zovet** . . ." (He sings to me . . . He sings to me . . . [He] calls). In poem V, Cvetaeva again hears him: "Ja tebe **vnemlju**" (I listen to you), and in poem VI his visual radiance is transformed into an auditory metaphor:

> Шли от него **лучи** —
> Жаркие **струны** по снегу.   (VI)

(Beams of light emanated from him —/ Hot musical strings along the snow.)

A similar synesthetic image appears in poem IX, where the poet's voice is likened to a ray of light: "Kak slabyj **luč** . . ./ Tak **golos tvoj**" (Like a weak beam of light . . ./ Your voice). Elsewhere the intonations of Blok's voice merge with other sonant phenomena—the swan's call, the howling of the snowstorm, or the proverbial music of the singing reeds:

> Блаженная тяжесть!
> Пророческий певчий камыш!   (XIV)

(O blessed burden!/ O prophetic singing reeds!)

Even death does not silence Blok's sound; in poem XV, for example, he is identified with Orpheus, whose head continues to "ring" after his body is dismembered by bacchanalian revelers:

> Не эта ль
> Серебряным **звоном** полна,
> Вдоль сонного Гебра
> Плыла голова?   (XV)

(Was it not this head/ Which floated/ Down the sleepy Hebrus,/ Of silver ringing full?)

Blok's image in the cycle is largely an acoustic one which undergoes a number of metaphoric permutations.

The idea of Blok's sound, however, is present in the cycle not only as motif but as concrete reality, since Cvetaeva literally echoes Blok's words in her own text. The cycle's first poem is the key since it presents the essence of her approach. There Cvetaeva plays with the sound of the word "Blok," getting a tactile sensation of it, continually returning to the feel of the name on her tongue, lips and throat:

> Имя твое — льдинка **на языке**.
> Одно-единственное **движенье** губ.
>
> . . . .
>
> Серебряный бубенец **во рту**.
>
> . . . .
>
> Имя твое — **поцелуй** в глаза,
>
> . . . .
>
> Имя твое — **поцелуй** в снег.
> Ключевой, ледяной, голубой **глоток**.   (I)[7]

If one considers that Blok's surname is the first word that belonged to him—even before his Christian name, even before his first coherent utterance—it becomes apparent that Cvetaeva's cycle represents a consistent effort to re-articulate and mediate the other poet's word through her own speech. In a sense, it is a dialogue carried on by a single articulatory apparatus.

Re-articulation of Blok's word is conspicuous in the reminiscences from his poetry that are scattered throughout the cycle. Their greatest concentration occurs in poem IX, where Cvetaeva records her impressions of Blok's recitation on May 9, 1920. From this poem is is even possible to reconstruct partially the evening's program since the textual parallels are quite strong. The program must have included, for instance, "Pesn' Ada" ("Hell's Canto"):

CVETAEVA	BLOK
Как слабый луч **сквозь** черный **морок адов** —	Знакомый Ад глядит в пустые очи.
Так **голос** твой **под** рокот рвущихся снарядов.	. . . .
	Средь ужасов и **мраков** потонуть.
. . . .	. . . .
Оповещает голосом глухим, —	Далеких **утр** неясное мерцанье
Откуда-то из древних **утр туманных**	. . . .
. . .	Под **утренним** холодным поцелуем
	В глубь зеркала **сквозь утренний туман**.
	. . . .

И вопрошаю **голосом** чуть внятным.

. . . .

И **голос** говорит из пустоты:

. . . .

И **мрак** был глух. И долгий вечер
мглист.

. . . .

И не кляни **повествований** странных.[8]

CVETAEVA: (Like a weak beam of light through the black darkness of
            hells—/ Is your voice beneath the rumble of exploding shells/
            . . ./ He narrates in a muffled voice,—/ Somewhere from the
            ancient hazy mornings . . .)

BLOK: (Familiar Hell peers into my empty gaze/ . . ./ To drown amidst the
            terrors and darknesses/ . . ./ The faint glimmer of distant morn-
            ings/ . . ./ Beneath the cold morning kiss/ . . ./ Deep into the mir-
            ror through the morning haze/ . . ./ I question in a barely audible
            voice/ . . ./ And a voice speaks out from the emptiness:/ . . ./ And
            the darkness was impenetrable. And the long evening foggy dim./
            . . ./ And don't abjure the strange narratives.)

Blok must have recited also "O doblestjax, o podvigax, o slave . . ." (Of
valorous, glorious deeds, of fame . . .) (1908):

CVETAEVA	BLOK
За **синий плащ**, за вероломства — грех . . .	Ты в **синий плащ** печально завернулась . . .
	. . . .
	Я крепко сплю, мне снится **плащ** твой **синий** . . .

CVETAEVA: (For the blue raincoat, for blasphemies — sin . . .)
BLOK: (Sorrowfully you wrapped yourself in the blue raincoat/ . . ./ I
            sleep soundly, I dream of your blue raincoat . . .)

As well as the poem "Golos iz xora" ("Voice from the Chorus") (1914):

CVETAEVA	BLOK
. . . . И еще о том, Какие **дни** нас **жудт**, как бог **обманет**, Как станешь **солнце звать** — и как **не встанет** . . .	Холод и мрак грядущих **дней**! . . . . Весны, дитя, ты будешь **ждать** — Весна **обманет**. Ты будешь **солнце** на небо **звать** — **Солнце не встанет**.

CVETAEVA: (And also about/ What days await us, how God will deceive
            us,/ How you will call the sun — and it will not rise . . .)
BLOK: (The cold and darkness of days to come!/ . . ./ You will await the
            spring, child,/ Spring will deceive you./ You will call the sun into
            the heavens,—/ The sun will not rise.)

Elsewhere in the cycle Cvetaeva continually echoes Blok—sometimes unmistakably as above, sometimes more subtly via repetition of motifs familiar from his lyric trilogy.[9] From the opening poem of "Stixi o Prekrasnoj Dame" ("Verses about the Beautiful Lady"), the central cycle of Blok's first volume, for instance, Cvetaeva draws the image of the "blue windows":

CVETAEVA	BLOK
Он поет мне	Купол стремится в лазурную высь.
За **синими окнами**.	**Синие окна** румянцем зажглись.
(Poem II)	(I, 74)

CVETAEVA: (He sings to me/ Behind blue windows.)
BLOK: (The cupola reaches for the azure height./ Blue windows are lit with red glow.)

Certain leitmotifs (*zarja, riza, kryl'ja*) are also derived principally from Blok's first volume, although no single poem serves as their source. Somewhat more prevalent are reminiscences from the second volume; calling Blok "snegovoj pevec" (singer of snows) (poem II) and repeated allusions to "metel'"/"v'juga" (snowstorm) naturally bring to mind the poet's romance with the Snow Mask and Faina, different manifestations of the second volume's principal heroine. In one instance Cvetaeva quotes verbatim from the poem "Kogda v listve syroj i ržavoj . . ." (When in the damp and rust-colored leaves . . .) (1907), which Blok included in the cycle "Faina":

CVETAEVA	BLOK
В **руку**, бледную от лобзаний,	Когда палач **рукой** костлявой
Не **вобью** своего **гвоздя**.	**Вобьет** в ладонь последний **гвоздь** . . .
(Poem III)	(II, 263)

CVETAEVA: (I shall not drive my stake/ Into the hand which has paled from caresses.)
BLOK: (When the executioner, with his bony hand,/ Has driven the last stake into the palm . . .)

Much of the imagery in poem XII is derived from Blok's programmatic lyric, "Syn i mat'" ("Son and Mother") (1906), also from the second volume:

CVETAEVA	BLOK
Матерь, ужель не узнала *сына*?	Вот он, **сын** мой, в светлом **облаке**,
Это с **заоблачной**—он— версты,	В шлеме утренней зари!
Это последнее—он—прости.	. . . .
. . . .	Точит грудь его пронзенная
Рваные ризы, крыло в **крови** . . .	**Кровь** и горние хвалы . . .
(Poem XII)	. . . .

В сердце **матери** оставленной
Золотая радость есть:
Вот он, **сын** мой, **окровавленный**!
(II, 108-109)

CVETAEVA: (Mother, did you not recognize your son?/ That was he from the milestone beyond the clouds,/ That was he sending his last farewell./ . . ./ Torn vestments, his wing covered with blood . . .)

BLOK: (There he is, my son, in the bright cloud,/ In the helmet of dawn!/ . . ./ His pierced breast gushes/ Blood and praises on high/ . . ./ In the heart of the mother who was left behind/ There is a golden joy:/ There he is, my son, covered in blood!)

The cycle is especially rich in reminiscences from Blok's third volume. The image of the "swan's call," for instance, clearly invokes "Na pole Kulikovom" ("On the Kulikovo Plain") (1907):

CVETAEVA	BLOK
Длинным **криком**,	За Непрядвой **лебеди кричали**,
Лебединым кликом —	И опять, опять они **кричат** . . .
Зовет. (Poem II)	(III, 250)
—	—
А над равниной —	Слышал я Твой голос сердцем вещим
Крик лебединый. (Poem XII)	в **криках лебедей**. (III, 250)
	—
	Опять за туманной рекою
	Ты **кличешь** меня издали . . .
	(III, 251)

CVETAEVA: (In a long shout,/ In a swan's call —/ He summons me); (And above the plain/ I hear a swan's call.)

BLOK: (Beyond the Neprjadva the swans shouted,/ And again, again they shout . . .); (With my prescient heart I heard Your voice/ In the swans' shouts); (Again beyond the hazy river/ You call me in the distance . . .)

In poem II there is a fleeting echo of Blok's "Žizn' moego prijatelja" ("The Life of My Companion") (1913–15):

CVETAEVA	BLOK
Так, по перьям,	Говорит **Смерть**:
Иду к **двери**,	А сам к моей блаженной **двери**
За которой — **смерть**.	Отыскивает вяло путь.
(Poem II)	(III, 53)

CVETAEVA: (Thus stepping on the feathers,/ I move towards the door/ Behind which is death.)

BLOK: (Death Speaks: And he himself listlessly seeks out the path/ To my blissful door.)

The word *čelovek* 'human being' in Cvetaeva's poem VI ("Dumali—čelo-vek!/ I umeret' zastavili") (They thought he was a human being!/ And forced him to die) also recalls Blok's late poetry and the play "Pesnja Sud'by" ("Song of Fate") (1908), where this image is allied with Christ's passion:

Раздался голос: *Ecce homo!*
Меч выпал. Дрогнула рука . . .   (III, 30)

—

Но я — **человек**. И, паденье свое признавая,
Тревогу свою не смирю я: она всё сильнее.
То ревность по дому, тревогою сердце снедая,
Твердит неотступно: Что делаешь, делай скорее.
                                                  (III, 46)

—

Се **человек**.
(Толпа уже отвлечена слухом о казни.)
                                                  (IV, 130)

(A voice resounded: *Ecce homo!*/ My sword fell. My hand shuddered . . .); (But I am a human being. And acknowledging my fall,/ I shall not pacify my agitation: it is ever stronger./ That is the zeal of my house, devouring my heart in agitation,/ That repeats unrelentingly: That thou doest, do quickly (John 2:17; 13:27)); (Behold a human being. (The crowd is distracted by a rumor about execution).)

Here Cvetaeva even reproduces the intonational break that follows the word in Blok's texts. Such intonational reminiscences, which capture the melodic patterns of Blok's poetic speech, are evident elsewhere as well; compare, for instance, the tri-partite formula "Za sinij plašč, za verolomstva — grex" (poem IX) with Blok's "O doblestjax, o podvigax, o slave . . .".

To determine what larger function these reminiscences serve, one must consider the dynamics of the cycle as a whole.

Two features of "Stixi k Bloku" are typical of Cvetaeva's method as a cyclic poet: 1) she uses a single basic dramatic situation and modulates it variously in successive poems, often with the effect of generating a certain plot momentum; 2) she tends to rework existing myth (broadly understood) rather than create her own (in this respect her cyclic technique is closer to Vjačeslav Ivanov's than Blok's). Like Blok, Cvetaeva tends to make her cycles into lyric narratives, but unlike Blok she usually borrows a dramatic situation and superimposes upon it her own lyric experience, her own bio-graphical subtext. In "Stixi k dočeri" ("Verses to My Daughter") (1916–19), for instance, the borrowed mythic situation is the Virgin-Mother's relation to the Christ-child; in "Marina" (1921), which is about her relation to the

Revolution, it is Marina Mnišek's role in the Time of Troubles; in "Georgij" (1921), which deals with her husband's participation in the Civil War, it
is the legend of St. George, the dragon-slayer. In this sense Cvetaeva's
cycles usually involve a framing situation (taken from life) and a framed
situation (taken from literature, folklore, or history).

In "Stixi k Bloku" we find a similar phenomenon. The framing situation
is Cvetaeva's desire to commune with Blok as a human being ("čelovek"),
even as an object of erotic affection. The framed situation is the myth of
Blok's own lyric "trilogy" in its various component scenarios. Moreover
there is in the disposition and selection of these scenarios a rationale
resembling plot movement.

This is apparent in the way Cvetaeva treats the theme of the **path**, the
central mythic construct of Blok's trilogy[10] Tracing this motif through the
cycle reveals a pattern which, though not followed rigidly, represents a recognizable trajectory of thought:

> HE IS MOVING/EN ROUTE   →   SHE IS MOVING/EN ROUTE
> SHE IS STATIONARY   →   HE IS STATIONARY

Early in the cycle the hero (Blok's image) is depicted in movement along a
path: "Ty proxodiš' na zapad solnca . . . Ty projdeš' . . . Nerušima tvoja
stezja . . . postup'ju veličavoj/ Ty prošel . . . I proxodiš' ty" (You pass by
moving toward the sunset . . . You will pass by . . . Your path is inviolable
. . . In stately gait/ You passed by . . . And you pass by) (poems III, V).
The hero is associated with the sound of horses' hooves ("V legkom ščel-
kan'e **kopyt**") (I) and carriage bells ("On poet mne/ **Bubencami** dalekimi")
(II). The heroine (Cvetaeva's image), by contrast, is generally motionless:
the hero **passes by** her **windows** in poem III, and she **stands (still)** as he
passes in poem V. This circumstance is familiar from Blok's "Stixi o Prekrasnoj Dame," where the poet is typically a wanderer while the Lady's
prime attribute is **immobility** (nepodvižnost'). Here Cvetaeva strives to
relate to Blok, essentially, via the myth of his first volume. Later in the
cycle these roles are reversed. The heroine becomes a traveler (VII) and
moves amid the native Russian landscape (VIII). As the hero's journey
comes to an end (XII, XV) and his image is transmuted into that of the
swaddled Christ-child awaiting discovery (XIV), the heroine's journey is
just beginning:

> Великим обходом
> Пойду по российской земле.   (XIV)

(In a great pilgrimage/ I shall wander about the Russian land.)

Here Cvetaeva is working with scenarios of Blok's third volume: the myth of reincarnation, as for example in the cycle "Venecija" ("Venice"), and the myth of passage through the homeland, as presented in the cycle "Rodina" ("Native Land"). Hence Cvetaeva seeks to commune with Blok first through his early poetry, then through his late poetry, and in this respect the design of her cycle mimics the outline of his trilogy.[11]

Reminiscences from "Snežnaja Maska" ("The Snow Mask") and "Faina," the core cycles of Blok's second volume, represented by contrast a negative model for Cvetaeva; these cycles are identified with a destructive stage in the biography of Blok's lyric hero ("V ruku . . ./ Ne vob'ju svoego gvozda" (III), whose gruesome lesson need not be repeated:

> — И снова родиться,
> Чтоб снова метель замела?!
>
> Рвануть его! Выше!
> Держать! Не отдать его лишь! (XIV)

(And [is he] to be born again,/ To be smothered again by the snowstorm?!/ Yank him up! Higher!/ Hold him! Don't dare give him up!)

Unlike the Snow Mask, who pursues, overtakes and annihilates the poet, Cvetaeva's lyric heroine chooses not to follow the poet on his journey and is content to maintain her distance:

> Восковому, святому лику
> Только издали поклонюсь. (III)

(Only from afar shall I worship/ His waxen, sacred countenance.)

Apparently, what frightens Cvetaeva most about "Snežnaja Maska" and "Faina" is that they involve an elemental erotic drive and sexual intimacy. With this possibility Cvetaeva flirts at first and then shies away, and the dynamic of this behavior is traced in her treatment of the name motif. The cycle's first poem, as we saw, depicts an almost erotic fascination with the poet's name; we observe something similar in Blok's cycle "Faina":

> Я слушаю говор открытый,
> Я тонкое **имя** люблю!   (II, 278)
>
> —
>
> Но **имя** тонкое твое
> Твердить мне дивно, больно, сладко . . .
>   (II, 282)
>
> —
>
> Хочу по **имени** назвать,
> Дышать и жить с тобою рядом . . . (II, 288)

(I listen to unmuffled speech, I love your slender name); (But for me to repeat your slender name/ Is wondrous, painful, sweet . . .); (I want to call you by name,/ To breathe and live beside you . . .)

Here, and in Cvetaeva's first poem to Blok, the name is a metonym for the person, and intimacy with the name sublimates physical intimacy with its owner. All of this is alien to Blok's use of the word *imja* 'name' in "Verses about the Beautiful Lady" and lyrics closely allied with their imagery:

> Отошла Я в снега без возврата,
> Но, холодные вихри крутя,
> На черте огневого заката
> Начертала Я **Имя**, дитя . . .   (I, 213)
> —
> Из огня душа твоя скована
> И вселенской мечте предана.
> Непомерной мечтой взволнована —
> Угадать Ее **Имена**.   (I, 293)
> —
> Ты в поля отошла без возврата.
> Да святится **Имя** Твое!   (II, 6)

(I have moved away into the snows without return,/ But spinning the cold whirlwinds,/ I have traced My Name, child,/ On the boundary of the burning sunset . . .); (Your soul is forged out of fire/ And entrusted to the universal dream./ Agitated by an immeasurable dream—/ One must guess Her Names.); (You have moved away into the planes without return./ Hallowed be Thy Name!)

Here "Imja" is not a concrete, but a mystic, often unknown quantity—an object of reverence rather than erotic gratification.

For Cvetaeva, Blok's name is known and concrete, but her attitude toward it evolves; if in poem I it is primarily an erotic object, in subsequent poems it becomes more an object of worship, although these categories are not entirely separate—the shift is more a change of emphasis. In poem III, for instance, the "name" is both sacred and erotic:

> И по **имени** не окликну,
> И руками не потянусь.
> . . . .
> И во **имя** твое святое
> Поцелую вечерний снег . . .   (III)

(And I shall not call you by name,/ And I shall not reach my arms out to you./ . . ./ And in your holy name/ I shall caress the evening snow . . .)

The first two lines establish the equivalency "po imeni okliknut'"—"rukami potjanut'"; here to "call by name" means to seek physical closeness. But in the last two lines the name is something holy; the erotic gesture of "kissing" is simultaneously an act of reverence. In poem IV glorifying the name ("slavit'/Imja") is contrasted specifically with feminine wiles ("ženščine lukavit'"); and in poem VIII Blok's name is something hallowed:

> И имя твое, звучащее словно: ангел. (VIII)

(And your name, sounding like the word 'angel'.)

This shift in emphasis is a sign of the heroine's evolving relation to the hero: her erotic, possessive love, which is strongest in poem I, ultimately yields to a different kind of love, which is akin to religious piety and imbued with the spirit of community. This is the sense of the cycle's final poem:

> Не свой любовный произвол
> Пою — своей отчизны рану.
>
> . . . .
>
> Русь — Пасхою к тебе плывет,
> Разливом тысячеголосым.
>
> Так, сердце, плачь и славословь!
> Пусть вопль твой — тысяча который? —
> Ревнует смертная любовь.
> Другая — радуется хору. (XVI)

(I sing not my own amorous whim/ But my fatherland's wound./ . . ./ Russia floats toward you at Easter,/ In its thousand-voice flood./ So, heart, weep and raise praise!/ Let mortal love be jealous of/ Your cry—Which thousandth is it?—/ Another love is joyful for the chorus.)

"Ljubovnyj proizvol" (amorous whim) and "smertnaja ljubov'" (mortal love) characterize that attitude and sentiment which the heroine explores in the first poem but then renounces as the cycle unfolds.

As we have seen, however, Blok's name is a metonym not only for the man, but for his poetic word. To "glorify his name" (IV) implies also paying homage to his poetic legacy. Olga Peters Hasty suggests this when she writes, apropos of the first poem's last stanza, that "child-like images are replaced by those associated with Blok's poetry."[12] The idea is captured vividly in Catherine Chvany's "sound effect" translation of the first poem's thirteenth line ("Imja tvoe—ax, nel'zja!").

> Praised be Thy Name . . . but I must not . . .
> **Whatever your own hallowed words prompt.**

Throughout the cycle Cvetaeva is repeating Blok's "name" in this sense—reproducing his poetic imagery, echoing intonations of his muse as modulated through her own voice. This is as intimate a dialogue as can exist between two people, more meaningful than the exchange of pleasantries which might have occurred May 14, 1920, had Cvetaeva introduced herself to Blok at the crowded Palace of the Arts in Moscow. Blok's silent reply, his knowing smile, suggests that he understood this; and as he read Cvetaeva's cycle he may well have recalled his own verses to the Beautiful Lady:

> Так — белых птиц над океаном
> Неразлученные сердца
> Звучат призывом за туманом,
> Понятным им лишь до конца.   (I, 78)

(Thus the inseparable hearts/ Of white birds soaring above the ocean/ Ring out beyond the mist like a call/ Whose ultimate meaning is grasped by them alone.)

Tufts University

NOTES

[1]Quoted by Margaret Ann Troupin in her dissertation "Marina Cvetaeva's *Remeslo*: A Commentary" (Harvard University, 1974), 62.

[2]Cvetaeva describes the circumstances of this non-meeting in a letter to Pasternak from February 1923; see her *Izbrannye proizvedenija* (M–L: "Sovetskij pisatel'," 1965), 735.

[3]A. Saakjanc, "Marina Cvetaeva ob Aleksandr Bloke," in *V mire Bloka: Sbornik statej* (M: "Sovetskij pisatel'," 1981), 426.

[4]I am using the texts and numbering of poems as given in *Izbrannye proizvedenija*, 92-103. Originally the cycle appeared in Marina Cvetaeva, *Stixi k Bloku* (Berlin: "Ogon'ki," 1922), 11-37; there the poems are split into two sections—one written before Blok's death, the other after—which are numbered separately.

[5]The Russian Orthodox phraseology in Cvetaeva's cycle is discussed in greater detail by Catherine Chvany in her companion article, this volume.

[6]*Anatomy of Criticism: Four Essays* (Princeton: Princeton University Press, 1971), 249-250.

[7]For translations of this poem see Chvany, this volume.

[8]Aleksandr Blok, *Sobranie sočinenij v vos'mi tomax* (M–L: "Xudožestvennaja literatura," 1960-63), III, 15-018; subsequent references to this edition will be given in the text.

[9]In referring to the "volumes" of Blok's "trilogy," I will use its final, so-called "canonical" version published 1918-22. Cvetaeva, of course, could not have know this version when she started writing the cycle, but she may have known its penultimate redaction, which began appearing in April 1916, the same month she composed poem I.

[10]On the importance of this theme in Blok see D. E. Maksimov's seminal article, "Ideja puti v poètičeskom mire Al. Bloka," in his *Poèzija i proza Al. Bloka* (L.: "Sovetskij pisatel'," 1981), pp. 6-151.

[11]For analysis of the "trilogy's" cyclic design, see my forthcoming book, *Aleksandr Blok and the Dynamics of the Lyric Cycle.*

[12]Olga Peters Hasty, "'What's in a Name?': Cvetaeva'a Onomastic Verse," ms., read at the Yale Colloquium on Marina Cvetaeva, New Haven, April 12-14, 1984.

THE INTERPRETATION OF POLITICS: SOME PROBLEMS IN RUSSIAN-ENGLISH SIMULTANEOUS INTERPRETATION

Lynn Visson

Interpretation has the dubious honor of being among the world's oldest professions, dating back to the tower of Babel (Genesis 11). And in his first letter to the Corinthians St. Paul orders, "If any man speak in an unknown tongue let it be by two, or at most by three . . . and let one interpret." (14:27).

As distinguished from written translation, interpretation is an oral process.[1] In consecutive interpretation the speaker continues for several sentences while the interpreter takes notes; the speaker then pauses to allow for interpretation.[2] Consecutive is used at a few State Department conferences, disarmament negotiations, formal dinners with toasts, and was used at the United Nations until 1951.[3] Simultaneous interpretation, during which the interpreter does not wait for the speaker to pause, but interprets simultaneously, is used at most State Department conferences, almost all United Nations meetings, and many conferences in the private and business sphere.

While interpretation from one language into another has existed for centuries, modern simultaneous interpretation with microphones, earphones, and sound equipment is a relatively new phenomenon. In the nineteenth century there was no need for interpretation, since French was the universal language of diplomacy. Consecutive was first used at the Paris peace conference of 1919, and simultaneous at the sixth congress of the Comintern held in Russia in 1928. Simultaneous interpretation first emerged on the world scene at the Nuremburg trials, and many of those interpreters went on to work at the newly founded United Nations. In 1948 the first school for interpreters was opened in Geneva, and in 1962 Moscow's Thorez institute began its training program. Schools also exist in London and Heidelberg; in the U.S. training is available at Georgetown University and the Monterey Institute of International Studies (Russian is available only at Monterey). There are two major professional organizations for conference interpreters, The American Association of Language Specialists (TAALS) and the Association Internationale des Interprètes de Conference (A.I.I.C.). During the last twenty years literature on interpretation has grown steadily; basic Russian works include G. V. Černov, *Teorija i praktika sinxronnogo perevoda* (Moscow: Meždunarodnye otnošenija, 1978) and A. F. Širjaev, *Sinxronnyj perevod* (Moscow: Voenizdat, 1979).[4]

Any conference using several languages usually works on a system of booths, i.e. the target language. Interpretation into English is carried out by the English booth, into Russian by the Russian booth, etc. The United Nations has six booths, one for each of the official languages: English, French, Spanish, Russian, Chinese and Arabic. The first four booths work solely into these languages, while the Chinese and Arabic booths interpret both into Chinese and Arabic and from them into English or French. Because of the extra burden of working into and from the native language, the Chinese and Arabic booths at a meeting have three interpreters, while the English, French, Spanish and Russian have two. In the English booth one person (known as the *russifiant*) works into English from French and Russian, while his colleague (known as an *hispanisant*) works from French and Spanish. Similarly, in the French booth one interpreter works into French from English and Russian while the other works from English and Spanish. If a Russian-speaking delegate takes the floor while the *russifiant* is out of the English booth, his colleague listens to the interpretation of Russian into French and translates that into English. This process obviously requires close coordination to ensure that both *russifiants*—or both *hispanisants*—do not walk out at the same time; generally, work is divided into half-hour shifts. Elaborate versions of the game of "Telephone" can result at a meeting: e.g., Russian is interpreted into French, then into English, and then into Chinese—a triple interpretation within a couple of seconds.

Given the extreme pressure of simultaneous interpretation, it is clearly advisable to have the interpreter work into his native language. Even some bilinguals have difficulty interpreting into one of their two languages; it is a bit like asking a train to switch tracks in a split second at a complicated railroad crossing. Two requirements for an interpreter are total fluency in the target language, and total comprehension of the foreign language. Different language skills serve different purposes, and there is no automatic connection between one skill and another. A person may speak Russian well and write it badly, or read with total comprehension but have no oral fluency. The skills can be taught and developed separately, too. Teachers of Russian are sometimes startled to realize that superb Russian-English interpreters could starve to death on the streets of Moscow, for some of the world's best interpreters cannot—or will not—speak the languages from which they interpret. The job requires aural comprehension, not active speaking ability.

The simultaneous interpreter translates speeches, statements, documents, and informal conversation. A delegate may distribute the text of a statement in advance, allowing the interpreter to consult a dictionary or colleagues and to prepare the translation. Many texts, however, are marked "check against delivery," and there is no guarantee that the delegate will not make last minute changes, additions, or omissions; he may in fact monitor the interpretation to check whether the changes have been included in the translation. In some cases the interpreter is given both the original text of a speech and a translation into English, an item known as a Van Doren, an appellation which harks back to Charles Van Doren's apparently spontaneous performance on the $64,000 Question television show for which the answers had in fact been rehearsed in advance. Even with a Van Doren, the interpreter must remain alert, since the quality of the translation can vary and there may be changes in the actual text delivered.

One of the biggest hurdles for the interpreter is a delegate who gallops through his speech at inhuman speed. Interpreters who work from English into Russian have a particularly difficult problem since the sheer length of Russian words and the structure of the language cause interpretation into Russian to take thirty-three per cent longer than the time required for Russian-English translation. As a result the Russian interpreter is often forced to condense the text to avoid falling far behind the speaker. Studies have shown that with a delegate speaking English at a rate of 166-180 syllables per minute the interpreter works into Russian at an average of 206 syllables per minute, and the degree of condensation of the text (as compared to a standard written translation of the material) is zero per cent. With the speaker at 226-240 syllables per minute the interpreter is averaging 222 syllables in Russian, and the rate of condensation rises to 28.2%.[5] In interpreting from any language, however, the intellectual effort required to condense a text often takes more energy and time than does an attempt to speed up to match the speaker's tempo. And regardless of how fast the speaker is going—or what language the interpreter is speaking—it is of paramount importance that the interpreter finish, or "wrap up" his sentence; a dangling phrase will cause the listener to lose confidence in the translator.

One of the biggest problems for the Russian-English simultaneous interpreter is that of syntax. Participial phrases are especially tricky, e.g. a sentence beginning "*Odobrennaja dvadcat' pervogo dekabrja delegatami iz soroka stran na zasedanii našej rabočej gruppy* . . . ." The interpreter cannot wait for the magic word "*rezoljucija*," for if he does so he risks losing the entire sentence. A solution is to insert a temporary subject and then replace it: e.g. "Something which was adopted," + rest of sentence + "namely, the resolution," or "I am referring to the resolution."

Russian syntax also tends toward *tema* position locative construction which translate awkwardly into English. Sentences beginning "*V stranax tret'ego mira*" or "*V ètom doklade obsuždaetsja*" are often best interpreted on the principle Think nominative: "The countries of the third world," "The report deals with," etc. The nominative *tema* allows for a reordering of the *rema* to produce a much more elegant English sentence.

Tenses—and the relative lack of them in Russian—are another potential stumbling block for the Russian-English interpreter. Each Russian verb confronts the interpreter with a problem of choice. English may prefer a continuous tense, or a perfect; nor is the best rendering always clear at the time the interpreter launches into the translation of the Russian sentence. A clause which pops up later in a phrase may make the interpreter wish he had taken a different decision.

The following sentences illustrate a frequently met construction:

Mongol'skaja delegacija s samogo načala vozražala i vozražaet protiv obsužde-nija ètogo voprosa. My sčitali i sčitaem, čto obsuždenie ètogo nadumannogo voprosa, vopreki vole afganskogo naroda . . .

Rather than repeating each verb, the interpreter might simplify the sentence into "From the outset, the Mongolian delegation has objected to . . ." The "*sčitali i sčitaem*" can be compressed to "We continue to believe that," avoiding awkward repetition of the verb. "Continues" is also a useful solution in interpreting a construction such as "*Sovetskij sojuz i vpred' budet zaščiščat' prava*"—"The Soviet Union will continue to defend the rights" or "*SSSR i teper' vystupaet za nezamedlitel'noe prinjatie mer*"—"The USSR continues to favor," etc.

Words are an interpreter's best friends, but also his worst enemies. Context and meaning must always be uppermost in the interpreter's mind. The word "shot," for example, could refer to a gun, a camera, some vodka, outer space, or an injection. In political language, Russian and English cognates may acquire somewhat different connotations than those they retain in everyday speech—e.g. "*revoljucija*" and "revolution." In Russian the word always means a radical and progressive change in any field of life; in English it could refer to either a progressive or reactionary event. A sentence such as "Revolutions are a common occurrence in Latin America" would therefore translate as "*Gosudarstvennye perevoroty — obyčnoe javle-nie v Latinskoj Amerike.*" Speaking of a palace revolution, English might well prefer "coup d'état." The word "*idealizm*" (idealism) also takes on different shades of meaning in Russian and English. Russian political language uses the word to mean a philosophical trend of thought hostile to materialism; in English it implies advocacy of lofty ideals over practical considerations.

Sometimes entirely different words express phenomena which vary from one social system to another. A Russian referring to American "*služaščie i raboče*" means white and blue collar workers. The expression "full employment" could be translated into Russian literally as "*polnaja zanjatost'*" or by the more common Russian term "*otsutstvie bezraboticy.*" And then there are always the dangerous "*ložnye druz'ja perevodčika*" lurking about, ready to trip up the unwary interpreter. An "*aktual'nyj vopros*" is an urgent, pressing, or relevant issue. "Decade" in English means ten years, but in Russian "*dekada*" refers to ten days.

Puns, jokes, proverbs, and idiomatic expressions also seem created expressly to plague the interpreter. Sometimes paraphrase and English-language equivalents are imperative, as for example in dealing with "*Pokažu ja vam kus'kinu mat'*," or "*motat' sebe na us.*" Great care must be exercised in translating such expressions, for excessive creativity can land the interpreter in deep trouble. If he decides to say "put it in your pipe and smoke it" for "*kus'kina mat'*," an English-speaking delegate may well pick up on the expression and retort to his Soviet colleague, "We've all stopped smoking," "yes, let's smoke a peace pipe," or "let's find the smoking gun." The result—an utterly confused Russian delegate violently insisting he never said anything about smoking, and a very sheepish interpreter. One of the main differences between written translation and oral interpretation at meetings is that the listener—as opposed to the reader—can and will give a response to the translation. Those flights of fancy which get students A's in class will get F's in a political forum where passions run high, talk goes quickly, and a phrase or even a single word can communicate highly sensitive material relating to government policies or decision making. In this situation "We'll show you," or 'We'll give it to you" would be a safe bet for "*kus'kina mat'*," and "make a mental note of it" a reasonable rendering of "*motat' sebe na us.*"

Even when there does seem to be a perfect English parallel to a Russian expression the interpreter must use great caution. The translator who seizes upon "a pig in a poke" as the ideal rendering of "*kot v meške*" may bitterly regret his flash of brilliance if the speaker's cat then proceeds to meow or arch its back. The speaker's next sentence, or his further development of a metaphor cannot be predicted. Expressions with highly colored language are often best translated literally. An interpreter who rephrased Gromyko's "*V meždunarodnyx delax namerevajutsja vesti sebja po principu — čto levoj noge zablagorassuditsja*"[6] as "whatever one feels like doing" or "according to their whim" would be in an awkward position when faced with the next sentence of this text: "*Vot i stupajut po čužim zemljam kovanym soldatskim sapogom — to levym, to pravym.*" A translation of "*mež dvux ognej*" by "between the devil and the deep blue sea" or of "*posle doždika v četverg*" by "till hell freezes over" would be ill advised because of the English theological implications which do not exist in the Russian expressions.

The interpreter's major problem goes far beyond the rendering of idiomatic expressions or individual words. His number one task is to make Russian political prose sound like normal English. The goal of the interpreter, after all, is comprehension by a listener, who is unaware of the specific words used in the original Russian. It is up to the interpreter not to let himself be dragged along lamely by the Russian words; his job is to process, to make the linguistic raw material he hears into a fully finished product. He must make sense—and English—out of the Russian text in a minimum amount of time. Slavists would do their students a great service if they stressed from Lesson I on the importance of using good English when translating from Russian, even if the translation involves no more than a drill on the use of participles or time expressions. The habit of bad or literal translation into English is not easily broken, and the place to instil a respect for English as well as for Russian is the language classroom.

A Russian sentence may need reworking—at the expense of individual lexical units—to transform it into palatable English. Take for example, "*Meždunarodnaja atmosfera snova načala osložnjat'sja, a zatem i nakaljat'-sja.*" The idea expressed by "*osložnjat'sja*" is one of worsening or deterioration rather than of complexity. A literal rendering of "*nakaljat'sja*" by "heating" or "tempering" fails to work in English. The point of the verb is that the situation has reached an extreme; it has become critical. So too, a literal rendering of "*èta politika obankrotilas'*" might leave the listener puzzled, while "this policy is now discredited" would shed light on the speaker's intention. Another example are the "*tuči voiny*" which in Russian tend to "*sguščat'sja.*" English-speaking clouds, however, prefer to "gather" rather than to darken or pile up.

Individual words, too, take on different meanings when translated in a political context. "Fault" or "guilt" automatically come to mind as translations for "*vina,*" but in a sentence such as "*I èto ne po vine sovetskogo sojuza*" a different word is appropriate: "And for this the Soviet Union is not to blame." "*Napravlenie*" if we are speaking of "*dannoe napravlenie v mirovoj politike*" is more often "area" than "direction"; and something which is "*principial'no važno*" may be "extremely important." A document which contains a "*kompleksnaja programma*" has far or wide ranging rather than "complex" information, and a "*rjad*" of *zadači* or *problemy* are much happier being a "number" of issues rather than a "series" in English.

The problem of stylistics is made particularly difficult by time pressure. It is often hard enough to come up with a correct or appropriate word, let alone a stylistically happy one. Yet Russian statements are often highly verbally colored, especially when they are critical in tone. Such critical texts tend to make heavy use of two stylistic levels, an elevated language based mainly on Church Slavonic roots, and an extremely colloquial, almost slangy plane of Russian. For example:

> *Obrečennye istoriej rasisty . . . ne smogli by tvorit' prestupnye **dejanija** bez opory na èti krugi.*
>
> *Prinimaemye rezoljucii jakoby nedoocenivajut značenie ètix **blagodejanij** . . . èti dremučie skazki o položitel'nom kolonializme uže nikogo ne mogut vvesti v zabluždenie.*
>
> *Sjuda izdavna ustremljalis' alčnye vzory čužezemnyx zaxvatčikov.*
>
> *V Belom dome s pompoj prinimajut ee glavarej. V dekabre prošlogo goda v gosdepartamente bylo organizovano provokacionnoe sborišče, na kotorom s učastiem predvoditelej banditskogo otreb'ja . . . obsuždalis' voprosy aktivizacii . . . pomošči naemnym bandam.*[7]

If the interpreter has the luxury of a few extra seconds to reflect, he may wish to translate "*dejanija*" as "deeds" rather than "actions"; "*dremučie skazki*" might come across as "hoary tales" or, depending on the speaker's tone in the rest of the speech, as "time-worn chestnuts." "*Sborišče*" could be rendered by "get-together," and "*otreb'e*" as "riffraff," "rabble," or "mob." Here too, though, extreme caution must be used to avoid distorting the precise meaning a delegate wishes to convey to his listeners. Sometimes a speaker may monitor the interpretation, and may correct the interpreter if he disagrees with the translation or finds that the interpreter has taken too many stylistic liberties. In the highly charged sphere of political discourse, neutrality is often the best policy.

While stylistics is the icing on the interpreter's cake, such political texts could provide interesting material for classroom discussion and translation in advanced level Russian courses. More attention to translation problems—with stress on English as well as on Russian—would help students to express themselves better in both languages. Translators and interpreters, after all, deal with the same linguistic raw materials as do teachers of Russian, and today's students are tomorrow's translators. Closer cooperation would benefit teachers, students, and interpreters as well.

United Nations

NOTES

[1]The author is heavily indebted to Stephen B. Pearl, Chief, English Section, Interpretation Service, United Nations; Cyril Muromcew, Language Services, U.S. Department of State; and Vadim Milstein, INION of the USSR Academy of Sciences, for much of the information in this paper. All judgments and errors are mine alone.

[2]Nearly all interpreters, even those who know a shorthand system, take notes in the form of symbols—e.g., a drawing of a flag for "country," a question mark for "issue" or "problem," a frowning face for "disagreement." Apparently there is a Vygotskian symbolic stratum involved in the shift from one lexical system to another. On this cf. D. H. Garretson, "A Psychological Approach to Consecutive Interpretation," *Meta*, 26, #3, 1981.

[3]Consecutive continued to be used in the Security Council until 1970, when a shift was made to simultaneous interpreting.

[4]See also:

C. Andronikov, "Servitude et grandeur de l'interprète," *Babel*, 8, #1, 1962.

A. H. Birse, *Memoirs of an Interpreter*, New York: Coward McCann.

D. Gerver, "A Psychological Approach to Simultaneous Interpretation," *Meta*, 20, #2, 1975.

E. A. Gofman, "K istorii sinxronnogo perevoda," *Tetradi perevodčika*, 1. Moscow: Meždunarodnye otnošenija, 1963.

G. G. Judina, *Učites' perevodit'*. Moscow: Meždunarodnye otnošenija, 1962.

―――, *Improve Interpreting Skills*. Moscow: Meždunarodnye otnošenija, 1976.

P. Longley, *Conference Interpreting*. London: 1968.

R. K. Minjar-Beloručev, *Posledovatel'nyj perevod*. Moscow: Voenizdat, 1969.

―――, *Posobie po ustnomu perevodu*. Moscow: Vysšaja škola, 1969.

R. Neubert, "Einige Uberlegungen zum Sprechakt beim Dolmetschen," *Fremdsprachen*, #2, 1971.

T. Nilski, "Translators and Interpreters—Siblings or a Breed Apart?" *Meta*, 12, #2, 1967.

E. Weintraub, M. Lederer, and J. de Clarens, "Enseigner l'interprétation," *Études de linguistique appliquée*, Paris, #12, 1973.

These are only a few titles from the extensive number of works written on interpretation. For further bibliography see Černov, *op. cit.*, pp. 201-07.

[5]Širjaev, *op. cit.*, pp. 86-87.

[6]Speech to the 39th Plenary Session of the United Nations General Assembly by A. A. Gromyko, document A/39/PV.10/63.

[7]Quotations are from Ukrainian and Belorussian speeches given at the 39th session of the United Nations General Assembly, November–December 1984. Since almost all United Nations speeches are given in one of the six official languages—English, French, Spanish, Russian, Chinese, and Arabic—the Ukrainian and Belorussian statements are written in Russian.

FORMAL AND AESTHETIC FUNCTIONS OF DIMINUTIVES IN THE RUSSIAN LAMENT

Dean S. Worth

1. One of the most characteristic stylistic features of Russian folk verse in general, and of the Russian funeral lament in particular, is the unusually high frequency of hypocoristic (diminutive) forms. They are especially frequent among substantives (времечко, головушка, живленьице) and adverbs (ранешенько, тошнешенько, теперечко), and can also be seen in verbs with the non-spatial (attenuative) prefix при-. Hardly a lament line is without some form of diminutive or other, and they frequently occur two or three to the line, as for example in the following passage from Barsov 1872:[1]

> Резвы *ноженьки* у нас да все *при*топчутся,
> Белы руч*еньки* у нас да *при*махаются,
> Сила могуча во плеч*юшках при*держится;
> Без мороз*ушку* серд*ечко при*рострескает;
>
> (13.49-52)

The meaning of these misnamed "diminutives" is not, of course, really diminutive at all: the плечюшки which contain а сила могуча are clearly not narrow, nor is the 'ocean-sea' of

> Во это в океан — да сине морюшко (6.112)

presented as in any way diminished in size. The function of these hypocoristic forms is not referential but purely emotive, reflecting the direct emotional response of the lament singer to the entire physical and emotional world by which she is surrounded (солнышко, лесушки, реченька, ветероченьки; платьице, подвесточка, окошечко, стульица; живленьице, кручинушка, разлукушка, смеретушка, etc.). These suffixes create a deictic bond between the bereaved person and the world she lives in, a bond which forces all of nature to share in, and hence to lighten, the lonely grief of the individual. The ensuing, intensely emotional tonality of the Russian lament is obvious.

However, in addition to this general, emotive function, diminutives in the Russian lament serve other, more specifically poetic purposes. These purposes are both formal and aesthetic,[2] dealing with syllabic and colon structure on the one hand, and with the aesthetics of phonological and semantic patterning on the other. These formal and aesthetic functions will be discussed in sections **2** and **3** below.

2. Formal functions. Hypocoristic suffixes serve two separate but interrelated formal (in the broad sense, metrical) purposes. On the one hand, they serve as metrical (syllabic) fillers, and on the other, they mark the line-end and the line's internal division into cola.

2.1. Syllabic fillers. The most frequent lament type has thirteen syllables with ictuses on the odd-numbered syllables and strong ictuses (fulfilled by the stresses of major parts of speech) on the third, seventh, and eleventh; the first and/or last syllable may be omitted. Less frequent types have nine or (more rarely) eleven syllables. The most obvious function of hypocoristics is to complete the metrical line; that is, they fill out those syllables which the underlying morphosyntactic component of the line has not occupied with obligatory elements. One can assume, for example, that the line

> Со стадушком оно да со детиною   (1.7)

has an underlying structure something like

> {s# stad-...om s# detinoj(u)}

(plus the syntactic bracketing characterizing this string), and that the surface manifestation of this underlying structure is adjusted to meet the metrical requirements of the lament. This adjustment is accomplished in two steps. First, the line is expanded by exploiting the syllabic variability of the underlying structure, namely, by (a) repeating the preposition {s#} and vocalizing both instances of it to co, (b) choosing the long variant -ою of the fem. instr. ending {-#j[u]}, and (c) adding the hypocoristic suffix {uš#k} to the stem {stad-}. In this way, the bare five syllables of the obligatory base are expanded to nine, namely

> /so staduškom so det'inoju/.

Second, the resulting nine-syllable line is further expanded by repeating both the clitic да and the anaphoric оно from the preceding lines

> Укатилося красное солнышко
> За горы *оно да* за высокия,
> За лесушка *оно да* за дремучии,
> За облачка *оно да* за ходячии,
> За часты звезды *да* за подвосточныя!
> Покидать меня победную головушку   (1.1-6),

whence   Со стадушком *оно да* со детиною;   (1.7).

Line 7 is now—except for the shortened anacrusis (syllable one of the thirteen-syllable line is missing)—a metrically perfect lament line. The choice of the suffix {uš#k}, rather than a clitic filler resulting in such a line as

*Со стадом *же* оно да со детиною,

is motivated by complex and poorly understood syntactic and metrical factors that cannot be approached in the framework of an article; cf., however, the remarks on colon structure below.

The example beginning Со стадушком . . . showed a hypocoristic at work filling out weak syllables after the first strong ictus in syllable three (in the given instance, with shortened anacrusis, two). The same function is fulfilled after the second strong ictus in, for example,

Чорным вороном в окошко залетела,   (3.43).

In this example, however, the underlying morphosyntactic structure itself occupies eleven syllables, namely

$$
\begin{array}{c}
1\ \ 2 \quad\ \ 3\ 4\ \ 5 \qquad 6 \qquad 7\ 8\ \ 9\ 10\ 11 \\
\{\text{čorn-im voron-om v# ok#n-o za=lete-l-a}\},
\end{array}
$$

which, except for the shortened clausula, leaves only a single syllable to be supplied. The addition of {š#k}, which displaces the ending -но of окно one syllable to the right, is all that is needed to produce another metrically perfect line (the trochaic clausula being dictated by the highly restricted choice of line-final clitics).[3]

Metrical filling is most frequent of all after the third strong ictus (syllable eleven), because of the nearly obligatory dactylic clausula; the twelfth and thirteenth syllables are unstressed 99% and 97% of the time, whereas the final syllables of the first and second cola (syllables five and nine, respectively) are filled by phonologically stressed vowels in app. 30% and 21% of the lines respectively.[4] For example, in all three of the lines

Не утай, скажи, спорядной мой суседушко
Моей милоей, законноей сдержавушке:
Как посли своей надежноей головушки   (15.51-16.2)

the suffix {uš#k} provides the necessary dactylic clausula. What actually transpires, however, is different in each of the three lines. In (16.1) the base form {s#=deržav-} would have given the acceptable though not preferred trochaic clausula *. . . сдержаве, which is simply "stretched out" by {uš#k} to form the dactyl . . . сдержавушке. In (15.51), the o-stem base {sused-} could only have resulted in the absolutely unacceptable line-final stress *. . . сусéд, and {uš#k} provides not only the unstressed syllable уш but also the vocalic ending -о, again resulting in the dactyl . . . сусéдушко. Finally, the underlying end-stressed {golov-} of (16.2) could have given only the unacceptable final-stressed *. . . головы́, while the addition of {uš#k} again provides the needed dactyl . . . голо́вушки.[5] The extent to which hypocoristics serve as syllabic fillers can be seen from the following table, which shows, for the 1193 lines of Barsov 1872:1-44, the number of times each of the line's thirteen syllables is filled by part of a hypocoristic but would not have been filled by its base (e.g., резвы но́жень*ки* compared to резвы но́ги):

Syllable:	1	2	3	4	5	6	7	8	9	10	11	12	13
Hyp. fillers:	0	0	1	16	116	0	2	31	98	0	14	128	548

One can compare the absolute and percentage figures for each of the three cola, as follows:

	FIRST COLON				*SECOND COLON*				*THIRD COLON*			
Syll:	2	3	4	5	6	7	8	9	10	11	12	13
No.	0	1	16	116	0	2	31	98	0	14	128	548
%:	0	1	12	87	0	2	24	75	0	2	19	79

The fact that the absolute figures are much larger for the third than for the first two cola reflects the fact that hypocoristics in this position mark not only the colon, but also the line-end boundary. We can also combine the figures for the three cola, in order to show which otherwise unfilled syllables of the colon, in general, have been supplied by hypocoristics:

	FIRST ARSIS (2,6,10)	*STRONG ICTUS* (3,7,11)	*SECOND ARSIS* (4,8,12)	*WEAK ICTUS* (5,9,13)
No.	0	17	175	762
%	0	2	18	80

These distributional data lead naturally into a discussion of the delimitative functions of hypocoristics in *2.2* below.

2.2. Delimitative functions. Hypocoristics serve not only as syntactic fillers, but also as border signals, marking both the line-end and the internal segmentation of the line into cola.

The 13-syllable lament line consists of a monosyllabic anacrusis (54% ˘, 46% —) followed by three tetrasyllabic cola, usually of the form ˘ — ˘ ˘, but ˘ — ˘ — in app. 30% of the first and 21% of the second colon respectively. The second syllable of each colon is obligatorily stressed, and the fourth may be stressed as well.[6] The delimitative role of hypocoristics results from the interaction of their overwhelmingly dactylic stress pattern (see fn. 3 above) with the metrical contour of the colon: the stressed vowels of the hypocoristics must occupy the 3d, 7th or 11th syllables of the line (= the second syllable [strong ictus] of each colon) and their final unstressed syl-

lables must therefore coincide with the 5th, 9th or 13th syllable of the line
(= the fourth and final syllable [weak ictus] of each colon). That is, the
interaction of line metrics and hypocoristic stress puts a word boundary
(and, often, a phrase boundary as well) after the 5th and/or 9th and/or
13th syllable(s).[7] Some examples (with / marking the colon and // the line
boundaries):

У *окошечка* / ведь смерть да не / давалася //	(2.40);
Наливали бы / ей *питьица* / медвянова //	(3.53);
Кабы видели / злодийную / *смеретушку* //	(3.46);

or, with more than one colon so marked:

Што томным идешь / *суседушка* / *томнешенько* //	(33.58);
Во *гостибище* / у вашего / у *батюшки* //	(32.25);
За *обиденкой* / *молебенок* / пропели бы //	(26.34).

3. Aesthetic functions. As we have seen, hypocoristic suffixes often occur
in structurally correlated positions within a line or between lines. For this
reason, they contribute substantially to the morphosyntactic and phonological parallels and, in general, to the replications that are the core of lament
aesthetics. A full treatment of this topic would take us far beyond the confines of an article, but we can at least sketch in a few of the aesthetic effects
in which hypocoristics participate.

3.1. Homeoteleuton. The repetition of diminutive suffixes in identical
syllables of adjacent lines, or within a line, creates near-identical colon or
line ends, that is, homeoteleuton or even canonical rhyme. Homeoteleuton
can occur in any of the three cola. In the first, for example:

Я без бетр*ышка* горюша нынь шатаюся,	
На работ*ушку*, победна, призамаюся;	
Надо сил*ушка* держать да мне звериная,	(39.68-70)

Second-colon homeoteleuton is less frequent, a fact which is probably
explained by the historically secondary origin of this colon:[8]

Отдали ходишь, сус*едушка*, туляешься	
Со мной на речи, поб*еднушка*, не ставишься,	(9.4-5).

Similar near-rhymes are, as expected, most frequent of all in the third
colon, as for example in the following lines:

Не утай, скажи, спорядной мой сус*едушко*	
Моей милоей, законноей сдерж*авушке*:	
Как посли своей надежноей гол*овушки*	(15/51-16.1).

Canonical rhyme, incidentally, tends to occur not with nominal, but with
adverbial diminutives, e.g.

> Аль по утрышку да ждать тебя ран*ешенько*,
> Аль по вечеру да ждать тебя позд*ешенько*?   (19.9-11)

whereas nominal hypocoristics usually result in less complete phonological
parallels, as in the examples already adduced.

Rhyme-like correspondences can be created within as well as among
lines. In the following examples, the parallels are between the first and
second cola:

> Скрозь *хоромишки воронишки* летают   (14.14)
> Станут *детушек победнушек* подергивать   (18.51).

Such correspondences are often established both within and between lines.
The two couplets below show internal ("horizontal") rhyme between the
first and third cola of each of the two lines, as well as between each of these
cola in the first and the second lines:

> Тут не *хлебушки* тебя да не *надиюшка*,
> Твоим *детушкам* ведь тут не прибер*егушка*.   (23.34-35);

> [Не прошу да я победна горепашица —]
> Со поло*сынки* у вас да я доли*ночки*
> Не со по*женки* у вас да я трети*ночки*,   (32.13-15).

Finally, the following example shows both horizontal and vertical rhyme
sets in the second and third cola:

> Накопилося кручи*ночки* в голо*вушко*,
> Все несносныя тоски*чюшки* в серде*чюшко*;   (12.12-13).

3.2.   Semantic sets and meta-sets. The second major aesthetic function of
hypocoristics is the creation not only of phonological, but also of semantic
replications, that is, the creation of sets of words semantically correlated by
one of several relations, e.g.

(a) synonyms, at least within the immediate context, e.g. the 'children'
and the 'poor things' of

> Станут *детушек победнушек* подергивать   (18.51),

or the 'neighbor' and 'poor thing' of

> Отдали ходишь, сус*едушка*, туляешься
> Со мной на речи, поб*еднушка*, не ставишься,   (9.4-5);

(b) equipollent members of some semantic set, e.g. 'arm', 'leg', and
'head' as members of the set 'body parts', or 'trees', 'clouds', 'mountains'
as members of 'natural phenomena', etc., e.g.

Накопилося кручиночки в *головушко*.
Все несносныя тоскичюшки в *сердечюшко*;   (12.12-13),

or

Резвы *ноженьки* у нас да все притопчутся,
Белы *рученьки* у нас да примахаются;   (13.49-50);

(c) antonymic members of a binary set, e.g. 'early' and 'late' as polarized members of the set 'time scale';

Аль по *утышку* да ждать тебя *ранешенько*,
Аль по *вечеру* да ждать тебя *поздешенько*?   (19.9-11);

(d) various metaphoric and metonymic sets too complex to be dealt with here, e.g.

На *работушку*, победна, призамаюся;
Надо *силушка* держать да мне звериная,   (39.69-70).[9]

The greater the morphosyntactic parallelism of the rest of the lines, —that is, of all of two adjacent lines except the juxtaposed hypocoristics— the stronger is the effect of their juxtaposition. In the two lines from (19.9-11) cited above, for example, nearly the entire lines are identical:

Аль по . . .-у да ждать тебя . . .-ешенько
Аль по . . .-у да ждать тебя . . .-ешенько,

which makes the contrast of утро and вечер and of рано and поздно particularly salient. The two, paired sets 'morning' : 'evening' and 'early' : 'late' create what might be called a meta-set, each of the two members of which is itself a synecdochic set, namely 'morning' : 'early' and 'evening' : 'late'. Similarly, another adverbal set,

По уличке *ходить* надо *тихошенько*,
Буйну голову *носить* надо *низешенько*   (21.38-39),

confronts the two pairs ходить : носить and тихо : низко, which results in the meta-set ходить : тихо :: носить : низко, which might be translated as 'act' : 'restraint'. A full description of all such sets and meta-sets would approximate a description of the semantic universe of the lament genre.

The preceding survey, while of necessity introductory and cursory, illustrates at least some of the complex interrelations of morphology, metrics, and aesthetics in the Russian lament. This fascinating genre warrants further and more detailed investigation.

University of California, Los Angeles

NOTES

[1]Barsov's spelling has been modernized in our examples: ѣ = e, i = и, prefixal з before voiceless consonants = c, final ъ = zero. Identification in parentheses is by page and line(s).

[2]In a sense, the formal functions in a poetic text are but one of the text's aesthetic components; the distinction between them is largely a descriptive convenience.

[3]For reasons which are not entirely clear, such otherwise frequent clitic fillers as -(т)ко, -ка, же are not permitted in the clausula (only the verbal -ся is at all regular in that position).

[4]These figures come from 1193 lines of 13-syllable verse in Barsov 1872.

[5]One may note in passing that hypocoristic formation often results in ready-made dactyls, that is, in stems which remain metrically constant in all case-number forms. Whereas base forms like сторона or голова have shifting stress that greatly restricts their appearance in various syntactic positions (сторона́, сто́роны, сторо́н; голова́, го́ловы, голо́в), their diminutives have fixed antepenult stress permitting them to appear (for example) at line end, no matter what case-number form is required by the syntactic environment (сторо́нушка, сторо́нушки, сторо́нушек, shortened instr. plur. сторо́нушкам; голо́вушка, голо́вушки, голо́вушек, etc.). The effect of hypocoristic formation is therefore to simplify the fit between morphosyntax and metrics by increasing the stock of available ready-made dactyls; whereas, say, fixed-stress кручи́на and mobile-stress сторона́ have radically different distributional constraints within the line, their hypocoristics кручи́нушка and сторо́нушка have identical distribution patterns. This fact, in turn, simplifies the aesthetic exploitation of hypocoristics to be discussed below.

[6]See Jakobson 1952:35-39 and Taranovsky 1954:350-351. These scholars' pioneering descriptions are phrased in terms of metrical feet (specifically, trochaic hexameter) rather than cola, but their observations are equally pertinent in the latter framework.

[7]As we shall show in another place, the boundary between the first and second cola clearly falls between the 5th and 6th syllables, but that between cola two and three is less sharply marked, wavering between 8-9 and 9-10).

[8]There is some evidence indicating that the "long" or 13-syllable lament grew out of the "short" or 9-syllable type; this topic will be examined in an article now in preparation.

[9]See Worth 1983:524-525.

REFERENCES

Barsov, E. V.
1872 *Pričitanija severnogo kraja. Čast' I: Plači poxoronnye, nadgrobnye i nadmogil'nye*, Moscow.

Jakobson, R.
1952 "Studies in comparative Slavic metrics," *Oxford Slavonic papers*, III, pp. 21-66 (reprinted 1962).

Taranovski, K.
1954 [review of] "Roman Jakobson, *Studies in comparative Slavic metrics (Oxford Slavonic Papers*, Vol. III. 1952, pp. 21-66), *Prilozi za književnost, jezik, istoriju i folklor*, XX, 3-4, pp. 350-360.

Worth, D. S.
1983 "On 'rhyme' in the Russian lament," *Russian poetics. Proceedings of the International Colloquium at UCLA, September 22-26, 1975* (T. Eekman, D. S. Worth, edd.) (= *UCLA Slavic Studies*, 4), Columbus, 1983, pp. 515-529.

APPENDIX

As illustrations of the syllable-filling function of hypocoristics, we adduce below a representative but not exhaustive list of contrastive lines from Barsov 1872:

бессчастье — бессчастьице
   Во большом углу *бессчастьицо* садилося,
   Впереди да шло *бессчастье* ясным соколом,   (8.51-52)

вдова — вдовушка
   Сирота бедна *вдова* да оставляется —   (11.12)
   Не окинься, бедна *вдовушко* молóдая,   (22.19)

ветры — ветерки — ветрушки (ветрышки) — ветероченьки
   Вийте буйны, вийте *ветры*, столько *ветрушки*   (28.107)
   Буйна гóлова без *ветрышка* шатается   (11.43)
   Приовиют тонки *ветерки*   (35.30)
   Столько вийте-тко вы буйны *ветероченьки*   (28.113)

время — времячко (времечко)
   Не во пору, не во *время*—   (56.28)
   Кабы в эту пору *времечко*   (54.59)

горы — горушки
   За *горы* оно да за высокия.   (1.2)
   За *горушки* она за высокия,   (131.134)

горюха — горюша — горюшица
   Со мной *горюхой*-сúротой!   (59.28)
   Оставлять меня *горюшу* горегорькую   (1.8)
   Как мне жить, бедной *горюшице*.   (59.34)

дитя — дитятко — детушки
   Она грубо стане нá *дитя* поглядывать   (84.107)
   Возбуждать пойду сердечно свое *дитятко*:   (173.35)
   Да ты ходишь с сердечныма *детушкам*   (239.58)

дорожка — дороженька
   На широку путь *дорожку* колесистую: (34.71)
   Путь *дорожинька* вот им да не торнешенька;   (1.14)

зима — зимушка
   Западут *зимой* снежком оны перистым;   (155.31)
   Вы студеной этой *зимушкой* согрейте-тко   (155.14)

крылечко — крылечико — крылечушко
   Со *крылечка* на *крылечико* ставаютца   (157.93)
   На *крылечушке* светик-братец стретает,   (89.24)

лавка — лавочка
   Были *лавочки* теперечко не отперты,
   Нонь купцов да все во *лавках* не сгодилося,   (15.39-40)

лебеди — лебедушки
  Налетело *лебедей* стадо,
  Все стоят да ведь *лебедушки*   (75.25-26)

лиходийка — лиходеица
  Со оружия, *лиходийку*, застрелила бы,   (61.6)
  Она крадчи шла, злодийка, *лиходеица*,   (61.8)

лица — личко — личюшко
  На *лицо* оны ведь е да все ласко́выи   (25.21)
  Без дождя *личко* повымокло: (55.73)
  Да то *личюшко* ведь блеклое   (49.6)

люди — людушки
  Он народу — сговорил да *людям* добрыим   (263.371)
  Во потай сули без добрых — ты без *людушек*,   (250.49)

могила — могилушка
  Хоть обкладена *могилушка* сырой землей,
  Заросла эта *могила* муравой травой;   (33.38-39)

нешутки — нешутушки
  У ветляныих *нешуток* домагалася;
  Как гордливыя ветляныя *нешутушки*   (30.150-151)

нога — ножка — ноженька ﹅
  Тут правой *ногой* она стане прищалкивать   (221.46)
  Без воды да резвы *ножки* подмывает   (44.210)
  На свои да стань могучи резвы *ноженьки*;   (29.132)

ночка — ноченька
  Или в полночь — *ночку* темную,   (59.39)
  Я не вижу, кое день, кое темная-де *ноченька*;   (63.62)

обида — обидушка
  Рассадить-ли мне *овиду* по темным лесам?
  Уже тут моей *обидушке* не местечко,   (17.29-30)

обидня (= обедня) — обидинька
  Сослужили бы *обидню* полуденную;
  За *обидинкой* молебенок пропели бы,   (26.33-34)

озеро — озерышко
  У *озер* нет перегребных малых лоточек,   (91.96)
  Кругом шла да как ты малого *озерышка*,   (232.17)

окно — окошко — окошечко — околенко
  Из *окна* в *окно* кидалася,   (51.48)
  И *окошка* запиратися,   (51.67)
  Прорублены решотчаты *окошечка*,
  Врезаны стекольчаты *околенка*,   (27.62-63)

Онега — Онегушко
    Ловцы ездят на *Онеге* незнакомыи,   (111.26)
    С горя кинуся ко синему *Онегушку*—   (111.19)

платье — платьице
    Как твое хорошо скруто — *платье* цветное;   (107.16)
    У тя *платьица* не здешнии,   (45.8)

племнятка — племяннички
    При слезах стоят любимы мои *племнятка*,   (150.271)
    Вас сердечных, любимых *племянничков*.   (153.8)

поле — полюшко
    Повытают снежечки со чиста *поля*,   (6.107)
    Будут пахари на чистыих на *полюшках*,   (6.115)

пора — порушка
    В кою *пору*, в кое времечко,   (59.37)
    Во эту как во *порушку*   (45.17)

птичка — птиченька — пташечка
    Из за морь *птички* слетаются   (54.36)
    Я быв *птиченька* в темном лесе пугаюся;   (86.139)
    Малой *пташечкой* в окошко залетела   (61.11)

разговор — разговорушка
    И прелестной *разговор* их да надсмечливой;   (22.28)
    Разговорушки у ей да нехорошии.   (23.48)

река — ричка — риченька
    Рути слезы, горюша, в быстру *реку*;
    Камышок от *рички* не откатится,   (14.61-62)
    Ты выдь-то там ко быстроей ко *риченьке*,   (14.57)

свет — светик — светушко
    Наталья *свет* Ивановна?   (79.2)
    На крылечушке *светик*-братец стретает.   (89.24)
    Светушко-братец — родимой?   (88.11)

светлица — светелочка
    По светлой повзыщем его *светлице*,   (219.4)
    Ты пройди да нонь во светлую *светёлочку*,   (139.99)

сестрица — сестричушка
    Аль боялась ты *сестрица* неможеньица?   (137.25)
    Отлишилися *сестричушки* родимой;   (137.32)

сирота — сиротинушка — сиротиночка
    Хоть говорю я, бедна *сирóта*,   (76.57)
    Допусти-тко, *сиротинушку*,   (53.4)
    Засмотри меня бессчастну *сиротиночку*;   (65.14)

слово — словечушко
   Была на́ *слово* она да не спесивая,   (82.30)
   Обиждать буду *словечушком* обидным,   (156.69)

смерть — смеретка — смеретушка
   Как убиту эту *смерть* он получил;   (249.11)
   Вы голодноей *смерёткой* не морите-тко!   (222.84)
   Как не видла взять *смерётушка*   (45.20)

соловей — соловеюшко — соло́вьюшко
   Соловей стал потихошеньку посвистывать,   (26.48)
   Соловеюшко садился под окошечко,   (26.46)
   Запосвистывать *соло́вьюшко*;   (69.41)

сродчи — сродники — сроднички
   Не в росска́з было *сродчам* — милым *сродникам*,   (83.49)
   Мои милые вы *сродчи* — столько *сроднички*!   (99.3)

стол — столик
   Круг *стола* стану горюшица похаживать,   (41.143)
   Ко *столикам* садитесь-ко дубовыим—   (171.11)

сторона — сторонушка
   Со *стороны* да от добрых людей
   Про чюжу дальну *сторонушку*,   (78.26-27)

строенье — строеньице — построеньице
   Как зглянула на хоромное *строеньице*,
   Што *строенье* приклонилось ко сырой земли,   (149.262-263)
   С добрым, хоромным *построеньицем*,   (121.2)

стряпня — стряпе́юшка
   Скоро стряпала *стряпню* я суетливую,   (27.88)
   У стола была любимая *стряпе́юшка*,   (117.6)

сусед — суседка — суседушка
   Все *суседы* порядовыи,
   Все *суседки*, малы детушки.   (36.33-34)
   Сговорит да им *суседям* таково слово:
   Вы *суседушки* живите во согласьице.   (160.45-46)

тоска — тоскичюшка
   Как долит *тоска* великая *тоскичюшка*:   (11.4)

HIGH FREQUENCY VOCABULARY IN RUSSIAN AND AMERICAN ENGLISH: A SOCIOLINGUISTIC COMPARISON

Olga Yokoyama

1. Introduction.

The purpose of this paper is to examine the highest frequency 1000 words of Contemporary Edited Russian (R) in comparison with Contemporary Edited American English (AE), and to see what differences exist between the two languages with respect to seven semantic groups ranging from ideological/historical/political to religious/moral. Statistical data were drawn from *Častotnyj Slovar' Russkogo Jazyka* (ČSRJ) edited by L. N. Zasorina (Moscow, 1977), and *Computational Analysis of Present-day American English* (CAPAE) by Henry Kučera and W. Nelson Francis (Providence, 1967).

Every statistical study has its limitations. The composition of the corpus and its size are of primary importance, and the differences in these respects between ČSRJ and CAPAE must be pointed out before we begin our examination. Both corpuses had slightly above 1,000,00 running words, and can thus be judged to be comparable, and equally meaningful, especially in the high frequency items, of which we examine only the first thousand. As for the composition of the samples, two major differences can be pointed out between the two sources. First, ČSRJ made an effort to reflect oral speech by using its closest written semblance, i.e. drama texts, which constitute 27.2% of the sample text. CAPAE made the opposite decision in this respect: drama, as well as any other prose text that happened to have more than 50% dialogue, were excluded from the corpus, and the proportion of fiction and journalistic writing was correspondingly increased.

The second difference lies in the essentially normative approach of ČSRJ, as opposed to the non-normative principles of CAPAE. The compilers of ČSRJ acknowledge their indebtedness to Larin's theory of the formation of the lexicon of Contemporary Russian. This theory holds that the **norm** of Modern Russian is determined through the interaction of four different lexical spheres: literary fiction, colloquial speech, scientific and social writing, and business language (ČSRJ, p. 8). In following this theory, ČSRJ not only reflects these four spheres in the proportion of its samples, but also attempts to capture the sources that influence the formation and the development of the Modern Russian **norm** by including such influential texts (ČSRJ, p. 9) as Lenin's articles and speeches, and Gorky's prose. Thus the samples used by ČSRJ date back as far as the turn of the century. This contrasts sharply with the strictly synchronic principles of CAPAE, which limits itself to texts printed in 1961. In contrast to this, only one quarter of the ČSRJ sample, namely journalistic prose, was chosen according to the synchronicity principle, limiting the samples to those printed in 1968.

Although it would be ideal to compare statistics produced by more similar corpuses, we shall see below that the trends observed are even more striking **because** of the presumably more colloquial nature of the ČSRJ corpus. As we proceed with the comparison, then, we must keep in mind the differences mentioned above.

In comparing two languages with regard to the frequency of certain semantic fields it is impossible to be statistically rigorous because of differences in the two linguistic systems. First of all, there is hardly ever a complete overlap in seemingly corresponding items in the two languages. For example, *pravda* is *truth* (and *justice*), while *justice* is also *spravedlivost'* (and *justicija*, and *sud'ja*), while *spravedlivost'* is also *fairness*. To compensate for this problem, we compared the sums of such synonym groups, rather than individual lexical items.

Some differences between the languages that lie in their structure, rather than in their lexicon, affect the frequency of certain lexical items. *Be* in English can be expected to be much more frequent than *est'* in Russian because the Russian equivalent is usually deleted in the present tense. Similarly, the extremely high frequency of English *way* is likely to be due to expressions like *this way, my way, the other way, no way,* which in Russian do not use the same noun but are rendered by adverbs instead (e.g. *tak, po-moemu, inače, nikak*). Words which are likely to behave in this way were excluded from comparison at our discretion.

Finally, there were purely technical problems due to the computer-based nature of the data. CAPAE follows a graphic principle, and as a result of this there is a separate entry for each distinct allograph. Thus, *write, wrote, writes,* etc. all have separate entries and separate ranks, and the true rank of the lexeme *write* can only be approximated by adding the frequencies of all these allographs. Such a sum becomes only an approximation because one of the effects of the graphic method is the increase of the total accumulated number of word-tokens in CAPAE, resulting in the lowering of the ranks of individual items progressively, as the ranks descend. While on the one hand increasing the number of entries by counting each allograph of a verb or a noun (*doctor, doctors, doctor's, doctors', Dr.*) as a separate entry, CAPAE also decreases the number of potentially different dictionary entries by lumping homographs together. Thus there is only one entry *state*, which is the sum of the noun, the verb, and the adjective, rendered as at least three different words in Russian. Since the number of such homographs is much higher in English than in Russian, lumping of homographs is likely to affect the comparative ranking of tokens in the two languages. The problem of homographs in Russian is very limited (a list of homonyms and homographs found in ČSRJ, e.g. *peč'* (verb and noun), has only 109 items); with respect to allographs, moreover, ČSRJ lists only the basic forms (the infinitive of verbs and the nominative singular of nouns). One fact of Russian, however, contributes to increasing the number of entries in Russian as compared with English, namely aspect. ČSRJ gives separate entries and frequencies for each member of aspectual oppositions, as well as for reflexive and non-reflexive forms, in effect giving up to four entries for one verbal concept.

Since technical problems of this kind are especially complicated with respect to verbs, we limited our comparison to nouns and adjectives. To compensate for the fact that CAPAE lists the singular and the plural forms separately, we treated their sums as a group contrasting with the basic nominative singular form in Russian. The differences between the two languages, and the two sociolinguistic backgrounds, emerge very clearly despite the limited data, as we shall see below.

2. Non-characteristic frequencies.

Some words show frequencies which in themselves are not characteristic for comparison between R and AE sociolinguistically. Thus, some words are so basic to human experience (or to the experience of these two cultures, which are after all similar), that they are likely to be frequent in both languages. Similarly, there are words which are so specific to a given way of life that their likelihood of existing in another language is null. The following words, for example, are very general and are included in the highest frequency 200 words in both ČSRJ and CAPAE:

    verbs: be, can, say, know, come, go, take, have, think, make
    nouns: time, man, year, life, day, house, home, place, water
    adjectives: new, other, last, great
    adverbs: here, now, more, well, always

Comparing their frequencies in R and AE is of no particular interest. Among words which are, on the contrary, very country-specific, and which exist in the other language mostly in transliteration (if at all), are words like *rubl', gektar, kolxoznik*. The fact that such words are much more frequent in Russian than in English is only to be expected, and contributes little to our understanding of the two sociolinguistic systems. It is only when we compare the frequency of *ruble* in R to the frequency of *dollar* in AE, or the frequency of *dollar* in R to the frequency of *ruble* in AE, that numbers have non-trivial implications.

3. Characteristic frequencies.

It is the area between the (almost) universally human and the country-specific that will be the object of the following examination. Seven semantic fields were chosen, which covered the fields that deviate in certain ways from basic daily human experience (e.g. human body, family, household). The highest frequency 1000 words were examined in both languages, and all the nouns and adjectives that could be judged to belong to these semantic fields were recorded. When a word ranked within the first 1000 in one language but not in the other, its frequency and rank in the other language was also recorded. The results are given in the charts below. The numbers given after the words indicate the number of occurrences of the word in the one million corpus (e.g., *bor'ba*, the first Russian word in the chart in section 3.1, was found 903 times in the corpus of one million). When two numbers appear after AE equivalents, the first one is singular, the second one is plural (e.g., in the same chart, the first American English word *labor* occurs 145 times, and its plural form *labors* occurs 2 times in the corpus of one million). Words joined with a plus sign (+) are treated as an equivalent group for the reasons discussed in section 1 above (e.g., in the same chart, *vlast'* and *sila* in Russian are compared as a sum to the English *power* and *strength* as a sum). Not all of the words in a group may be of high frequency, or even of the same meaning, but they had to be included to balance the group as a whole when compared to its AE or R equivalent(s). In cases when the AE equivalent(s) were noticeably more frequent than their counterparts, the AE equivalents were capitalized (e.g., GOVERN-MENT in the chart below: its frequency was 417, as opposed to 267 of *pravitel'stvo*). In the following presentation, each chart will be followed by a brief discussion.

3.1   Ideology, History, Politics.

rank	Russian	American English
0	bor'ba 903, trud 683, partija 532 + partijnyj 158, obščestvo 472, klass 423 +	labor 145+2, party 216+59, society 237+41, class 207+85,

klassovyj 136, revoljucija 407,	
istorija 382,	history 286+11,
kommunističeskij 373 + kommunist 244,	
vlast' 364 + sila 986,	power 342+73 + strength 136+4,
socialističeskij 333 + socialist 31,	
obščestvennyj 331 +	societal 4 + public 14 + social 380,
social'nyj 142 + publičnyj 14,	
sovet 316, zakon 315,	council 103+4 + advice 51,
	LAW 299+88,
buržuazija 312, političeskij 302,	political 258,
socializm 271, pravitel'stvo 267,	GOVERNMENT 417,
meždunarodnyj 257,	international 155,
kommunizm 256, pobeda 244,	
respublika 244, politika 242,	policy 222 + politics 67,
revoljucionnyj 255 +	
revoljucioner 17, kapitalističeskij 196+	
kapitalist 70, kapitalizm 194,	
geroj 191, stroj 181,	
programma 179, svoboda 178,	PROGRAM 394+139,
buržuaznyj 173, slava 173,	
istoričeskij 167, čelovečestvo 153,	
mirnyj 143,	
material'nyj 139 + material 322,	material 174,
organ 134	

1000		democratic 109
1000	demokratičeskij 96	
		struggle 62+3, victory 61+7,
		hero 52+17, mankind 39 +
		humanity 28, council 103+4 +
		advice 51, revolution 70+7,
		communist 97, communism 70,
2000		historical 71 + historic 23
3000		republic 43+6
4000		organ 12+14
		glory 21+4, regime 23+2,
		revolutionary 21, socialism 20,
5000		socialist 21
7000		capitalism 14
9000		
10,000		capitalist 6 + capitalistic 2
16,000		
50,000		bourgeois 3, bourgeoisie 1
		peaceful 0

Corresponding to 36 words (or word groups) in R that can be reasonably well characterized as predominantly associated with topics in ideology, history or politics, only 16 are of comparable rank in AE. Moreover, their frequency is generally much higher in R: of the 15 overlapping words, only three (*law, government,* and *program*) are significantly more frequent in AE. There is one word (*democratic*) which is included in the first 1000 in AE, but not in R. The AE equivalents which did not make the first 1000 are spread from the second 1000 all the way below the first 50,000. The greater representation of this semantic field in R high frequency vocabulary is thus quite obvious. It is interesting to note that ideologically-oriented vocabulary is highly represented not only when it refers to **Soviet** society (e.g. *kommunističeskij, socialističeskij*) but also when it refers to *Western* society (*buržuazija, kapitalističeskij,* etc.). In AE, neither *communist* nor *capitalist* are as high as their counterparts in R, although *communism* and *socialism* are discussed more frequently than *capitalism* and *bourgeoisie.*

3.2 Economy.

rank	Russian	American English
0	zavod 628 + fabrika 89 + mel'nica 48 + rastenie 361,	plant 125+59 + factory 32+24 + mill 11+32,
	razvitie 535, proizvodstvo 500 + produkcija 161,	development 334+59, production 148+7 + product 87+108,
	xozjajstvo 462 + èkonomija 75,	
	plan 407, den'gi 323,	plan 113+205, money 265,
	stroitel'stvo 280 + konstrukcija 45, promyšlennost'	industry 171+36,
	271 + industrija 24,	
	èkonomičeskij 266,	economic 243,
	predprijatie 216, rubl' 205,	
	inžener 186, texničeskij 183 +	technical 120 + technological 18,
	texnologičeskij 53,	
	bogatstvo 175, procent 172,	
	ximičeskij 12, tonna 162,	
	semja 162, gektar 157 + ar 4 +	
	akr 3, kollektiv 157 +	
	kollektivnyj 25, krest'janin 157 +	
	kolxoznik 63 + kolxoznica 8,	
	traktor 145, cena 140,	price 108+61,
	zerno 136, èkonomika 135	
1000		CENT 158, industrial 143, FISCAL 116 + FINANCIAL 86, DOLLAR 46+97

2000	promyšlennyj 98 + industrial'nyj 22, dollar 85	economy 79, construction 95+4, engineer 42+32, chemical 60, seed 41+42, farmer 56
3000	finansovyj 54 + otčetnyj 19	enterprise 31+14, percent 52, ton 13+28, grain 27+20
4000		collective 32, tractor 24+7
5000		riches 2 + wealth 22
6000		economics 17
9000		acre 9
25,000		
40,000	cent 1	
50,000		
		ruble 0, hectare 0

Economy-oriented vocabulary exhibits the same differences between R and AE. Corresponding to 25 words that can be judged to belong to this field among the highest frequency 1000 words in R, only 9 AE equivalents can be established within the same rank; the AE equivalents are, moreover, generally of lower frequency than the R items. There are 4 items which are highly frequent in AE whose equivalents in R do not rank as high; two of them, however, are the country-specific terms *cent* and *dollar*. Of the remaining two (*industrial* and *fiscal* + *financial*) the actual frequency of *industrial* runs close to that of the R equivalents. Thus only *fiscal* 141 *financial* represent a topic that seems to be discussed much more often in AE as compared with R. The remaining 16 AE equivalents which did not make the first 1000 are spread, again, from the second 1000 all the way to below 50,000. Noticeable, again, is the tendency for R to have more use for *dollar* than AE does for *ruble*. The tendency to favor quantitative terms like *procent, tonna,* and *gektar* is another characteristic trait of R.

3.3 Culture.

rank	Russian	American English
0	slovo 1039, kniga 691 gazeta 433, pis'mo 410 + bukva 55, reč' 277, pisatel' 271, kul'tura 269, kartina 259, iskusstvo 242, xudožestvennyj 211, avtor 202,	word 274+274, book 193+96, letter 115+145, writer 73+41 picture 162+68 art 208+66,

	pesnja 200, literatura 194, stranica 194,	song 70+59, literature 133+1,
	čitatel' 192, teatr 188, rasskaz 183, korrespondent 160,	story 153+35,
	xudožnik 149, muzej 146,	artist 57+55,
	muzyka 144, risunok 140,	MUSIC 216,
1000	radio 132,	radio 120+7
2000		newspaper 65+38, speech 61+21, culture 58+12, author 46+23, page 66+31, reader 43+37, theater/theatre 52/11+29/1, drawing 40+21
3000		artistic 33, museum 32+10,
5000		
6000		correspondent 12+5

As opposed to the ideological and economic fields, in which the difference between the high concentration of items in the first 1000 in R sharply
contrasted with their distribution across ranks in AE, the difference between the two languages is not as great in the field of culture. It is clear,
however, that R uses culture-related vocabulary much more often than AE
does. Corresponding to 23 such words within the first 1000 in R, there are
only 12 equivalents in the same ranks in AE. Of these, only one word is
noticeably more frequent in AE (*music*). The remaining 11 equivalents in
AE rank between the second 1000 (8 out of 11) and no lower than the 6th
1000. Concern with culture thus appears to be higher in R, although not as
strikingly as with ideology and economy.

3.4   Military affairs.

rank	Russian	American English
0	vojna 825, armija 557, voennyj 485, soldat 419, kapitan 352, komandir 325, boj 305, matros 263 + morjak 120,	war 464+26, army 132+15, military 212,
	oficer 257, lejtenant 220, oružie 200, flot 162, vojska 154, štab 140, vintovka 71 + ruž'e 59 + pistolet 28	officer 101+83, arms 121, forces 175, GUN 118+42 + RIFLE 63+23,
1000	zaščita 114 + zaščitnyj 13 + oborona 65 + oboronnyj 11	defense 167 + defensive 17, nuclear 115
2000	jadernyj 84	soldier 39+56, captain 85+1, headquarters 1+65

3000	commander 28+6, combat 27, fleet 17+1 + navy 37
4000	lieutenant 29+3
6000	
7000	sailor 5+8

Military vocabulary exhibits approximately the same trend as cultural vocabulary. R once again has more vocabulary that ranks within the first 1000 than AE; those AE words which did not make the first thousand are distributed between the second and the seventh 1000. One word (*nuclear*) made the first 1000 in AE, but only the second 1000 in R. One item, namely *gun + rifle*, is noticeably higher in frequency than its Russian counterpart (everybody in America can buy a gun!). The match in the distribution between cultural and military vocabulary of the two languages is thus almost perfect, including the fact that in both languages culture-related terms are more frequent than military terms (more so in R than in AE).

3.5 Science.

rank	Russian	American English
0	nauka 581 + naučnyj 291, veščestsvo 453, ènergija 351, učenyj 271, vrač 216 + doktor 139,	science 131+35 + scientific 86, substance 33+23 + matter 308+64, energy 100+11, physician 14+6 + doctor 100+30 +
1000	znanie 170, atom 145	Dr. 192+5, knowledge 145
2000		atom 37+41
3000		scholar 36+17

There is almost no discrepancy between the two languages in this area, although R again has more science-related words among the first 1000 than AE does. The frequency of these words is also much greater in R. Of the two AE equivalents that did not make the first 1000, none rank below 3000, however, and the number of words in this field that made the first 1000 is comparable in both languages.

3.6 Education.

rank	Russian	American English
0	škola 298 + škol'nyj 42, institut 274 + institutskij 6 + universitet 81 + universitetskij 5, student 163 + studentik 8 + studentka 7 + učenik 60 + učenica 3	SCHOOL 492+195, INSTITUTE 50+1 + UNIVERSITY 214+32 + COLLEGE 267+39 STUDENT 131+213 + PUPIL 20+25,

	obrazovanie 163 + vospitanie 141	education 214 + upbringing 1 +
1000		training 156

Education is the area in which AE has finally caught up with R. In fact, not only do all of the AE equivalents also rank within the first 1000, but the actual frequency of most of the items is higher in AE than in R. Both academic institutions and students attending them are mentioned in AE from two to three times more often than in R. A curious detail is obvious in R due to the gender marking of the language: the masculine counterparts of "students" appear to be discussed much more often than the feminine ones (*student* 163 vs. *studentka* 7, *učenik* 60 vs. *učenica* 3). Although references to students as a mixed group should appear in the plural forms of the masculine nouns due to their being the unmarked forms, sexist reality must be at least partly responsible for these numbers. Note that a highly marked masculine form *studentik* 8 is still more frequent than the standard feminine form *studentka* 7. (Cf. also *kolxoznik* 63 vs. *kolxiznica* 8 in Section 3.2.) The AE equivalents are not marked for gender, but there are good reasons to believe that sexism is not any more characteristic to R than it is to AE. According to CAPAE, the frequency of *he* and *she* in AE (which in English almost exclusively refer to persons) is as follows: *he:she* = 9543:2859.

3.7 Religion, morals.

rank	Russian	American English
0	pravda 579, bog 474, čert 259 + d'javol 29, sud'ba 181, cerkov' 150, gospod' 137 + lord 7, dux 134, moral 88 + moral'nyj 66 + nravstvennyj 32 + nravstvennost' 26	truth 126+4, God 318+14, CHURCH 348+96, SPIRIT 182+44, moral 142
1000		RELIGIOUS 165, CHRISTIAN 144, RELIGION 119, JUSTICE 114, faith 111
2000		lord 93+3
3000	spravedlivost' 53, vera 96	fate 33+3
4000	religija 33	devil 25+2
5000		
6000	religioznyj 21	
8000		
9000	xristianskij 10 + xristianin 1	

This field shows a clear reversal of the trends seen in the fields of ideology, economy, culture, and the military. This is the only area of the seven areas examined in which it is the Russian equivalents that spread into the lower ranks, and in which AE has more items that clear the first 1000. The difference is not great (AE 10 vs. R 8), but if we take into account the fact that *čert* and *gospod'* are almost exclusively used as interjections or swear words, and therefore do not really belong in this semantic field, the difference becomes bigger. Once these two words are excluded, the total number of words that are included in the first 100 becomes 6 for R, as opposed to 10 in English. The frequency of these words is also much higher in AE: of the 10 AE words in the first 1000, 6 are significantly more frequent than their R counterparts. While the low frequency of such institutional terms as *religija* and *xristianskij* is understandable, given the official position of religion in the Soviet Union, the difference in the frequencies of *sud'ba* 181 and *fate* 36, and *spravedlivost'* 53, and *justice* 114 is curious.

4. Conclusions.

The examination of the highest frequency first 1000 words of R vocabulary in comparison with AE shows that the two languages, while sharing basic vocabulary pertaining to the human condition, differ with respect to less general semantic fields. Assuming that frequency of usage reflects concern, genuine or rhetorical, we are led to conclude that there is a much greater concern with both ideology and economy in the Soviet Union than in the United States; that the Soviet Union is also much more concerned with cultural life and military matters, although the difference between the two countries is not as great in these two fields. Scientific vocabulary is also somewhat more prevalent in R, although to a much lesser degree than in the four fields mentioned above. In the fields of education and religion, the United States shows a greater concern than the Soviet Union; this is especially striking in religion, where the distribution approximately reverses that observed in military vocabulary. The ranking of the seven fields within the first 1000 in R is as follows: ideological, economical, cultural, military, scientific, religious (excluding interjectional *čert* and *gospod'*), and educational. For AE the order is: ideological, economical, cultural, religious, military, scientific, and educational. The number of items in each of these fields ranges between a maximum of 36 for ideology and a minimum of 4 for education in R, and a maximum of 16 for ideology and a minimum of 4 for education in AE. Items or concepts that are noticeably more frequent in AE are: law, government, program, financial, music, guns, schools and colleges, students, church, spirit, religion, Christianity, justice. Otherwise, the majority of words are considerably more frequent in R. Among more general trends, it is possible to point to a greater concern with the West in R than there is with the Socialist bloc in AE, a tendency to be more quantitative in R, and a tendency to swear more by God and the devil in R than in AE. Both languages share sexist tendencies of giving more prominence to the male.

Some of these conclusions are less surprising than others, and in any case a Slavist will find that, upon reflection, most of the results are consistent with his/her intuitions and thereby confirm them. What is significant, however, is the fact that an examination of such a small fraction of such seemingly bare and mechanical linguistic data presents a picture so surprisingly accurate and consistent with other evidence known from much more extensive and complex studies.[1] This brings into relief the significance of word frequency in sociolinguistic research. It demonstrates that the lexical component, being the most open and the most flexible part of language, reflects social conditions most readily and has a great capacity to reflect relatively young changes in the society that uses a given language. From the point of view of teaching R as a foreign language, these facts justify the introduction of high frequency vocabulary even when it includes such seemingly useless words as *predprijatie* 216, or *komandir* 325 (both rank within the first 1000), because they tell us no less about the country where Russian is spoken than such colorful favorites of Russian textbooks as *samovar* 61 (ranks between 2000 and 3000).

Harvard University

NOTE

[1]Cf. N. P. Vakar, *A Word Count of Spoken Russian*, Columbus: OSU Press, 1966, who also points out the validity of observations based on a relatively small sample.